The
Chinese Communist Regime

DOCUMENTS AND COMMENTARY

DS777.55
C394

951.05
C42c

The
Chinese Communist Regime

DOCUMENTS AND COMMENTARY

EDITED BY

Theodore H. E. Chen

FREDERICK A. PRAEGER, *Publishers*

New York · Washington · London

MAY 1 1968

122532

FREDERICK A. PRAEGER, Publishers
111 Fourth Avenue, New York, N.Y. 10003, U.S.A.
77-79 Charlotte Street, London W.1, England

Published in the United States of America in 1967
by Frederick A. Praeger, Inc., Publishers

© 1967 by Frederick A. Praeger, Inc.

All rights reserved

Library of Congress Catalog Card Number: 67-18969

*This book is Number 191 in the series of
Praeger Publications in Russian History and World Communism*

Printed in the United States of America

Preface

This volume is an outgrowth of classroom experience gained in a course taught every year since 1950 for the specific purpose of studying the nature of the Communist regime in China. It is felt that the students would have the best chance of forming objective opinions if they could read the official documents (in translation) at first hand instead of depending on secondary sources.

The documents have been selected with the central purpose of enabling the reader to understand how the Chinese Communist government and Party are organized, how they exercise their control, and what their major policies of economic and social development are. The contents can be broken down into three parts: The first part, Chapter I, gives a brief survey of developments since 1949. The second section, the next three chapters, deals with the organization of the government and the Party. Finally, the last two chapters present documents purporting to show the general direction of economic and social change.

The selection of documents involved difficult decisions. Many important documents had to be left out in order to keep the volume within manageable size. An effort has been made to include documents that show the salient features of the Communist regime, its basic policies, the general pattern of control by the Party-state and its auxiliary agencies, and the major goals of the Communist revolution. No attempt has been made to keep up with current events or the fast-moving changes in the execution of basic policies.

A complete study of policies might well devote a chapter to educational and cultural change and a chapter to foreign relations. Documents dealing with these important areas have not been included because of space limitations. Fortunately, many of them are already available to the public.*

---

* See, for example, Stewart Fraser, *Chinese Communist Education* (New York: John Wiley & Sons, 1966); Chang-tu Hu, *Chinese Education under Communism* (New York: Teachers College, Columbia University, 1952); G. V. Ambekar and V. D. Divekar, *Documents on China's Relations with South and Southeast Asia, 1949-1962* (New York: Paragon Book Reprint Corp., n.d.); G. F. Hudson, Richard Lowenthal, and Roderick MacFarquhar, *The Sino-Soviet Dispute* (New York: Frederick A. Praeger, 1961); and John Gittings, *The Sino-Soviet Dispute, 1956-63: Extracts from Recent Documents* (New York: Oxford University Press, 1964).

Most of the documents are laws and directives that form the basis of policy. There are a few official policy statements, but speeches as such have been avoided. The documents are those of the regime since its establishment; the only pre-1949 document is Mao Tse-tung's analysis of classes in Chinese society (D4) .†

Most of the translations used are those of the Foreign Languages Press in Peking; the remainder were prepared either by the American Consulate General in Hong Kong (indicated by an asterisk in the table of contents) or by the author (indicated by a double asterisk in the table of contents). As far as possible, the official translation of the Foreign Languages Press has been followed. Minor editorial changes were made, however, where the official version resulted in awkward or confusing phrasing or to make spelling and punctuation conform to more standard usage. Because more than one translation of the same document has sometimes been issued by the Foreign Languages Press, the reader may find that the exact wording of the same text may vary slightly in different documents.

The author wishes to acknowledge his indebtedness to Miss Juliana Pennington for proofreading the documents and Mrs. Elois Jenkins for typing a large part of the manuscript.

THEODORE H. E. CHEN

Los Angeles, California
January, 1967

---

† The designation "D" followed by a numeral refers to the document as numbered; "D5" means Document No. 5.

Contents

vii

I
The
Chinese Communist Regime:
A Brief Survey

EARLY BEGINNINGS

The Chinese Communists came to power in 1949. Official policy during the period immediately following the establishment of the new regime was marked by caution and moderation. The Communists did not want to alarm the people, who had been more interested in peace and the cessation of civil strife than in ideology or party politics. To allay public fears, they declared that there would be no abrupt changes. Business people were encouraged to carry on and assured of due profit. Teachers were told that their work would not be interrupted. Even the missionaries were given the impression that they would be able to continue their educational and evangelical work without drastic curtailment.

Official declarations during this initial period promised to protect private property and private enterprise. Religious freedom was guaranteed. The peasants were given land and the satisfaction of private ownership of the land they tilled. Little was said about socialism and Communism; these were distant goals to be attained only after a long transitional period in which the major concern was to build up a strong, independent, and prosperous nation.

This period of moderation did not last long. Its termination was hastened when, in 1950, the new regime decided to play a major role in the Korean War. In the name of a national emergency, the Communists adopted repressive measures to stamp out latent as well as overt opposition and to tighten their control over the population. A campaign for the "suppression of counterrevolutionaries" was launched in the latter part of 1950, and the ensuing months saw a crescendo of mass trials, mass executions, and wholesale persecution of all who were believed or suspected to be hostile to the new regime. At the same time, a fierce "class war" was waged against landlords in the countryside and the bourgeoisie in the cities, resulting in further persecution and more deaths. Millions of people met sudden and violent death; many more were condemned to long-term hard labor in camps. These campaigns against the "enemies of the people" left no doubt among the people that the Communists would brook no interference with what they were setting out to do.

Reporting to the Fourth Session of the First National People's Progress on June 26, 1957, Prime Minister Chou En-lai noted with

3

satisfaction the success of the new regime in consolidating its power and using it to lead the country toward socialism. Five major campaigns, he said, had paved the way for the consolidation of state power: (1) the agrarian reform to destroy feudalism and the landlord class; (2) the Resist America and Aid Korea movement to combat American imperialism and root out its evil influences on Chinese life; (3) the suppression of counterrevolutionaries to liquidate opposition; (4) the "three anti" and "five anti" campaigns[1] against the bourgeoisie; and (5) ideological remolding to change the outlook, thought patterns, and basic loyalties of the Chinese people, especially the intellectuals. These campaigns were the instruments by which control was tightened during the period from 1950 through 1952.

By the end of 1952, the Communists felt confident enough to terminate officially the initial period of moderate policies and to launch openly their plans for socialism as a prelude to Communism. The Korean War was entering a quiescent phase, with negotiations in process toward some kind of formal armistice. The rural and urban population had been brought under control, and the intellectuals had undergone intensive "thought reform." The First Five-Year Plan was launched on January 1, 1953.

FIVE-YEAR PLANS

Then followed five years of intensive reconstruction marked by positive achievements and substantial material progress. A good start was made in industrialization. New buildings and wide streets gave Peking and other big cities a look of modernization. New roads, new irrigation works, and new schools were being constructed. Production rose; manufactured goods were exported to other lands as proof to China's neighbors of the success of the Five-Year Plan. Visitors from abroad were impressed by the cleanliness and orderliness of the streets, as well as the immense energy of the people engaged in constructive enterprises. They saw a new China rising, united and moving ahead under the leadership of a stable and efficient government.

The Communists were at the height of their pride and confidence at the beginning of 1958. The Second Five-Year Plan, which was to be even more spectacular than the first, was announced with much fanfare. The nation would not only move at an increased pace; it would take a "Great Leap Forward." China was to overtake Britain industrially in fifteen years. The farms and factories would produce "more, faster, better, and more economically."

The year of the Great Leap Forward was also the year of the dramatic steel drive and the communes. Most of these grandiose plans,

---

[1] See the introduction to Chapter V.

however, remained on paper. A combination of circumstances led to economic dislocations and reverses which nullified many of the gains made under the First Five-Year Plan. Industrialization virtually came to a halt. Agricultural production lagged. Shortage of food and consumer goods caused a decline in public morale. Refugees sought haven in Hong Kong or abroad.

The economic crisis, which became more acute after 1959, continued until 1962. Realizing the necessity of major changes in policy, the Communists adopted emergency measures that finally checked the deterioration of the economy. It took time, however, to put new life into the economy and to offset the losses sustained during the period of dislocations. Before further progress was possible, it was first necessary to try to return to the level of development attained in 1957–58. The Second Five-Year Plan, scheduled to last until 1962, had faded away without even an obituary. Three years of "adjustment" intervened before a mild Third Five-Year Plan was announced, to begin in 1966.

CULTURAL REVOLUTION

The ideological aspect of its program also posed serious problems for the regime. It has been noted that ideological remolding was one of the "five big campaigns" that the regime relied upon for the consolidation of its power. Actually, thought reform was involved in all the five campaigns: The class struggle against the landlords and the bourgeoisie, the attack on American influence on Chinese life, and the assault on "bourgeois ideology" and bourgeois behavior all constituted important phases of the Communist "ideological struggle."[2] It should also be observed that ideological remolding cannot be accomplished in one stroke; it is a continuous campaign with intermittent periods of relative intensity and severity. Among these periods in China have been the thought reform of 1951–52, with intellectuals making confessions of their failings; the anti-rightist campaign that followed the "contending of the Hundred Schools and blooming of the Hundred Flowers"[3] in 1957; the subsequent demand that intellectuals sign pledges of "heart surrender," vowing to surrender their whole heart, without reservation or condition, to the Communist Party; and the controversy over "Redness versus expertness," in which the official line maintained that it was not enough to train persons with expert knowledge and skills but, even more important, they should be imbued with the correct political ideology in order to become thoroughly "Red."

[2] See Theodore H. E. Chen, *Thought Reform of the Chinese Intellectuals* (Hong Kong: University of Hong Kong Press; New York: Oxford University Press, 1960), Part I.

[3] This refers to a brief period in 1957 when the intellectuals were encouraged to speak their minds. The result was a flood of severe criticism of the Communists.

New problems have continued to arise to disturb and distress the ideological molders, and the pressure for thought reform has had to persist unabated.

The Sino-Soviet dispute produced serious problems not only in the economic and political realms, but also in the ideological struggle. Antirevisionism injected a new stimulant into the campaign for ideological orthodoxy and led to a witch hunt for any indications of thought or attitude that might be at variance with the Party line. A campaign against nonconforming historians, philosophers, and writers seemed to merge in 1966 with a struggle for power within the Communist Party. Important figures in the Party hierarchy and well-known intellectuals who had enjoyed official approbation were put on the black list of "revisionists" and "anti-Party conspirators." Scholars were accused of teaching and spreading anti-Marxist ideas by minimizing the importance of the class struggle or stressing the material aspects of happiness, such as food and comfort. Writers were attacked for voicing indirect criticism of the regime through political satire and ridicule of historical rulers who had ignored the welfare of the people. Even some Party leaders were branded "revisionists" because they did not fully support the program of large-scale collectivization. To combat the rising wave of bourgeois ideas, a "great cultural revolution" of vast proportions was launched. The full effects of this revolution remain to be seen; they are likely to go far beyond the political field and leave deep scars in the fabric of social and cultural life on the Chinese mainland.

FORCES AT WORK

In 1966, Communist China did not have the poise and confidence it had exhibited in 1958. In terms of political unity and national stability, the regime seemed to have retrogressed. The popular enthusiasm and the vitality of a dynamic society that so impressed the world in the 1950's seemed to have been overshadowed by internal strife and tensions. What had happened?

The positive achievements of the 1950's stemmed from a combination of circumstances. At the time of the Communist assumption of power, China had emerged from an eight-year war with Japan, only to find itself torn by intensified civil strife. Political instability and economic chaos had discouraged constructive work, and there had been little incentive for long-range planning. History, however, provides ample evidence of the capacity of the Chinese people for hard work and creative activities. Some of the greatest achievements of China have taken place during periods of relative peace and stability—in the long dynasties of Chou, Han, T'ang, Sung, Ming, and the early years of

Ch'ing. But the disheartening experiences of a weakened and hard-pressed nation in the nineteenth and the twentieth centuries discouraged and frustrated the people, who were unable to give expression to their latent abilities and creative energies.

In the 1930's, under a government that could at least claim nominal unity after years of division and warlordism, and in a wave of national patriotism stimulated in part by the threat of external aggression, there had been a release of energy resulting in a few years of constructive progress. During the few years prior to the outbreak of war in 1937, China made substantial progress in education, public health, fiscal reform, road-building, rural development, and various phases of material reconstruction. Foreign observers who visited China or served as advisers in various capacities at this time had high praise for the accomplishments of the regime. Optimists averred that a new era was dawning.

The prospect of progress and prosperity came to an abrupt end with the outbreak of war in 1937. What happened to wartime China and the declining morale of the people in the postwar years is a story that does not need to be told here. Suffice it to say that after eight years of a devastating war with Japan, followed by a prolonged civil war, the people of China wanted peace more than anything else. They wanted a stabilization of conditions which would enable them to work and plan in order to get things accomplished. They welcomed the cessation of civil strife that came with Communist victory, and they were eager and relieved to settle down to a peaceful and industrious life.

This brief review of past events suggests that a large part of the credit for the achievements of the 1950's belongs to the hard-working people of China, apart from the government. The material progress and economic prosperity that the island of Taiwan has seen since 1950 also lends support to the contention that, given a reasonable degree of peace and stability, the people of China are capable of outstanding accomplishments, regardless of the form of government under which they live.

At the same time, due recognition must be made of the ability of the Communists to arouse the enthusiasm of the people and to stimulate their pride in positive achievements. Communist propaganda made a strong appeal to national pride; the slogan "The Chinese people have now stood up" helped to raise national morale from the abyss of dejection and depression. Inspired by the vision of a strong and prosperous nation, the people responded enthusiastically to the call for hard work and sacrificial devotion.

Credit must also be given to the Communists for their ability to mobilize the people and marshal their energies and capabilities in the fulfillment of projected plans. The Communists did bring something new to the Chinese scene. Their experience in discipline and organization enabled them to introduce efficiency and orderliness in public enterprises. They forged an intricate system of government and Party administration that exercised authority in all parts of the country. They established a network of mass organizations reaching into all phases of social, economic, and political life. They extended the "iron discipline" of their Party to the nation at large and brought all sectors of the population under their control. By means of rectification campaigns and such devices as criticism and self-criticism in small groups, and by an unrelenting effort to prevent and weed out any "deviations" in thought and action, they were able to reduce corruption and assure the enforcement of orders and decrees.

Effective control was facilitated by a unified leadership that showed few signs of factionalism. The top leaders were singularly devoted to what they believed to be the right cause. By a combination of astute propaganda, effective organization, strict discipline, and a unified and dedicated leadership, the Communists were able to direct the energies and capabilities of the Chinese people into constructive projects. They cleverly combined an appeal to idealism and national pride with veiled forms of coercion, and the fact that punitive action by a powerful Party-state could be quick and relentless made it easier to obtain the "voluntary" submission of the masses. Ruthless suppression of any latent as well as overt opposition also served to convince the population that it would be wiser to submit than to resist.

It took tremendous feats of organization to assemble hundreds of thousands of people to work on the construction of dams, to stage the huge rallies celebrating such events as the founding of the new regime on October 1, or to arrange for simultaneous demonstrations all over the country on a designated day to oppose American imperialism. It was no simple matter to develop mass organizations embracing major sectors of the population—for example, the Sino-Soviet Friendship Association, trade unions, youth groups, the women's federation, and organizations of teachers, scientists, writers, artists—with each local group subordinate to the next higher one in a hierarchy culminating at the national headquarters. It was no easy task to get millions of people to go out on the streets to kill flies, mosquitoes, or sparrows on a given day, or to take part in a fertilizer-collecting drive. These things the Communists were able to achieve on a nation-wide scale.

SETBACK

A different picture, however, presented itself in the 1960's. The popular enthusiasm that characterized the earlier mass campaigns and made possible the production records of the First Five-Year Plan seemed to have declined. The image of a united and dedicated leadership was blurred by what appeared to be a deep-seated factional struggle among the upper echelons of the Party. Unrest among intellectuals was still prevalent after successive campaigns of ideological remolding. Even young people—products of Communist indoctrination—were found wanting in ideological firmness, sometimes hostile to the established order. Somehow or other, the slogans and the propaganda appeals that had stirred the masses in the first decade no longer seemed effective. The shake-up within the Party leadership, the renewed attack upon intellectuals, and a demand for drastic changes in education testified to the fact that the regime was in the midst of a crisis that went deeper than economic difficulties.

The waning of popular enthusiasm probably began with the economic shortages of 1959 and afterward, and with the institution of the communes,[4] demanding radical changes in the Chinese way of life. The decline of production in the communes was in no small measure due to a lack of motivation. People who had in the first decade responded to the call to work hard for a strong and prosperous country now wondered if they had labored only to lose what they considered precious —their land, their family life, and their traditions. They had accepted the need to sacrifice present comforts for a better tomorrow, but now they began to wonder if tomorrow would ever come. True, the Communists quickly revised their initially ambitious plans for communization; they did not push collectivization beyond the public mess halls, service centers, and nurseries for the care of infants. Moreover, they gave a part of the collectivized land to the peasants to be cultivated as private plots. The very fact that the private plots proved to be the healthiest part of the rural economy showed that the peasants had no enthusiasm for the communes and the collectivization program of the Communists.

From another point of view, the Sino-Soviet dispute must have exacerbated the internal psychological problems confronting the Communists. During the first few years of the regime, the Sino-Soviet Friendship Association was the biggest mass organization in the country. Headed by no less a person than Liu Shao-ch'i, it flooded the country with intensive propaganda praising "the Soviet Union, our teacher" and honoring Joseph Stalin, "the savior of mankind." During the "Hundred Flowers" period of "free criticism," no one was allowed to criticize the Soviet Union. Soviet advisers were exalted as "Big Brothers" who had come to assist China in the most selfless spirit. The Soviet model was held up as a guide in industry, in education, and in

---

[4] See Chapter V for further discussion of the communes.

all reforms. Russian replaced English as the most important foreign language.

Then the Party line was completely reversed when the Sino-Soviet dispute became acute. No longer selfless "Big Brothers," the Russian "revisionists" were now attacked and reviled as severely as the imperialist Americans. The erstwhile Russian model was now shunned, and the Russian language was no longer stressed. The intellectuals and the nationalist-minded patriots who in early years had been skeptical of the wholesale introduction of Russian influence may have been secretly amused by the belated realization that Soviet dominance was no better than any other form of foreign influence, but the masses must have been greatly confused by the switch of Party line. The reversal of what had been repeatedly affirmed in nation-wide propaganda must have created in many minds a serious doubt as to the veracity of the "truths" imparted in Communist propaganda. Once such doubts begin to grow in the public mind, the whole structure of Communst propaganda, a major pillar of the regime, may start to weaken.

In the upheaval of the mid-1960's, therefore, the Communists were not grappling with economic or political problems as such, but with the state of mind that had created them. While the popular enthusiasm of the first decade was the product of popular attitudes that the Communists were able to exploit and direct to fulfill their plans, the decline of morale in the 1960's was the result of a state of mind that tended to question or even resist the official plans and policies. In the opinion of this writer, it is a recognition of the need to change the public mood that lies behind the new emphasis on a "cultural revolution."

BASIC DIFFICULTIES

This task has assumed various forms. A violent form is the purge of individuals accused of "anti-Party" ideas and activities. A milder form is a kind of political indoctrination known as "class education," which has been given fresh emphasis since 1960. Its essence is to stress "class" as a central concept in the proletarian ideology and to instill a deep "class-consciousness" and a firm determination to wage a relentless struggle against class enemies, and all antiproletarian ideas and actions. Its aim is to produce class warriors motivated by powerful emotions of hate toward the enemies and love for the revolution. It is hoped that an intensified program of class education will produce devoted revolutionaries who accept hardship without complaint and gladly sacrifice the present for the future, personal interests for the collective good. The chief method is to tell the people how bad conditions were before "liberation,"[5] and how much life has improved

---

[5] The Communists call their 1949 victory the "liberation" of China.

for the liberated people of China, so that they may appreciate the present and support current policies, and, at the same time, fight militantly to prevent the return of pre-liberation conditions and influences.

The Communists decided on this program of class education because they saw popular enthusiasm dwindling and discontent spreading among the people. Economic difficulties had led to complaints about shortages of food and goods. The communes and collectivization program had encountered resistance from the people and even raised doubts among cadres and Party members. T'ao Chu, then first secretary of the South Central China Bureau of the Communist Party's Central Committee and a vice-premier of the State Council, spoke of "rightist opportunists" who had opposed agricultural cooperation—that is, collectivization. He gave the impression that their number was not negligible.[6] Even within the Communist Party, T'ao said, there were rightist opportunists who were "subject to the influence of the bourgeoisie" and who "did their best to find pretexts to oppose" the Party program. It was therefore necessary to "arouse the masses" and wage an uncompromising war against all rightist opportunists and revisionists. (Subsequent intra-Party strife, in which T'ao himself was purged as a revisionist, brought to light the fact that an astonishing number of people within the Party opposed the official policy directed by Mao Tse-tung.)

The Communist leaders have also been concerned with the problem of succession. Recognizing their own advancing age, they ask if the second echelon of leaders will be ready to take over responsibility. They fear that the younger generation, without the personal experience of the life-and-death struggle which deepened the dedication of the old veterans, may be too far removed from the fierce battles of the early years to realize fully the importance of ideological vigilance and continued class struggle. Lacking depth and firmness in their convictions, they may be easily influenced by bourgeois infiltrators. Some of them may be too absorbed in the practical affairs of management and the technical details of administration, and pay insufficient attention to ideological matters, such as the indispensable class struggle. These cadres and Party members, as well as the population in general, need intensive political indoctrination to stir up their emotions and heighten their revolutionary zeal.

There is a basic difficulty, however, in maintaining mass emotions at a high pitch. The mass campaigns[7] are used to stir up public emo-

---

[6] See *Peking Review*, August 20, 1965, p. 7.

[7] For example, the "three anti" and "five anti" campaigns, discussed in Chapter V, the Resist America and Aid Korea campaign, and the campaign against counter-revolutionaries.

tions, on which their success in turn depends. The slogans, the production drives, the rallies and demonstrations consist in large part of emotional appeals. But there are indications that continuous stimulation may produce emotional fatigue, and it may become increasingly difficult to rekindle enthusiasm and revolutionary zeal. The effort to arouse the masses, therefore, may be met with diminishing returns.

DOCTRINAIRISM VS. REALISM

Many of the difficulties of the Communists stem from their commitment to ideological dogmas. They won much support in China by their advocacy of reforms, but their preaching of the class struggle met with cold response. Their program of modernization and national reconstruction inspired eager participation and strong support, but their goal of socialism and Communism was not greeted with any great enthusiasm by the people at large. In the execution of their program, the Communists have at times been realistic and reasonable, but at other times they have been led by inflexible dogmas into blind alleys. Since they came to power, they have many times reversed their economic, political, social, and educational policies. The shifts of policy are often traceable to a continuing tug of war between realism and doctrinairism.

When Mao Tse-tung said that any popular revolution in China must first of all be a peasant revolution, and that the best way to win over the peasants is to give them what they want most—namely, land—he was being eminently realistic. When he proposed agricultural cooperation without depriving the peasants of the legal ownership of land, he was still guided by realism. But when he ordered full-scale collectivization and moved on from collectives to communes, he was led by Marxist dogmas—and this could only mean trouble.

When the communes failed to measure up to original expectations, the Communists were realistic enough to take a few steps backward. Realism compelled them to allow private plots and free trading of products, and this paid off in some degree of economic recovery. But after such concessions to private initiative, the Communists began to worry about the rebirth of capitalism—a concern that reflected their Marxist dogmas.

Vacillation between realism and doctrinairism is seen in the Communist policy toward intellectuals. As early as 1939, the Communists had declared a policy of "absorbing and reforming" the intellectuals. They realized that they must win over the intellectuals, not only because the services of the intellectuals were badly needed, but also because of the prestige and influence of intellectuals in Chinese society. Yet they have always distrusted the intellectuals as products of bourgeois education and purveyors of bourgeois ideas. They demand that intellectuals must be thoroughly reformed before they can be of genuine service to the new society.

In pursuing this dual policy, however, the Communists sometimes put more emphasis on absorption, other times on reform. Realism dictates the former, doctrinairism the latter. Consequently, there have been alternate periods of relaxation and rigidity of control. When the need to win over the intellectuals was the major consideration, the Communists adopted a relatively liberal policy, such as that in 1956, when "socialist construction" was the order of the day and effort was made to get the intellectuals to contribute more actively to it. The intellectuals were accorded better treatment, not only in the material aspects of daily living, but also in the accessibility of research materials, such as books and periodicals from capitalist countries. This period of liberalism culminated in the short-lived policy of permitting "a Hundred Schools to contend, a Hundred Flowers to bloom." When the "contending" and "blooming" got out of hand, however, the doctrinaires moved in to take charge. They ordered an anti-rightist campaign. Another round of organized attacks, of self-criticism and confessions, signaled the return of doctrinairism as the determinant of policy.

In education, one finds the same vacillation between realistic policy and policy dictated by dogma. Which is more important— academic learning or political indoctrination? Should students be selected and promoted on the basis of academic achievement or political background? Is there any place in the schools for "old intellectuals" of unquestionable academic competence who take a rather indifferent attitude toward politics? In the making of "Red experts," should education give equal consideration to both or prior consideration to "Redness" or politics? In periods of realism, educational policy has stressed the quality of academic learning, but in periods of doctrinaire ascendancy, education becomes a cheap tool of politics. It is therefore not surprising that during the purge of "anti-Party" scholars and writers in 1966, the regime ordered a shortening of the college course and a change of entrance requirements to make sure that only those who were politically reliable were admitted to higher schools.

It is possible to view major Communist policies in terms of the relative dominance of these two forces, realism and doctrinairism. Realism has produced policies that have won popular support and enhanced the prestige of the regime, while doctrinairism has led to rigidity, regimentation, and negative reactions from the people. The future of the regime may, in part, depend upon the relative strength of these conflicting forces.

The trouble is that the Communists are often caught between the horns of dilemmas that cannot be easily resolved: absorption versus reform of intellectuals, quantity versus quality in education, Redness versus expertness, private plots versus collectivization in agriculture.

INHERENT DILEMMAS

There are dilemmas that are inherent in the Party line. To bolster public morale and confidence, Communist propaganda emphasizes the improvement of the present over the past and tells of the even better things that are to come. But when the people really expect a better livelihood and ask for more food, better clothing, and more adequate housing, they are criticized for "bourgeois" tastes and desires, and they are told that it is wrong to think of personal comfort and individual welfare when the revolution still requires many long years of hardship and sacrifice. The trouble is that many of what the Communists criticize as bourgeois evils are normal human aspirations for a better life. Actually, the Communists are caught in their own contradictions. They advocate universal education, but they set definite limits to the freedom of the mind. They urge people to go to school, but after providing minimum basic schooling they carry on extensive propaganda to persuade people not to seek entrance to higher schools. They whet appetites that they cannot satisfy. They release forces that push beyond prescribed limits and threaten to upset their neat planning. In an attempt to solve these difficult problems, they have launched a gigantic campaign—a "great cultural revolution"— to teach a "new concept of happiness," to implant a revolutionary outlook on life, and to stamp out any vestige of "bourgeois individualism." They believe they can change and remold human nature. But they have not found this easy to accomplish.

The crisis confronting the Communists in 1966 had political, ideological, cultural, and psychological ramifications. The Communists consider "struggle" a key concept of their ideology; they speak of the class struggle, the production struggle, the ideological struggle, among others. In 1966, they were engaged in struggles on at least four different fronts. One was the political front, with the top leaders of the Party fighting for personal power and supremacy in anticipation of Mao Tse-tung's death or incapacitation. Secondly, there was the ideological front; a controversy had evidently been raging between the doctrinaires and those within the Communist Party who held more realistic views of economic and technical development and had questioned the dogma-ridden policies of the communes, the Great Leap, the stress on labor, etc. Thirdly, the recalcitrant intellectuals continued to be a source of trouble and worry; even those who had seemingly cast their lot with the new regime had once in a while given expression, directly or indirectly, to their mental reservations and to an independence of thought incompatible with the complete surrender demanded of them. Finally, something had to be done about the public state of mind, to bolster the morale of the people and to instill in them the kind of revolutionary zeal that would make them disregard personal desires and ambitions and sacrifice pleasure or comfort without complaint. These are grave problems, presenting a direct challenge to the fundamental nature of Communism and its dogmas. The way they are handled will, in a large degree, determine the future of the Communist regime in China.

THE SPECTER OF REVISIONISM

The Chinese Communists have launched an all-out campaign against revisionism and revisionists. The Sino-Soviet dispute is only a phase of the antirevisionist campaign; the purges of 1966 seem to indicate that the Chinese Communists are even more alarmed by the threat of revisionism at home. And they have good reason to be alarmed, for the potential forces of revisionism within China are legion. By way of summary, a few major forces may be mentioned:

There are many patriotic Chinese who are moved by nationalism, but not by Communism. They want to do all they can to rid China of foreign domination—to help build a strong and independent China. But they have no enthusiasm for any ideology or even for any political party as such.

There are liberals who in the early years supported the Communist proposals for reform because they, too, were deeply dissatisfied with the old social order. However, they are not interested in ideology, which the Communists consider essential to their program. Furthermore, the Communists attack "reformism" and "reformers" as incompatible with their stress on "revolution" and "revolutionaries." The advocacy of gradual reform or partial change is an ideological deviation in the Communist view.

The masses want a better livelihood today. Their demands run counter to the Communist requirements of disciplined living, acceptance of hardships, toughness of character, and sacrifice of personal comfort and welfare.

Many people in China do not subscribe to the Marxist theory of class and "class struggle." To the doctrinaire Communists, however, class-consciousness is the essence of a revolutionary outlook.

The intellectuals do not readily fall in line. They tend to assert their independence and express "bourgeois" or "antiproletarian" ideas even after they outwardly conform and submit to the demand for thought reform.

Old traditions and cultural values persist despite strong condemnation. Among them are attachment to the home and the family, aversion to collective life, prejudice against soldiery, Confucianism and its way of life, and long-established customs reinforced by deep sentiments. They resist change and stand in the way of the social remolding and total revolution that the Communists want. The cultural revolution of 1966 may be considered a frenzied, all-out effort to stamp out these entrenched traditions of the old society.

Technologists and professionals resent political interference with their activities. They do not accept the principle of letting politics take command. They value technological and professional competence above political or ideological orthodoxy. Among them are educators who want to put more emphasis on academic learning, technicians who feel that Marxism-Leninism and the thought of Mao Tse-tung cannot take the place of technical skills, and even military leaders[8] who are more concerned with building a strong modern army than with political indoctrination or the use of soldiers for "productive labor" or construction work.

Even among the Communists themselves, there is the young generation which lacks the experience of "bitter struggle" that characterized the early years of the Communist movement in China, and consequently does not share the fiery and single-minded dedication of the veterans.

There are among the Communists some who are more realistically inclined. They are afraid that a dogmatic approach will alienate public support and arouse more opposition. They advise, among other things, less haste in collectivization and more attention to the practical tasks of building a strong nation and a healthy economy.

There is always the danger that the socialist changes will be gradually weakened and ultimately nullified by the rebirth of capitalism. Private plots for agriculture, material incentives for work, the unpopularity of public mess halls—all of these pose threats to socialism and collectivism.

More may be added to the list. What the doctrinaires call revisionism is likely to rear its head from many sections of the population and various areas of national life. Their antirevisionist campaign, therefore, must necessarily be long in duration and pervasive in scope.

OVERVIEW

It is not difficult to see that the basic problems and dilemmas mentioned above lie at the root of the turmoil that shook the regime in 1966 and will probably continue for some time. In the long run, the

---

[8] For example, P'eng Teh-huai in 1958.

power struggle, in the form of personal rivalry to succeed Mao, is less crucial than the ideological dispute between the dogmatists and the realists and the continuing struggle to remold the intellectuals and the masses.

The rampaging Red Guards who began their campaign in 1966 are used by Mao and his faction as an instrument to oust the realists and revisionists from power, and to demand a complete change in the hearts and minds of the people. Their slogan is to "destroy the four old and establish the four new." Old habits, old customs, old ideas, and the old culture are to be stamped out and replaced by new ones. This is, indeed, a task of no small proportions. Two basic questions are involved: First, is it possible to achieve a revolution and build a country with ideological dogmas? Even among the Communist leaders themselves, as we have seen, there are many who believe that it is necessary to temper dogmas with a realistic assessment of actual conditions, such as the psychology and motivation of the people. The second basic issue is: Is it possible to remold the hearts and minds of the people in defiance of their past heritage and regardless of their personal desires, hopes, aspirations, and plans?

To summarize, when the Communists came to power in 1949, their first business was the political revolution, by which they aimed to consolidate their power and forge an effective system of state and Party control throughout the country. By the ruthless suppression of opposition, by the astute use of propaganda, and by virtue of their ability for organization and discipline, they achieved considerable success in their political revolution.

Next came the economic revolution. The agrarian reform not only eliminated the landlord class, but paved the way for the collectivization of agriculture. The First Five-Year Plan, inaugurated in 1953, impressed the world with its accomplishments. In the urban areas, a class war against the bourgeoisie destroyed its position in Chinese society and resulted in what seemed to be a peaceful transition from private enterprise to socialist industry, commerce, and handicrafts.[9]

But then the Communists found that political and economic changes would not suffice. The people must be changed as well. To make the new system work, it was necessary to "remold" the people—their habits, customs, ideas, attitudes, emotions, loyalties, and motivations. Hence the cultural revolution, for the old ideas and attitudes are the outgrowth of traditional culture, and unless and until the old culture is replaced by the new, the hearts and minds of the people will remain fundamentally unchanged. Whether the dogmatists or the realists gain ascendancy, they must eventually grapple with this problem of the

---

[9] See Chapter V on economic policy.

cultural revolution, if they continue to subscribe to the goals of Communism.

The cultural revolution will doubtless prove to be much more difficult than the political or economic revolution. Changing people will not be so easy as changing systems or institutions. In the main, it may be said that the Communists have shown that they can pass the political and economic tests. They have yet to pass the test of the cultural revolution.

II

The Birth of
a New Regime

The People's Republic of China was formally proclaimed on October 1, 1949—the culmination of months of careful preparation and important conferences. A brief review of the preparatory measures leading to this climactic event may aid the reader to understand more clearly the nature and spirit of the new government.

POSTWAR PEACE TALKS

It will be recalled that the approach of V-J Day in 1945 greatly stimulated the hopes of the Chinese nation that a way might be found to resolve the long-standing conflict between the Kuomintang and the Communists and to bring about a truly united nation ready to enjoy the fruits of victory and to undertake the tasks of postwar rehabilitation and reconstruction. Public opinion was becoming more and more articulate in demanding that the dissenting political parties place the welfare of the nation above partisan interests. In response to public pressure, the leaders of the parties agreed to speed up negotiations for a peaceful settlement of their differences.[1] Hopes were raised when Mao Tse-tung flew from his base at Yenan to the wartime capital city of Chungking on August 28, 1945, to confer with Chiang Kai-shek on concrete issues. The two leaders and their aides were engaged in private conferences lasting some seven weeks, and they were reported to have arrived at a general agreement in regard to broad principles. Unfortunately, the talks failed to prevent the flare-up of open hostilities in the northern and northeastern areas of the country.

THE POLITICAL CONSULTATIVE CONFERENCE OF 1946

With the purpose of using its influence to help achieve "the unification of China by peaceful, democratic means," the U.S. Government announced on November 27, 1945, the appointment of General George C. Marshall as a special envoy "to persuade the Chinese Government to call a national conference of representatives of the major political elements to bring about the unification of China and, concurrently, to effect a cessation of hostilities, particularly in north China."[2] Marshall's arrival in Chungking gave a new impetus to the

---

[1] For a summary of previous negotiations, see *United States Relations with China* (Washington, D.C.: U.S. Department of State, 1949) pp. 53–55, 73–86, 100–112.

[2] *Ibid.*, p. 605.

21

peace efforts. With his help, representatives of the Kuomingtang and the Communist Party reached an agreement on January 10, 1946, for the cessation of hostilities. On the same date a peace conference called the Political Consultative Conference (PCC) [3] was convened in Chungking. Of the thirty-eight members who attended the conference, eight represented the Kuomingtang, seven the Communists, fourteen were nominated by other political parties, and the other nine were prominent national leaders belonging to no political party. The conference was in session for three weeks; the issues discussed fell into five categories: the reorganization of the National Government, a program for peaceful national reconstruction, military problems, the convening of a National Assembly, and a revision of the Draft Constitution of 1936. Obviously, these problems were interrelated. The main problem was the establishment of a new government representing all political groups and exercising authority over the entire nation.

The PCC passed resolutions on each of the major issues. The resolutions seemed to indicate agreement among the conferees not only in regard to general principles, but also on the concrete steps to be taken in the immediate future toward a democratic and united China. According to the plan, one-party government by the Kuomintang was to be replaced by a coalition government in which all political parties would be represented; the armed forces were to be reorganized to create a national army belonging to the state rather than any political party; the Draft Constitution of 1936, which the Communists had opposed on the grounds that it was promulgated by the Kuomintang without consultation with other parties, would now be revised by a newly created committee representing the various political parties; and the plan for a National Assembly was to be modified in order to insure the representation of all political groups and to prevent domination by the Kuomintang. The conference also adopted a Program of Peaceful National Reconstruction, which set forth guiding principles for political reform, economics and finance, education and culture, relief and rehabilitation, etc. Democracy and the safeguarding of human rights were emphasized in the program.

The PCC adjourned in what seemed a harmonious atmosphere. Its proposals, if really carried out, would have ended civil strife and ushered in a united government more democratic than any that China had known. Unfortunately, the optimism it engendered was again short-lived. In spite of the truce agreement, hostilities continued. The Kuomintang and the Communists blamed each other for violating the truce. Charging the Kuomintang with not acting in good faith,

---

[3] The PCC was not a new idea; it had been proposed in preliminary negotiations prior to the Marshall mission.

the Communists decided to boycott what they considered insincere measures to carry out the PCC resolutions. They refused to nominate candidates for the newly proposed State Council, for posts in the proposed coalition government, and for the committee for the revision of the Draft Constitution. Further efforts at negotiations failed to produce results. When, in the spring of 1947, Chiang Kai-shek's government finally declared its reorganization and convened the National Assembly, the absence of Communist representation made these developments very different from what had been intended by the PCC.

At the same time, a split had taken place among the other political parties. The Democratic Socialist Party and the Youth Party withdrew from the Democratic League and joined the Kuomintang in the reorganized government and the National Assembly. On the other hand, the remaining elements of the Democratic League sided with the Communists and attacked the government reorganization and the National Assembly as empty gestures producing no real change in the one-party regime of the Kuomintang. Thus the minor parties lost their status of neutrality, and the issue became even more clearly a contest between the Kuomintang and the Communists. As the gulf between the dissenting parties widened, the civil war became more intense and spread into wider areas. In the midst of runaway inflation, intensified poverty and suffering, increasing popular discontent, and postwar disillusionment, events moved rapidly toward the collapse of the National Government in Nanking and a Communist victory on the mainland.

PREPARING FOR A NEW PCC

Contending that the PCC had failed to bring about national unity because the Kuomintang had sabotaged its resolutions, the Communists declared in favor of a new PCC in 1947. On May 1, 1948, the Communist Party issued an appeal to all anti-Kuomintang groups and anti-Chiang Kai-shek elements within the Kuomintang and invited their cooperation in plans for a new conference as a prelude to what might be considered a coalition government. Responding to the invitation, representatives of groups sympathetic to the Communist program assembled in Harbin, Manchuria, on November 25, 1948, to discuss concrete plans for a Preparatory Commission for the new PCC. A list was made of twenty-three groups or units to be invited to send delegates to the Preparatory Commission. Groups or individuals considered eligible for participation must be opposed to American imperialism, Kuomintang reactionary rule, feudalism, and bureaucratic capitalism.[4]

---

[4] Report of Lin Po-Ch'u, member of the Central Committee of the Chinese Communist Party, at the meeting of the Chinese People's Political Consultative Conference, September 22, 1949.

It was decided that the Preparatory Commission should determine the units or groups to be represented in the new PCC and should draft the documents to be presented and approved by the conference. It was further agreed that the new PCC should be convened some time in 1949 and should be charged with two specific tasks: the formulation of a Common Program and the establishment of the Central Government of the People's Republic of China.

The Preparatory Commission for the new PCC was convened on June 15, 1949, in Peking. It was attended by 134 members who had been chosen to represent 23 designated units or groups. The following groups were approved for representation:

1) The Chinese Communist Party.
2) The Kuomintang Revolutionary Committee. This group, organized in January, 1948, by anti–Chiang Kai-shek Kuomintang members then gathered in Hong Kong, stressed friendly relations with the CCP and with the Soviet Union.
3) The Democratic League. Organized in 1941 as an alliance of small political parties each of which was too weak to exert any great influence, the League originally included the Youth Party, the National Socialist Party (later renamed the Democratic Socialist Party), the National Salvation Association, the Rural Reconstruction Party, the Vocational Education Group, and the Democratic Party of Peasants and Workers. In 1948, the Youth Party and the Democratic Socialist Party withdrew from the League, which then moved more openly to the side of the Communists.
4) The Association for Democratic National Reconstruction. Organized in 1946, this group opposed the civil war and urged reconstruction through increased production.
5) Nonpartisan "democratic elements" in China. Not an organized group. Six intellectuals sympathetic to the Communist program were chosen to represent this segment of the population.
6) The Association for the Advancement of Chinese Democracy. Formed in 1946 by a group of intellectuals and industrial leaders in Shanghai.
7) The Democratic Party of Peasants and Workers. Organized in 1927 in protest against Chiang Kai-shek's policy of purging the Kuomintang of the Communists, this group was originally known as the Third Party. It is also a constituent unit of the Democratic League.
8) The National Salvation Association. Organized in 1936, this group was opposed to the policies of the Kuomintang. Among its members were the "Seven Gentlemen" who were arrested by the Nationalist Government and put in jail for their anti-government views. It is also a unit in the Democratic League.
9) The Association of San Min Chu I Comrades. This group is not unlike the Kuomintang Revolutionary Committee.
10) The Kuomintang Association for the Advancement of Democracy. Closely affiliated with the Kuomintang Revolutionary Committee.

11) Chih-Kung-Tang. This organization, also known as Hung-Men-Chih-Kung-Tang, has a long history extending as far back as the Manchu dynasty. It was active in inciting revolt against the Manchus. After the T'aip'ing Rebellion, this secret society became most active in the United States. It has branch organizations in Cuba, Mexico, and Canada.

12) The People's Liberation Army. The name of the Red Army in China.

13) All-China Federation of Labor.

14) Peasants' organizations in the liberated areas.

15) "Democratic elements" from the productive enterprises.

16) "Democratic elements" from the cultural fields.

17) "Democratic" professors.

18) All-China Federation of Democratic Youth.

19) All-China Federation of Democratic Women.

20) All-China Student Federation.

21) Shanghai Federation of People's Organizations.

22) Minority races in China.

23) "Democratic elements" from among the overseas Chinese.

A few characteristics of these participating units deserve attention. All of them were selected and approved by the Communists. Many of them had been organized in the postwar period and represented elements who were opposed to Chiang Kai-shek and were favorable to the Communists. Some were organized under the aegis of the Communists. Moreover, there was a good deal of overlapping; the same people were often active in several groups, and the constituent units of the Democratic League were represented both in the League and independently. The long list, however, looked impressive to the uncritical eye and seemed to indicate wide support from different sections of the population. It is further to be noted that the delegates attending the Preparatory Commission were not elected by the groups they were supposed to represent, but were hand-picked by the planners to serve as "representatives" of their group, just as the planners at the Harbin Conference had been hand-picked by the Communists to constitute a "representative" body.

The Preparatory Commission was in session June 15–19, 1949. From among its members, twenty-one persons were elected to constitute a Standing Committee, with Mao Tse-tung as chairman and Chou En-lai as one of the five vice-chairmen. Six additional committees were established, one for each of the following tasks: (1) to make a list of the units to be represented in the new PCC and name the delegates for each unit; (2) to draft the Organic Law of the new PCC; (3) to draft the Common Program; (4) to formulate a plan for the Government of the Chinese People's Democratic Republic; (5) to draft a public declaration of the new regime; and (6) to adopt a national flag, anthem, emblem, etc. The work of the Commission was done entirely by these committees and the Standing Committee.

Meeting again on September 17–19, 1949, the Preparatory Commission heard the reports of the committees and accepted their recommendations as the unanimous resolutions of the Commission. It was decided that the new PCC should now be officially named the Chinese People's Political Consultative Conference (CPPCC) and should have 510 delegates representing 45 units, with 77 alternates and 74 other delegates chosen from among the "democratic elements" of Chinese society at large, thus making a total of 661 persons. The names of the candidates were to be submitted to the Preparatory Commission for approval, with the list to be enlarged or modified at the discretion of the Committee. Besides the apportionment of delegates for the CPPCC, the Commission passed resolutions concerning the organization and agenda of the CPPCC, the Common Program to be adopted, and the organization of the Central People's Government of the People's Republic of China; in short, it settled all important issues concerning the CPPCC except the national flag, anthem, and emblem.

The thoroughness with which the Communists had planned the sequence of events is attested by the fact that the 661 delegates were ready to be called into action within a couple of days. The CPPCC was convened on September 21, 1949, only two days after the adjournment of the Preparatory Commission which selected the delegates for the conference. Yet fewer than 30 of the chosen delegates failed to attend, and all the rest of the 661 were in Peking two days after they were designated as delegates.

The 45 units represented in this history-making body consisted of 14 political parties, including the 11 represented in the Preparatory Commission; 9 geographical areas (e.g., the north China liberated area, the central China liberated area, the south China liberated area) ; 6 army units (e.g., the Headquarters of the People's Liberation Army, the various Field Forces) ; and 16 "people's organizations" (e.g., the Labor Federation, peasants' organizations, the Women's Federation, the Preparatory Committee for the Congress of Educational Workers, the Preparatory Committee for the Congress of National Science Workers).[5] There were 7 delegates and an alternate representing "democratic elements" from among the religious groups—5 Christians, 2 Buddhists, and 1 Mohammedan. No Catholic was invited because of the open hostility between the Communists and the Catholic Church.

---

[5] Some of the new groups had been organized between the two sessions of the Preparatory Commission, at the instigation of the Commission; for example, the National Federation of Literature and Fine Arts, and the Preparatory Committee for the Congress of Social Science Workers.

THE CPPCC

The keynote of the Conference was pronounced by Mao Tse-tung, who declared: "This conference has materialized today because we have defeated in war the Kuomintang reactionary government supported by American imperialism. . . . This is a conference representing the people of the entire nation. . . . Our revolutionary task is not yet complete. The imperialists abroad and the reactionaries within the country will not readily accept defeat. Internationally, we must unite with all peace-loving and freedom-loving nations and peoples of the world, but we must first of all unite with the Soviet Union and the New Democracies." Again, he blamed the Kuomintang for the failure of the PCC of 1946. Other speakers, elaborating on this theme, attributed the failure of the old PCC to the domination of the reactionaries, to the intervention of American imperialism in the form of the hypocritical Marshall mission, and to the fact that the objectives of the old PCC had been formulated within the framework of the outworn capitalistic democracy instead of the New Democracy. It was emphasized that the CPPCC was so constituted as to represent all the people of China, and that all the delegates were opposed to imperialism, feudalism, and bureaucratic capitalism so that, unlike its predecessor of 1946, it was entirely free from reactionary influences.

The CPPCC was declared to be more democratic than the old PCC not only because it gave representation to many political parties, but also because it represented workers and peasants constituting the majority of the Chinese people: "The Chinese People's Political Consultative Conference, composed of the representatives of the Communist Party of China, of all democratic parties and groups and people's organizations, of all regions, of the People's Liberation Army, of all national minorities, overseas Chinese, and patriotic democratic elements, is the form of organization of the Chinese People's democratic united front."[6] The Communists also pointed with pride to the fact that the Communist Party had no more representatives—sixteen, plus two alternates—than the Democratic League or the Kuomintang Revolutionary Committee. What they did not publicize was the fact that names of influential Communists appeared in the delegations from the liberated areas, from the Field Forces of the Liberation Army, and from organizations of labor, peasants, women, etc.; and therefore the actual number of Communists in the conference was many times greater than the sixteen officially listed as representatives of the Party. At any rate, the resolutions of the CPPCC faithfully followed in the minutest

---

[6] This statement appears in the preamble of the Common Program adopted by the CPPCC.

details the theories and plans the Communist leaders had advanced for the New Democracy and the People's Republic.

The CPPCC was in session September 21–30, 1949. It made history by giving birth to a new regime, the People's Republic of China, officially proclaimed on October 1, 1949. To emphasize the beginning of a new era, the conference adopted a new national flag: a red flag with five yellow stars (a large star surrounded by four small stars) on the upper left corner. The large star is supposed to represent the Communist Party, while the four small stars symbolize the four major classes of people (workers, peasants, petty bourgeoisie, and national bourgoisie) who under the leadership of the Communist Party combine to establish and support the new People's Republic of China. For the national anthem, it was decided to use temporarily the popular war song "The Marching Song of the Volunteers,"[7] pending the adoption of a new anthem. No decision was made in regard to the national emblem. Peking—the Kuomintang-sponsored name Peiping is now rejected—was chosen as the capital of the People's Republic. A sharp break with the past was further emphasized by the adoption of the Gregorian calendar instead of the calendar year according to the age of the Chinese Republic (the latter system is still used in Taiwan).

October 1 now replaced October 10 as the national holiday of the "New China." At a mammoth rally in Peking on October 1, 1949, Mao Tse-tung proclaimed the birth of the new regime (D1). At the same

---

[7] This song is commonly known by its popular name "Ch'i Lai." The words have been translated as follows:

Arise
Ye who refuse to be bond slaves,
With our very flesh and blood
Let us build our new Great Wall.
China's masses have met the day of danger
Indignation fills the hearts of all our countrymen.

Arise! Arise! Arise!
Many hearts with one mind
Brave the enemy's gunfire!
March on!
Brave the enemy's gunfire!
March on! March on! March on!

In 1966, T'ien Han, the author of the lyrics, was denounced as an "anti-Party" writer. There was talk of dropping his song, and a proposal was made to substitute "The East in Red Glow" in public gatherings. The words of that song's first stanza are:

From the red east rises the sun
In China appears Mao Tse-tung.
He works for the people's welfare.
He is the people's savior.

time, three basic documents were formally promulgated which constituted the legal basis of the regime: the Common Program of the Chinese People's Political Consultative Conference (D2), the Organic Law of the Central People's Government of the People's Republic of China (D3), and the Organic Law of the Chinese People's Political Consultative Conference (not included in this volume). These documents spell out the organization of the central government and its basic policies. They were prescribed as the basic materials for the "study sessions" and indoctrination classes which became practically compulsory for the entire population.

The most important of the three documents is the Common Program (D2). It was so called because the Communists contended that the new regime was a coalition of a number of political parties,[8] and that these parties must agree on a set of principles governing their common effort, or a Common Program which all parties would support. Actually, the content of the Common Program represented what the Communists call their "minimum program," or the preliminary phase of their revolution prior to the advent of socialism.

THE NEW DEMOCRACY

The new regime is called the New Democracy. The blueprint for this program was drawn by Mao Tse-tung in the decade before the establishment of the regime.[9] The basic premise is that Chinese society is not yet ready for a full-fledged proletarian-socialist revolution and that it is consequently necessary to divide the revolution into two stages. The first stage, called the New Democracy, represents a transition from "feudal" and "semicolonial" China to a proletarian-socialist China.

The New Democracy is not yet ready for the "dictatorship of the proletariat." Since the proletariat is still too weak to take over completely the power of the state, it is necessary for the working class to cooperate or "ally" with other classes. The New Democracy, therefore, is characterized by the "joint dictatorship" of four "revolutionary classes" (again, the workers, peasants, petty bourgeoisie, and national bourgeoisie). The four classes are not of equal status.[10] The workers, it is emphasized, are the "fundamental force of the revolution" and the leader of the four classes. Their chief ally is the peasantry, which constitutes the majority of China's masses. Next in the scale comes the petty bourgeoisie; the national bourgeoisie, the capitalists who are

---

[8] See D5 for the names of the other political parties.

[9] The nature of the New Democracy and of the regime established in 1949 was explained in Mao's "On New Democracy" (1940), "On Coalition Government" (1945), and "On People's Democratic Dictatorship" (1949).

[10] See D4 for Mao's analysis of classes in Chinese society.

willing to put themselves at the service of the "people's state," are the least "dependable" allies, have to be watched, and sometimes must be chastised.

The four classes constitute the "people" in the People's Republic of China. The word "people" assumes a new meaning in this context. Outside the four classes there are persons who are not qualified for participation in the New Democracy. Among them are reactionary elements, feudal elements, "lackeys of imperialism," "bureaucratic capitalists," and "enemies of the people." They do not qualify as "people," but they are "nationals" subject to the laws of the new state. Only the "people" are given the freedom stipulated in Article 5 and other articles of the Common Program. Only the "people" may enjoy the privileges of the "People's Democracy." The reactionary elements and the "enemies of the people" are to be suppressed, punished or "reformed." The "people's state," it is said, is a "Democratic Dictatorship" (democracy for the "people" and dictatorship for the "enemies of the people").

The government established in 1949 was a temporary one. With the adoption of the Constitution in September, 1954, the government was reorganized, and the general provisions of the Common Program were translated into more concrete policies or replaced by more specific stipulations of the Constitution. For a clear understanding of what the Constitution and the new organic laws of the government and the CPPCC evolved from, however, it is important to have an accurate knowledge of the system that existed from 1949 to 1954. Moreover, the Constitution may in some ways be considered the elaboration and the further implementation of the Common Program, which still remains as an important document setting forth the framework within which the new regime pushes on from the transitional stage to the next, or "higher," phase of the revolution.

COMMUNIST LEADERSHIP

Attention has been called to the continuity of planning since the Harbin Conference of November, 1948, which produced the Preparatory Commission, which in turn elected Mao Tse-tung as chairman. The work of the Commission was carried on by committees under the direction of the Standing Committee elected by the Commission, and Mao was the chairman of the Standing Committee. The CPPCC in its plenary session elected a National Committee, which was to exercise the power of the "representative" body in the absence of the plenary session. The National Committee of 180 members in turn elected a Standing Committee of 28 members, which had authority to act when the National Committee was not in session. Mao Tse-tung was chairman of the National Committee as well as its Standing Committee.

The multiple responsibilities of Mao Tse-tung illustrate not only the Communist principle of "democratic centralism" but also the firm "leadership" of the Communist Party in the new state. Just as the working class is the leader of the "people," so the Communist Party, as the "organized vanguard of the working class," must be the accepted leader of the other political parties. The highest governmental body, in which were concentrated legislative and judiciary as well as executive powers, was the Central People's Government Council, consisting of the chairman, six vice-chairmen, and fifty-six councilors. All were "elected" by the CPPCC. Naturally enough, Mao Tse-tung, who now served as the head of the government as well as the head of the Communist Party, was made the chairman.

Of the six vice-chairmen, three were influential Communists: Liu Shao-Ch'i, organizer and chief theoretician of the CCP; Chu Teh, veteran commander in chief of the Red Army; and Kao Kang, then the head of the Manchurian Government.[11] The three non-Communists were Madame Sun Yat-sen, Li Chi-Shen of the Kuomintang Revolutionary Committee, and Chang Lan of the Democratic League. Of the fifty-six councilors, twenty-seven were Party members.

The control of the Communist Party was made sure in many ways. First, the same persons occupied the key positions in Party and government. Second, the parties and non-Communist personnel who participated in the "joint dictatorship" were hand-picked by the Communist leaders. Third, the Communist Party was not merely one of several political parties; it was the leader calling the tune. Fourth, the Common Program and the theoretical basis of the new regime stemmed directly from the ideology of the Communists. Last, major policies and decisions were initiated by the Communist Party, passed on to the CPPCC to be endorsed and publicized as the resolutions of the national "united front" body, and then transmitted to the government for execution.

Take, for example, the Agrarian Reform Law of 1950. The initiative for a new law came from the Communist Party. After the Party's Central Committee completed the drafting of the new law, the National Committee of the CPPCC took up the matter and put its stamp of approval on the draft law. The proposal then went to the Central People's Government as the recommendation from the CPPCC. Finally, the law was promulgated by the Central People's Government as the Agrarian Reform Law of the People's Republic of China.

In regard to the relation between the New Democracy of the People's

---

11 He was to be a victim of the purge in 1955.

Republic of China and the Communist program of proletarian-socialist revolution, it would be best to quote from Mao Tse-tung's "On New Democracy." "The Communist Party" he wrote, "has its present program and its future program, or its minimum program and its future program. For the present, New Democracy, and for the future, socialism—these are two parts of an organic whole, guided by one and the same Communist ideology." Elsewhere in the same treatise, he declared that even in the early stage of the New Democracy, the Chinese revolution "has become a part of the proletarian-socialist world revolution."

DOCUMENT 1

PROCLAMATION OF THE CENTRAL PEOPLE'S GOVERNMENT OF THE PEOPLE'S REPUBLIC OF CHINA

[Read by Mao Tse-tung at a rally on October 1, 1949]

The people throughout China have been plunged into bitter sufferings and tribulations since the Chiang Kai-shek Kuomintang reactionary government betrayed the motherland, conspired with imperialists, and launched the counterrevolutionary war. However, our People's Liberation Army, supported by the people throughout the country, fighting heroically and selflessly to defend the territorial sovereignty of the motherland, to protect the people's lives and property, to relieve the people of their suffering, and to struggle for their rights, has eliminated the reactionary troops and overthrown the reactionary rule of the Nationalist Government.

Now, the war of the people's liberation has been fundamentally won, and the majority of the people throughout the country have been liberated.

On this foundation, the first session of the Chinese People's Political Consultative Conference, composed of the delegates of all democratic parties and groups, people's various regions, various nationalities, overseas Chinese, and patriotic democratic elements of the whole country has been convened. Representing the will of the people throughout the country, this session of the Chinese People's Political Consultative Conference has enacted the Organic Law of the Central People's Government of the People's Republic of China, elected Mao Tse-tung as chairman of the Central People's Government, and Chu Teh, Liu Shao-ch'i, Soong Ch'ing-ling, Li Chi-shen, Chang Lan and Kao Kang as vice-chairmen of the Central People's Government, and Ch'en Yi, Ho Lung, Li Li-san, Lin Po-ch'u, Yeh Chien-ying, Ho Hsiang-ning, Lin Piao, P'eng Teh-huai, Liu Po-ch'eng, Wu Yu-chang, Hsu Hsiang-chien, P'eng Chen, Po Yi-p'o, Nieh Jung-chen, Chou En-lai, Tung Pi-wu, Saifudin, Jao Shu-shih, Tan Kah-kee, Lo Jung-huan, Teng Tsu-hui, Ulanfu, Hsu Teh-li, Ts'ai Ch'ang, Liu K'e-ping, Ma Yin-ch'u, Ch'en Yun, Kang Sheng, Lin Feng, Ma Hsu-lun, Kuo Mo-jo, Chang Yun-yi, Teng Hsiao-ping, Kao Chung-min, Shen Chun-ju, Shen Yen-ping, Ch'en Shu-tung, Seeto Meitong, Li Hsi-chiu, Huang Yen-p'ei, Ts'ai T'ing-k'ai, Hsi Chung-hsun, P'eng Tse-min, Chang chih-chung, Fu Tso-yi, Li Chu-ch'en, Li Chang-ta, Chang Po-chun, Cheng Ch'ien, Chang Hsi-jo, Ch'en Ming-shu, Tan Ping-shan, Chang Nan-hsien, Liu Ya-tsu, Chang Tung-sun, and Lung Yun as council members to form the Central People's Government Council, proclaimed the founding of the People's Republic of China, and decided that Peking shall be the capital of the People's Republic of China.

The Central People's Government Council of the People's Republic of China took over office today in this capital and unanimously made the following decisions:

Proclamation of the formation of the Central People's Government of the People's Republic of China;

Adoption of the Common Program of the Chinese People's Political Consultative Conference as the policy of the Government;

Election of Lin Po-ch'u among the council members as secretary-general of the Central People's Government Council;

Appointment of Chou En-lai as premier of the State Administration Council and concurrently as minister of the Ministry of Foreign Affairs, Mao Tse-tung as chairman of the People's Revolutionary Military Council of the Central People's Government, Chu Teh as commander-in-chief of the People's Liberation Army, Shen Chun-ju as chief justice of the Supreme People's Court, and Lo Jung-huan as procurator-general of the Supreme People's Procuratorate and entrusting them with the task of early formation of the various organs of the Government to carry out the work of the Government.

At the same time, the Central People's Government Council decided to declare to the governments of all other countries that this Government is the sole legal government representing all the people of the People's Republic of China. This Government is willing to establish diplomatic relations with any foreign government that is willing to observe the principles of equality, mutual benefit, and mutual respect of territorial integrity and sovereignty.

DOCUMENT 2

THE COMMON PROGRAM OF THE CHINESE PEOPLE'S POLITICAL CONSULTATIVE CONFERENCE

[Adopted by the First Plenary Session of the Chinese People's Political Consultative Conference on September 29, 1949, in Peking.]

PREAMBLE

The great victories of the Chinese people's War of Liberation and of the people's revolution have put an end to the era of the rule of imperialism, feudalism, and bureaucratic capitalism in China. From the status of an oppressed people, the Chinese have risen to become masters of a new society and a new state, and have replaced the Kuomintang's reactionary rule of feudal, comprador, fascist dictatorship with the Republic of the People's Democratic Dictatorship.

The Chinese People's Democratic Dictatorship is the state power of the people's democratic united front, composed of the Chinese working class, peasantry, petty bourgeoisie, national bourgeoisie, and other patriotic democratic elements, based on the alliance of workers and peasants, and led by the working class. The Chinese People's Political Consultative Conference, composed of the representatives of the Communist Party of China, of all democratic parties and people's organizations, of all regions, of the People's Liberation Army, of all national minorities, overseas Chinese, and other patriotic democratic elements, is the organizational form of the people's democratic united front.

The Chinese People's Political Consultative Conference, representing the will of the people of the whole country, proclaims the establishment of the People's Republic of China and forms the people's own central government. The Chinese People's Political Consultative Conference unanimously agrees that New Democracy, *i.e.*, the People's Democracy, shall be the political foundation for the national construction of the People's Republic of China. It has also adopted the following Common Program which should be observed by all units participating in the Conference, by the people's government at all levels, and by the people of the whole country.

CHAPTER I. GENERAL PRINCIPLES

Article 1. The People's Republic of China is a New Democratic or a People's Democratic state. It carries out the People's Democratic Dictatorship—led by the working class, based on the alliance of workers and peasants, and uniting all democratic classes and all nationalities in China. It opposes imperialism, feudalism, and bureaucratic capitalism, and strives for the independence, democracy, peace, unity, prosperity, and strength of China.

Article 2. The Central People's Government of the People's Republic of China shall undertake to wage the people's War of Liberation to the very end, to liberate all the territory of China, and to achieve the unification of China.

Article 3. The People's Republic of China shall abolish all the prerogatives of imperialist countries in China. It shall confiscate bureaucratic capital and place it into the possession of the people's state. It shall systematically transform the feudal and semifeudal land ownership system into a system of peasant land ownership. It shall protect the public property of the state and the property of the cooperatives and shall protect the economic interests and private property of workers, peasants, the petty bourgeoisie, and the national bourgeoisie. It shall develop the people's economy of New Democracy and steadily transform the country from an agricultural into an industrial one.

Article 4. The people of the People's Republic of China shall have the right to elect and to be elected according to law.

Article 5. The people of the People's Republic of China shall have freedom of thought, speech, publication, assembly, association, correspondence, person, domicile, change of domicile, religious belief, and freedom to hold processions and demonstrations.

Article 6. The People's Republic of China shall abolish the feudal system which holds women in bondage. Women shall enjoy equal rights with men in political, economic, cultural, educational, and social life. Freedom to choose whom they shall marry shall be put into effect for men and women.

Article 7. The People's Republic of China shall suppress all counterrevolutionary activities and severely punish all Kuomintang counterrevolutionary war criminals and other leading incorrigible counterrevolutionary elements who collaborate with imperialism, commit treason against the motherland, and oppose the cause of People's Democracy. Feudal landlords, bureaucratic capitalists, and reactionary elements in general, after they have been disarmed and have had their special powers abolished, shall, within a required period, be deprived of their political rights in accordance with law. But, at the same time, they shall be given some means of livelihood and shall be compelled to reform themselves through labor so as to become new men. If they continue to engage in counterrevolutionary activities, they will be severely punished.

Article 8. It is the duty of every national of the People's Republic of China to defend the motherland, to abide by the law, to observe labor discipline, to protect public property, to perform public and military service, and to pay taxes.

Article 9. All nationalities within the boundaries of the People's Republic of China shall have equal rights and duties.

Article 10. The armed forces of the People's Republic of China, *i.e.,* the People's Liberation Army, the people's public security forces, and the people's police belong to the people. It is the tasks of these armed forces to defend the independence, territorial integrity, and sovereignty of China, and to defend the revolutionary gains and all legitimate rights and interests of the Chinese people. The Central People's Government of the People's Republic of China shall endeavor to consolidate and strengthen the people's armed forces, so as to enable them to carry out their tasks effectively.

Article 11. The People's Republic of China shall unite with all peace-loving and freedom-loving countries and peoples throughout the world—first of all, with the U.S.S.R., all People's Democracies, and all oppressed nations. It shall take its stand in the camp of world peace and democracy, to oppose imperialist aggression and defend lasting world peace.

CHAPTER II. ORGANS OF STATE POWER

Article 12. The state power of the People's Republic of China belongs to the people. The people's congresses and the people's governments at all levels are the organs for the exercise of state power by the people. The people's congresses at all levels shall be elected by universal franchise. The people's congresses at all levels shall elect the people's governments at their respective levels. The people's governments shall be the organs for exercising state power at their respective levels when the people's congresses at their respective levels are not in session.

The All-China People's Congress shall be the organ of state power. The Central People's Government shall be the supreme organ for exercising state power when the All-China People's Congress is not in session.

Article 13. The Chinese People's Political Consultative Conference is the organizational form of the people's democratic united front. It shall be composed of the representatives of the working class, the peasantry, the revolutionary armed forces, intellectuals, the petty bourgeoisie, the national bourgeoisie, national minorities, the overseas Chinese, and other patriotic democratic elements.

Pending the convocation of the All-China People's Congress elected by universal franchise, the Plenary Session of the Chinese People's Political Counsultative Conference shall exercise the functions and powers of the All-China People's Congress, enact the Organic Law of the Central People's Government of the People's Republic of China, elect the Central People's Government Council of the People's Republic of China and vest it with the authority to exercise state power.

After the convocation of the All-China People's Congress elected by universal franchise, the Chinese People's Political Consultative Conference may submit proposals on fundamental policies relating to national construction work and on other important measures to the All-China People's Congress or to the Central People's Government.

Article 14. In all places newly liberated by the People's Liberation Army, military control shall be exercised, and the Kuomintang reactionary organs of state power shall be abolished. The Central People's Government or the military and administrative organs at the front shall appoint personnel to organize military control commissions and local people's governments. These shall lead the people in establishing revolutionary order and suppressing counterrevolutionary activities and, when conditions permit, shall convene people's representative conferences.

Pending the convocation of the local people's congresses elected by universal franchise, the local people's representative conferences shall gradually exercise the functions and powers of the local people's congresses.

The duration of military control shall be determined by the Central People's Government according to the military and political conditions prevailing in the different localities.

In all places where military operations have completely ended, where agrarian reform has been thoroughly carried out, and people of all circles have been fully organized, elections based on universal franchise shall be held immediately for the purpose of convening local people's congresses.

Article 15. The organs of state power at all levels shall practice democratic centralism. The main principles shall be: the people's congresses shall be responsible and accountable to the people; the people's government councils shall be responsible and accountable to the people's congresses. Within the people's congresses and within the people's government councils, the minority shall abide by the decisions of the majority; the appointment of the people's governments of each level shall be ratified by the people's government of the higher level; the people's government at the lower levels shall obey the people's government at the higher levels; and all local people's government throughout the country shall obey the Central People's Government.

Article 16. The jurisdiction of the Central People's Government and the local people's governments shall be defined according to the nature of the various matters involved, and shall be prescribed by decrees of the Central People's Government Council so as to satisfy the requirements of both national unity and local expediency.

Article 17. All laws, decrees, and judicial systems of the Kuomintang reactionary government that oppressed the people shall be abolished. Laws and decrees protecting the people shall be enacted and the people's judicial system shall be established.

Article 18. All state organs of the People's Republic of China shall enforce a revolutionary working style, embodying honesty, simplicity, and service to the people. They shall severely punish corruption, forbid extravagance, and oppose the bureaucratic working style, which alienates the masses of the people.

Article 19. People's supervisory organs shall be set up in the people's governments at county and municipal level and above, to supervise the performance of duties by the state organs at various levels and by government personnel of all types, and to propose that disciplinary action be taken against state organs and government personnel who violate the law or are found negligent in the performance of their duties.

The people or people's organizations shall have the right to file charges with the people's supervisory organs or people's judicial organs against any state organs or any government personnel who violate the law or are found negligent in the performance of their duties.

CHAPTER III. MILITARY SYSTEM

Article 20. The People's Republic of China shall build up a unified army, *i.e.*, the People's Liberation Army and people's public security forces, which shall be placed under the command of the People's Revolutionary Military Council of the Central People's Government; it shall institute unity of command, system, formation, and discipline.

Article 21. The People's Liberation Army and the people's public security forces shall, in accordance with the principle of unity between the officers and the rank and file and between the army and the people, set up a system of political work and shall educate the commanders and rank and file of these forces in a revolutionary and patriotic spirit.

Article 22. The People's Republic of China shall strengthen its modernized army and shall establish an air force and a navy in order to consolidate national defense.

Article 23. The People's Republic of China shall put into effect the militia system to safeguard local order and to lay the foundation for national mobilization. It shall make preparations to enforce a system of obligatory military service at the appropriate time.

Article 24. The armed forces of the People's Republic of China shall, during peacetime, systematically take part in agricultural and industrial production in order to assist in national construction work, provided such work does not interfere with their military duties.

Article 25. Dependents of those who have given their lives for the revolution, as well as dependants of members of the revolutionary forces who are in need, shall receive preferential treatment from the state and society. The people's government shall make appropriate arrangements for disabled or retired servicemen who have participated in the revolutionary war, providing them with the means of livelihood or with occupations.

CHAPTER IV. ECONOMIC POLICY

Article 26. The basic principle for the economic construction of the People's Republic of China is to develop production and bring about a prosperous economy through the policies of taking into account both public and private interests, of benefiting both labor and capital, of mutual aid between the city and countryside, and circulation of goods between China and foreign countries. The state shall coordinate and regulate the state-owned, cooperative, individual peasant and handicraft, private capitalist, and state capitalist sectors of the economy, in their spheres of operations, supply of raw materials, marketing, labor conditions, technical equipment, policies of public and general finance, etc. In this way all sectors of the social economy can, under the leadership of the state-owned economy, carry out division and coordination of labor and play their proper parts in promoting the development of the social economy as a whole.

Article 27. Agrarian reform is the indispensable condition for the development of the nation's productive power and for its industrialization. In all areas where agrarian reform has been carried out, the ownership of the land acquired by the peasants shall be protected. In areas where agrarian reform has not been carried out, the peasant masses must be set in motion to establish peasant organizations and to put into effect the policy of "land to the tiller" through such measures as the elimination of local bandits and despots, the reduction of rent and interest, and the distribution of land.

Article 28. State-owned economy is an economy of a socialist nature. All enterprises relating to the economic life of the country and exercising a dominant influence over the people's livelihood shall be under the unified operation of the state. All state-owned resources and enterprises are the public property of all the people and are the main material basis on which the People's Republic will develop production and bring about a prosperous economy. They are the leading force of the entire social economy.

Article 29. Cooperative economy is an economy of a semisocialist nature and is an important sector of the people's economy as a whole. The people's government shall foster its development and accord it preferential treatment.

Article 30. The people's government shall encourage the active operation of all private economic enterprises beneficial to the national welfare and to the people's livelihood and shall assist in their development.

Article 31. The economy jointly operated by state and private capital is an economy of a state capitalist nature. Whenever necessary and possible, private capital shall be encouraged to develop in the direction of state capitalism, in such ways as doing processing work for state-owned enterprises, jointly operating enterprises with the state, or in the form of concessions exploiting state-owned resources.

Article 32. The system of workers' participation in the administration of production shall, for the present period, be established in state-owned enterprises. This means that factory administrative committees shall be set up under the leadership of the factory managers. In privately owned enterprises, in order to carry out the principle of benefiting both labor and capital, collective contracts shall be signed by the trade union, representing the workers and staff members, and by the employer. For the present period, an eight- to ten-hour day should in general be enforced in publicly and privately operated enterprises, but under special circumstances this matter may be dealt with at discretion. The people's government shall fix minimum wages according to the conditions prevailing in various localities and trades. Labor insurance shall be gradually established. The special interests of juvenile and women workers shall be safeguarded. Inspection of industries and mines shall be carried out in order to improve their safety precautions and sanitary facilities.

Article 33. The Central People's Government shall strive to draw up, as soon as possible, a general plan for rehabilitating and developing the main sectors of the public and private economy of the entire country. It shall also fix the scope of the division and coordination of labor between the Central People's Government and local governments in economic construction, and shall coordinate the activities of the economic departments of the Central People's Government and local governments. Under the unified leadership of the Central People's Government, its various economic departments and those of the local governments shall give full play to their creativity and initiative.

Article 34. Agriculture, forestry, fisheries and animal husbandry: In all areas where agrarian reform has been thoroughly carried out, the central task of the people's government shall be the organization of the peasants and of all manpower available for allocation to the development of agricultural production and secondary occupations. The people's government shall also guide the peasants step by step in the organization of various forms of mutual aid in labor and cooperation in production, according to the principle of willingness and mutual benefit. In newly liberated areas, every step in agrarian reform shall be linked with reviving and developing agricultural production.

The people's government shall, in accordance with the state plan and the material requirements of the people, strive to restore and surpass the prewar output of grain, industrial raw materials, and export goods as soon as possible. Attention shall be paid to construction and repair of irrigation works, to prevention of floods and droughts, to restoration and development of animal husbandry, to increasing the supply of fertilizers to improvement of farm implements and seeds, to prevention of pest damage and plant diseases, to relief work in the

event of natural calamities, and to planned settlement for land reclamation.

Forests shall be protected and afforestation shall be developed according to plan.

Coastal fisheries shall be protected and the marine products industry
shall be developed.

Livestock raising shall be protected and developed and preventive
measures shall be taken against plague.

Article 35. Industry: In order to lay the foundation for the industrialization of the country, the central focus of industrial work shall
be the planned, systematic rehabilitation and development of heavy
industry, such as mining, iron and steel production, power, machine-
making, electricity, the main chemical industries, etc. At the same time,
the production of the textile industry and other light industries beneficial to the national welfare and to the people's livelihood shall be
restored and increased so as to meet the needs of the people's daily
consumption.

Article 36. Communications: Railways and highways shall be swiftly
restored and gradually extended. Rivers shall be dredged and water
transportation expanded. Postal and telecommunications shall be improved and developed. Various communications facilities shall be built
up and civil aviation established step by step according to plan.

Article 37. Commerce: All legitimate public and private trade shall
be protected. Control shall be exercised over foreign trade and a policy
of protecting trade shall be adopted. Freedom of domestic trade shall
be established under a unified state economic plan, but disturbing the
market through commercial speculation shall be strictly prohibited.
State-owned trading organizations shall assume the responsibility of
adjusting supply and demand, stabilizing commodity prices, and assisting the people's cooperatives. The people's government shall adopt
the measures necessary to encourage the people to save, to facilitate
remittances from overseas Chinese, and to channel into industry and
other productive enterprises all idle capital and commercial capital
that are not beneficial to the national welfare and to the people's livelihood.

Article 38. Cooperatives: The broad masses of working people shall
be encouraged and assisted to develop cooperative enterprises on a
voluntary basis. Supply and marketing cooperatives, as well as consumers', credit, producers', and transport cooperatives shall be organized in towns and villages. Consumers' cooperatives shall first be organized in factories, government offices, and schools.

Article 39. Currency and Banking: Financial enterprises shall be
strictly controlled by the state. The right of issuing currency belongs

to the state. The circulation of foreign currency within the country shall be prohibited. The buying and selling of foreign exchange, foreign currency, gold, and silver shall be managed by the state banks. Private financial enterprises operating in accordance with the law shall be subjected to supervision and direction by the state. All who engage in financial speculation and undermine the financial enterprises of the state shall be subject to severe punishment.

Article 40. Public finance: A budget and financial statement system shall be instituted. The spheres of financial administration of the Central People's Government and local governments shall be defined. Economizing and frugality shall be enforced. The budget shall be gradually balanced and capital accumulated for the country's production.

The taxation policy of the state shall be based on the principle of ensuring supplies for the revolutionary war, and giving consideration to the rehabilitation and development of production and the requirements of national construction. The taxation system shall be simplified and equitable distribution of burden effected.

CHAPTER V. CULTURAL AND EDUCATIONAL POLICY

Article 41. The culture and education of the People's Republic of China shall be New Democratic—national, scientific, and popular. The main tasks of the people's government in cultural and educational work shall be the raising of the cultural level of the people, the training of personnel for national construction work, the eradicating of feudal, comprador, and fascist ideologies, and the cultivation of the idea of service to the people.

Article 42. Love of the motherland, love of the people, love of labor, love of science, and care of public property shall be promoted as the public spirit of all nationals of the People's Republic of China.

Article 43. Efforts shall be made to develop the natural sciences in order to serve industrial, agricultural, and national defense construction. Scientific discoveries and inventions shall be encouraged and rewarded and scientific knowledge shall be disseminated among the people.

Article 44. The application of a scientific-historical viewpoint to the study and interpretation of history, economics, politics, culture, and international affairs shall be promoted. Outstanding works in social science shall be encouraged and rewarded.

Article 45. Literature and the arts shall be promoted to serve the people, to awaken their political consciousness, and to enhance their enthusiasm for labor. Outstanding works of literature and art shall be encouraged and rewarded. The people's drama and cinema shall be developed.

Article 46. The method of education of the People's Republic of China shall be the unification of theory and practice. The people's government shall reform the old educational system, subject matter, and teaching methods in a planned and systematic manner.

Article 47. In order to meet the extensive requirements of revolutionary and national construction work, universal education shall be carried out, secondary and higher education shall be strengthened, technical education shall be stressed, the spare-time education of workers and of cadres at their posts shall be strengthened, and revolutionary political education shall be accorded to both young and old-style intellectuals. All this is to be done in a planned and systematic manner.

Article 48. Universal physical culture shall be promoted. Public health and medical services shall be expanded and attention shall be paid to the protection of the health of mothers, infants, and children.

Article 49. The freedom to report the news truthfully shall be safeguarded. The utilization of the press for slander, for undermining the interests of the state and the people, and for provoking world war shall be prohibited. The people's broadcasting and publishing enterprises shall be developed. Attention shall be paid to publishing popular books and journals beneficial to the people.

CHAPTER VI.   POLICY TOWARD NATIONALITIES

Article 50. All nationalities within the boundaries of the People's Republic of China are equal. They shall establish unity and mutual aid among themselves, and shall oppose imperialism and their own public enemies, so that the People's Republic of China will become a big fraternal and cooperative family composed of all its nationalities. Nationalism and chauvinism shall be opposed. Acts involving discrimination, oppression, and disrupting the unity of the various nationalities shall be prohibited.

Article 51. Regional autonomy shall be exercised in areas where national minorities are concentrated, and various kinds of autonomous organizations for the different nationalities shall be set up according to the size of the respective populations and regions. In places where different nationalities live together and in the autonomous areas of the national minorities, the different nationalities shall each have an appropriate number of representatives in the local organs of state power.

Article 52. All national minorities within the boundaries of the People's Republic of China shall have the right to join the People's Liberation Army and to organize local people's public security forces in accordance with the unified military system of the state.

Article 53. All national minorities shall have freedom to develop their spoken and written languages, to preserve or reform their traditions, customs, and religious beliefs. The people's government shall assist the masses of all national minorities in their political, economic, cultural, and educational development.

CHAPTER VII. FOREIGN POLICY

Article 54. The foreign policy of the People's Republic of China is based on the principle of protection of the independence, freedom, integrity of territory, and sovereignty of the country, upholding lasting international peace and friendly cooperation between the peoples of all countries, and opposing the imperialist policy of aggression and war.

Article 55. The Central People's Government of the People's Republic of China shall examine the treaties and agreements concluded between the Kuomintang and foreign governments, and shall recognize, abrogate, revise, or renegotiate them according to their respective contents.

Article 56. The Central People's Government of the People's Republic of China may, on the basis of equality, mutual benefit, and mutual respect for territorial sovereignty, negotiate with foreign governments that have severed relations with the Kuomintang reactionary clique and that adopt a friendly attitude toward the People's Republic of China, and may establish diplomatic relations with them.

Article 57. The People's Republic of China may restore and develop commercial and trade relations with foreign governments and peoples on a basis of equality and mutual benefit.

Article 58. The Central People's Government of the People's Republic of China shall do its utmost to protect the legitimate rights and interests of Chinese residing abroad.

Article 59. The people's government of the People's Republic of China protects law-abiding foreign nationals in China.

Article 60. The People's Republic of China shall accord the right of asylum to foreign nationals who seek refuge in China because they have been oppressed by their own governments for supporting the people's interests and for taking part in the struggle for peace and democracy.

THE ORGANIC LAW OF THE CENTRAL PEOPLE'S GOVERNMENT OF THE PEOPLE'S REPUBLIC OF CHINA

[Adopted by the First Plenary Session of the Chinese People's Political Consultative Conference on September 27, 1949, in Peking.]

CHAPTER I. GENERAL PRINCIPLES

Article I. The People's Republic of China is a state of the People's Democratic Dictatorship, led by the working class, based on the alliance of workers and peasants, and uniting all democratic classes and all the nationalities within the country.

Article 2. The Government of the People's Republic of China shall be established by the All-China People's Congress on the principle of democratic centralism.

Article 3. Prior to the convocation of the All-China People's Congress, to be elected by universal franchise, the Plenary Session of the Chinese People's Political Consultative Conference shall perform the functions and exercise the powers of the All-China People's Congress, enact the Organic Law of the Central People's Government of the People's Republic of China, elect the Central People's Government Council of the People's Republic of China, and vest it with the authority to exercise state power.

Article 4. The Central People's Government Council represents the People's Republic of China in international relations and assumes the leadership of the state apparatus at home.

Article 5. The Central People's Government Council shall set up the Government Administration Council as the highest executive body for state administration; the People's Revolutionary Military Council as the supreme military command of the state; and the Supreme People's Court and the Supreme People's Procuratorate as the highest judicial and supervisory bodies of the state.

CHAPTER II. THE CENTRAL PEOPLE'S GOVERNMENT COUNCIL

Article 6. The Central People's Government Council shall consist of a chairman and six vice-chairmen of the Central People's Government and of fifty-six council members elected by the Plenary Session of the Chinese People's Political Consultative Conference. It shall have a secretary-general elected by and from the Central People's Government Council.

Article 7. The Central People's Government Council shall exercise the following authority, in accordance with the Common Program enacted by the Plenary Session of the Chinese People's Political Consultative Conference:

1. Enacting and interpreting the laws of the state, promulgating decrees, and supervising their execution;

2. Determining the administrative policies of the state;

3. Annulling or revising any decisions and orders of the Government Administration Council that do not conform to the laws and decrees of the state;

4. Ratifying, abrogating, or revising treaties and agreements concluded by the People's Republic of China with foreign countries;

5. Dealing with questions of war and peace;

6. Approving or revising the state budget and financial statement;

7. Promulgating acts of general amnesty and pardon;

8. Instituting and awarding orders, medals, and titles of honor of the state;

9. Appointing or removing of government personnel as follows:

a) Appointment or removal of the premier and vice-premiers and members of the Government Administration Council; secretary-general and assistant secretaries-general of the Government Administration Council; chairmen, vice-chairmen, and members of the various committees and commissions; ministers and vice-ministers of the various ministries; president and vice-presidents of the Academy of Sciences; directors and deputy directors of the various administrations; and manager and assistant managers of the People's Bank;

b) Appointment or removal or confirmation of the appointment or removal, on the recommendation of the Government Administration Council, of chairmen, vice-chairmen, and chief administrative personnel of people's governments in various major administrative areas, provinces, and municipalities;

c) Appointment or removal of ambassadors, ministers, and plenipotentiary representatives to foreign states;

d) Appointment or removal of the chairmen, vice-chairmen, and members of the People's Revolutionary Military Council, and of the commander-in-chief, deputy commander-in-chief, chief-of-staff, deputy chiefs-of-staff, director, and assistant director of the General Political Department of the People's Liberation Army;

e) Appointment or removal of the president and vice-presidents and committee members of the Supreme People's Court, and the procurator-general, deputy procurators-general, and committee members of the Supreme People's Procuratorate;

10. Preparing for and convening the All-China People's Congress.

Article 8. The chairman of the Central People's Government shall preside over the meetings of the Central People's Government Council and shall direct its work.

Article 9. The vice-chairman and secretary-general of the Central People's Government shall assist the chairman in the discharge of his duties.

Article 10. Sessions of the Central People's Government Council shall be convened by the chairman once every two months. The chairman may convene the session earlier or postpone it when conditions demand it or upon the request of more than one third of the members of the Central People's Government Council or upon the request of the Government Administration Council. More than half of the council members constitute a quorum; the adoption of any resolution demands the concurrence of over half the members present at the session.

Article 11. The Central People's Government Council shall have a secretariat and may set up other subordinate working bodies when necessary.

Article 12. The Central People's Government Council shall enact its own organizational regulations.

CHAPTER III. THE GOVERNMENT ADMINISTRATION COUNCIL

Article 13. The Government Administration Council shall consist of a premier, a number of vice-premiers, a secretary-general, and a number of council members appointed by the Central People's Government Council.

Members of the Government Administration Council may concurrently hold posts as chairmen of the various committees or commissions or as ministers of the various ministries.

Article 14. The Government Administration Council shall be responsible and accountable to the Central People's Government Council. When the Central People's Government Council adjourns, the Government Administration Council shall be responsible and accountable to the chairman of the Central People's Government.

Article 15. The Government Administration Council shall exercise the following authority on the basis of the Common Program of the Chinese People's Political Consultative Conference, and of the laws and decrees of the state and of the administrative policies stipulated by the Central People's Government Council:

1. Issuing decisions and orders and supervising their execution;

2. Annulling or revising the decisions and orders of the committees, ministries, commissions, Academy of Sciences, administrations, and the People's Bank, and governments at all levels, that do not conform to

the laws and decrees of the state and to the decisions and orders of the Government Administration Council;

3. Submitting bills to the Central People's Government Council;

4. Coordinating, unifying, and directing the interrelations, the internal organizations, and the general work of the committees, ministries, commissions, administrations, and the People's Bank, and other subordinate bodies;

5. Directing the work of local people's governments throughout the country;

6. Appointment or removal, or confirming the appointment or removal of the chief administrative personnel of county and municipal level and above, not included in Article 7, Section 9b.

Article 16. The premier of the Government Administration Council shall direct the Council's affairs. The vice-premiers and the secretary-general of the Government Administration Council shall assist the premier in the discharge of his duties.

Article 17. Once a week the Government Administration Council shall hold meetings convened by the premier. The premier may convene the meeting earlier or postpone it when conditions demand it, or upon the request of more than one third of the council members. Over half of the members of the Government Administration Council constitute a quorum, and the adoption of a resolution demands the concurrence of over half the members present at the meeting.

The decisions and orders of the Government Administration Council shall come into force either when signed by the premier or when signed by the premier and countersigned by the heads of the committees, ministries, commissions, Academy of Sciences, administrations, or the People's Bank.

Article 18. The Government Administration Council shall set up committees of Political and Legal Affairs, of Financial and Economic Affairs, of Cultural and Educational Affairs, and of People's Control, and shall set up the following ministries, commissions, Academy of Sciences, administrations, and the People's Bank, which shall direct their respective departments of state administration:

Ministry of the Interior, Ministry of Foreign Affairs, Information Administration, Ministry of Public Security, Ministry of Finance, People's Bank, Ministry of Trade, Customs Administration, Ministry of Heavy Industry, Ministry of Fuel Industry, Ministry of Textile Industry, Ministry of Food Industry, Ministry of Light Industry (industries not included in the four mentioned above), Ministry of Railways, Ministry of Posts and Telecommunications, Ministry of Communications, Ministry of Agriculture, Ministry of Forestry and Land

Reclamation, Ministry of Water Conservation, Ministry of Labor, Ministry of Cultural Affairs, Ministry of Education, Academy of Sciences, Press Administration, Publications Administration, Ministry of Public Health, Ministry of Justice, Commission of Legislative Affairs, Commission of the Nationalities Affairs, and the Commission of Overseas Chinese Affairs.

The Committee of Political and Legal Affairs shall direct the work of the Ministry of the Interior, the Ministry of Public Security, the Ministry of Justice, the Commission of Legislative Affairs, and the Commission of the Nationalities Affairs.

The Committee of Financial and Economic Affairs shall direct the work of the Ministries of Finance, of Trade, of Heavy Industry, of Fuel Industry, of Textile Industry, of Food Industry, of Light Industry, of Railways, of Posts and Telecommunications, of Communications, of Agriculture, of Forestry and Land Reclamation, of Water Conservation, of Labor, the People's Bank, and the Customs Administration.

The Committee of Cultural and Educational Affairs shall direct the work of the Ministry of Cultural Affairs, the Ministry of Education, the Ministry of Public Health, the Academy of Sciences, the Press Administration, and the Publications Administration.

In order to carry out their work, the responsible committees may issue decisions and orders to the ministries, the commissions, the Academy of Sciences, the administrations, and the People's Bank under their direction and to other subordinate bodies and shall supervise the execution of these orders.

The Committee of People's Control shall be responsible for supervising the execution of duties by government offices and government employees.

Article 19. The ministries, commissions, Academy of Sciences, administrations, and the People's Bank may announce decisions and issue orders within their jurisdiction and shall supervise their execution.

Article 20. The Government Administration Council shall have a secretariat to deal with the routine work and to take charge of the files, archives, the printing of official seals, etc.

Article 21. The organizational regulations of the Government Administration Council, the committees, ministries, commissions, the Academy of Sciences, the administrations, the People's Bank, and the secretariat shall be enacted or ratified by the Central People's Government Council.

Article 22. The Central People's Government Council may, when necessary, decide on the increase or reduction of the number or on the merging of the committees, ministries, commissions, the Academy of Sciences, administrations, the People's Bank, and the secretariat.

CHAPTER IV. THE PEOPLE'S REVOLUTIONARY MILITARY COUNCIL

Article 23. The People's Liberation Army and other people's armed forces throughout the country shall come under the unified control and command of the People's Revolutionary Military Council.

Article 24. The People's Revolutionary Military Council shall have a chairman, a number of vice-chairmen, and a number of council members.

Article 25. The organization of the People's Revolutionary Military Council and the system of its administration and command shall be determined by the Central People's Government Council.

CHAPTER V. THE SUPREME PEOPLE'S COURT AND THE SUPREME PEOPLE'S PROCURATORATE

Article 26. The Supreme People's Court is the highest judicial body in the country, and is charged with the direction and supervision of the work of judicial bodies at all levels throughout the country.

Article 27. The Supreme People's Court shall have a president, a number of vice-presidents, and a number of committee members.

Article 28. The Supreme People's Procuratorate shall have supreme supervisory power to ensure the strict observance of the law by all government offices and government personnel as well as by nationals of the country.

Article 29. The Supreme People's Procuratorate shall have a procurator-general, a number of deputy procurators-general, and a number of committee members.

Article 30. The organizational regulations of the Supreme People's Court and of the Supreme People's Procuratorate shall be enacted by the Central People's Government Council.

CHAPTER VI. RIGHT OF AMENDMENT AND INTERPRETATION OF THIS ORGANIC LAW

Article 31. The right of amendment of the Organic Law of the Central People's Government belongs to the Plenary Session of the Chinese People's Political Consultative Conference; when the latter is not in session, it belongs to the Central People's Government Council. The right of interpretation of this Organic Law belongs to the Central People's Government Council.

MAO TSE-TUNG'S ANALYSIS OF CLASSES IN CHINESE SOCIETY

[Quotations are from *The Chinese Revolution and the Communist Party of China, 1939.*]

THE LANDLORD CLASS

The big landlords are the "remaining feudal elements" and the "mainstay of the Chinese society under the imperialist rule." They constitute the majority of the landowning class. They exploit and oppress the peasantry. They are the enemies of the revolution who should be suppressed and eliminated.

The petty landlords, especially those who are bankrupt or nearly bankrupt, may remain neutral or may even take part in the revolution against the imperialists and the big landlords. The "intelligentsia who have sprung up from this stratum and who have had a scientific education" may be especially helpful.

THE BOURGEOISIE

The comprador upper bourgeoisie serve and are nurtured by the imperialistic foreign capitalists. They are close to the semifeudal elements. They are enemies of the revolution and must be "resolutely crushed." When imperialist powers clash with one another or when the revolution is fighting against a certain imperialist power, the comprador class in the service of an opposing imperialist power may be temporarily helpful to the revolution, but they are in the long run unreliable.

The national bourgeoisie is mainly a middle bourgeoisie and has suffered from the oppression of the imperialists and the remaining feudal elements. Though it is weak economically and politically, "at a certain period and under certain circumstances," it can be a "comparatively good ally." But at other times, it may assist the upper bourgeoisie and other antirevolutionary forces, and so "we must exercise caution in dealing with this class stratum."

THE PETTY BOURGEOISIE

The intelligentsia and the students who are poverty stricken or threatened by unemployment are "quite revolutionary." Possessing a high political consciousness, they can become the vanguard of the revolution. It was among them that the study of Marxism-Leninism had its start. The revolution needs them.

The poor people of urban districts: "This class stratum includes bankrupt handicraftsmen, hawkers, peasants who left their homes and remain unemployed in towns, and other laborers without fixed jobs." Their status is like that of the poor peasants. They are the "semi-proletariat" and "a natural ally of the proletariat."

The employees of industrial and commercial organizations, as well as government offices and cultural institutions, "earn their living through mental labor or technical abilities." They are "indispensable in all economic, national, and cultural reconstruction."

Handicraftsmen and free professional men: The latter refer to "doctors and others"; the former, to independent producers who "now bear the burden of Chinese economic reconstruction. . . . Some of them hire a small number of laborers, while others work on their own." They can become "a part of the revolutionary force."

THE PEASANTRY

Rich farmers, about 5 per cent of the rural population, are the country bourgeoisie; strictly speaking, they are not a part of the peasantry. Though most of them are "imbued with semifeudal characteristics and are related to the town bourgeoisie," their products are "indispensable within a certain period."

Middle peasants, about 20 per cent of the rural population, are self-sufficient economically, but they do not exploit others and "most of them do not own enough land and enjoy no political privileges at all." They are "a reliable ally of the proletariat."

Poor peasants and farm laborers comprise about 70 per cent of the peasantry. "The poor peasants either do not possess any land or do not possess enough land and form a semiproletariat of the peasantry. They form the strongest force of the Chinese Revolution, the natural and most reliable ally of the proletariat and the main force of the Chinese Revolution."

THE PROLETARIAT

"The Chinese proletariat includes approximately 2.5 million modern industrial workers, 12 million town handicraftsmen and hired laborers, and also a large number of country proletariat." They are oppressed by three forces: the imperialists, the bourgeoisie, and the feudal elements. Under the leadership of the Communist Party of China, they are "the fundamental force of the revolution."

"Without the proletariat, no revolution can succeed."

DOCUMENT 5

POLITICAL PARTIES OTHER THAN THE COMMUNIST PARTY

[Summarized by the author and based on information from "Political Parties in China," *People's China*, November 16, 1956.]

1. *The Kuomintang Revolutionary Committee.* This group was organized in January, 1948, by former members of the Kuomintang gathered in Hong Kong who were all opposed to Chiang Kai-shek.

2. *The China Democratic League* is an alliance of small political parties organized in 1941. The more conservative groups later left the League, abandoning it to the more or less leftist elements.

3. *The China Democratic National Reconstruction Association.* Organized in 1945, this group consists mainly of industrialists, businessmen, and intellectuals engaged in industry and commerce. It has played a major role in the "socialist remolding" of the capitalists and in persuading them to put their enterprises under state control.

4. *The China Association for Promoting Democracy* draws its members from educational and cultural workers.

5. *The Chinese Peasants' and Workers' Democratic Party* was originally known as "The Third Party" and was organized in protest against Chiang Kai-shek's anti-Communist purge of 1927, which ended the Kuomintang-Communist cooperation.

6. *Chih-Kung-Tang.* The name of the group has a long history; it began with overseas Chinese who supported the revolution of Sun Yat-sen against the Manchus. The present group in China came into being in 1947, and its mission is to appeal to Chinese abroad on behalf of the Communists.

7. *Chiu-san Society.* Organized in 1945, this group recruits its members from intellectuals in scientific and technical fields.

8. *Taiwan Democratic Self-Government League.* This very small group of persons from Taiwan agitates for the return of Taiwan to the motherland.

III

The Organization of
the Government

When the New Democracy was established in 1949, there was no indication how long this transition period would last. Mao Tse-tung in his writings had stressed the need of gradual transition and had given the impression that socialism for China was a distant goal.[1] In "On New Democracy," he wrote:

> The task of the revolution at present is to oppose imperialism and feudalism. Before this task is accomplished, it is useless to talk about socialism. The Chinese revolution must be divided into two steps: the first is the New Democracy and the second is socialism. Moreover, the period of the first step is by no means short. It cannot be achieved overnight. We are not impractical visionaries; we cannot ignore the actual conditions before our eyes.

In his address "On Coalition Government" five years later (1945), he repeated the same view and cautioned against Communist Party members who "talk glibly about socialism and Communism":

> In China it will be necessary to struggle for [the New] democracy for a long time yet. Without the united nation of the New Democracy, without the growth of the economy of the New Democracy, without the development of private capitalism and cooperative economy . . . without a new and thorough bourgeois-democratic revolution, it would be an empty dream to establish socialism on the barren waste of colonial, semicolonial, and semifeudal society.

The affirmation that the transitional period would be "by no means short" led people to believe that the more moderate policies would be continued for a long time, that "private capitalism" would not be in any danger of early liquidation, and that private ownership would be given due protection. Mao, however, did not specify how many years would be considered a "long" transitional period. At any rate, few people suspected in 1949 that the New Democracy would be replaced by socialism in five years.

THE ELECTIONS

As far as government structure was concerned, the Common Program stipulated that state power belonged to the people and the people would exercise their sovereign power through elected representatives.

---

[1] According to Communist theory, socialism is a prelude to Communism. China as a "semifeudal, semicolonial" country was not ready for socialism.

Conditions in 1949, however, were not considered ripe for election, and no specific date for elections was set. The Common Program stated in Article 14 that three conditions must be met before elections could be held: termination of military operations, completion of agrarian reform, and the organization of "people of all circles." These were not simple tasks that could be accomplished in a short time.

What the Communists considered favorable conditions for elections arrived sooner than expected. The strong measures adopted in 1950–52 had enabled them to exercise sufficient control over the population to assure general compliance. By 1953, they felt ready to begin their first five-year plan and to hold elections for a reorganization of the government. The new mood of confidence was clearly reflected in the resolution to hold elections (D6). It is to be noted that the "glorious victories" which, according to the resolution, made possible the "ripe" conditions for elections included not only the three prerequisites specified in Article 14 of the Common Program, but also the "five big campaigns" previously mentioned.

The fact is that the Communists were not disposed to take any chances with elections unless they could be sure they had everything under control. After the Electoral Law (D7) was promulgated, large numbers of cadres especially trained in the interpretation and enforcement of the law were dispatched to different parts of the country to teach people how to register and vote. Universal franchise is the general principle, but certain classes of undesirable citizens (Article 5 of the law) are deprived of the right to vote. The registration of voters and the nomination of candidates are under the supervision of election committees. The law further provides for punishment of those guilty of "unlawful practices" in connection with elections.

The representative bodies are known as congresses and the representatives as deputies. Only the congresses of the local basic levels are elected directly by the people. As indicated in Article 56 of the Constitution (D8), the congresses of the provinces and counties as well as the National Congress are elected by the congresses of the next lower level; in other words, the deputies to the National Congress are elected by the provincial congresses, and the deputies to each provincial congress are elected by the county congresses in the province.

THE NATIONAL PEOPLE'S CONGRESS

According to official figures, 278,093,100 persons, constituting 85.88 per cent of registered voters, went to the polls to elect 5,669,144 deputies to the people's congresses at the primary level (D7, Article 3). The local people's congresses then met to elect deputies to the people's congresses of the next higher level, and the highest body thus indirectly elected was the National People's Congress.

The first National People's Congress, with 1,226 deputies, was convened in Peking on September 15, 1954. It was in session until September 28. Its most important task was the adoption of the Constitution, which formally terminated the transitional period of the New Democracy (1949–54). The nation entered the era of socialism, and "socialist construction" became the goal of all effort. The Constitution is supposed to be "based on the Common Program" and "a further development of it." A crucial difference is that the term "New Democracy" is hardly mentioned, but socialism and the attainment of a socialist society are repeatedly stressed.

The Common Program had, in its Article 11, pledged unity with other People's Democracies, "first of all, the U.S.S.R." This policy is reaffirmed in the preamble of the Constitution, with specific mention of the "indestructible friendship with the great U.S.S.R. and the People's Democracies." In domestic policy, however, there is a distinct difference: While the Common Program prescribes a moderate program for the transitional stage of the New Democracy, the Constitution calls for a positive program of socialism and definite measures to curb private enterprise and promote a socialist economy. For example, Article 3 of the Common Program states that the new regime "must protect the economic interests and *private property* of workers, peasants, the petty bourgeoisie, and the national bourgeoisie [italics added]," and specifies "a system of peasant land ownership," and Article 30 states that "the people's government shall encourage the active operation of all private economic enterprises beneficial to the national welfare . . . and shall assist in their development." The Constitution, on the other hand, adopts a more restrictive policy. It is stated in Article 8 that "the policy of the state toward rich-peasant economy is to restrict and gradually eliminate it," and in Article 10 that "the policy of the state toward capitalist industry and commerce is to use, restrict, and transform them." It will be seen more clearly in Chapter V that "transformation" of private enterprises into socialist enterprises means the elimination of the former.

The government structure has also been changed. As provided in Article 13 of the Common Program, the CPPCC exercised the functions of the elected congresses until elections were held. Mao Tse-tung was "elected" chairman of the People's Republic by the CPPCC. According to the Constitution, the government, known as "people's council," of each administrative level—province, county, district, etc.—is elected by the people's congress of the corresponding level. Democratic centralism, however, prescribes that the decisions and actions of every congress below the National Congress are subject to the approval or veto of the congress of the next higher level. Likewise, although a local people's council is elected by and carries out the decisions of the local congress, its actions are subject to the approval or veto of the administrative organs of higher levels. The election of representative bodies, therefore, does not diminish the power and authority of the central authorities.

GOVERNMENT CHANGES

The Constitution abolished the Central People's Government Council. The CPPCC now became an unimportant body, with advisory functions only (D11). The State Council,[2] with the premier, as well as the Supreme People's Court and the Supreme People's Procuratorate are directly responsible to the chairman of the republic and the chairman of the Standing Committee of the National People's Congress (NPC),[3] without the intervening authority of the Central People's Government Council. A new top-level organ was added: the Supreme State Council, a body for the consideration of high policy,[4] with the chairman of the republic serving as chairman and convener. The People's Revolutionary Military Council was replaced by the Council of National Defense, with the chairman of the republic serving as its ex-officio chairman and commander in chief of the armed forces. By such provisions, the Constitution vested the chairman of the republic with more power and authority than he possessed under the Common Program.

The number of vice-chairmen was reduced from six to one. The NPC in 1954 elected Mao Tse-tung as chairman of the republic, and Chu Teh as vice-chairman; Liu Shao-ch'i was elected chairman of the Standing Committee of the NPC; and Chou En-lai was again appointed premier, to preside over the State Council. Unlike the appointments in 1949, non-Communists were absent from the highest political offices in the reorganization of 1954. The chief procurator, the president of the supreme court, and the ten vice-premiers were all high-ranking members of the Communist Party.

The NPC and the highest officials of the central government are elected for a term of four years, lower congresses and "people's councils" for two years. The terms may be prolonged and elections postponed; the top leaders of the Party and the state decide on such matters.

---

[2] The new name for the Government Administrative Council, or the cabinet.
[3] See Article 30 of the Constitution.
[4] See Article 43.

The second NPC was convened in April, 1959, and the third NPC was held in December, 1964. It was announced on the eve of the second NPC that Mao had decided to relinquish his post as chairman in order to devote his attention to Party affairs and ideological problems. In the power struggle of 1966, however, the Maoist faction charged that Mao had been forced to give up his position as chief of state by an anti-Mao group in the Politburo, presumably headed by Liu Shao-ch'i.

The second NPC elected Liu Shao-ch'i chairman of the People's Republic and Chu Teh chairman of its Standing Committee. The number of vice-chairmen of the Republic was increased to two; Tung Pi-wu, a Party member since the inception of the Communist movement in China, and Soong Ch'ing-ling (Madame Sun Yat-sen) were elected. The post of premier again went to Chou En-lai.

In 1964, 3,040 deputies were elected to the third NPC. Most of the original 1,226 deputies were re-elected, but a number of important names associated with Soviet revisionism or with opposition to the Great Leap Forward were dropped.[5] The increase in the size of the NPC was a result of changes in the ratio of representation. For example, the provinces elected one deputy for every 400,000 persons, thus doubling the number provided in Article 20 of the Electoral Law. Deputies were also increased for the municipalities, the mining and industrial centers, and the armed forces. Wider representation was given to workers, peasants, and technical personnel. Eighteen per cent of the deputies were women—among them, the wives of Mao Tse-tung, Liu Shao Ch'i, Chou En-lai, and other top Communists. The third NPC made no modification in the government structure or in the top-level personnel of the central government.

How the state extends its authority to the local levels can be seen in the Organic Regulations of Urban Inhabitants' Committees (D12), the Organic Regulations of Urban Street Offices (D13), and the Organic Regulations of Public Security Substations (D14). Official and quasi-official agencies intertwine to make state control effective in all parts of the country. Mention has been made of the various mass organizations as the eyes and ears of the Party and the state. How an "autonomous mass organization" functions as an arm of the government is clearly seen in the Regulations of the Urban Inhabitants' Committees (D12). Set up as neighborhood organizations, they operate under the direction of the government or the local people's council.

---

[5] Among them were P'eng Teh-huai, formerly minister of defense; Chang Wen-t'ien, erstwhile ambassador to the U.S.S.R.; and Yang Hsien-chen, lecturer on Marxism now accused of revisionist ideas.

They control the daily life of the people, down to the intimate details of personal and family life. They help the government by explaining official policies to the people and seeing to it that all inhabitants obey and conform. They bring the power of the Party-state into every household and into the life of every individual. They work hand in hand with the urban street office (D13) and the local security agency (D14). This well-organized system of local supervision and control, in the words of a Canadian reporter who visited the Chinese mainland, "make complete the lack of privacy in Communist China."[6]

[6] Report by David Lancashire, in the *Christian Science Monitor*, December 16, 1956.

RESOLUTION ON CONVOCATION OF THE ALL-CHINA PEOPLE'S CONGRESS IN 1953

[Adopted by the Central People's Government Council on January 13, 1953.]

As stipulated in Article 12 of the Common Program, "The state power of the People's Republic of China belongs to the people. All levels of the people's congress and all levels of the people's government are the organs for exercising state power by the people. All levels of the people's congress shall be elected through universal suffrage by the people. All levels of the people's congress shall elect the respective levels of the people's government. The various levels of the people's government shall be the organs for exercising state power at their respective levels when their respective people's congresses are not in session. The All-China People's Congress is the supreme organ of state power. The Central People's Government shall be the supreme organ for exercising state power when the All-China People's Congress is not in session. As stipulated in Article 2 of the Organic Law of the Central People's Government of the People's Republic of China, "The government of the People's Republic of China will be established by the All-China People's Congress on the principle of democratic centralism." Upon the founding of our nation three years ago, many aspects of revolutionary work were barely started, the masses were not adequately mobilized, and the conditions were not ripe for the convocation of the All-China People's Congress. Consequently, at that moment, the principles stipulated in Article 13 of the Common Program were followed to enable the First Plenary Session of the People's Political Consultative Conference to exercise the functions and powers of the All-China People's Congress, to formulate the Organic Law of the Central People's Government of the People's Republic of China, elect the Central People's Government Council of the People's Republic of China, and vest it with the authority to exercise state power.

For the past three years, as a result of the leadership of the Chinese Communist Party and of Chairman Mao, and the concerted efforts of all the nationalities in China, the democratic classes, the democratic parties and groups, and the people's organizations, we have basically completed agrarian reform on a national scale, implemented democratic reforms and other reforms in industrial and mining enterprises, victoriously carried out the Resist America and Aid Korea movement, carried out the "three anti" and "five anti" movements and the ideological reform of the intellectuals, vigorously suppressed the counter-revolutionary elements, and liquidated the remnant bandits; and in particular, by adopting the correct steps to stabilize the price level, to restore and elevate the level of agricultural production, and to struggle for a basic turn for the better in economic conditions, have succeeded in gaining preliminary improvements in the living standards of the people.

The above series of glorious victories greatly improved the people's state of organization and level of consciousness, consolidated the People's Democratic Dictatorship, and laid the ground for the First Five-Year Plan for national construction. Hereafter, the center of our work shall lie in, on the one hand, keeping up the struggle for final victory in the Resist America and Aid Korea movement; and on the other hand, the organization and education of the people for the realization of all our construction plans. To further the organization and education of the people, it behooves us to abide by the principles stipulated in the Common Program for the timely convocation of the All-China People's Congress through universal suffrage, in place of the present practice of entrusting the Plenary Session of the People's Political Consultative Conference with the powers of the All-China People's Congress; and for the election through universal franchise of various people's congresses in place of the present practice of entrusting various local congresses of all groups of people with the powers of the people's congress. Thus shall the ties between the people's government and the people be strengthened, and the state system of the People's Democratic Dictatorship rendered more perfect, so as to meet the needs of planned national construction.

It is the opinion of the Central People's Government Council that current conditions are ripe for the convocation of the All-China People's Congress. On the basis of Item 10 of Article 7 of the Organic Law of the Central People's Government of the People's Republic of China, it has now been decided to convene in 1953 the various grades of *hsiang, hsien,** and provincial (municipal) people's congresses elected through universal franchise, and then to convene, on this basis, the All-China People's Congress. The All-China People's Congress shall draft our constitution, ratify the Five-Year Plan of national construction, and elect a new Central People's Government.

---

* *Hsiang* means village; *hsien* means county.

DOCUMENT 7

ELECTORAL LAW OF THE PEOPLE'S REPUBLIC OF CHINA

[Promulgated by the Central People's Government on March 1, 1953.]

CHAPTER I. GENERAL PROVISIONS

Article 1. The All-China People's Congress and local people's congresses of all levels of the People's Republic of China shall be elected by the people of all nationalities on the basis of universal suffrage, in accordance with Article 12 of the Common Program of the Chinese People's Political Consultative Conference.

Article 2. Deputies to the All-China People's Congress; deputies to the people's congress of a province, county, *hsiang* (or town) ; deputies to the people's congress of a municipality, or of a municipal district; and deputies to the people's congress of a national autonomous region shall be elected according to the existing divisions of administrative areas.

Article 3. Deputies to the All-China People's Congress and deputies to the people's congress of a province, county, or municipality divided into districts, shall be elected by the people's congress at the next lower level. Deputies to the people's congress of a *hsiang*, town, municipal district, or a municipality not divided into districts, shall be elected directly by the electors.

Article 4. All citizens of the People's Republic of China who have reached the age of eighteen shall have the right to elect and to be elected irrespective of nationality, race, sex, occupation, social origin, religion, education, property status, or residence.

Women shall have the right to elect and to be elected on equal terms with men.

Article 5. None of the following shall have the right to elect or to be elected:

1. Elements of the landlord class whose status has not yet been changed according to law;

2. Counterrevolutionaries who have been deprived of political rights according to law;

3. Others who have been deprived of political rights according to law;

4. Insane persons.

Article 6. Each elector shall have one vote only.

Article 7. The people's armed forces and overseas Chinese may conduct separate elections. Regulations governing such elections shall be made separately.

Article 8. Election expenses for the All-China People's Congress and the local people's congresses of all levels shall be disbursed by the national treasury.

CHAPTER II.   NUMBER OF DEPUTIES TO LOCAL PEOPLE'S CONGRESSES
AT ALL LEVELS

Section 1.   *Hsiang* and Towns

Article 9. Number of deputies to the people's congress of a *hsiang* or town:

A *hsiang* or town with a population not exceeding 2,000 shall elect 15 to 20 deputies; a *hsiang* or town with a population exceeding 2,000 shall elect 20 to 35 deputies.

A *hsiang* or town with an exceptionally small population may elect less than 15 but not less than 7 deputies; a *hsiang* or town with an exceptionally large population may elect more than 35 but not more than 50 deputies.

Section 2.   Counties

Article 10. Number of deputies to the people's congress of a county:

A county with a population not exceeding 200,000 shall elect 100 to 200 deputies; a county with a population exceeding 200,000 shall elect 200 to 350 deputies.

A county where the population and the number of *hsiang* are exceptionally small shall elect less than 100 but not less than 30 deputies; a county where the population and the number of *hsiang* are exceptionally large shall elect more than 350 but not more than 450 deputies.

Article 11. Number of deputies to be elected from a *hsiang* to a county people's congress:

A *hsiang* with a population not exceeding 2,000 shall elect one deputy; a *hsiang* with a population of more than 2,000 but less than 6,000 shall elect 2 deputies; a *hsiang* with a population of more than 6,000 shall elect 3 deputies. In counties where the population and the number of *hsiang* are exceptionally small, each *hsiang* with a population below 2,000 may nevertheless elect 2 deputies.

One deputy shall be elected for every 500 persons in cities and towns under a county and in important industrial and mining districts within the boundaries of a county. One deputy may nevertheless be elected in places where the population is less than 500 but more than 250. A city or town under a county where the population and number of towns are exceptionally large may elect 1 deputy for every 1,000 persons.

Article 12. The number of deputies to be elected from the people's armed forces to a county people's congress shall be from 1 to 5.

Section 3. Provinces

Article 13. Number of deputies to a provincial people's congress:

A province with a population not exceeding 20 million shall elect from 100 to 400 deputies; a province with a population exceeding 20 million shall elect from 400 to 500 deputies. In a province where the population and the number of counties are exceptionally small, the number of deputies may be less than 100 but not less than 50; where the population and the number of counties are exceptionally large, the number of deputies may exceed 500 but shall not exceed 600.

Article 14. Number of deputies to be elected from a county to a provincial people's congress:

A county with a population not exceeding 200,000 shall elect 1 to 3 deputies; a county with a population exceeding 200,000 and up to 600,000 shall elect 2 to 4 deputies; a county with a population exceeding 600,000 shall elect 3 to 5 deputies.

One deputy shall be elected for every 20,000 of the population in provincial municipalities and towns and in important industrial and mining districts within the boundaries of a province. One deputy may nevertheless be elected in those places where the population is less than 20,000 but more than 10,000.

Article 15. The number of deputies to be elected from the people's armed forces to a provincial people's congress shall be from 3 to 15.

Section 4. Municipalities

Article 16. Number of deputies to a municipal people's congress:

A municipality with a population not exceeding 100,000 shall elect 1 deputy for every 500 to 1,000 persons; a municipality with a population of more than 100,000 but less than 350,000 shall elect 1 deputy for every 1,000 to 2,000 persons; a municipality with a population of more than 350,000 but less than 750,000 shall elect 1 deputy for every 2,000 to 3,000 persons; a municipality with a population of more than 750,000 but less than 1,500,000 shall elect 1 deputy for every 3,000 to 5,000 persons; a municipality with a population exceeding 1,500,000 shall elect 1 deputy for every 5,000 to 7,000 persons.

The number of deputies to a municipal people's congress shall be not less than 50 and not more than 800. The number of persons represented by 1 deputy from a municipal suburban district shall be greater than the number of persons represented by 1 deputy from a municipal urban district.

Article 17. The number of deputies to be elected from the people's armed forces to a municipal people's congress shall be from 2 to 10.

Article 18. Number of deputies to the people's congress of a municipal district:

One deputy shall be elected for every 500 to 2,000 of the population, but the total number of deputies shall be not less than 35 and not more than 200.

CHAPTER III.   NUMBER OF DEPUTIES TO THE ALL-CHINA PEOPLE'S CONGRESS

Article 19. Deputies to the All-China People's Congress shall be elected by the people's congresses of provinces, municipalities directly under the Central People's Government, industrial municipalities with a population of more than 500,000 directly under a provincial government, national minority administrative units directly under the Central People's Government, the people's armed forces, and by the overseas Chinese.

Article 20. The number of deputies to be elected from a province to the All-China People's Congress shall be on the basis of 1 deputy for every 800,000 persons. The number of deputies from a province with an exceptionally small population shall be not less than 3.

The number of deputies to be elected to the All-China People's Congress from a municipality directly under the Central People's Government and from an industrial municipality with a population of more than 500,000 directly under a provincial government shall be on the basis of 1 deputy for every 100,000 persons.

Article 21. The national minorities throughout the country shall elect 150 deputies to the All-China People's Congress.

Article 22. The people's armed forces shall elect 60 deputies to the All-China People's Congress.

Article 23. The overseas Chinese shall elect 30 deputies to the All-China People's Congress.

CHAPTER IV.   ELECTIONS AMONG NATIONAL MINORITIES

Article 24. In deciding on the distribution of the 150 deputies to be elected to the All-China People's Congress by the national minorities throughout the country, the Central People's Government shall take into consideration the size and distribution of the population and other factors relating to the national minorities.

Notwithstanding the provisions of the preceding paragraph, national minority electors who are otherwise elected as deputies to the All-China People's Congress shall not be included in the figure of 150 deputies mentioned above.

Article 25. Election of national minority deputies to the All-China People's Congress:

Deputies from a national minority administrative unit directly under the Central People's Government shall be elected by the administrative unit concerned; deputies of a national minority in any other area shall be elected by the provincial or municipal people's congress.

Article 26. The number of deputies to be elected from among national minorities to a local people's congress shall be included in the number of deputies as stipulated in the articles of Chapter II of this Law.

Article 27. Every national minority, wherever concentrated, shall have its own deputy or deputies to the local people's congress.

Where the total population of a national minority concentrated in an area exceeds 10 per cent of the total population of the area, the number of persons represented by each of its deputies shall be approximately equal to the number of persons represented by any other deputy to the local people's congress, as stipulated in the provisions concerning the number of deputies in Chapter II of this Law.

Where the total population of a national minority concentrated in an area is less than 10 per cent of the total population of the area, the number of persons represented by each of its deputies may be correspondingly less than the number represented by any other deputy to the local people's congress, but in principle it shall be not less than half that number. But even where the population is exceptionally small, the national minority shall elect 1 deputy.

Where, in accordance with the preceding clause, the number of deputies to a local people's congress exceeds the number stipulated in the articles of Chapter II of this Law, the case shall be submitted for approval to the people's government at a higher level.

Article 28. The number of deputies to the people's congresses in a national autonomous region shall be appropriately determined in accordance with the administrative status of the region and the size of its population, and shall be submitted for approval to the people's government at the next higher level.

Article 29. In a national autonomous region, deputies to the local people's congresses from among the other national minorities concentrated in the area shall be elected in accordance with the stipulations of Article 27 of this Law.

Where Hans are concentrated in a national autonomous region and in areas where national minorities are concentrated, elections of Han* deputies to the people's congresses at all levels shall be similarly governed by Article 27 of this Law.

---

* "Han" is the name of the majority Chinese race, as distinguished from the Mongols, the Tibetans, and other "national minorities."

Article 30. Dispersed groupings of all national minorities may take part in the elections of deputies to the people's congresses of all levels. The number of their deputies shall be proportionate to their population. The number of persons represented by each national minority deputy may be less than the number of persons represented by any other deputy to the local people's congress, but in general it shall be not less than half that number.

Where Hans are dispersed in a national autonomous region and in areas where national minorities are concentrated, elections of Han deputies to the people's congresses at all levels shall be governed by the above paragraph.

Article 31. Deputies to the people's congresses in a national autonomous region equivalent to people's congresses in *hsiang,* towns, municipal districts, and municipalities not divided into districts shall be directly elected by the electors. Deputies to people's congresses at other levels shall be elected by the people's congresses of the next lower level.

The above paragraph shall apply to the election of national minority deputies to the people's congresses at all levels in localities where national minorities are concentrated.

Article 32. The election of deputies to people's congresses in *hsiang,* towns, municipal districts, and municipalities not divided into districts where national minorities reside may be carried out by the national minority electors separately or jointly, according to existing relations between the nationalities and their residential distribution.

Where Hans are concentrated or dispersed in a national autonomous region and in areas where national minorities are concentrated, elections of Han deputies to the people's congresses at all levels shall be governed by the above paragraph.

Article 33. Other matters relating to elections among national minorities shall be dealt with by referring to the relevant articles of this Law.

Article 34. In those national minority areas where conditions for universal suffrage do not yet exist, methods of election shall be stipulated separately by the people's government at a higher level.

CHAPTER V. ELECTION COMMITTEES

Article 35. The Central Election Committee and local election committees of all levels shall be set up under the Central People's Government and the local people's governments at all levels. The central and local election committees at all levels shall be the organs dealing with all matters pertaining to the election of the All-China People's Congress and the local people's congresses at all levels.

The Central Election Committee shall be appointed by the Central People's Government Council. The local election committees at all levels shall be appointed by the people's government at the next higher level.

Article 36. Composition of the Central Election Committee and the local election committees at all levels shall be as follows: The Central Election Committee shall consist of a chairman and 28 members; provincial (or municipal) election committees shall consist of a chairman and 8 to 20 members; election committees at the level of provincial municipalities, municipal districts, and counties shall consist of a chairman and 6 to 12 members; election committees at *hsiang* (or town) level shall consist of a chairman and 4 to 8 members.

The staff for the central and local election committees at all levels shall be appointed by the election committees concerned.

Article 37. The functions of the Central Election Committee shall be as follows:

1. To direct and supervise the correct application of this Law throughout the country and to issue directives and decisions in accordance with the provisions of this Law;

2. To direct the work of the local election committees at all levels;

3. To prescribe the forms for the register of electors, electors' certificates, and certificates of election to duly elected deputies of the people's congresses at all levels, and the design of official seals for the electoral committees at all levels;

4. To deal with information concerning unlawful practices during elections and charges thereof, and to decide on final measures to be taken; and

5. To register the deputies duly elected to the All-China People's Congress, to publish a list of the deputies elected, and to issue them certificates of election.

Article 38. The functions of election committees at the level of a province, county, or municipality divided into districts shall be as follows:

1. To supervise the correct application of this Law in the areas under their respective jurisdiction;

2. To direct the work of election committees at the lower levels;

3. To deal with information concerning unlawful practices during elections and charges thereof in areas under their respective jurisdiction, and to decide on measures to be taken; and

4. To register the deputies duly elected to the people's congresses at their corresponding levels, to publish lists of the deputies elected, and to issue them certificates of election.

Article 39. The functions of election committees at the level of *hsiang,* town, municipal district, and municipality not divided into districts shall be as follows:

1. To supervise the correct application of this Law in the areas under their respective jurisdiction;

2. To register the electors, and to examine and publish the register of electors;

3. To deal with objections to the register of electors in the areas under their respective jurisdiction, and to decide on measures to be taken;

4. To register and publish the list of candidates;

5. To define the limits of electoral districts in accordance with the residential distribution of the electors;

6. To fix the date and method of election, and to convene and conduct election meetings;

7. To issue electors' certificates; and

8. To count the ballots, determine who is elected, publish the list of deputies duly elected, and issue them certificates of election.

Article 40. After an election, the election committee shall transfer to the people's government at the corresponding level for safekeeping all documents concerning the election, and shall forthwith submit reports summing up the election to the people's government and to the election committee at a higher level.

Article 41. Election committees shall be dissolved after they have completed their work.

CHAPTER VI.   REGISTRATION OF ELECTORS

Article 42. An election committee of a *hsiang,* town, municipal district, or municipality not divided into districts shall register electors and issue them electors' certificates before an election.

Article 43. An elector shall register only once.

Article 44. The register of electors shall be published thirty days before an election.

Article 45. Anyone who objects to the published register of electors may bring his complaint before the election committee concerned. The committee shall make a decision regarding the complaint within five days. If the person who has made such objections is dissatisfied with the decision, he may take his case to a people's tribunal or a people's court, whose decision shall be final.

Article 46. An elector who changes his residence during the period of an election shall be transferred to the register of electors of the district he moves into, after he has obtained a transfer certificate from the election committee of his former place of residence.

CHAPTER VII.   NOMINATION OF CANDIDATES FOR ELECTION

Article 47. A candidate who stands for election as deputy to the All-China People's Congress or local people's congress shall be nominated according to electoral districts or electoral units.

The Communist Party of China, the various democratic parties, the various people's organizations, and electors or representatives who are not affiliated to the parties or organizations mentioned above, may all nominate candidates for election as deputies, either jointly or separately, according to electoral districts or electoral units.

Article 48. A candidate who stands for election as deputy to the All-China People's Congress or local people's congress at the same level shall be eligible for election only in one electoral unit or in one electoral district.

Article 49. In electing deputies to a people's congress at a higher level, a local people's congress shall not limit the list of candidates for election to its own deputies.

Article 50. The list of candidates shall be published in advance.

Article 51. An elector may vote in accordance with the list of candidates or for any other elector he may choose.

CHAPTER VIII.   PROCEDURE OF ELECTIONS

Article 52. Elections of deputies to the people's congress of a *hsiang,* town, municipal district, or municipality not divided into districts shall be held at a fixed date, in accordance with the decision of the people's government at a higher level.

Article 53. Elections of deputies to the people's congress of a *hsiang,* town, municipal district, or municipality not divided into districts shall be held at election meetings called separately in each district, defined in accordance with the residential distribution of the electors.

Article 54. An election meeting in a *hsiang,* town, municipal district, or municipality not divided into districts shall be held only in the presence of a representative of the election committee concerned. The presidium of an election meeting shall be comprised of three persons: the representative of the election committee as *ex officio* chairman of the presidium, and two other members elected at the meeting.

A local people's congress, in electing deputies to a people's congress at the next higher level, shall be presided over by its own presidium.

Article 55. The election of deputies to the people's congress of a *hsiang,* town, municipal district, or municipality not divided into districts, and the election of *hsiang* or town deputies to a county people's congress, may be conducted by a show of hands or by secret ballot. Election to a people's congress at and above the county level shall be conducted by secret ballot.

An elector who is unable to write because of illiteracy or infirmity may ask any other elector to record his vote for him.

Article 56. At an election meeting or people's congress, an election shall be held only when more than half of the electors or deputies are present. If the number of electors or deputies present is less than the required quorum, the election committee or the presidium shall fix a date for convening another meeting to proceed with the election. At the second meeting, the election shall be held even if the number of electors or deputies present is less than half of the total.

Article 57. When the voting is over, examiners elected by the meeting shall check the number of voters and votes cast and draw up a report to be signed by the chairman of the meeting.

Article 58. An election shall be invalid if the number of votes cast is more than the number of voters. It shall be valid if the number of votes cast is less than the number of voters.

A ballot shall be invalid if more candidates are voted for than the number stipulated. It shall be valid if fewer candidates are voted for than the number stipulated.

Article 59. Candidates who stand for election as deputies to a people's congress shall be deemed elected if they receive more than half of the votes cast by the electors or deputies present. Another election shall be held if no candidate receives more than half of the number of votes cast by the electors or deputies present.

Article 60. Election returns shall be declared valid or invalid in accordance with this Law and announced by the election committee or the presidium.

Article 61. During his tenure of office a deputy may be recalled and replaced in accordance with legal procedure if the majority of his voters or his electoral unit so desire.

CHAPTER IX. PUNISHMENT FOR SABOTAGING ELECTIONS

Article 62. Unlawful practices such as violence, intimidation, fraud, or bribery, to sabotage an election or to prevent an elector from freely exercising his right to elect or to be elected, shall be regarded as offenses liable to penalty of imprisonment for a maximum period of two years, to be imposed by a people's court or a people's tribunal.

Article 63. Any member or employee of a people's government or election committee who is found guilty of such offenses as forgery of election documents, falsifying the number of votes, suppression of facts, or deception shall be liable to penalty of imprisonment for a maximum period of three years, to be imposed by a people's court or a people's tribunal.

Article 64. All persons have the right to give information concerning unlawful practices during an election and to bring charges thereof before an election committee or the judicial organ of a people's government. No organization or individual shall suppress this right or take any retaliatory measures against those giving information. Offenders shall be liable to penalty of imprisonment for a maximum period of three years, to be imposed by a people's court or a people's tribunal.

CHAPTER X. SUPPLEMENTARY PROVISIONS

Article 65. A provincial (or municipal) people's government may draw up detailed regulations for the carrying out of elections in accordance with this Law, and shall submit such regulations to the Central People's Government for approval.

Article 66. This Law shall be promulgated and put into effect upon adoption by the Central People's Government Council. The right to interpret this Law is vested in the Central Election Committee.

DOCUMENT 8

CONSTITUTION OF THE PEOPLE'S REPUBLIC OF CHINA

[Adopted on September 20, 1954, by the First National People's Congress.]

PREAMBLE

In 1949, after more than a century of heroic struggle, the Chinese people, led by the Communist Party of China, finally achieved their great victory in the people's revolution against imperialism, feudalism, and bureaucratic capitalism; thereby bringing to an end their long history of oppression and enslavement, and founded the People's Republic of China, a People's Democratic Dictatorship. The system of People's Democracy—New Democracy—of the People's Republic of China guarantees that China can peacefully banish exploitation and poverty and build a prosperous and happy socialist society.

The period from the founding of the People's Republic of China to the attainment of a socialist society is one of transition. During the transition the fundamental tasks of the state are, step by step, to bring about the socialist industrialization of the country and, step by step, to accomplish the socialist transformation of agriculture, handicrafts, capitalist industry, and commerce. In a few short years our people have successfully carried out a series of large-scale struggles: the reform of the agrarian system, resistance to American aggression and aid to Korea, the suppression of counterrevolutionaries, and the rehabilitation of the national economy. As a result, the necessary conditions have been created for planned economic construction and the gradual transition to socialism.

The First National People's Congress of the People's Republic of China, at its first session held in Peking, the capital, solemnly adopted the Constitution of the People's Republic of China on September 20, 1954. This Constitution is based on the Common Program of the Chinese People's Political Consultative Conference of 1949, and is a further development of it. It consolidates the gains of the Chinese people's revolution and the new victories won in the political and economic fields since the founding of the People's Republic of China; moreover, it reflects the basic needs of the state in the period of transition, as well as the general desire of the people to build a socialist society.

In the course of the great struggle to establish the People's Republic of China, the people of our country forged a broad people's democratic united front, composed of all democratic classes, democratic parties and groups, and popular organizations, and led by the Communist Party of China. This people's democratic united front will continue to play its part in mobilizing and rallying the whole people in the common struggle to fulfill the fundamental tasks of the state during the transitional period and to oppose enemies within and without.

All the nationalities in our country are united in one great family of free and equal nationalities. This unity of China's nationalities will continue to gain in strength, founded as it is on ever-growing friendship and mutual aid, and on the struggle against imperialism, against public enemies of the people within the nationalities, and against both chauvinism and local nationalism. In the course of economic and cultural development, the state will concern itself with the needs of the different nationalities, and, in the matter of socialist transformation, pay full attention to special characteristics in the development of each.

China has already built an indestructible friendship with the great Union of Soviet Socialist Republics and the People's Democracies, and the friendship between our people and peace-loving people in all other countries is growing day by day. Such friendship will be constantly strengthened and broadened. China's policy of establishing and extending diplomatic relations with all countries on the principles of equality, mutual benefit, and mutual respect for each other's sovereignty and territorial integrity, which has already yielded success, will continue to be carried out. In international affairs our firm and consistent policy is to strive for the noble cause of world peace and the progress of humanity.

CHAPTER I. GENERAL PRINCIPLES

Article 1. The People's Republic of China is a people's democratic state led by the working class and based on the alliance of workers and peasants.

Article 2. All power in the People's Republic of China belongs to the people. The organs through which the people exercise power are the National People's Congress and the local people's congresses.

The National People's Congress, the local people's congresses, and all other organs of state practice democratic centralism.

Article 3. The People's Republic of China is a unified, multinational state.

All the nationalities are equal. Discrimination against or oppression of any nationality, or any act that undermines the unity of the nationalities, is prohibited.

All the nationalities have freedom to use and foster the growth of their spoken and written languages, and to preserve or reform their own customs or ways.

Regional autonomy shall be exercised in areas entirely or largely inhabited by national minorities. Such national autonomous areas are inalienable parts of the People's Republic of China.

Article 4. The People's Republic of China, by relying on the organs of state and the social forces, and by means of socialist industrialization and socialist transformation, ensures the gradual abolition of systems of exploitation and the building of a socialist society.

Article 5. In the People's Republic of China the ownership of the means of production today mainly takes the following forms: state ownership, that is, ownership by the whole people; cooperative ownership, that is, collective ownership by the working masses; ownership by individual working people; and capitalist ownership.

Article 6. State-owned economy is socialist economy owned by the whole people; it is the leading force in the national economy and the material basis on which the state carries out socialist transformation. The state ensures priority for the development of state-owned economy.

All mineral resources, waters, forests, undeveloped land, and other resources owned by the state are the property of the whole people.

Article 7. Cooperative economy is either socialist economy when collectively owned by the working masses, or semisocialist economy, when in part collectively owned by the working masses. Such partial collective ownership by the working masses is a transitional form by means of which individual peasants, individual handicraftsmen, and other individual working people organize themselves in their advance toward collective ownership by the working masses.

The state protects the property of the cooperatives and encourages, guides, and helps the development of cooperative economy. It regards the promotion of producers' cooperatives as the chief means for the transformation of individual farming and individual handicrafts.

Article 8. The state protects peasant ownership of land and other means of production according to law.

The state guides and helps individual peasants to increase production and encourages them to form cooperatives in production, supply and marketing, and credit.

The policy of the state toward rich-peasant economy is to restrict and gradually eliminate it.

Article 9. The state protects the ownership of the means of production by handicraftsmen and other nonagricultural individual working people according to law.

The state guides and helps individual handicraftsmen and other nonagricultural individual working people to improve the management of their affairs and encourages them to form cooperatives in the fields of production and supply and marketing.

Article 10. The state protects the ownership by capitalists of the means of production and other capital according to law.

The policy of the state toward capitalist industry and commerce is to use, restrict, and transform them. The state makes use of the positive qualities of capitalist industry and commerce that are beneficial to national welfare and the people's livelihood, restricts their negative qualities that are not beneficial to national welfare and the people's livelihood, and encourages and guides their transformation to various forms of state-capitalist economy, gradually replacing capitalist ownership with ownership by the whole people. This it does by means of control exercised by administrative organs of state, the leadership given by state-owned economy, and supervision by the workers.

The state forbids any kind of illegal activity by capitalists that endangers the public interest, disturbs the social or economic order, or undermines the economic plan of the state.

Article 11. The state protects the right of citizens to possess lawfully earned income, savings, houses, and other means of subsistence.

Article 12. The state protects the right of citizens to inherit private property according to law.

Article 13. The state may, in the public interest, buy, requisition, or nationalize land and other means of production, both in cities and in the countryside, according to provisions of law.

Article 14. The state forbids any person to use his private property to the detriment of the public interest.

Article 15. The state directs the growth and transformation of the national economy through economic planning to secure constantly increasing production, thus enriching the material and cultural life of the people and consolidating the independence and security of the country.

Article 16. Work is a matter of honor for every citizen of the People's Republic of China who is able to work. The state encourages enthusiasm and creative activity of citizens in their work.

Article 17. All organs of state must rely on the masses of the people, constantly maintain close contact with them, heed their opinions, and accept their supervision.

Article 18. All persons working in organs of state must be loyal to the people's democratic system, observe the Constitution and the law, and strive to serve the people.

Article 19. The People's Republic of China safeguards the people's democratic system, suppresses all treasonable and counterrevolutionary activities, and punishes all traitors and counterrevolutionaries.

The state deprives feudal landlords and bureaucratic capitalists of political rights for a specific period of time according to law; at the same time it provides them with a way to live, in order to enable them to reform through work and become citizens who earn their livelihood by their own labor.

Article 20. The armed forces of the People's Republic of China belong to the people; their duty is to safeguard the gains of the people's revolution and the achievements of national construction, and to defend the sovereignty, territorial integrity, and security of the country.

CHAPTER II. THE STATE STRUCTURE

Section 1. The National People's Congress

Article 21. The National People's Congress of the People's Republic of China is the highest organ of state power.

Article 22. The National People's Congress is the only organ exercising the legislative power of the State.

Article 23. The National People's Congress is composed of deputies elected by provinces, autonomous regions, municipalities directly under the central authority, the armed forces, and Chinese residents abroad.

The number of deputies to the National People's Congress, including those representing national minorities, and the manner of their election are prescribed by electoral law.

Article 24. The National People's Congress is elected for a term of four years.

Two months before the term of office of the National People's Congress expires, its Standing Committee must carry out the election of deputies to the next National People's Congress. Should exceptional circumstances arise preventing such an election, the term of office of the National People's Congress may be prolonged until the first session of the next National People's Congress.

*Article 25.*The National People's Congress meets once a year, convened by its Standing Committee. It may also be convened whenever its Standing Committee deems this necessary, or when one-fifth of the deputies so propose.

Article 26. When the National People's Congress meets, it elects a presidium to conduct the session.

Article 27. The National People's Congress exercises the following functions and powers:

1. To amend the Constitution;
2. To enact laws;
3. To supervise the enforcement of the Constitution;
4. To elect the chairman and the vice-chairman of the People's Republic of China;
5. To decide on the choice of the premier of the State Council upon recommendation by the chairman of the People's Republic of China, and of the component members of the State Council upon recommendation by the premier;
6. To decide on the choice of the vice-chairman and members of the Council of National Defense upon recommendation by the chairman of the People's Republic of China;
7. To elect the president of the Supreme People's Court;
8. To elect the procurator-general of the Supreme People's Procuratorate;
9. To decide on the national economic plan;
10. To examine and approve the state budget and the financial report;
11. To ratify the status and boundaries of provinces, autonomous regions, and municipalities directly under the central authority;
12. To decide on general amnesties;
13. To decide on questions of war and peace; and
14. To exercise such other functions and powers as the National People's Congress considers necessary.

Article 28. The National People's Congress has power to remove from office:

1. The chairman and the vice-chairman of the People's Republic of China;
2. The premier and vice-premiers, ministers, heads of commissions, and the secretary-general of the State Council;
3. The vice-chairman and members of the Council of National Defense;

4. The president of the Supreme People's Court;

5. The chief procurator of the Supreme People's Procuratorate.

Article 29. Amendments to the Constitution require a two-thirds majority vote of all the deputies to the National People's Congress.

Laws and other bills require a simple majority vote of all the deputies to the National People's Congress.

Article 30. The Standing Committee of the National People's Congress is the permanent body of the National People's Congress.

The Standing Committee of the National People's Congress is composed of a chairman, a vice-chairman, a secretary-general, and members, all of whom shall be elected by the National People's Congress.

Article 31. The Standing Committee of the National People's Congress exercises the following functions and powers:

1. To conduct the election of deputies to the National People's Congress;

2. To convene the sessions of the National People's Congress;

3. To interpret the laws;

4. To adopt decrees;

5. To supervise the work of the State Council, the Supreme People's Court, and the Supreme People's Procuratorate;

6. To annul decisions and orders of the State Council that contravene the Constitution, laws, or decrees;

7. To revise or annul inappropriate decisions of the organs of state power of provinces, autonomous regions, and municipalities directly under the central authority;

8. To decide on the appointment or removal of any vice-premier, minister, head of commission, or the secretary-general of the State Council when the National People's Congress is not in session;

9. To appoint or remove the vice-presidents, judges, and members of the Judicial Committee of the Supreme People's Court;

10. To appoint or remove the deputy procurator-general, procurators, and members of the Procuratorial Committee of the Supreme People's Procuratorate;

11. To decide on the appointment or recall of plenipotentiary envoys to foreign states;

12. To decide on the ratification or abrogation of treaties concluded with foreign states;

13. To institute military, diplomatic, and other special titles and ranks;

14. To institute and decide on the award of state orders, medals, and titles of honor;

15. To decide on the granting of pardons;

16. To decide, when the National People's Congress is not in session,

on the proclamation of a state of war in the event of armed attack against the state or in fulfillment of international treaty obligations concerning common defense against aggression;

17. To decide on general or partial mobilization;

18. To decide on the enforcement of martial law throughout the country or in certain areas; and

19. To exercise such other functions and powers as are vested in it by the National People's Congress.

Article 32. The Standing Committee of the National People's Congress exercises its functions and powers until the next National People's Congress elects a new Standing Committee.

Article 33. The Standing Committee of the National People's Congress is responsible to the National People's Congress and reports to it.

The National People's Congress has the power to recall members of its Standing Committee.

Article 34. The National People's Congress establishes a Nationalities Committee, a Bills Committee, a Budget Committee, a Credentials Committee, and other necessary committees.

The Nationalities Committee and the Bills Committee are under the direction of the Standing Committee of the National People's Congress when the National People's Congress is not in session.

Article 35. Investigation committees may be constituted to inquire into specific questions when the National People's Congress, or its Standing Committee if the National People's Congress is not in session, deems it necessary.

All organs of state, people's organizations, and citizens concerned are obliged to supply necessary information to these committees when they conduct investigations.

Article 36. Deputies to the National People's Congress have the right to address questions to the State Council, or to the ministries and commissions of the State Council, which are under obligation to answer.

Article 37. No deputy to the National People's Congress may be arrested or placed on trial without the permission of the National People's Congress or, when the National People's Congress is not in session, of its Standing Committee.

Article 38. Deputies to the National People's Congress are subject to the supervision of the units which elect them. These electoral units have the power to replace at any time the deputies they elect, according to the procedure prescribed by law.

Section 2. The Chairman of the People's Republic of China

Article 39. The chairman of the People's Republic of China is elected by the National People's Congress. Any citizen of the People's

Republic of China who has the right to vote and stand for election and has reached the age of thirty-five is eligible for election as chairman of the People's Republic of China.

The term of office of the chairman of the People's Republic of China is four years.

Article 40. The chairman of the People's Republic of China, in accordance with decisions of the National People's Congress or the Standing Committee of the National People's Congress, promulgates laws and decrees; appoints or removes the premier, vice-premiers, ministers, heads of commissions, and the secretary-general of the State Council; appoints or removes the vice-chairmen and members of the Council of National Defense; confers state orders, medals, and titles of honor; proclaims general amnesties and grants pardons; proclaims martial law; proclaims a state of war; and orders mobilization.

Article 41. The chairman of the People's Republic of China represents the People's Republic of China in its relations with foreign states, receives foreign envoys, and, in accordance with decisions of the Standing Committee of the National People's Congress, appoints or recalls plenipotentiary envoys to foreign states and ratifies treaties concluded with foreign states.

Article 42. The chairman of the People's Republic of China commands the armed forces of the country, and is chairman of the Council of National Defense.

Article 43. The chairman of the People's Republic of China convenes a Supreme State Conference whenever necessary and acts as its chairman.

The vice-chairman of the People's Republic of China, the chairman of the Standing Committee of the National People's Congress, the premier of the State Council, and other persons concerned take part in the Supreme State Conference.

The chairman of the People's Republic of China submits the views of the Supreme State Conference on important affairs of state to the National People's Congress, its Standing Committee, the State Council, or other bodies concerned for their consideration and decision.

Article 44. The vice-chairman of the People's Republic of China assists the chairman in his work. The vice-chairman may exercise such part of the functions and powers of the chairman as the chairman may entrust to him.

The provisions of Article 39 of the Constitution governing the election and term of office of the chairman of the People's Republic of China apply also to the election and term of office of the vice-chairman of the People's Republic of China.

Article 45. The chairman and the vice-chairman of the People's Republic of China exercise their functions and power until the new chairman and vice-chairman elected by the next National People's Congress take office.

Article 46. Should the chairman of the People's Republic of China be unable to perform his duties over a long period of time for reasons of health, the vice-chairman exercises the functions and powers of chairman on his behalf.

Should the office of chairman of the People's Republic of China fall vacant, the vice-chairman succeeds to the office of chairman.

Section 3.   The State Council

Article 47. The State Council of the People's Republic of China, that is, the Central People's Government, is the executive of the highest organ of state power; it is the highest administrative organ of state.

Article 48. The State Council is composed of the premier, the vice-premiers, the ministers, the heads of commissions, and the secretary-general.

The organization of the State Council is determined by law.

Article 49. The State Council exercises the following functions and powers:

1. To formulate administrative measures, issue decisions and orders, and verify their execution, in accordance with the Constitution, laws, and decrees;

2. To submit bills to the National People's Congress or its Standing Committee;

3. To coordinate and lead the work of ministries and commissions;

4. To coordinate and lead the work of local administrative organs of state throughout the country;

5. To revise or annul inappropriate orders and directives issued by ministers or by heads of commissions;

6. To revise or annul inappropriate decisions and orders issued by local administrative organs of state;

7. To put into effect the national economic plan and provisions of the state budget;

8. To control foreign and domestic trade;

9. To direct cultural, educational, and public health work;

10. To administer affairs concerning the nationalities;

11. To administer affairs concerning Chinese residents abroad;

12. To protect the interests of the state, to maintain public order, and to safeguard the rights of citizens;

13. To direct the conduct of external affairs;

14. To guide the building up of the defense forces;

15. To ratify the status and boundaries of autonomous *chou**, counties, autonomous counties, and municipalities;

16. To appoint or remove administrative personnel according to provisions of law; and

17. To exercise such other functions and powers as are vested in it by the National People's Congress or its Standing Committee.

Article 50. The premier directs the work of the State Council and presides over its meetings.

The vice-premiers assist the premier in his work.

Article 51. The ministers and heads of commissions direct the work of their respective departments. Ministers and heads of commissions may issue orders and directives within the jurisdiction of their respective departments and in accordance with laws and decrees, and with the decisions and orders of the State Council.

Article 52. The State Council is responsible and reports to the National People's Congress or, when the National People's Congress is not in session, to its Standing Committee.

Section 4. The Local People's Congresses and the Local People's Councils

Article 53. The administrative division of the People's Republic of China is as follows:

1. The country is divided into provinces, autonomous regions, and municipalities directly under the central authority;

2. Provinces and autonomous regions are divided into autonomous *chou,* counties, autonomous counties, and municipalities;

3. Counties and autonomous counties are divided into *hsiang,* nationality *hsiang,* and towns.

Municipalities directly under the central authority and other large municipalities are divided into districts. Autonomous *chou* are divided into counties, autonomous counties, and municipalities.

Autonomous regions, autonomous *chou,* and autonomous counties are all national autonomous areas.

Article 54. People's congresses and people's councils are established in provinces, municipalities directly under the central authority, counties, municipalities, municipal districts, *hsiang,* nationality *hsiang,* and towns. Organs of self-government are established in autonomous regions, autonomous *chou,* and autonomous counties. The organization and work of organs of self-government are specified in Section 5 of Chapter II of this Constitution.

---

* *Chou* is a unit larger than the county.

Article 55. Local people's congresses at all levels are the local organs of state power.

Article 56. Deputies to the people's congresses of provinces, municipalities directly under the central authority, counties, and municipalities divided into districts are elected by the people's congresses at the next lower level; deputies to the people's congresses of municipalities not divided into districts, municipal districts, *hsiang*, nationality *hsiang*, and towns are directly elected by the voters.

The number of deputies to local people's congresses and the manner of their election are prescribed by the Electoral Law.

Article 57. The term of office of the provincial people's congresses is four years. The term of office of the people's congresses of municipalities directly under the central authority, counties, municipalities, municipal districts, *hsiang*, nationality *hsiang*, and towns is two years.

Article 58. The local people's congresses at every level ensure the observance and execution of laws and decrees in their respective administrative areas, draw up plans for local economic construction and cultural development and for public works, examine and approve local budgets and financial reports, protect public property, maintain public order, and safeguard the rights of citizens and the equal rights of national minorities.

Article 59. The local people's congresses elect and have power to recall members of the people's councils at corresponding levels.

The people's congresses at county level and above elect and have power to recall the presidents of people's courts at corresponding levels.

Article 60. The local people's congresses adopt and issue decisions within the limits of the authority prescribed by law.

The people's congresses of nationality *hsiang* may, within the limits of the authority prescribed by law, take specific measures appropriate to the characteristics of the nationalities concerned.

The local people's congresses have the power to revise or annul inappropriate decisions and orders of people's councils at corresponding levels.

The people's congresses at county level and above have the power to revise or annul inappropriate decisions of people's congresses at the next lower level, as well as inappropriate decisions and orders of people's councils at the next lower level.

Article 61. Deputies to the people's congresses of provinces, municipalities directly under the central authority, counties, and municipalities divided into districts are subject to supervision by the units which elect them; deputies to the people's congresses of municipalities not divided into districts, municipal districts, *hsiang*, nationality *hsiang*, and towns are subject to supervision by their electors. The electoral units and electorates that elect the deputies to the local people's congresses have the power at any time to recall their deputies according to the procedure prescribed by law.

Article 62. Local people's councils, that is, local people's governments, are the executive organs of local people's congresses at corresponding levels, and are the local administrative organs of state.

Article 63. A local people's council is composed, according to its level, of the provincial governor and deputy provincial governors, or the mayor and deputy mayors of municipalities, or the county head and deputy county heads, or the district head and deputy district heads, or the *hsiang* head and the deputy *hsiang* heads, or the town head and deputy town heads, as the case may be, together with council members.

The term of office of a local people's council is the same as that of the people's congress at the corresponding level.

The organization of local people's councils is determined by law.

Article 64. The local people's councils administer their respective areas within the limits of their authority as prescribed by law.

The local people's councils carry out the decisions of people's congresses at corresponding levels and decisions and orders of administrative organs of state at higher levels.

The local people's councils issue decisions and orders within the limits of their authority as prescribed by law.

Article 65. The people's councils at county level and above direct the work of all their subordinate departments and of people's councils at lower levels, as well as appointing or removing personnel of organs of state according to provisions of law.

The people's councils at county level and above have the power to suspend the execution of inappropriate decisions issued by people's congresses at the next lower level, and to revise or annul inappropriate orders and directives issued by their subordinate departments or by people's councils at lower levels.

Article 66. The local people's councils are responsible and accountable to the people's congresses at corresponding levels and to the administrative organs of state at the next higher level.

The local people's councils throughout the country are administrative organs of state under the unified leadership of, and subordinate to, the State Council.

Section 5. The Organs of Self-government of National Autonomous Areas

Article 67. The organs of self-government of all autonomous regions, autonomous *chou,* and autonomous counties are formed in accordance with the basic principles governing the organization of local organs of state, as specified in Section 4 of Chapter II of this Constitution. The form of each organ of self-government may be determined in accordance with the wishes of the majority of the people of the nationality or nationalities enjoying regional autonomy in a given area.

Article 68. In all autonomous regions, autonomous *chou,* and autonomous counties where a number of nationalities live together, each nationality is entitled to appropriate representation in the organs of self-government.

Article 69. The organs of self-government of all autonomous regions, autonomous *chou,* and autonomous counties exercise the functions and powers of local organs of state, as specified in Section 4 of Chapter II of this Constitution.

Article 70. The organs of self-government of all autonomous regions, autonomous *chou,* and autonomous counties exercise autonomy within the limits of their authority as prescribed by the Constitution and by law.

The organs of self-government of all autonomous regions, autonomous *chou,* and autonomous counties administer their own local finances within the limits of their authority as prescribed by law.

The organs of self-government of all autonomous regions, autonomous *chou,* and autonomous counties organize their local public security forces in accordance with the military system of the state.

The organs of self-government of all autonomous regions, autonomous *chou,* and autonomous counties may draw up regulations governing the exercise of autonomy and other special regulations suited to the political, economic, and cultural characteristics of the nationality or nationalities in a given area and submit any such regulations to the Standing Committee of the National People's Congress for approval.

Article 71. In performing their duties, organs of self-government of all autonomous regions, autonomous *chou,* and autonomous counties employ the spoken and written language or languages commonly used by the nationality or nationalities in a given area.

Article 72. The higher organs of state should fully safeguard the right of organs of self-government of all autonomous regions, autonomous *chou,* and autonomous counties to exercise autonomy, and should assist the various national minorities in their political, economic, and cultural development.

Section 6.   The People's Courts and the People's Procuratorates

Article 73. In the People's Republic of China judicial authority is exercised by the Supreme People's Court, local people's courts, and special people's courts.

Article 74. The term of office of the president of the Supreme People's Court and presidents of local people's courts is four years.

The organization of people's courts is determined by law.

Article 75. The system of people's assessors applies, in accordance with law, to judicial proceedings in the people's courts.

Article 76. Cases in the people's courts are heard in public unless otherwise provided by law. The accused has the right to defense.

Article 77. Citizens of all nationalities have the right to use their own spoken and written languages in court proceedings. The people's courts are required to provide interpreters for any party unacquainted with the spoken or written language commonly used in the locality.

In an area entirely or largely inhabited by a national minority or where a number of nationalities live together, hearings in people's courts are conducted in the language commonly used in the locality, and judgments, notices, and all other documents of the people's courts are made public in that language.

Article 78. In administering justice the people's courts are independent, subject only to the law.

Article 79. The Supreme People's Court is the highest judicial organ.

The Supreme People's Court supervises the judicial work of local people's courts and special people's courts; people's courts at higher levels supervise the judicial work of people's courts at lower levels.

Article 80. The Supreme People's Court is responsible and accountable to the National People's Congress or, when the National People's Congress is not in session, to its Standing Committee. Local people's courts are responsible and accountable to the local people's congresses at corresponding levels.

Article 81. The Supreme People's Procuratorate of the People's Republic of China exercises procuratorial authority over all departments of the State Council, local organs of state, persons working in organs of state, and citizens, to ensure observance of the law. Local organs of the people's procuratorates and special people's procuratorates exercise procuratorial authority within the limits prescribed by law.

Local organs of the people's procuratorates and the special people's procuratorates work under the leadership of the people's procuratorates at higher levels, and all work under the unified leadership of the Supreme People's Procuratorate.

Article 82. The term of office of the chief procurator of the Supreme People's Procuratorate is four years.

The organization of people's procuratorates is determined by law.

Article 83. In the exercise of their authority local organs of the people's procuratorate are independent and are not subject to interference by local organs of state.

Article 84. The Supreme People's Procuratorate is responsible and accountable to the National People's Congress or, when the National People's Congress is not in session, to its Standing Committee.

CHAPTER III. FUNDAMENTAL RIGHTS AND DUTIES OF CITIZENS

Article 85. Citizens of the People's Republic of China are equal before the law.

Article 86. Citizens of the People's Republic of China who have reached the age of eighteen have the right to vote and stand for election whatever their nationality, race, sex, occupation, social origin, religious belief, education, property status, or length of residence, except insane persons and persons deprived by law of the right to vote and stand for election.

Women have equal rights with men to vote and stand for election.

Article 87. Citizens of the People's Republic of China have freedom of speech, freedom of the press, freedom of assembly, freedom of association, freedom of procession, and freedom of demonstration. By providing the necessary material facilities, the state guarantees citizens enjoyment of these freedoms.

Article 88. Citizens of the People's Republic of China have freedom of religious belief.

Article 89. Freedom of the person of citizens of the People's Republic of China is inviolable. No citizen may be arrested except by decision of a people's court or with the sanction of a people's procuratorate.

Article 90. The homes of citizens of the People's Republic of China are inviolable, and privacy of correspondence is protected by law.

Citizens of the People's Republic of China have freedom of residence and freedom to change their residence.

Article 91. Citizens of the People's Republic of China have the right to work. To guarantee enjoyment of this right, the state, by planned development of the national economy, gradually creates more employment, improves working conditions, and increases wages, amenities, and benefits.

Article 92. Working people in the People's Republic of China have the right to rest and leisure. To guarantee enjoyment of this right, the state prescribes working hours and holidays for workers and office employees; at the same time it gradually expands material facilities to enable working people to rest and build up their health.

Article 93. Working people in the People's Republic of China have the right to material assistance in old age and in case of illness or disability. To guarantee enjoyment of this right, the state provides social insurance, social assistance, and public health services, and gradually expands these facilities.

Article 94. Citizens of the People's Republic of China have the right to education. To guarantee enjoyment of this right, the state establishes and gradually extends the various types of schools and other cultural and educational institutions.

The state pays special attention to the physical and mental development of young people.

Article 95. The People's Republic of China safeguards the freedom of citizens to engage in scientific research, literary and artistic creation, and other cultural activities. The state encourages and assists citizens engaged in science, education, literature, art, and other fields of culture to pursue their creative work.

Article 96. In the People's Republic of China women enjoy equal rights with men in all spheres—political, economic, cultural, social, and domestic.

The state protects marriage, the family, and the mother and child.

Article 97. Citizens of the People's Republic of China have the right to bring complaints against any person working in organs of state for transgression of law or neglect of duty by making a written or verbal statement to any organ of state at any level. People suffering loss because their rights as citizens have been infringed by persons working in organs of state have the right to compensation.

Article 98. The People's Republic of China protects the proper rights and interests of Chinese residents abroad.

Article 99. The People's Republic of China grants the right of asylum to any foreign national persecuted for supporting a just cause, taking part in the peace movement, or engaging in scientific activity.

Article 100. Citizens of the People's Republic of China must abide by the Constitution and the law, uphold discipline at work, keep public order, and respect social ethics.

Article 101. The public property of the People's Republic of China is sacred and inviolable. It is the duty of every citizen to respect and protect public property.

Article 102. It is the duty of citizens of the People's Republic of China to pay taxes according to law.

Article 103. It is the sacred duty of every citizen of the People's Republic of China to defend the homeland.

It is the honorable duty of citizens of the People's Republic of China to perform military service according to law.

CHAPTER IV. NATIONAL FLAG, STATE EMBLEM, CAPITAL

Article 104. The national flag of the People's Republic of China is a red flag with five stars.

Article 105. The state emblem of the People's Republic of China is:

*T'ien An Men** under the light of five stars, framed with ears of grain, and with a cogwheel at its base.

Article 106. The capital of the People's Republic of China is Peking.

ORGANIC LAW OF THE PEOPLE'S COURTS

[Adopted by the First National People's Congress on September 21, 1954.]

CHAPTER I. GENERAL PRINCIPLES

Article 1. The judicial authority in the People's Republic of China shall be exercised by the local people's courts; the special people's courts; and the Supreme People's Court.

The local people's courts shall be divided into basic people's courts, intermediate people's courts, and higher people's courts.

Article 2. The Ministry of Justice shall seek approval of the State Council for the establishment of the higher people's courts and special people's courts; the judicial organs of provinces, autonomous regions, and municipalities directly under the central authority shall seek approval of the provincial and municipal people's councils or the self-government organs of autonomous regions for the establishment of intermediate people's courts and basic people's courts.

Article 3. The tasks of the people's courts shall consist in adjudicating criminal and civil cases and, through adjudication activities, in punishing all kinds of criminals and settling civil disputes, thereby safeguarding the people's democratic system, maintaining public order, protecting public property, protecting the rights and legitimate interests of citizens, and ensuring the smooth progress of the socialist construction and socialist transformation of the country.

The people's courts shall educate the citizens to be loyal to the motherland and conscientiously observe laws.

Article 4. In administering justice the people's courts are independent, subject only to the law.

Article 5. In adjudicating cases the people's courts shall apply the law equally to all citizens irrespective of their nationality, race, sex, occupation, social origin, religious belief, educational standard, property status, or length of residence.

---

* Literally, "Gate of Celestial Peace."

Article 6. The citizens of all nationalities shall have the right to use their own spoken and written languages in court proceedings. The people's courts are to provide interpreters for any party unacquainted with the spoken or written language commonly used in the locality. In an area entirely or largely inhabited by a national minority or where a number of nationalities live together, hearings in people's courts shall be conducted in the language commonly used in the locality, and judgments, notices, and other documents of the people's courts shall be made public in that language.

Article 7. A case in the people's courts shall be heard in public unless otherwise provided for by law. The accused has the right to defense.

In addition to exercising his or her right to defense, the accused may entrust a lawyer with the defense of his or her case, may arrange for citizens recommended by people's bodies or approved by the people's courts to defend his or her case, or may arrange for his or her next of kin or guardian to defend his or her case. When necessary the people's courts may designate an attorney to defend his or her case.

Article 8. The system of people's asssessors shall be applied to hearing of cases of the first instance in the people's courts with the exception of simple civil cases, minor criminal cases, and other cases provided by law.

Article 9. Cases in the people's court shall be heard in full court.

With the exception of simple civil cases, minor crimnal cases, and other cases provided for by law, cases of the first instance in the people's courts shall be heard in full court composed of judges and people's assessors.

Appeals and objections in the people's courts shall be heard in full court composed of judges.

The president or division president shall designate a judge to act as chief judge in the full court. The president or division president shall act as chief judge when taking part in the hearing of cases.

Article 10. The people's courts shall establish adjudication committees. The task of the adjudication committees shall consist in summing up adjudication experience and discussing important or doubtful cases and other cases connected with adjudication work.

Members of the adjudication committees of the local people's courts shall be appointed and removed by the people's councils at the corresponding level upon the recommendation of the presidents of the people's courts; members of the Adjudication Committee of the Supreme People's Court shall be appointed and removed by the Standing Committee of the National People's Congress upon the recommendation of the president of the Supreme People's Court.

The presidents shall preside over the meetings of the adjudication committees of the people's courts, while the procurator-general of the people's procuratorate at the corresponding level shall have the right to attend the meetings.

Article 11. The system of one appeal shall be applied to cases adjudicated by people's courts.

With regard to the judgments and rulings on cases of the first instance passed by the people's courts, the party concerned may appeal to the people's court at the higher level according to the procedures prescribed by law, and the people's procuratorate may raise an objection in the people's court at the higher level according to the procedures prescribed by law.

The judgments and rulings of the people's courts on cases of the first instance shall be judgments and rulings of legal effect if the party does not appeal and if the people's procuratorate does not raise objection during the period of appeal.

The judgments and rulings of the intermediate people's courts, the higher people's courts, and the Supreme People's Court on cases of the second instance as well as the judgments and rulings of the Supreme People's Court on cases of the first instance shall be judgments and rulings of the last instance, i.e., judgments and rulings of legal effect.

With regard to sentences of death passed by the intermediate people's courts and the higher people's courts of the last instance, the party concerned may appeal to the people's court at the higher level for reconsideration if he or she objects to the sentence. Sentences of death passed by the basic people's courts and sentences of death passed by the intermediate people's courts should be carried out after obtaining approval from the higher people's courts, if the party concerned does not appeal and does not ask for reconsideration of the case.

Article 12. The presidents of the people's courts are under obligation to bring forward before the adjudication committees for action their court judgments and rulings of legal effect if they discover any mistake in the determination of facts or in the application of law.

With regard to judgments and rulings of the people's courts at all levels that have taken legal effect, the Supreme People's Court has the right to bring the case forward for trial or order the people's court of the lower level to try the case again if the Supreme People's Court discovers any mistakes in the judgments and the rulings. With regard to judgments and rulings of the people's courts at a lower level which have taken legal effect, the people's court of the higher level has the right to bring the case forward for trial or order the people's court of the lower level to try the case again upon discovery of any mistake in the judgments and rulings.

With regard to judgments and rulings of the people's courts at all levels that have taken legal effect, the Supreme People's Procuratorate has the right to raise objections according to procedures of judicial supervision upon discovery of any mistake. With regard to judgments and rulings of the people's courts at the lower level that have taken legal effect, the people's procuratorate of the higher level has the right to raise objections according to the procedures of judicial supervision upon discovery of any mistake.

Article 13. If the party concerned considers a judge to be incapable of being impartial in the trial on account of personal interests in the case or other reasons, he has the right to ask the judge to withdraw from the trial. Whether the judge should withdraw shall be decided by the president of the court.

Article 14. The Supreme People's Court is responsible to the National People's Congress and reports to it, or to the Standing Committee of the National People's Congress when the National People's Congress is not in session. Local people's courts are responsible to the local people's congresses at corresponding levels and report to them.

The adjudication work of the people's courts at the lower level are subject to supervision of the people's courts at the higher level.

The judicial administration of the people's courts shall be handled by the organs of judicial administration.

CHAPTER II.   ORGANIZATION, FUNCTIONS, AND POWERS OF THE
PEOPLE'S COURTS

Section 1.   Basic People's Courts

Article 15. The basic people's courts shall include *hsien* and municipal people's court, autonomous *hsien* people's courts, and municipal *ch'ü* people's courts.

Article 16. A basic people's court shall be composed of one president, one or two vice-presidents, and a certain number of judges.

A basic people's court may set up a criminal division or civil division, each with one division president and, if necessary, one deputy division president.

Article 17. A basic people's court may set up a certain number of people's tribunals according to areas, population, and conditions of cases. The people's tribunals are components of the basic people's court and their judgments and rulings are judgments and rulings of the basic people's court.

Article 18. The basic people's courts shall adjudicate criminal and civil cases of the first instance with the exception of cases separately provided for by laws and decrees.

The basic people's courts may request transfer to the people's court at the higher level for trial of criminal and civil cases that they have accepted but that they consider to be so important as to call for trial by the people's court at the higher level.

Article 19. In addition to adjudicating cases, the basic people's courts shall attend to the following business:

1. To deal with civil disputes and minor criminal cases that do not call for hearing in court;

2. To direct the work of people's mediation committees; and

3. To manage judicial administration within the limits of authority granted by organs of judicial administration of the higher level.

Section 2.   Intermediate People's Courts

Article 20. The intermediate people's courts shall consist of intermediate people's courts established in provinces and autonomous regions according to district, intermediate people's courts established in municipalities directly under the central authority, intermediate people's courts established in larger municipalities, and intermediate people's courts of autonomous *chou.*

Article 21. The intermediate people's court shall be composed of one president, one or two vice presidents, and a number of division presidents, deputy division presidents, and judges.

An intermediate people's court shall set up a criminal division and a civil division and, if necessary, other divisions.

Article 22. The intermediate people's courts shall adjudicate the following cases:

1. Cases of the first instance within their sphere of competency as prescribed by laws and decrees;

2. Cases of the first instance transferred from the basic people's courts;

3. Appeals against and objections to the judgments and rulings of the basic people's courts;

4. Objections raised by the people's procuratorate according to the procedures of judicial supervision.

The intermediate people's courts may request transfer to the people's courts at the higher level for adjudication of those criminal and civil cases that they have accepted but that, in their opinion, are so important in nature as to require adjudication by the people's court at a higher level.

Section 3.   The Higher People's Courts

Article 23. The higher people's courts shall consist of the higher people's courts of provinces, the higher people's courts of autonomous regions, and the higher people's courts of municipalities directly under the central authority.

Article 24. The higher people's court shall be composed of one president, a certain number of vice-presidents, and a number of division presidents, deputy division presidents, and judges.

The higher people's court shall set up a criminal division and a civil division and, if necessary, other divisions.

Article 25. The higher people's court shall adjudicate the following cases:

1. Cases of the first instance within their sphere of competency as prescribed by laws and decrees;

2. Cases of the first instance transferred from the people's court of the lower level;

3. Appeals against and objections to the judgments and rulings of the people's courts of the lower levels; and

4. Objections raised by the people's procuratorate according to the procedures of judicial supervision.

Section 4.   Special People's Courts

Article 26. The special people's courts shall consist of the military courts, railway transportation courts, and water transportation courts.

Article 27. The organization of the special courts shall be separately provided by the Standing Committee of the National People's Congress.

Section 5.   The Supreme People's Court

Article 28. The Supreme People's Court is the highest adjudication organ. The Supreme People's Court shall supervise the adjudication work of local people's courts and special people's courts.

Article 29. The Supreme People's Court shall be composed of one president, a number of vice-presidents, a number of division presidents and deputy division presidents, and a number of judges.

The Supreme People's Court shall set up a criminal division and a civil division and whatever other divisions are required.

Article 30. The Supreme People's Court shall adjudicate the following cases:

1. Cases of the first instance that fall within its sphere of competency as prescribed by laws and decrees, and that it considers should be adjudicated by itself;

2. Appeals against and objections to the judgments and rulings of the higher people's courts and special people's courts;

3. Objections raised by the Supreme People's Procuratorate according to procedures of judicial supervision.

CHAPTER III.   JUDGES AND OTHER PERSONNEL OF THE PEOPLE'S COURTS

Section 1.   Presidents, Division Presidents, and Judges

Article 31. Citizens who have reached the age of twenty-three and have the right to elect and to be elected may be elected as presidents of the people's courts or may be appointed as vice-presidents, division presidents, deputy division presidents, judges, or assistant judges of the people's courts, with the exception of those deprived of political rights.

Article 32. The presidents of local people's courts shall be elected by the local people's congresses and the vice presidents, division presidents, deputy division presidents, and judges shall be appointed or removed by local people's councils.

The presidents of the intermediate people's courts established in provinces according to district, and in municipalities directly under the central authority shall be elected by the people's congresses of provinces and municipalities directly under the central authority; the vice-presidents, division presidents, deputy division presidents, and judges shall be appointed or removed by the people's congresses of provinces and municipalities directly under the central authority.

The presidents, vice-presidents, division presidents, deputy division presidents, and judges of local people's courts established in regions of national autonomy shall be elected or appointed or removed by the organs of self-government of various levels.

The president of the Supreme People's Court shall be elected by the National People's Congress; the vice-presidents, division presidents, deputy division presidents, and judges of the Supreme People's Court shall be appointed or removed by the Standing Committee of the National People's Congress.

Article 33. The term of office of the presidents of people's courts is four years.

The people's congresses have the right to remove the presidents of the people's courts elected by them.

Article 34. The people's courts may have assistant judges according to requirements.

The assistant judges of local people's courts shall be appointed or removed by the organs of judicial administration at the next higher level. The assistant judges of the Supreme People's Court shall be appointed or removed by the Ministry of Justice.

Upon the recommendation of the president of the court and with the approval of the adjudication committee, an assistant judge may temporarily carry on the duties of a judge.

Section 2.   People's Assessors

Article 35. With the exception of those deprived of political right, citizens who have reached the age of twenty-three and have the right to elect and to be elected may be elected as people's assessors.

The number, term of office, and method of selection of the people's assessors of the people's courts shall be separately provided for by the Ministry of Justice.

Article 36. The people's assessors are members of the courts in which they take part and enjoy the same right as the judges during the period in which they perform their duties in the people's courts.

Article 37. The people's assessors are under obligation to attend the people's courts to carry out their duties at the time indicated in the notice of the people's courts.

The people's assessors shall be paid their usual wages by the work units to which they belong while performing their duties at the people's courts; those having no wage income shall be given an appropriate allowance by the people's courts.

Section 3.   Other Personnel

Article 38. The local people's courts shall appoint bailiffs to carry out the judgments and rulings on civil cases and to execute that part of the judgments and rulings on criminal cases relating to property.

Article 39. The people's courts shall appoint clerks to record the court proceedings and to handle other relevant business.

Article 40. The personnel organization of the people's courts and the operating machinery of the people's courts shall be separately provided by the Ministry of Justice.

DOCUMENT 10

ORGANIC LAW OF THE PEOPLE'S PROCURATORATES

[Adopted by the First National People's Congress on September 21, 1954.]

CHAPTER I.   GENERAL PRINCIPLES

Article 1. The People's Republic of China shall establish the Supreme People's Procuratorate, the local people's procuratorates, and the special people's procuratorates.

The local people's procuratorates shall consist of people's procuratorates of provinces, autonomous regions, municipalities directly under the central authority, autonomous *chou, hsien,* municipalities, and autonomous *hsien.* The people's procuratorates of provinces, autonomous regions, and municipalities directly under the central authority may set up branch procuratorates. The people's procuratorates of municipalities directly under the central authority and of municipalities divided into *ch'ü** may set up municipal *ch'ü* people's procuratorates according to their needs.

The organization of the special people's procuratorates shall be separately provided for by the Standing Committee of the National People's Congress.

Article 2. The people's procuratorates shall each have one procurator-general, a number of deputy procurators-general, and a number of procurators.

The procurators-general shall direct the work of the people's procuratorates.

The people's procuratorates shall set up procuratorial committees. Under the leadership of the chief procurators, the procuratorial committees shall deal with important questions of procuratorial work.

Article 3. The Supreme People's Procuratorate shall exercise procuratorial authority over all departments of the State Council, all local organs of the state, persons working in organs of state, and citizens to ensure an observance of the law.

Article 4. The local people's procuratorates shall exercise the following authority, in accordance with the procedures laid down in Chapter II of this Organic Law:

1. To supervise the decisions, orders, and measures of local state organs to ensure their conformity with law, and to supervise persons working in organs of state and citizens to ensure observance of the law;

2. To inquire into criminal cases, conduct public prosecution, and support public prosecution;

3. To supervise the inquiring activities of the organs of inquiry to ensure their conformity with law;

4. To supervise adjudication activities of the people's courts to ensure their conformity with law;

5. To supervise the execution of the judgments on criminal cases and the activities of the organs for reform through work to ensure their conformity with law; and

6. To exercise the right to prosecute or join in prosecution important civil cases involving the interests of the state and the people.

Article 5. The people's procuratorate shall apply the law equally

---
* Ch'ü means district.

to all citizens irrespective of their nationality, race, sex, occupation, social origin, religious belief, educational standard, property status, or length of residence.

Article 6. The local people's procuratorates are independent in the exercise of their authority and are not subject to interference by local state organs.

Local people's procuratorates and the special people's procuratorates shall work under the leadership of the people's procuratorates at higher levels, and all shall work under the unified leadership of the Supreme People's Procuratorate.

Article 7. The Supreme People's Procuratorate is responsible to the National People's Congress and reports to it, or to its Standing Committee when the National People's Congress is not in session.

CHAPTER II. PROCEDURES FOR THE EXERCISE OF AUTHORITY BY THE PEOPLE'S PROCURATORATES

Article 8. The Supreme People's Procuratorate shall have the power to protest against the decisions, orders, and measures of the departments of the State Council and local state organs that contravene the law.

The local people's procuratorates shall have the power to demand correction of the decisions, orders, and measures of the state organs of the corresponding level that contravene the law; if their demand is not accepted, they should request the people's procuratorate at the next higher level to lodge a protest with the state organs at the next higher level. The local people's procuratorate should request the people's procuratorate at the next higher level to take action upon discovery of any decisions, orders, and measures of the departments of the State Council and of the local state organs at the higher levels that contravene the law.

The people's procuratorates shall have no power directly to annul, change, or stop execution of the decisions, orders, and measures that contravene the law.

The state organs concerned shall be under obligation to deal with and reply to the demand or protest of the people's procuratorates.

Article 9. Upon discovery of unlawful acts on the part of persons working in state organs, the people's procuratorates should notify the organs concerned to correct the unlawful acts; the people's procuratorates should investigate the criminal responsibility if such unlawful acts have constituted a crime.

Article 10. Upon discovery and establishment of a crime, the people's procuratorates should institute a criminal case and, according to the procedures prescribed by law, conduct inquiries or hand over the case to the public security organs for investigation; if, upon conclusion of inquiries, it is found necessary to investigate the criminal responsibility of the accused, the people's procuratorates should conduct public prosecution before the people's court.

Article 11. The people's procuratorates should notify the public security organs at the corresponding level to correct their investigation activities that contravene the law.

Criminal cases instituted by the public security organs, in which prosecution is found necessary upon conclusion of investigations, should be handed over, according to the provisions of law, to the people's procuratorates for consideration and decision as to whether prosecution is to be conducted or not.

Article 12. Except for decision by the people's court, arrest of any citizen must be subject to approval of the people's procuratorate.

Article 13. The public security organs shall have the right to express their views to or to place a charge before the people's procuratorate at the next higher level, in case they find any mistake in the decision of the people's procuratorate not to approve the demand for arrest of the public security organs and not to conduct prosecution of the cases handed over to it by the public security organs.

Article 14. With regard to cases in which public prosecution is conducted by the people's procuratorates, the procurator-general or procurator designated by him shall attend the court as the public prosecutor of the state, to support the public prosecution and supervise the adjudication activities to ensure their conformity with law. The procurator-general may also send a representative to take part in and supervise the hearing of cases that are not prosecuted by the people's procuratorates.

The procurator-general should attend the court or designate a procurator to attend the court when the people's court decides that the people's procuratorate must send a representative to attend the court.

Article 15. The local people's procuratorates shall have the right to raise objections according to the procedures of appeal, in case they find any mistake in the judgments and decisions of the people's courts at the corresponding level on cases of the first instance.

Article 16. The Supreme People's Procuratorate shall have the right to raise objections according to the procedures of judicial supervision, in case it finds any mistake in the judgments and decisions of the people's courts that have taken legal effect. The people's procuratorate at the higher level shall have the right to raise objections according to the procedures of judicial supervision, in case it finds any mistake in the judgments and decisions of the people's court at the lower level that have taken legal effect.

Article 17. The procurator-general of the Supreme People's Procuratorate shall attend the meetings of the Judicial Committee of the Supreme People's Court, and he shall have the right to request the Standing Committee of the National People's Congress to consider and deal with the case if he does not agree with the decision of the Judicial Committee.

The procurators-general of the local people's procuratorates shall have the right to attend the meetings of the judicial committees of the people's courts at the corresponding level.

Article 18. The people's procuratorates shall supervise the execution of the judgments on criminal cases, and they should notify the executive organs to correct the execution in case they discover any violation of law.

The people's procuratorates shall supervise the activities of the organs for reform through work, and they should notify the competent organs to correct any of their activities that contravene the law.

Article 19. For the purpose of carrying out their procuratorial duties, the people's procuratorates shall have the right to send men to attend the meetings of relevant organs and the right to gain access to the necessary decisions, orders, files, and other documents of the relevant organs, enterprises, cooperatives, and social bodies. The relevant organs, bodies, and personnel are under obligation to supply the necessary information and explanations to the people's procuratorates.

CHAPTER III. APPOINTMENT AND REMOVAL OF THE PERSONNEL OF THE PEOPLE'S PROCURATORATES

Article 20. The procurator-general of the Supreme People's Procuratorate shall be elected by the National People's Congress. His term of office shall be four years.

The deputy procurator-general of the Supreme People's Procuratorate shall be appointed or removed by the Standing Committee of the National People's Congress.

The procurators and members of the Procuratorial Committee of the Supreme People's Procuratorate shall be appointed or removed by the Standing Committee of the National People's Congress upon the recommendation of the procurator-general of the Supreme People's Procuratorate.

Article 21. The procurators-general, deputy procurators-general, procurators, and members of the procuratorial committees of the people's procuratorates of provinces, autonomous regions, and municipalities directly under the central authority shall be appointed or removed by the Supreme People's Procuratorate, with approval of the Standing Committee of the National People's Congress. The procurators-general, deputy procurators-general, procurators, and members of the procuratorial committees of the branch people's procuratorates of provinces, autonomous regions, and municipalities directly under the central authority and of the people's procuratorates of the *hsien, chou,* autonomous *chou,* autonomous *hsien,* and municipal *ch'ü* shall be appointed or removed by the people's procuratorates of provinces, autonomous regions, and municipalities directly under the central authority, with the approval of the Supreme People's Procuratorate.

   Article 22. The personnel organization and operating machinery of the people's procuratorates shall be provided separately by the Supreme People's Procuratorate.

DOCUMENT 11

CONSTITUTION OF THE CHINESE PEOPLE'S POLITICAL CONSULTATIVE CONFERENCE

[Adopted by the Second National Committee of CPPCC on December 25, 1954.]

GENERAL PRINCIPLES

In their great revolutionary struggle against imperialism, feudalism, and bureaucratic capitalism, the Chinese people have formed the people's democratic united front, led by the Communist Party of China. In September, 1949, the Chinese People's Political Consultative Conference, the organization of the Chinese people's democratic united front, based on the great victory of the Chinese people's revolution, held its First Plenary Session, exercised the functions and power of the National People's Congress, enacted the Common Program, organized the Central People's Government, and, representing the will of the whole nation, proclaimed the founding of the People's Republic of China.

   The First Plenary Session of the CPPCC elected the National Committee; in local areas the provincial and municipal consultative councils exercised the functions and power of local committees on its behalf. In the past five years and more, the National Committee and provincial and municipal consultative councils have played an important role in various social reforms; in the great Resist America and Aid Korea struggle for defending the motherland and safeguarding peace; in assisting the government in mobilizing the people to take part in the construction work in political, economic, and cultural spheres; in strengthening and enlarging the organization of the united front; and in carrying out ideological remolding work.

The first session of first National People's Congress of the People's Republic of China has been held and the Constitution of the People's Republic of China has been proclaimed. The Common Program of the CPPCC, whose basic contents have been incorporated into the Constitution, has been replaced by the Constitution. The task of the Plenary Session of the CPPCC in exercising the functions and power of the NPC has come to an end, but the CPPCC will continue to exist as an organization of the people's democratic united front for rallying all nationalities, democratic classes, democratic parties and groups, people's bodies, overseas Chinese, and other patriotic democrats. As stated in the Preamble of the Constitution, "In the future, the Chinese people's democratic united front will continue to play its part in mobilizing and rallying the whole people in the common struggle to fulfill the fundamental tasks of the state during the transitional period and to oppose enemies within and without."

At the First Plenary Session of the second National Committee, held in December, 1954, the CPPCC agreed that the people's democratic system, led by the working class and based on the alliance of workers and peasants, had opened a broad way to the socialist development of our country. To intensify the struggle against internal and external enemies, to consolidate the people's democratic system, and to realize the central task of the state in the transition period so as to enable our country to gradually eliminate exploitation and build a socialist society by peaceful means, it is all the more necessary to unify and concentrate the strength of the whole nation. For this reason, the Chinese people's democratic united front must be consolidated and developed further, and the role of the Communist Party of China as its leading force must be further strengthened. The Chinese People's Political Consultative Conference, under the leadership of the Communist Party of China and through the unity of democratic parties and groups and people's bodies, will continue to unite the people of all nationalities to exert common efforts and overcome difficulties in the struggle for building a great socialist country.

The First Plenary Session of the second National Committee of the CPPCC enacted this Constitution and laid down the following guiding principles to be observed in common by all units participating in the CPPCC:

1. To support the Constitution of the People's Republic of China and enforce it with every effort.

2. To consolidate the people's democratic system, led by the working class and based on the alliance of workers and peasants.

3. To assist the state organs and set the social forces in motion in translating the construction plans for socialist industrialization and socialist transformation into reality.

4. To maintain close contact with the masses, reflect the views of the masses, and make proposals to relevant state organs.

5. To strengthen the work of unity, manifest patriotic spirit, sharpen revolutionary vigilance, defend national construction, and persist in the struggle against internal and external enemies among the people of all nationalities.

6. To continue to consolidate and develop the alliance between China and the U.S.S.R. and the unbreakable friendship with the People's Democracies, promote the friendship between China and all peace-loving countries, strengthen the friendship between the Chinese people and all peace-loving peoples of the world, oppose aggressive war, safeguard world peace, and uphold the righteous cause of mankind.

7. To study Marxist-Leninist theories on a voluntary basis, study state policy, raise the level of political affairs, practice criticism and self-criticism, and strive for ideological remolding.

CHAPTER I. GENERAL RULES OF ORGANIZATION

Article 1. The Chinese People's Political Consultative Conference shall be organized on the basis of the democratic parties and groups and people's bodies.

Article 2. The Chinese People's Political Consultative Conference shall set up a National Committee and local committees.

Article 3. All units and individuals on the National Committee and local committees of the CPPCC shall be under obligation to observe and carry out the Constitution of the CPPCC.

Article 4. All resolutions of the plenary sessions of the National Committee and its Standing Committee, and all resolutions of the plenary sessions of the local committees and their standing committees, must be passed by a simple majority of their total members. All units and individuals participating in the conferences should observe and carry out the resolutions adopted by the conferences. In case of any objections to the resolutions, they may reserve their objections for discussion at the next conference but should carry out the resolutions without fail according to the principle of the minority obeying the majority; in case of fundamental objections to important resolutions, they are free to announce withdrawal from the CPPCC.

Article 5. Units or individuals on the National Committee of the CPPCC who seriously violate the Constitution of the CPPCC or the resolutions of the National Committee, shall be cautioned, disqualified as members, or disqualified as units from participating in the Committee by the National Committee, according to the circumstances of the case.

Units or individuals on the local committees of the CPPCC who violate the Constitution of the CPPCC, the resolutions of the National Committee, or the resolutions of local committees, shall be cautioned, disqualified as members, or disqualified as units from participating in the committees, according to the circumstances of the case.

Units or individuals subject to such disciplinary action may request reconsideration while units or individuals on the local committees may appeal to the committee at the higher level if they object to the action.

Article 6. Local committees of the CPPCC are under obligation to observe and carry out the national resolutions and calls of the National Committee.

Article 7. The relation between the National Committee of the CPPCC and local committees at the lower level shall be one of the higher level directing the lower level.

CHAPTER II.   THE NATIONAL COMMITTEE

Article 8. The National Committee of the CPPCC shall be composed of representatives of democratic parties and groups and people's bodies and, if necessary, individuals. Minority nationalities and overseas Chinese should have an appropriate number of representatives on the National Committee.

The units, number of persons, and members participating in each National Committee shall be determined by the Standing Committee of the last National Committee through consultations.

Any increase or change in the units or number of persons, or any decision on election of members that is necessary during the term of office of each National Committee shall be determined by the Standing Committee of the present National Committee through consultations.

Article 9. In accordance with the General Principles of the Constitution of the CPPCC, the National Committee of the CPPCC shall hold consultations and carry out work in connection with important matters concerning the political life of the country and the people's democratic united front.

Article 10. The National Committee of the CPPCC is elected for a term of four years.

Article 11. The National Committee of the CPPCC has one honorary chairman, one chairman, several vice-chairmen, and a secretary-general.

Article 12. The National Committee of the CPPCC shall set up a Standing Committee to take charge of the affairs of the Committee.

The Standing Committee shall be composed of the chairman, several vice-chairmen, the secretary-general of the National Committee, and several Standing Committee members.

Article 13. The Plenary Session of the National Committee of the CPPCC shall be held once every year to be convened by the Standing Committee. The Standing Committee may advance or postpone the date of session if it considers it necessary.

Article 14. The following functions and power of the National Committee of the CPPCC must be exercised by the Plenary Session: revision of the Constitution of the CPPCC; recommendation of the honorary chairman of the National Committee and election of the chairman, vice-chairmen, secretary-general, and Standing Committee members of the National Committee; and hearing and consideration of the work report of the Standing Committee.

Article 15. The National Committee of the CPPCC shall have several deputy secretaries-general, to be selected and appointed by the Standing Committee, and shall set up a secretariat to work under the leadership of the secretary-general.

Article 16. The National Committee of the CPPCC may, according to work requirements, set up a certain number of teams to work under the leadership of the secretary-general.

Each team shall have one head and several deputy heads, to be designated by the Standing Committee.

CHAPTER III. LOCAL COMMITTEES

Article 17. Provincial committees, autonomous district committees, committees of municipalities directly under the Central People's Government, and municipal committees shall be set up respectively in provinces, autonomous districts, municipalities directly under the Central People's Government, and municipalities. Local committees may also be set up in other localities if necessary.

Article 18. A local committee of the CPPCC shall be composed of representatives of local democratic parties and groups and people's bodies and, if necessary, of individuals to be invited. Local minority nationals should have an appropriate number of representatives on the committee.

The units, number of persons, and members of each local committee shall be determined by the Standing Committee of the last local committee through consultations.

Any increase or change in the units or number of persons, or any decision on election of members that is necessary during the term of office of each local committee shall be determined by the standing committee of the present local committee through consultations.

Article 19. The local committees of the CPPCC are local organizations of the people's democratic united front; their tasks shall consist in observing and carrying out the Constitution of the CPPCC, implementing the national resolutions and calls of the National Committee of the CPPCC, and holding consultations over the local work of the people's democratic united front and carrying it out.

Article 20. The provincial committees and autonomous district committees of the CPPCC shall be elected for a term of four years; the committees of municipalities directly under the CPG, municipal committees, and other local committees shall be elected for a term of three years.

Article 21. A local committee of the CPPCC shall have one chairman and one or several vice-chairmen and may appoint a secretary-general according to needs.

Article 22. Local committees of the CPPCC shall set up standing committees to take charge of the affairs of committees.

A standing committee shall be composed of the chairman, one or several vice-chairmen, the secretary-general (if any) of the local committee, and several standing committee members.

Article 23. The plenary sessions of a local committee of the CPPCC shall be convened according to needs and at least once every year by the standing committee.

Article 24. The following functions and power of a local committee of the CPPCC must be exercised by the plenary session: election of chairman, vice-chairmen, secretaries-general (where secretaries-general are appointed), and standing committee members; and hearing and consideration of the work report of the standing committee.

Article 25. A local committee of the CPPCC may either set up work organs or appoint working personnel according to requirements.

A local committee with a secretary-general may appoint one or several deputy secretaries-general according to requirements.

DOCUMENT 12

ORGANIC REGULATIONS OF URBAN INHABITANTS' COMMITTEES

[Adopted by the Standing Committee of the National People's Congress on December 31, 1954.]

Article 1. For the purpose of strengthening the organization and work of street inhabitants in cities and furthering the public welfare of inhabitants, inhabitants' committees may be set up according to residential areas under the guidance of people's councils of municipal *ch'ü*, municipalities without *ch'ü* divisions, or their deputed organs.

Inhabitants' committees are mass and autonomous organizations of inhabitants.

Article 2. The tasks of inhabitants' committees are as follows:

1. To undertake public welfare work for inhabitants;

2. To reflect views and demands of inhabitants to local people's councils or their deputed organs;

3. To mobilize inhabitants to respond to government calls and observe laws;

4. To direct mass security work; and

5. To mediate disputes among inhabitants.

Article 3. Inhabitants' committees shall be organized as follows:

Inhabitants' committees should be set up according to the conditions of residence of inhabitants, with consideration given to the area demarcation under the jurisdiction of the population section of public security office, and in general should cover 100 to 600 households of inhabitants each.

Under inhabitants' committees are set up inhabitants' teams composed generally of fifteen to forty households each. The number of teams set up by each inhabitants' committee may not exceed seventeen.

An inhabitants' committee shall have seven to seventeen members, with one to be elected by each inhabitants' team; one chairman and one to three vice-chairmen shall be coopted from among the members; among them there should be one to take charge of women's work.

An inhabitants' team shall have one head, and in general the member of the inhabitants' committee should act as the head of the team concurrently; one to two deputy heads may be elected if necessary. In case a member of the inhabitants' committee is elected committee chairman or vice-chairman, the team which elected him may elect another team head.

An inhabitants' committee representing a small number of inhabitants shall in general not set up a work committee; its work shall be undertaken by its members with labor divided. An inhabitants' committee representing a large number of inhabitants may, according to requirements and with the approval of the people's council, set up permanent or provisional work committees to work under the unified leadership of the inhabitants' committee. Not more than five permanent work committees may be set up in such fields as social welfare (including care for dependents of martyrs and servicemen) ; security; culture, education, and health; mediation; and women's work. Temporary work committees should be abolished upon conclusion of their work.

Work committees should enlist activists among inhabitants in their work, but where possible one person should assume only one duty, so that they are not overburdened with work.

Elements subject to mass surveillance and elements disfranchised among inhabitants should be incorporated into inhabitants' teams, but are not allowed to act as members of inhabitants' committees, heads of inhabitants' teams, or members of work committees. When necessary, the head of an inhabitants' team has the power to stop their participation in certain meetings of the inhabitants' team.

Article 4. An inhabitants' committee shall be elected for a term of one year.

In case a member of an inhabitants' committee cannot assume his post for some reason, another member may be elected to replace him.

Article 5. In general, organs, schools, and large enterprises shall not participate in inhabitants' committees, but should send their representatives to the conferences called by the inhabitants' committees that are relevant to them, and should observe the resolutions and compacts of the inhabitants' committees concerning public interests of inhabitants.

In workers' residential areas in which office employees and workers of enterprises live together, and in large collective living quarters, either an inhabitants' committee should be set up under the unified guidance of the people's councils of municipal *ch'ü* or municipalities without *ch'ü* divisions or of their deputed organs, or else the committee of workers' dependents organized by trade unions may take up the work of the inhabitants' committee.

Article 6. In city areas where minority nationals live together, a separate inhabitants' committee may be set up for them; where the households of minority nationals are small in number, an inhabitants' team may be formed.

Article 7. In case it becomes necessary to assign tasks to inhabitants' committees or their work committees, the work departments of the people's councils of municipalities, municipal *ch'ü*, and other organs should make unified arrangements subject to approval by the people's councils of municipalities and municipal *ch'ü*. The work departments of the municipal people's councils and municipal *ch'ü* people's councils may exercise professional guidance over the relevant work committees of the inhabitants' committees.

Article 8. Inhabitants should observe the resolutions and compacts of inhabitants' committees concerning public interests. In carrying out their work, inhabitants' committees should, on the basis of democratic centralism and voluntary cooperation of the masses, fully manifest democracy and may not resort to coercion.

Article 9. Public and miscellaneous expense for inhabitants' committees and living allowance for members of inhabitants' committees shall be allocated under centralized plans by the people's councils of provinces and municipalities directly under the Central People's Government, according to scales to be separately fixed by the Ministry of the Interior.

Article 10. Expenses defrayed by inhabitants' committees for public welfare work may be collected from inhabitants on a voluntary basis, subject to concurrence of inhabitants and approval of the people's councils of municipal *ch'ü* and municipalities without *ch'ü* divisions. Apart from this, no donations may be collected and no funds may be raised among inhabitants.

Funds collected for public welfare and their accounts should be made public upon conclusion of business.

DOCUMENT 13

ORGANIC REGULATIONS OF URBAN STREET OFFICES

[Adopted by the Standing Committee of the National People's Congress on December 31, 1954.]

Article 1. For the purpose of strengthening the work among inhabitants and maintaining close contact between the government and inhabitants, the people's councils of municipal *ch'ü* and municipalities without *ch'ü* divisions may set up street offices according to work requirements as their deputed organs.

Article 2. Street offices may be set up in municipal *ch'ü* and municipalities without *ch'ü* divisions having 100,000 population and more and may also be set up in municipal *ch'ü* and municipalities without *ch'ü* divisions having less than 100,000 population and more than 50,000 population if work requirements actually need street offices. Generally, they shall not be set up in municipal *ch'ü* and municipalities without *ch'ü* divisions having less than 50,000 population.

Establishment of street offices shall be subject to approval by the people's council at the next higher level.

Article 3. The area under the jurisdiction of street offices should generally correspond to the area under the jurisdiction of public security substations.

Article 4. Street offices shall carry out the following tasks: undertake matters assigned by the people's councils concerning work among inhabitants; direct the work of inhabitants' committees; and reflect the views and demands of inhabitants.

Article 5. A street office shall have one director, several secretaries (according to the amount of work and size of area under jurisdiction), and one deputy director if necessary.

A street office shall have three to seven full-time cadres, including one to take charge of work among women.

Directors, secretaries, deputy directors, and cadres of street offices shall all be appointed by the people's councils of municipal *ch'ü* and municipalities without *ch'ü* divisions.

Article 6. Without approval of municipal people's councils and municipal *ch'ü* people's councils, the work departments of municipal and municipal *ch'ü* people's councils may not directly assign tasks to street offices.

Article 7. Operation expenses for street offices and wages for working personnel shall be allocated by the people's council's of provinces or municipalities directly under the Central People's Government under centralized plans.

DOCUMENT 14

ORGANIC REGULATIONS OF PUBLIC SECURITY SUBSTATIONS

[Adopted by the Standing Committee of the National People's Congress on December 31, 1954.]

Article 1. For the purpose of strengthening social security, maintaining public order, protecting public property, and safeguarding civil rights, municipal and *hsien* public security bureaus may set up public security substations in areas under their jurisdiction.

Public security substations are the deputed organs of municipal and *hsien* public security bureaus to take charge of security work.

Article 2. Public security substations shall carry out the following tasks:

1. Ensure enforcement of laws on public security and social order;
2. Suppress sabotage activities *flagrante delicto* of counterrevolutionaries;
3. Prevent and curb activities of bandits and other criminals;
4. Place counterrevolutionaries and other criminals under surveillance according to law;

5. Control the census;

6. Exercise control over theatres, cinemas, hotels, chop carvers,* and radio suppliers, as well as explosives, inflammable articles, and other dangerous articles;

7. Guard the scene of important criminal cases and assist the relevant department in breaking the cases;

8. Direct the work of security committees;

9. Conduct propaganda among inhabitants concerning increased revolutionary vigilance, observance of law, observance of public order, and respect to public morality; and

10. Take an active part and assist in welfare work for inhabitants.

Article 3. Public security substations should be set up according to the size of area, number of population, social conditions, and work requirements.

Article 4. A public security substation shall have one chief, one or two deputy chiefs, and several people's policemen.

Public security substations shall work under direct leadership of municipal and *hsien* public security bureaus or of public security sub-bureaus.

Article 5. Public security substations must maintain close contact with the masses, give serious attention to letters from the public, receive people's calls and make reports, and hear people's criticism and proposals at meetings of inhabitants or sessions of inhabitants' committees.

Article 6. Persons working in public security substations must fully observe laws, observe work discipline, and refrain from breaking laws or discipline and from encroachment upon civil rights of the people.

Article 7. In general, railway and water public security substations shall also be governed according to these regulations.

° In China, the seals, made of wood, soapstone, jade, or ivory, used in place of signatures on official documents were called "chops."

IV

The Chinese
Communist Party

Important as the organization of the government is, it is only the machinery for implementing the program of the Communist Party. Although the Constitution of the state details the relationship among various government agencies and vests the highest authority in the National People's Council and such governmental bodies as the State Council and the Supreme State Conference, no one in China has any doubt that the real source of all authority and power is the Communist Party.

Theoretically, there are nine political parties in China today. All eight other parties, however, accept the leadership and direction of the Communist Party, which is not merely the most important party, but is known in China as *"The* Party." Important state policies are often pronounced in directives jointly authorized by the State Council and the Central Committee of the Chinese Communist Party.

The Chinese Communist Party was officially organized on July 1, 1921, and became a part of the Comintern in 1922. Until it gained control of the Chinese mainland in 1949, it managed to survive in the face of extreme difficulties and hardships. It was a party known for its close-knit organization and iron discipline. The form of this tightly controlled organization is spelled out in the Constitution of the Party, but to understand how the Party functions it is important to try to understand its spirit and the measures taken to develop and preserve that spirit. Constant watchfulness against deviations, unceasing emphasis on ideological indoctrination, and the enforcement of a rigid discipline are among these measures.

Document 17 contains a few selected excerpts from the speeches and writings of Liu Shao-ch'i, who for decades was recognized as the voice of authority on matters of Party discipline and ideological orthodoxy. Although Liu was denounced as a revisionist and his writings were attacked as unsound in 1966, the ideas contained in these excerpts have exercised a powerful influence on Party life and help us understand how the Chinese Communist Party has vigilantly tried to maintain its discipline and homogeneity.

The Communist Party permeates every government agency, on the local as well as the national level; it determines policies and sees that they are carried out. It is the Big Brother who stands watch over every phase of national and individual life. It is referred to as "the organization," the symbol of collective life. There is a branch of the Party in every government office, every business organization, every factory, every rural organization, every school, and every small unit of the armed forces. It is assisted by the youth organizations (hence the inclusion of Documents 18 and 19 in this chapter).

RELATIONSHIP WITH OTHER PARTIES

The Communist Party is the vanguard of the revolution, the standard-bearer of the masses, the embodiment of proletarian virtues, and the guardian and interpreter of Marxist-Leninist-Maoist wisdom. To follow the masses is, in the Communist view, to follow the Communist Party; the way to serve the "people" is to serve the Communist Party; to work for the revolution is to accept the sure guidance of the Communist Party. Conversely, anyone who flouts the Party line is an enemy of the Party, and an enemy of the Party is synonymous with an enemy of the people. No other political party in China has an independent program of its own; the main function of the others, known as "democratic parties," is to support whatever is proposed by the Communist Party and to "mobilize" their members to support the program of the Communist Party.

The Constitution of the Communist Party (D15) frankly states that it is a "class organization." Since China has not yet arrived at the stage of the "dictatorship of the proletariat," there are at present other classes in Chinese society;[1] consequently, there is room for political parties representing classes other than workers and peasants. Each of the eight "democratic parties" (D5) recruits its members from a designated section of the nonproletarian population. For example, the Kuomintang Revolutionary Committee concentrates on persons who formerly belonged to the Kuomintang; the China Democratic League is active among the non-Communist but "progressive" scholars and college professors; the China Democratic National Construction Association works among the industrialists and business people; and so on. Just as the workers lead the four classes of "people" represented on the national flag, so the Communist Party, as the "vanguard of the working class," must be accepted as the leader over and above the eight "democratic parties." What appears to be a coalition, therefore, is actually the dictatorship of the Communist Party, assisted by eight subservient parties which serve as "mass organizations" for designated segments of the population. The existence of the "democratic parties" not only presents no threat to the supremacy of the Communist Party but makes it more effective by getting non-Communists to support the Communist program.

---

[1] See D4.

PARTY DISCIPLINE

The Communist Party permits no inactive or lukewarm members. Members are selected with great care and after a rigorous screening process. The probationary period affords further opportunity for close observation.[2] After a member has been admitted into the Party, strict discipline is maintained by a ceaseless program of "education," "criticism and self-criticism," and elaborate reports and close examination of each person's "revolutionary record." Any deviation in thought or action is promptly attacked and suppressed. Punitive action is swift and unrelenting. Frequent rectification and purification campaigns seek to ensure the unity of the Party. Some of the positive measures of indoctrination and "education" are described in excerpts from the writings of the veteran Party organizer Liu Shao-ch'i (D17).

The last paragraph of the preamble of the Party Constitution, under the heading "General Program," summarizes the obligations placed on Party members. They are stated in more specific detail in Article 2 of the Constitution. An examination of Articles 2 and 3 will show that the duties far outweigh the "rights," and that membership in the Party really means the acceptance of a life of hard work, rigid discipline, and sacrificial dedication. "We Communist Party members," said Liu Shao-ch'i, "are the most advanced revolutionaries in modern history and are the contemporary fighting and driving force in changing society and the world." To become a Party member is to join an elite group; it is an honor and a privilege in itself, and one must justify the honor by a life of complete surrender and fearless action.

MEMBERSHIP

There are several major sources from which new members are recruited. Among them are workers and peasants of "high political consciousness" or "revolutionary fervor"; activists and progressive elements in the "democratic parties" who have proven to be good revolutionary workers; cadres trained in specialized fields, such as industry, agriculture, or political work; and youth organizations. In the early 1950's, a special effort was made to increase the "proletarian elements" within the Party. Until 1949, the Communists had no chance to control urban areas (except during the brief period of the Wuhan government in 1926–27). Limited to rural bases, they had to rely on the peasants as the mainstay of the revolution. For Mao Tse-tung and his associates, however, the emphasis on the peasantry was a concession to practical necessity in agricultural China; ideologically, they have always been committed to the concept of the Communist Party as the vanguard of the working class. After they assumed national power, they set out

---

[2] See Articles 4-9 of Party Constitution.

to increase the proportion of proletarian elements in the Party membership. The new industrialization program had produced new urban centers with an emerging working class. A campaign was therefore launched to attract more workers to join the Party. The hope was expressed in 1950 that a third of the industrial workers of the country would be recruited to join the Party within three to five years.

In 1956–57, an effort was made to induce intellectuals to join the Party. That was a time when the Communists felt the need of more positive measures to win over China's intellectuals and to enlist their cooperation in the projected plans of "socialist construction." Much publicity was given to well-known intellectuals who decided to join the Party.[3] This effort proved to be of short duration. Not many intellectuals turned out to be the fiery revolutionaries considered ideal by the Communists. With the swing to more orthodox dogmas in 1965–66, priority in recruitment was again given to workers, peasants, and soldiers. The class-conscious Communists are extremely distrustful of persons of bourgeois background.

NUMERICAL STRENGTH

Despite the drive for proletarian members, the peasants still constitute the majority in the Party. Doctrinaire thinking leads the Communists to rely on workers and peasants, but illiterate workers and peasants, while strong in fiery "revolutionary spirit," are generally weak in technical knowledge or specific ability. According to official figures released in 1956,[4] workers constituted 14 per cent of total Party membership, peasants 69.1 per cent, intellectuals 11.7 per cent, and women about 10 per cent. Some of the problems arising from the character of the membership—for example, distinctions between the veteran Communists and the more recent recruits, distinctions between those who have had schooling and training and those lacking such opportunities—were mentioned by Liu Shao-ch'i in his 1961 address commemorating the fortieth anniversary of the Chinese Communist Party. He said:

> The Party today has 17 million members. Of these, 80 per cent joined the Party after the establishment of the People's Republic, and 70 per cent joined after 1953. They are the new blood of the Party, but they lack experience and many of them have not had systematic Marxist-Leninist education.
>
> Those Party members who joined before the Liberation passed through a bloody struggle and are today the backbone of our Party. But while they are well versed in revolutionary work, they have not had adequate

---

[3] See Chen, *op. cit.*, pp. 111–13.
[4] *Jen Min Jih Pao* (Peking *People's Daily*), September 14, 1956.

experience in socialist construction. Therefore a vast program of education and indoctrination is essential for both types of Party members.

Membership statistics for the early years are included in D16. Rapid increases in membership took place during several periods. The first was the period of "cooperation" between the Communist Party and the Kuomintang in 1924–27, when membership jumped from under 1,000 to nearly 58,000. The Long March of 1934–35 resulted in heavy losses so that on the eve of the Sino-Japanese War in 1937, total membership was reported to be no more than 40,000. The war years, theoretically the years of the "united front," witnessed another big spurt, and in 1945 the Party claimed to have 1,210,000 members. Steady growth took place in the postwar years and after the founding of the regime: 4.5 million members in 1949, 6.5 million in 1953, 10.7 million in 1956, and 13.96 million in 1959. No official figures have been released since Liu Shao-ch'i made his report in 1961, but the recruitment of new members has continued, possibly at the average rate of about a million a year. Most of this increase, however, has served to replace the "unsteady" and malcontent elements purged from the Party. Taking into account the loss of members by purge or by death, one would guess that the total membership stands somewhere near 18 million today. It is the largest Communist Party in the world.

PARTY ORGANIZATION

Democratic centralism is the guiding principle of organization in the Party (and in national life). Democracy does not mean freedom for individuals or local organizations; as a matter of fact, "ultrademocratism" is a serious deviation that the Party has always condemned. Democracy means that local organizations must keep in close touch with the masses in order to lead them, and that every member has an active role to play in the life of the Party. It demands wide and active participation of all members in the discussion and execution of plans. At the same time, centralism places on all individuals the obligation to follow the majority and on all local organizations to accept the authority of higher levels. As stated in the preamble, "solidarity and unity are the very life of the Party, the source of its strength." No one and no local branch may act independently; yet the responsibility of positive action and active participation lies with all members and all local branches. Thus an attempt is made to achieve the dual objective of centralized control and broad participation on local levels. The election of local Party congresses as the "leading bodies" is also claimed to be an expression of democracy.[5]

---

[5] See Article 19 of the Party Constitution.

The highest "leading body" is the National Party Congress. It elects the Central Committee and the Secretariat. The Central Committee, which has the power to act in the name of the Party, elects the Political Bureau,[6] which in turn elects the Standing Committee of the Political Bureau. While official resolutions are issued in the name of the Central Committee, it is obvious that the Political Bureau and its Standing Committee wield immense actual power. Moreover, the Central Committee decides whether the National Party Congress shall be called into session and whether elections for a new Congress shall be held, and the Political Bureau holds similar powers in the convening of the Central Committee. The irregularity of Party congresses in the past (D16) testifies to the wide powers of the top leaders in deciding whether conditions are suitable for the convening of a congress.

The Eighth National Party Congress, in 1956, re-elected Mao Tse-tung chairman of the Central Committee; Liu Shao-ch'i, Chou En-lai, Chu Teh, and Ch'en Yun as vice-chairmen; and Teng Hsiao-p'ing as general secretary. Lin Piao was added as another vice-chairman in 1958. These officers are currently those of the Political Bureau and the Secretariat. They also constitute the Standing Committee of the Political Bureau. To all intents and purposes, regardless of government positions, they are the rulers of mainland China.[7] The 1956 Constitution provided for the new post of honorary chairman of the Central Committee. It was rumored at that time that Mao Tse-tung was not in good health and might retire into an inactive role as Honorary Chairman, but the post has never been filled.

The Eighth Party Congress elected a Ceneral Committee of ninety-four full members and ninety-three alternate members. The Committee elected a Political Bureau of nineteen full members and six alternate members. Minor changes, the significance of which was not generally known, were made in subsequent reshuffles, but there were no major changes in the line-up of the top leadership until the power struggle of 1966. A special meeting of the Central Committee was convened in July–August, 1966, to elect a new Political Bureau. As a result of the shake-up, new names appeared in the membership of this powerful body, and Liu Shao-ch'i was relegated to a minor position, although his name still remained on the list.

LEADERS

Until recently, observers were impressed by the relative stability

---

[6] Also known as the Politburo.

[7] The reshuffling brought about by the power struggle of 1966 resulted in some changes in the personnel of the political bureau. At the time of writing, Liu Shao-ch'i is no longer vice-chairman, but remains on the political bureau. Teng Hsiao-P'ing, though severely condemned, retains his position as general secretary.

of the top CCP leadership. Deviations and deviators were attacked in successive rectification campaigns, but the Party was free from serious internal strife and factionalism. Nevertheless, top leaders have been ousted by intra-Party purges since the establishment of the regime. The first came in 1955 with the purge of Kao Kang, a prominent member of the Politburo and a vice-chairman of the People's Republic, and Jao Shu-shih, a member of the Central Committee. The two men were charged with heading an "anti-Party" faction to undermine Party solidarity and unity and engaging in a secret conspiracy against the leadership of the Party and state. A second top-level purge, in 1959, was directed against P'eng Teh-huai, then minister of defense and a member of the Politburo, and Huang K'o-ch'eng, vice-minister of defense and a member of the Central Committee. They were reported to have opposed some aspects of Party policy regarding the communes and the Great Leap Forward. In 1966, another big purge was instituted against high Party leaders. Among those suddenly toppled were P'eng Chen, Mayor of Peking and a member of the Politburo; Lo Jui-ch'ing, chief of the army general staff and a member of the Central Committee, who himself had directed bloody purges against "counter-revolutionaries" and "enemies of the people"; Lu Ting-yi, minister of culture, alternate member of the Politburo, and long-time director of the Propaganda Department of the Central Committee; Chou Yang, vice-minister of culture and an alternate member of the Central Committee, who had been the voice of the Party handing out the Party line to writers, artists, and "cultural workers," and constantly berating writers and artists for not heeding Mao's decree of literature and art for the proletarian masses; and a host of Party and non-Party intellectuals in high positions. Finally, two members of the Standing Committee of the Political Committee—Liu Shao-ch'i, the chief of state, and Teng Hsiao-p'ing, general secretary of the Central Committee of the Party—were attacked as leaders of a "black gang" of anti-Mao revisionists who were following the capitalist road.

The latest internal purge merged with the "great cultural revolution" of 1966 which, as has been noted, was in large part an intensification of a continuing war against China's intellectuals and their "bourgeois ideas." The Party purge was in part a personal struggle for supremacy and in part a struggle between the hard-line doctrinaires and those who questioned their policies. By mid-1966, Lin Piao was rapidly rising in power and position and was emerging as the main force behind the purge and power struggle. Liu Shao-ch'i, who had long been considered as the second in command and the most likely successor to Mao Tse-tung, was denounced, not only because he was considered to be the supporter of P'eng Chen, but also because of his pro-Soviet background.[8] Chou En-lai, normally considered a moderate, but a durable politician who had always managed to be on the winning team, seemed to be allied with Lin Piao in support of Mao Tse-tung and the ideologues. Chou was premier and foreign minister from 1949 to 1958. He gave up the post of foreign minister to his close friend Marshal Ch'en Yo in 1958, but retained the premiership. Besides Lin Piao and Chou En-lai, two other leaders of the Maoist camp are Mao's wife, Chiang Ch'ing, and Ch'en Po-ta, a writer and editor who is reported to have written many of Mao's speeches through the years.

The age of the top leaders is a factor in the current situation: Mao Tse-tung was born in 1893, Liu Shao-ch'i in 1898, Chou En-lai in 1899, Chu Teh in 1886, Lin Piao in 1907, Teng Hsiao-p'ing in 1904, Ch'en Yun in 1905.[9] There is a gap between these old veterans and the younger generation, or what may be considered the second echelon of Party leaders. Indications are that the veterans do not feel the younger leaders are ready to take over the responsibility for carrying on the revolution. Here lies a weakness in the leadership structure of the Chinese Communist Party. For some years, it was generally thought that Chou En-lai and Liu Shao-ch'i represented two rival factions among the top leaders. Teng Hsiao-p'ing was also considered a possible candidate for top leadership. Now, with the rapid rise of Lin Piao's influence and with the army playing a central role in the purges of 1966, the influence of the military in Party affairs may be considerably enhanced.

Regardless of the outcome of the power struggle, the turmoil of 1966 seems sure to result in a decline of the regime's prestige and authority. The downgrading of men who have long been in positions of power and authority is bound to discredit the Communists in the eyes of the people. Attacks of a personal nature will mar the public image of a dedicated, selfless leadership, and the denigration of heretofore high priests of indoctrination and propaganda is likely to make the people more skeptical of what they are told to think and believe. In addition to the increasing power of the military, there is also the threat of nascent localism to challenge the authority of the central government. Without the centralized control which it was able to exercise in the first decade, the new regime may not find it so easy to carry out its ambitious plans.

YOUTH ORGANIZATIONS

The Communist Youth League, known as the New Democratic Youth League before 1957, and the Young Pioneers are directly

---

[8] From the beginning of the regime, Liu had been a prime mover of the influential Sino-Soviet Friendship Association.

[9] See *Who's Who in Communist China* (Hong Kong: Union Research Institute, 1966).

sponsored and supervised by the Communist Party. The Communist Youth League is called "an assistant to the Communist Party" and "a school for the study of Communism" (D18). The League guides the activities of the Pioneers (D19).

The Youth League serves as a major reserve force for the Party; those with a good "revolutionary record" are recommended for membership in the Party when they reach the eligible age. Discipline is strictly observed. In schools, factories, villages, etc., the League works hand in hand with the local Party organizations and often shares the responsibility and authority of Party leadership. League members are required to spend time in ideological study and to conduct "education on class and class struggle" among young people who are not League members. They are supposed to lead in school work, production, and youth activities in general. They learn early to be militant revolutionaries who put the revolutionary cause above all else. They are expected "to play an exemplary role in labor, work, and study."[10]

League members and Young Pioneers are active leaders in the mass campaigns in their schools, their factories, or their communities. They lead in shouting the slogans and in militant demonstrations. They set examples in destroying mosquitoes and flies, in collecting fertilizers, in ferreting out "counterrevolutionaries," and "informing" the authorities on the political attitudes, thinking, and behavior of their acquaintances and their parents. During the early campaigns against the bourgeoisie and the counterrevolutionaries, Pioneers who denounced their bourgeois parents were taught to feel that the red scarf they wore was sufficient reward for putting their Party loyalty above their family loyalty.

A visitor to the mainland reported the following street scene. "In Canton I saw Young Pioneers chastise a man, then circle with chalk the spot on the sidewalk where he had spat, and inscribe his name alongside it—for all shocked passers-by to behold."[11] In such concrete ways, big and small, the Youth League and the Pioneers prepare for full membership in the militant Party, at the same time assisting in implementing the plan and programs of the Party in the home, in the school, in the factory, in the commune, and in the local community.

In 1965, in a massive campaign to educate the young generation in the Communist way of life, a decision was made to organize all young people from seven to fifteen. The Pioneers thus became an open organization, and the eligibility age was lowered from nine to seven. All children were to be given a chance to "wear red scarves and be

---

[10] See Article II of the Constitution of the League.
[11] Gerald Clark, *Impatient Giant: Red China Today,* (New York: David McKay, 1959), p. 48.

Chairman Mao's good children." The Young Pioneers were to become "a mass organization of teenagers and children and a Communist school for them." Under the direction of the Communist Youth League, a campaign was launched to draw all schoolchildren between seven and fifteen in key cities to join the Pioneers. Within a few months, membership in the Pioneers doubled, from 50 million to 100 million, with greater increases expected. Although more selective in character, the Youth League also stepped up its recruitment program and was reported to have admitted 8 million new members in 1965–66, pushing the total well beyond the 30 million mark.

The emergence of the Red Guards in 1966 posed a threat to the Youth League and the Pioneers. Under the direction of Lin Piao and Chiang Ch'ing, the Red Guards and other "revolutionary groups" created by the "great proletarian cultural revolution" threatened to displace the regular Party organizations and their affiliated youth organizations as official bodies vested with the authority of the Party. Both the local youth organizations and the local Party organizations have been charged with revisionist deviations. The Party organizations, however, have fought back with vigor and have proved too powerful to be easily overthrown. The youth organizations are still in existence, and it remains to be seen whether they will undergo any radical changes.

THE CONSTITUTION OF THE COMMUNIST PARTY OF CHINA

[Adopted by the Eighth National Party Congress on Sept. 26, 1956.]

GENERAL PROGRAM

The Communist Party of China is the vanguard of the Chinese working class, the highest form of its class organization. The aim of the Party is to achieve socialism and Communism in China.

The Communist Party of China takes Marxism-Leninism as its guide to action. Only Marxism-Leninism correctly sets forth the laws of development of society and correctly charts the path leading to the achievement of socialism and Communism. The Party adheres to the Marxist-Leninist world outlook of dialectical and historical materialism, and opposes the world outlook of idealism and metaphysics. Marxism-Leninism is not a dogma, but a guide to action. It demands that in striving to build socialism and Communism we should proceed from reality, apply the principles of Marxism-Leninism in a flexible and creative way for the solution of various problems arising out of the actual struggle, and thus continuously develop the theory of Marxism-Leninism. Consequently, the Party in its activities upholds the principle of integrating the universal truths of Marxism-Leninism with the actual practice of China's revolutionary struggle, and combats all doctrinaire or empiricist deviations.

In 1949, after long years of revolutionary struggle and revolutionary wars, the Communist Party of China and the people of the whole country overthrew the rule of imperialism, feudalism, and bureaucratic capitalism, and founded the People's Republic of China, a People's Democratic Dictatorship led by the working class and based on the alliance of workers and peasants. Following this, the Party led the people in accomplishing the task of the democratic revolution in most parts of the country and achieving great successes in the struggle for the establishment of a socialist society. During the period of transition from the founding of the People's Republic of China to the attainment of a socialist society, the fundamental task of the Party is to complete, step by step, the socialist transformation of agriculture, handicrafts, and capitalist industry and commerce, and to bring about, step by step, the industrialization of the country.

A decisive victory in every field has already been attained in the socialist transformation of our country. It is the task of the Communist

Party of China, by continuously adopting correct methods, to transform what now remains of capitalist ownership into ownership by the whole people, to transform what remains of individual ownership by working people into collective ownership by the working masses; and to uproot the system of exploitation and remove all the causes that give rise to such a system. In the process of building up a socialist society, the principle "from each according to his ability, to each according to his work" should be brought into effect step by step; and all former exploiters should be reformed in a peaceful manner to become working people living by their own labor. The Party must continue to pay attention to the elimination of capitalist factors and influence in the economic, political, and ideological fields, and make determined efforts to mobilize and unite all the positive forces throughout the country that can be mobilized and united for the purpose of winning a complete victory for the great cause of socialism.

The victory of the socialist revolution has opened up limitless possibilities for the development of the productive forces of society. It is the task of the Communist Party of China to develop the national economy in a planned way to bring about the industrialization of the country as rapidly as possible, and to effect the technological transformation of the national economy in a planned, systematic way so that China may possess a powerful modernized industry, a modernized agriculture, modernized communications and transport, and a modernized national defense. In order to achieve industrialization and bring about a continuous growth of the national economy, priority must be given to the development of heavy industry, but at the same time a just proportion must be maintained between heavy industry and light industry, and between industry as a whole and agriculture. The Party must do everything possible to stimulate progress in China's science, culture, and technology, so as to catch up with the world's more advanced countries in these fields. The basic object of all Party work is to satisfy as fully as possible the material and cultural needs of the people. Therefore, it is necessary that the living conditions of the people should, on the basis of increased production, gradually and continually improve. This is also necessary to enhance the people's enthusiasm for production.

Our country is a multinational state. For historical reasons, the development of many of the national minorities has been hindered. The Communist Party of China must make special efforts to raise the status of the national minorities, help them to attain self-government, endeavor to train cadres from among the national minorities, accelerate their economic and cultural advance, bring about complete equality between all the nationalities, and strengthen the unity and fraternal relations among them. Social reforms among the nationalities must be carried out by the respective nationalities themselves in accordance with their own wishes, and by taking steps in conformity with their special characteristics. The Party opposes all tendencies to chauvinism and local nationalism, both of which hamper the unity of nationalities. Special attention must be paid to the prevention and correction of tendencies of Hanism on the part of Party members and government workers of Han nationality.

The Communist Party of China must work untiringly to consolidate China's People's Democratic Dictatorship, which is the guarantee for the success of the socialist cause in China. The Party must fight for a fuller development of the democratic life of the nation and strive for the constant improvement of its democratic institutions. The Party must work in every way to fortify the fraternal alliance of workers and peasants, to consolidate the united front of all patriotic forces, and to strengthen its lasting cooperation with the other democratic parties as well as with democrats who have no party affiliations. Since the imperialists and counterrevolutionary remnants are bent on undermining the cause of the Chinese people, it is imperative for the Party to heighten its revolutionary vigilance and wage severe struggles against those forces that endanger our country's independence and security and those elements who try to wreck socialist construction in our country. The Party must work together with the people of the whole country to bring about the liberation of Taiwan.

The Communist Party of China advocates a foreign policy directed toward the safeguarding of world peace and the achievement of peaceful coexistence between countries with different systems. The Party stands for the establishment and development of diplomatic, economic, and cultural relations between China and other countries of the world, and for the broadening and strengthening of friendly relations between the Chinese people and the peoples of all other countries of the world. The Party is resolutely opposed to any act of aggression against China by imperialist countries and to any imperialist plans for a new war. It supports all efforts made by the peoples and governments of other countries to uphold peace and promote friendly relations between nations, and expresses its sympathy for all struggles in the world against imperialism and colonialism. The Party endeavors to develop and strengthen China's friendship with all other countries in the camp of peace, democracy, and socialism, headed by the Soviet Union; to strengthen the internationalist solidarity of the proletariat; and to learn from the experiences of the world Communist movement. It supports the struggle of the Communists, progressives, and the working people of the whole world for the progress of mankind, and educates its members and the Chinese people in the spirit of internationalism, as expressed in the slogan "Proletarians of all lands, unite!"

The Communist Party of China puts into practice all that it advocates through the activity of the Party organizations and membership among the masses, and through the conscientious efforts made by the people under its guidance. For this reason it is necessary to constantly develop the tradition of following the mass line in Party work. Whether the Party will be able to continue to give correct leadership depends on whether or not the Party will, through analysis and synthesis, systematically summarize the experience and opinions of the masses, turn the resulting ideas into the policy of the Party, and as a result of the Party's propaganda and organizational work among the masses, transform it into the views and action of the masses themselves, testing the correctness of Party policy and supplementing and revising it in the course of mass activity. It is the duty of the Party leadership to ensure that in the endless repetition of this process of "coming from the masses and going back to the masses" the Party members' level of understanding and that of the masses of the people are continually raised and the cause of the Party and the people is constantly advanced. The Party and its members must, therefore, maintain close and extensive ties with workers, peasants, intellectuals, and other patriots, and strive constantly to make such ties ever stronger and more widespread. Every Party member must understand that the interests of the Party and those of the people are one, and responsibility to the Party and responsibility to the people are identical. Every Party member must wholeheartedly serve the people, constantly consult them, pay heed to their opinions, concern himself with their well-being, and strive to help realize their wishes. Now that the Communist Party of China is a party in power, it must be especially careful to conduct itself with modesty and prudence, guard against conceit and impatience, and make the maximum effort in every Party organization, state organ, and economic unit to combat any bureaucratic practice which estranges the masses or leads to isolation from the realities of life.

The organizational principle of the Communist Party of China is democratic centralism, which means centralism on the basis of democracy and democracy under centralized guidance. The Party must take effective measures to promote democracy within the Party, encourage the initiative and creative ability of all Party members and of all local and primary Party organizations, and strengthen the lively contact between the higher and lower Party organizations. Only in this way can the Party effectively extend and strengthen its ties with the masses of the people, give correct and timely leadership, and adapt itself flexibly to various concrete conditions and local characteristics. And only in this way can Party life be invigorated and the cause of the Party advance on an ever wider scale and at an ever greater pace. Only on this basis, furthermore, can centralism and unity of the Party be consolidated and its discipline be voluntarily, not mechanically, observed. Democratic centralism demands that every Party organization should strictly abide by the principle of collective leadership coupled with individual responsibility and that every Party member and Party organization should be subject to Party supervision from above and from below.

Democracy within the Party must not be divorced from centralism. The Party is a united, militant organization, welded together by a discipline which is obligatory for all its members. Without discipline it would be impossible for the Party to lead the state and the people in overcoming their powerful enemies and bringing about socialism and Communism. As the highest form of class organization, the Party must strive to play a correct role as the leader and core in every aspect of the country's life and must combat any tendency toward departmentalism, that reduces the Party's role and weakens its unity. Solidarity and unity are the very life of the Party and the source of its strength. It is the sacred duty of every Party member to pay constant attention to the safeguarding of the solidarity of the Party and the consolidation of its unity. Within the Party, no action that violates the Party's political line or organizational principles is permissible; nor is it permissible to carry on activities aimed at splitting the Party or factional activities, to act independently of the Party, or to place the individual above the collective body of the Party.

No political party or person can be free from shortcomings and mistakes in work. The Communist Party of China and its members must constantly practice criticism and self-criticism to expose and eliminate their shortcomings and mistakes, so as to educate themselves and the people. In view of the fact that the Party plays the leading role in the life of the state and society, it is all the more necessary that it should make stringent demands on every Party organization and member and promote criticism and self-criticism. In particular, it should encourage and support criticism from below inside the Party as well as criticism of the Party by the masses of the people, and should prohibit any suppression of criticism. The Party must prevent and resist corruption by bourgeois and petty-bourgeois ways of thinking and styles of work, and guard against and defeat any rightist or "leftist" opportunist deviation inside the Party. In the case of Party members who have committed mistakes, the Party should, in the spirit of "curing the illness to save the patient," allow them to remain in the ranks and receive education and help them to correct their mistakes, provided such mistakes can be corrected within the Party and the erring Party member is prepared to correct his mistakes. As for those who persist in their mistakes and carry on activities detrimental to the Party, it is essential to wage a determined struggle against them, even to the point of expelling them from the Party.

The Communist Party of China requires all its members to place the Party's interests above their personal interests, to be diligent and unpretentious, to study and work hard, to unite the broad masses of the people, and to overcome all difficulties in order to build China into a great, mighty, prosperous, and advanced socialist state, and on this basis to advance toward the achievement of the loftiest ideal of mankind: Communism.

CHAPTER I.   MEMBERSHIP

Article 1. Membership of the Party is open to any Chinese citizen who works and does not exploit the labor of others, accepts the program and Constitution of the Party, joins and works in one of the Party organizations, carries out the Party's decisions, and pays membership dues as required.

Article 2. Party members have the following duties:

1. To strive to study Marxism-Leninism and unceasingly raise the level of their understanding;

2. To safeguard the Party's solidarity and consolidate its unity;

3. To faithfully carry out Party policy and decisions and energetically fulfill the tasks assigned them by the Party;

4. To strictly observe the Party Constitution and the laws of the state and behave in accordance with Communist ethics, no exception being made for any Party member, whatever his services and position;

5. To place the interests of the Party and the state, that is, the interests of the masses of the people, above their personal interests, and in the event of any conflct between the two, to submit unswervingly to the interests of the Party and the state, that is, the interests of the masses of the people;

6. To serve the masses of the people heart and soul, to strengthen their ties with the masses of the people, to learn from them, to listen with an open mind to their wishes and opinions and report these without delay to the Party, to explain Party policy and decisions to the people;

7. To set a good example in their work and constantly raise their productive skill and professional ability;

8. To practice criticism and self-criticism, expose shortcomings and mistakes in work and strive to overcome and correct them; to report

such shortcomings and mistakes to the leading Party bodies, up to and including the Central Committee; and to fight both inside and outside the Party against everything which is detrimental to the interests of the Party and the people;

9. To be truthful and honest with the Party and not to conceal or distort the truth; and

10. To be constantly on the alert against the intrigues of the enemy, and to guard the secrets of the Party and the state.

Party members who fail to fulfill any of the above-mentioned duties shall be criticized and educated. Any serious infraction of these duties, splitting of Party unity, breaking of the laws of the state, violation of Party decisions, damaging Party interests, or deception toward the Party constitutes a violation of Party discipline, and disciplinary action shall be taken against it.

Article 3. Party members enjoy the following rights:

1. To participate in free and practical discussion at Party meetings or in the Party press on theoretical and practical questions relating to Party policy;

2. To make proposals regarding the Party's work and give full play to their creative ability in their work;

3. To elect and be elected within the Party;

4. To criticize any Party organization or any functionary at Party meetings;

5. To ask to attend in person when a Party organization decides to take disciplinary action against them or to make an appraisal of their character and work;

6. To reserve their opinions or submit them to a leading body of the Party, in case they disagree with any Party decision, which, in the meantime, they must carry out unconditionally; and

7. To address any statement, appeal, or complaint to any Party organization, up to and including the Central Committee.

Party members and responsible members of Party organizations who fail to respect these rights of a Party member shall be criticized and educated. Infringement of these rights constitutes a violation of Party discipline, and disciplinary action shall be taken against it.

Article 4. Only persons of eighteen years old and older are eligible for Party membership.

Applicants for Party membership must undergo the procedure of admission individually.

New members are admitted to the Party through a Party branch. An applicant must be recommended by two full Party members, and is admitted as a probationary member after being accepted by the general membership meeting of a Party branch and approved by the next higher Party committee; he may become a full Party member only after the completion of a probationary period of one year.

Under special conditions, Party committees at county or municipal level and above have the power to admit new Party members to the Party directly.

Article 5. Party members who recommend an applicant for admission to the Party must be highly conscientious in furnishing the Party with truthful information about the applicant's ideology, character, and personal history, and must explain the Party program and Constitution to the applicant.

Article 6. Before approving the admission of an applicant for Party membership, the Party committee concerned must assign a Party functionary to have a detailed conversation with the applicant and carefully examine his application form, the opinions of the Party members who recommended him, and the decision made by the Party branch for his admission.

Article 7. During the probationary period, the Party organizations concerned shall give the probationary member an elementary Party education and observe his political qualities.

Probationary members have the same duties as full members. They enjoy the same rights as full members, except that they have no right to elect or be elected or to vote on any motion.

Article 8. When the probationary period of a probationary member has expired, the Party branch to which he belongs must discuss without delay whether he is qualified to be transferred to full membership. Such a transfer must be accepted by a general membership meeting of the Party branch and approved by the next higher Party committee.

When the probationary period of a probationary member has expired, the Party organization concerned may prolong it for a period not exceeding one year if it finds it necessary to continue to observe him. If a probationary member is found to be unfit for transfer to full membership, his status as probationary member shall be annulled.

Any decision by a Party branch to prolong the probationary period of a probationary member or to deprive him of his status as probationary member must be approved by the next higher Party committee.

Article 9. The probationary period of a probationary member begins from the day when the general membership meeting of a Party branch accepts him as probationary member. The Party standing of a Party member dates from the day when the general membership meeting of a Party branch accepts his transfer to full membership.

Article 10. Party members transferring from one Party organization to another become members of the latter organization.

Article 11. Party members are free to withdraw from the Party. When a Party member asks to withdraw, the Party branch to which he belongs shall, by decision of its general membership meeting, strike his name off the Party rolls and report the matter to the next higher Party committee for registration.

Article 12. A Party member who, over a period of six months and without proper reasons, fails to take part in Party life or to pay membership dues is regarded as having quitted the Party himself. The Party branch to which this member belongs shall, by decision of its general membership meeting, strike his name off the Party rolls and report the matter to the next higher Party committee for registration.

Article 13. Party organizations at all levels may, according to each individual case, take disciplinary measures against any Party member who violates Party discipline, such as warning, serious warning, removal from posts held in the Party, placing on probation within the Party, or expulsion from the Party.

The period in which a Party member is placed on probation shall not exceed two years. During this period, the rights and duties of the Party member concerned are the same as those of a probationary member. If, after a Party member has been placed on probation, the facts show that he has corrected his mistakes, his rights as full Party member shall be restored and the period in which he is placed on probation will be reckoned in his Party standing. If he is found to be unfit for Party membership, he shall be expelled from the Party.

Article 14. Any disciplinary measure taken against a Party member must be decided on by a general membership meeting of the Party branch to which he belongs and must be approved by a higher Party control commission or higher Party committee.

Under special conditions, a Party branch committee or a higher Party committee has the power to take disciplinary measures against a Party member, but these measures must be subject to approval by a higher Party control commission or higher Party committee.

Article 15. Any decision to remove a member or alternate member of the Party committee of a county, an autonomous county, a municipality, a province, an autonomous region, or a municipality directly under the central authority, or an autonomous *chou* from the said committee, to place him on probation or to expel him from the Party, must be taken by the Party congress that has elected that member. In conditions of urgency, such a decision may be taken by a two-thirds majority vote at a plenary session of the Party committee to which the member belongs, but it must be subject to approval by the next higher Party committee. A primary Party organization has no power to take decisions on the removal of a member or alternate member of a higher

Party committee from that committee, or of placing him on probation or expelling him from the Party.

Article 16. Any decision to remove a member or alternate member of the Central Committee of the Party from the Central Committee, to place him on probation, or to expel him from the Party must be taken by the National Party Congress. In conditions of urgency, such a decision may be taken by a two-thirds majority vote of the Central Committee at its plenary session, but it must be subject to subsequent confirmation by the next session of the National Party Congress.

Article 17. Expulsion from the Party is the most severe of all inner-Party disciplinary measures. In taking or approving such a decision, all Party organizations must exercise the utmost caution, thoroughly investigate and study the facts and material evidence of the case, and listen carefully to the statement made in his own defense by the Party member concerned.

Article 18. When a Party organization discusses or decides on disciplinary measure against a Party member, it must, barring special circumstances, notify the member concerned to attend the meeting to defend himself. When disciplinary action is decided on, the person against whom such action is taken must be told the reasons for it. If he disagrees, he may ask for a reconsideration of his case and address an appeal to higher Party Committees or to Party control commissions, up to and including the Central Committee. Party organizations at all levels must deal with such appeals seriously or forward them promptly; no suppression is permitted.

CHAPTER II. ORGANIZATIONAL STRUCTURE AND
ORGANIZATIONAL PRINCIPLES OF THE PARTY

Article 19. The Party is formed on the principle of democratic centralism.

Democratic centralism means centralism on the basis of democracy and democracy under centralized guidance. Its basic conditions are as follows:

1. The leading bodies of the Party at all levels are elected.

2. The highest leading body of the Party is the National Party Congress, and the highest leading body in each local Party organinzation is the local Party congress. The National Party Congress elects the Central Committee and the local Party congresses elect their respective local Party committees. The Central Committee and local Party committees are responsible to their respective Party congresses, to which they should report on their work.

3. All leading bodies of the Party must pay constant heed to the views of their lower organizations and the rank-and-file Party mem-

bers, study their experiences, and give prompt help in solving their problems.

4. Lower Party organizations must present periodic reports on their work to the Party organizations above them and ask in good time for instructions on questions which need decision by higher Party organizations.

5. All Party organizations operate on the principle of combining collective leadership with individual responsibility. All important issues are to be decided on collectively, and at the same time, each individual is enabled to play his part to the fullest possible extent.

6. Party decisions must be carried out unconditionally. Individual Party members shall obey the Party organization, the minority shall obey the majority, the lower Party organizations shall obey the higher Party organizations, and all constituent Party organizations throughout the country shall obey the National Party Congress and the Central Committee.

Article 20. Party organizations are formed on a geographical or industrial basis.

The Party organization in charge of Party work in a defined area is regarded as the highest of all the constituent Party organizations in that area.

The Party organization in charge of Party work in a particular production or work unit is regarded as the highest of all the constituent Party organizations in that unit.

Article 21. The highest bodies of the Party organizations at various levels are as follows:

1. For the whole country, the highest body of the Party organization is the National Party Congress. When the National Party Congress is not in session, it is the Central Committee elected by the National Party Congress.

2. For a province, autonomous region, or municipality directly under the central authority, it is the provincial, autonomous regional, or municipal Party congress. When the congress is not in session, it is the provincial, autonomous regional, or municipal Party committee elected by that congress.

For an autonomous *chou,* it is the autonomous *chou* Party congress. When the congress is not in session, it is the autonomous *chou* committee elected by that congress.

3. For a county, autonomous county, or municipality, it is the county, autonomous county, or municipal Party congress. When the congress is not in session, it is the county, autonomous county, or municipal committee elected by that congress.

4. For primary units (factories, mines and other enterprises, *hsiang,*

nationality *hsiang,* towns and agricultural producers' cooperatives, offices, schools, streets, companies of the People's Liberation Army, and other primary units) , it is the delegate meeting or the general membership meeting of the particular primary unit. When the delegate meeting or general membership meeting of the primary unit is not in session, it is the primary Party committee, the committee of a general Party branch, or the committee of a Party branch elected by the delegate meeting, or the general membership meeting.

Article 22. Party elections must fully reflect the will of the electors. The lists of candidates for election put forward by the Party organization or by electors must be discussed by the electors.

Election is by secret ballot. Electors shall be ensured of the right to criticize or reject any candidate, or nominate a person who is not on the list.

In an election in a primary Party organization, voting may be by a show of hands if voting by ballot is impossible. In such cases, each candidate shall be voted upon separately, and voting on a whole list of candidates is forbidden.

Article 23. Party electing units have the power to replace any member they have elected to a Party congress or Party committee during his term of office.

When a local Party congress is not in session, a higher Party committee, if it deems it necessary, may transfer or appoint responsible members of a lower Party organization.

Article 24. In places where, because of special circumstances, it is impossible for the time being to call Party congresses or general membership meetings to elect Party committees, such Party committees may be elected at Party conferences or appointed by higher Party organizations.

Article 25. The functions and powers of the central Party organizations and those of the local Party organizations shall be appropriately divided. All questions of a national character or questions that require a uniform decision for the whole country shall be handled by the central Party organizations, so as to contribute to the centralism and unity of the Party. All questions of a local character or questions that need to be decided locally shall be handled by the local Party organizations, so as to find solutions appropriate to the local conditions. The functions and powers of higher local Party organizations and those of lower local Party organizations shall be appropriately divided according to the same principle.

Decisions taken by lower Party organizations must not run counter to those made by higher Party organizations.

Article 26. Before decisions on Party policy are made by leading bodies of the Party, lower Party organizations and members of the Party committees may hold free and practical discussions inside the Party organizations and at Party meetings and submit their proposals to the leading bodies of the Party. However, once a decision is taken by the leading bodies of the Party, it must be accepted. Should a lower Party organization find that a decision made by a higher Party organization does not suit the actual conditions in its locality or in its particular department, it should request the higher Party organization concerned to modify the decision. If the higher Party organization upholds its decision, then the lower Party organization must carry it out unconditionally.

On policy of a national character, before the central leading bodies of the Party have made any statement or decision, departmental and local Party organizations and their responsible members are not permitted to make any public statement or make a decision at will, although they may discuss it among themselves and make suggestions to the central leading bodies.

Article 27. The newspapers issued by Party organizations at all levels must publicize the decisions and policy of the central Party organizations, of higher Party organizations, and of their own Party organizations.

Article 28. The formation of a new Party organization or the dissolution of an existing Party organization must be decided on by the next higher Party organization.

Article 29. To facilitate the direction of the work in various localities, the Central Committee may, if it deems it necessary, establish a bureau of the Central Committee as its representative body for an area embracing several provinces, autonomous regions, and municipalities directly under the central authority. A provincial or autonomous regional committee may, if it deems it necessary, establish a regional committee or an organization of equal status as its representative body for an area embracing a number of counties, autonomous counties, and municipalities. The Party committee of a municipality directly under the central authority, or of a municipality, county, or autonomous county may, if it deems it necessary, establish a number of district committees as its representative bodies within its area.

Article 30. Party committees at all levels may, as the situation requires, set up a number of departments, commissions, or other bodies to carry on work under their own direction.

CHAPTER III. CENTRAL ORGANIZATIONS OF THE PARTY

Article 31. The National Party Congress is elected for a term of five years.

The number of delegates to the National Party Congress and the procedure governing their election and replacement and the filling of vacancies shall be determined by the Central Committee.

A session of the National Party Congress shall be convened once a year by the Central Committee. Under extraordinary conditions, it may be postponed or convened before its due date as the Central Committee may decide. The Central Committee must convene a session of the National Party Congress if one-third of the delegates to the National Party Congress or one-third of the Party organizations at provincial level so request.

Article 32. The functions and powers of the National Party Congress are as follows:

1. To hear and examine the reports of the Central Committee and other central organs;

2. To determine the Party's line and policy;

3. To revise the Constitution of the Party; and

4. To elect the Central Committee.

Article 33. The Central Committee of the Party is elected for a term of five years. The number of members and alternate members of the Central Committee shall be determined by the National Party Congress. Vacancies on the Central Committee shall be filled by alternate members in order of established precedence.

Article 34. When the National Party Congress is not in session, the Central Committee directs the entire work of the Party, carries out the decisions of the National Party Congress, represents the Party in its relations with other parties and organizations, sets up various Party organs and directs their activities, and takes charge of and allocates Party cadres.

The Central Committee guides the work of the Central state organs and people's organizations of a national character through leading Party members' groups within them.

Article 35. The Party organizations in the Chinese People's Liberation Army carry on their work in accordance with the instructions of the Central Committee. The General Political Department in the People's Liberation Army, under the direction of the Central Committee, takes charge of the ideological and organizational work of the Party in the army.

Article 36. The Central Committee meets in Plenary Session at least twice a year, to be convened by the Political Bureau of the Central Committee.

Article 37. At its Plenary Session the Central Committee elects the Political Bureau, the Standing Committee of the Political Bureau and the Secretariat, as well as the chairman, vice-chairmen, and general secretary of the Central Committee.

When the Central Committee is not in Plenary Session, the Political Bureau and its Standing Committee exercise the powers and functions of the Central Committee.

The Secretariat attends to the daily work of the Central Committee under the direction of the Political Bureau and its Standing Committee.

The chairman and vice-chairmen of the Central Committee are concurrently chairman and vice-chairmen of the Political Bureau.

The Central Committee may, when it deems it necessary, have an honorary chairman.

CHAPTER IV. PARTY ORGANIZATIONS IN PROVINCES, AUTONOMOUS REGIONS, MUNICIPALITIES DIRECTLY UNDER THE CENTRAL AUTHORITY, AND AUTONOMOUS CHOU

Article 38. The Party congress for a province, autonomous region, or municipality directly under the central authority is elected for a term of three years.

The number of delegates to such a Party congress and the procedure governing their election and replacement and the filling of vacancies shall be determined by the Party committee in the given area.

The Party congress for a province, autonomous region, or municipality directly under the central authority shall be convened once a year by the Party committee in the area.

Article 39. The Party congress for a province, autonomous region, or municipality directly under the central authority hears and examines the reports of the Party committee and other organs in the area, discusses and decides on questions relating to policy and work of a local character in its area, elects the Party committee for the area, and elects delegates to the National Party Congress.

Article 40. The Party committee of a province, autonomous region, or municipality directly under the central authority is elected for a term of three years. The number of members and alternate members of the committee shall be determined by the Central Committee. Vacancies on the committee shall be filled by alternate members of the committee in established order of precedence.

The Party committee of a province, autonomous region, or municipality directly under the central authority shall, when the Party congress for the given area is not in session, carry out the decisions and directives of the Party in its area, direct all work of a local character, set up various Party organs and direct their activities, take charge of and allocate Party cadres in accordance with the regulations laid down by the Central Committee, direct the work of leading Party members' groups in local state organs and people's organizations, and systematically report on its work to the Central Committee.

Article 41. The Party committee of a province, autonomous region, or municipality directly under the central authority shall meet in full session at least three times a year.

The Party committee of a province, autonomous region, or municipality directly under the central authority elects its standing committee and secretariat at its plenary session. The standing committee exercises the powers and functions of the Party committee when the latter is not in session. The secretariat attends to the daily work under the direction of the standing committee.

The members of the secretariat and those of the standing committee of the Party committee of a province, autonomous region, or municipality directly under the central authority must be approved by the Central Committee. Members of the secretariat must be Party members of at least five years' standing.

Article 42. Party organizations in an autonomous *chou* carry on their work under the direction of a provincial or autonomous regional Party committee.

The Party congress and Party committee for an autonomous *chou* are constituted in the same manner as those for a province, autonomous region, or municipality directly under the central authority.

The Party congress and Party committee for an autonomous *chou* are elected for a term of two years.

An autonomous *chou* Party congress elects delegates to the provincial or autonomous regional Party congress.

The members of the secretariat and those of the standing committee of an autonomous *chou* Party committee must be approved by the Central Committee. The secretaries must be Party members of at least three years' standing.

CHAPTER V.   COUNTY, AUTONOMOUS COUNTY, AND MUNICIPAL PARTY
ORGANIZATIONS

Article 43. The Party congress for a county, autonomous county, or municipality is elected for a term of two years.

The number of delegates to the congress and the procedure governing their election and replacement and the filling of vacancies shall be determined by the Party committee in the area.

The Party congress for a county, autonomous county, or municipality shall be convened once a year by the Party committee in the area.

Article 44. The Party congress for a county, autonomous county, or municipality hears and examines the reports of the Party committee and other organs in the area, discusses and decides on questions relating to the policy and work of a local character in its area, elects the Party committee for the area, and elects delegates to the provincial or autonomous regional Party congress.

The Party congress for a county, autonomous county, or municipality under the jurisdiction of an autonomous *chou* elects delegates only to the Party congress of the said autonomous *chou*.

Article 45. The Party committee of a county, autonomous county, or municipality is elected for a term of two years. The number of members and alternate members of the committee shall be determined by the provincial or autnomous regional Party committee concerned. Vacancies on the committee shall be filled by alternate members of the committee in established order of precedence.

When the Party congress for a county, autonomous county, or municipality is not in session, the Party committee in the area carries out Party decisions and directives in its area, directs all work of a local character, sets up various Party organs and directs their activities, takes charge of and allocates Party cadres in accordance with the regulations laid down by the Central Committee, directs the work of leading Party members' groups in local government organs and people's organizations, and systematically reports on its work to higher Party committees.

Article 46. The Party committee of a county, autonomous county, or municipality shall meet in plenary session at least four times a year.

The county, autonomous county, or municipal Party committee elects at its plenary session its standing committee and secretary, and, if necessary, a secretariat. The standing committee exercises the powers and functions of the Party committee when the latter is not in plenary session. The secretary or the secretariat attends to the daily work under the direction of the standing committee.

The members of the secretariat and those of the standing committee must be approved by the provincial or autonomous regional Party committee. In the case of a city with a population of 500,000 or more or in the case of a key industrial city, such members must be approved by the Central Committee. The secretaries of the Party committee of a county, autonomous county, or municipality must be Party members of at least two years' standing. In the case of a city with a population of 500,000 or more, or in the case of a key industrial city, the secretaries of the Party committee must be Party members of at least five years' standing.

CHAPTER VI. PRIMARY ORGANIZATIONS OF THE PARTY

Article 47. Primary Party organizations are formed in factories, mines and other enterprises, in *hsiang* and nationality *hsiang,* in towns, in agricultural producers' cooperatives, in offices, schools, and streets, in companies of the People's Liberation Army, and in other primary units where there are three or more full Party members. When a primary unit contains less than three full Party members, no primary Party organization should be established, but these members together with the probationary members in their unit may either form a group or join the primary Party organization of a nearby unit.

Article 48. Primary Party organizations take the following organizational forms:

1. A primary Party organization with 100 or more Party members may, by decision of the next higher Party committee, hold a delegate meeting or a general membership meeting to elect a primary Party committee. Under the primary Party committee a number of general branches or branches may be formed in accordance with divisions based on production, work, or residence. Under a general Party branch a number of Party branches may be formed. The committee of a general Party branch is elected by a general membership meeting or a delegate meeting of that general branch. The committee of a Party branch is elected by the general membership meeting of that branch. The committee of the primary Party organization or of the general Party branch has the power to approve decisions made by a branch on the admission of new members and on disciplinary measures against Party members.

Under special conditions, individual primary Party organizations with less than 100 each may, by decision of the next higher Party committee, establish a committee of the said primary organizations.

2. A primary Party organization with fifty or more Party members may, by decision of the next higher Party committee, set up a general branch committee to be elected by a general membership meeting or a delegate meeting. Under a general branch committee a number of branches may be formed in accordance with divisions based on production, work, or residence. The general branch committee has the power to approve decisions made by a branch on the admission of new members and on disciplinary measures against Party members.

Under special conditions, a general branch committee may, by decision of the next higher Party committee, be set up in a primary Party organization whose membership is less than fifty but whose work requires a general branch committee, or in a primary Party organization whose membership numbers 100 or more but whose work does not require a primary Party committee.

3. A primary Party organization with less than fifty members may, by decision of the next higher Party committee, set up a branch committee to be elected by a general membership meeting, and has the power to make decisions on the admission of new members and on disciplinary measures against Party members.

4. Groups may be formed under a general Party branch or a Party branch.

Article 49. A primary Party organization which has set up its own primary committee shall convene a delegate meeting at least once a year. A general Party branch shall hold a general membership meeting or a delegate meeting at least twice a year. A Party branch shall hold a general membership meeting at least once in three months.

The delegate meeting or general membership meeting of a primary Party organization hears and examines the reports of the primary Party committee, the general branch committees, or the branch committees; discusses and decides on questions relating to its own unit; elects the primary Party committee, the general Party branch committees, or the branch committees, and elects delegates to the higher Party congress.

The primary Party committee, the general Party branch committee, and the branch committee are elected for a term of one year. The number of members of these committees shall be determind by their respective next higher Party committees.

A primary Party committee shall elect a secretary and from one to four deputy secretaries. If necessary, it may elect a standing committee. The general branch committee and the branch committee shall each elect a secretary, and, if necessary, one to three deputy secretaries.

A Party branch with less than ten members only elects a secretary or in addition a deputy secretary, but no branch committee needs to be formed.

A Party group shall elect a leader and, if necessary, a deputy leader.

Article 50. Primary Party organizations must cement the ties of the workers, peasants, intellectuals, and other patriotic people within the Party and its leading bodies. The general tasks of primary Party organizations are as follows:

1. To carry on propaganda and organizational work among the masses and put into practice the programs of the Party, and the decisions of higher Party organizations;

2. To pay constant heed to the sentiments and demands of the masses and report them to higher Party organizations, and to pay constant attention to the material and cultural life of the masses and strive to improve it;

3. To recruit new Party members, to collect membership dues, to

examine and appraise Party members, and to maintain Party discipline among the membership;

4. To organize Party members to study Marxism-Leninism and the Party's policy and experience, and raise the levels of their ideology and political understanding;

5. To lead the masses of the people to take an active part in the political life of the country;

6. To lead the masses to give full play to their activity and creative ability, to strengthen labor discipline, and to ensure the fulfillment of the production and work plans;

7. To promote criticism and self-criticism, to expose and eliminate shortcomings and mistakes in work, and to wage struggles against the violation of laws and discipline, against corruption and waste, and against bureaucracy; and

8. To educate the Party members and the masses to sharpen their revolutionary vigilance and to be constantly on the alert to combat the disruptive activities of the class enemy.

Article 51. Primary Party organizations in the enterprises, villages, schools, and army units should guide and supervise the administrative bodies and mass organizations in their respective units in the energetic fulfillment of the decisions of higher Party organizations and higher state organs, and in ceaselessly improving their work.

Since special conditions obtain in public institutions and organizations, the primary Party organizations therein are in no position to guide and supervise their work, but they should supervise ideologically and politically all Party members in the said institutions and organizations, including those who hold leading administrative posts. The primary Party organizations should also take a constant interest in improving the work in their respective units, strengthen labor discipline, combat bureaucracy, and report without delay any shortcomings in the work to the administrative chiefs of the given units and to higher Party organizations.

CHAPTER VII.   CONTROL ORGANS OF THE PARTY

Article 52. The Party's Central Committee, the Party committees of the provinces, autonomous regions, municipalities directly under the central authority, and autonomous *chou*, and the Party committees of the counties, autonomous counties, and municipalities shall set up control commissions. The Central Control Commission shall be elected by the Central Committee at its Plenary Session. A local control commission shall be elected by a plenary session of the Party committee for that locality, subject to approval by the next higher Party committee.

Article 53. The tasks of the Central and local control commissions are as follows: to examine and deal with cases of violation of the Party Constitution, Party discipline, Communist ethics, and the state laws and decrees on the part of Party members; to decide on or cancel disciplinary measures against Party members; and to deal with appeals and complaints from Party members.

Article 54. The control commissions at all levels function under the direction of the Party committees at corresponding levels.

Higher control commissions have the power to check up on the work of lower control commissions, and to approve or modify their decisions on any case. Lower control commissions must report on their work to higher control commissions, and present accurate reports on the violation of discipline by Party members.

CHAPTER VIII. RELATION BETWEEN THE PARTY AND THE
COMMUNIST YOUTH LEAGUE

Article 55. The Communist Youth League of China carries on its activities under the guidance of the Communist Party of China. The Central Committee of the Communist Youth League accepts the leadership of the Party's Central Committee. The Communist Youth League's local organizations are simultaneously under the leadership of the Party organizations at the corresponding levels and of higher League organizations.

Article 56. The Communist Youth League is the Party's assistant. In all spheres of socialist construction Communist Youth League organizations should play an active role in publicizing and carrying out Party policy and decisions. In the struggle to promote production, improve work, and expose and eliminate shortcomings and mistakes in work, the Communist Youth League organizations should render effective help to the Party, and have the duty to make suggestions to the Party organizations concerned.

Article 57. Party organizations at all levels must take a deep interest in the Communist Youth League's ideological and organizational work, give guidance to the Communist Youth League in imbuing all its members with Communist spirit and educating them in Marxist-Leninist theory, see to it that close contact is maintained between the Communist Youth League and the broad masses of young people, and pay constant attention to selecting members for the leadership of the Communist Youth League.

Article 58. Members of the Communist Youth League shall withdraw from the League when they have been admitted to the Party and have become full Party members, provided they do not hold leading posts or engage in specific work in the League organizations.

CHAPTER IX. LEADING PARTY MEMBERS' GROUPS IN
NON-PARTY ORGANIZATIONS

Article 59. In the leading body of a state organ or people's organization, where there are three or more Party members holding responsible
posts, a leading Party members' group shall be formed. The tasks
of such a group in that organ or organization are to assume the responsibility of carrying out Party policy and decisions, to fortify unity
with non-Party cadres, to cement the ties with the masses, to strengthen
Party and state discipline, and to combat bureaucracy.

Article 60. The composition of a leading Pary members' group shall
be decided by a competent Party committee. The group has a secretary,
and may, in case of need, also have a deputy secretary.

A leading Party members' group must in all matters accept the leadership of the competent Party committee.

DOCUMENT 16

NATIONAL CONGRESSES OF THE CHINESE COMMUNIST PARTY

[Condensed from an article in *People's China*, September 16, 1956.]

1) First National Party Congress, July, 1921: 12 delegates, representing 57 Party members, met in Shanghai. The Party was officially
founded.

2) Second National Party Congress, May, 1922: 12 delegates, representing 123 Party members, met in Shanghai. The Party joined the
Third International.

3) Third National Party Congress, June, 1923: 27 delegates, representing 432 Party members, met in Canton. Decision to cooperate with
the Kuomintang; Mao Tse-tung elected to the Central Committee.

4) Fourth National Party Congress, January, 1925: 20 delegates, representing 950 members, met in Shangai. Declaration of position on
ideological questions: leadership of working class, worker-peasant
alliance, role of Communist Party, etc.

5) Fifth National Party Congress, April, 1927: 80 delegates, representing 57,969 members, met in Hankow. Debate on the class struggle
and relations with the bourgeoisie; Ch'en Tu-hsiu criticized but

still elected General Secretary. August, 1927, emergency meeting of Central Committee expelled Ch'en Tu-hsiu from Central Committee.

6) Sixth National Party Congress, July, 1928: 118 delegates, representing 40,000 members, met in Moscow. Collapse of the united front, Ch'en Tu-hsiu ousted from leadership; Mao Tse-tung not present, but elected to Central Committee.

7) Seventh National Party Congress, April, 1945: 544 delegates and 208 alternate delegates, representing 1,210,000 members, met in Yenan. Adoption of a new Constitution for the Party; Mao Tse-tung spelled out the program for the New Democracy in his report "On a Coalition Government."

8) Eighth National Party Congress, September, 1956: 1,026 delegates and 107 alternate delegates, representing 10,730,000 members, met in Peking. Revision of Party Constitution; proposal for the Second Five-year Plan.

DOCUMENT 17

LIU SHAO-CH'I ON PARTY ORGANIZATION

[The following are excerpts from Liu Shao-ch'i's *How to Be a Good Communist* (1934), *On Inner-Party Struggle* (1941), and *On the Party's Mass Line* (1945).]

HOW TO BE A GOOD COMMUNIST

Ever since man came into the world, in order to be able to live, he has had to struggle against nature to produce the material values essential to his existence. However,

> men carry on a struggle against nature and utilize nature for the production of material values not in isolation from each other, not as separate individuals, but in common, in groups, in societies. Production, therefore, is at all times and under all conditions *social* production. In the production of material values men enter into mutual relations of one kind or another within production, into relations of production of one kind or another.*

---

* *The History of the Communist Party of the Soviet Union (Bolsheviks) Short Course* (Moscow: Foreign Languages Publishing House, 1951), pp. 188–89. (This footnote appears in the 1952 edition of Liu's treatise published by the Foreign Languages Press, Peking.—Ed.)

Thus, the struggle carried on by men against nature for production is social in character. It is a struggle of men as social beings against nature. It is in this ceaseless struggle against nature that human beings have been continuously changing nature and simultaneously changing themselves, and have changed their relations with one another. It is in the course of the long struggle of men as social beings against nature, that men's physical forms (hands, feet, posture, etc.), their social relations, their forms of social organization as well as their brains, ideology, etc. are all continuously being changed and improved. This is because:

> The first feature of production is that it never stays at one point for a long time and is always in a state of change and development, and that, furthermore, changes in the mode of production inevitably call forth changes in the whole social system, social ideas, political views, and political institutions. (*Ibid.* pp. 189–90)

Marx once told the workers: "You will have to go through fifteen, twenty, fifty years of civil wars and international conflicts, not only to change existing conditions, but also to change yourselves and to make yourselves capable of wielding political power."

In other words, men change themselves not only in their struggle against nature, but also in constant social struggle. The proletariat will also have to consciously go through a long period of social struggle to change society and itself.

We Communist Party members are the most advanced revolutionaries in modern history and are the contemporary fighting and driving force in changing society and the world. Revolutionaries exist because counterrevolutionaries still exist. Therefore, to conduct a ceaseless struggle against the counterrevolutionaries constitutes an essential condition for the existence and development of the revolutionaries. If they fail to carry on such a struggle, they cannot be called revolutionaries and still less can they advance and develop. It is in the course of this ceaseless struggle against the counterrevolutionaries that Communist Party members change society, change the world, and at the same time change themselves.

Not every revolutionary who has undergone the steeling of long years of revolutionary struggle can develop into a very good and experienced revolutionary, chiefly because his own efforts and self-cultivation are insufficient. But all those who have succeeded in becoming very good and experienced revolutionaries must certainly have gone through long years of steeling and self-cultivation in the revolutionary struggle. Hence, our Party members can make themselves politically inflexible revolutionaries of high quality only by steeling themselves, strengthening their self-cultivation, not losing their sense of the new, and by improving their reasoning power in the course of the revolutionary struggle of the broad masses under all difficulties and hardships.

The goal of Party members in steeling and cultivation should not merely be the standard of minimum qualifications, but should be the standard of maximum qualifications. At present we find it very difficult to define these maximum qualifications. However, we have before us the words and deeds, the achievements and qualities of Marx, Engels, Lenin, and Stalin throughout their lives as our examples and as the criterion of our cultivation. By cultivation is meant raising our own qualities in every respect to the same level as those of Marx, Engels, Lenin, and Stalin. Let us strive to become their best pupils.

We Communists must possess the greatest courage and revolutionary determination of mankind. Every Party member should gladly and seriously make up his mind about shouldering this unprecedented, great, and difficult task in human history—the realization of Communism. While we clearly see the difficulties confronting the cause of Communism, we are not in the least daunted by them, for we also clearly understand that these difficulties can certainly be overcome in the course of drawing into the revolution countless millions of people. We clearly understand that the cause of Communism is a "100-year great task." We must fulfill the great mission which historical evolution has devolved upon us. We have the support of great masses. We must accomplish a great part of the task of the cause of Communism in our generation and leave to posterity the final completion of the task. Comrades! The great vision and courage of us Communists has never been matched by that of any past heroes in the annals of mankind. In this respect we have every reason to be proud of ourselves.

Apart from clearly establishing his Communist outlook on life and his Communist world outlook, a Communist must also clearly define the correct relationship between his personal interests and the interests of the Party. The Marxist principle is that personal interests must be subordinated to the Party's interests, partial interests to total interests, temporary interests to long-range interests, and the interests of one nation to the interests of the world as a whole.

Whether or not a Communist Party member can absolutely and unconditionally subordinate his personal interests to the Party's interests under all circumstances is the criterion with which to test his loyalty to the Party, to the revolution, and to the Communist cause. Since the realization of Communism must depend upon the proletariat and the Communist Party, Communism will never be brought about if the interests of the proletariat and the Communist Party are impaired.

At all times and on all questions, a Communist Party member should take into account the interests of the Party as a whole, and place the Party's interests above his personal problems and interests. It is the highest principle of our Party members that the Party's interests are supreme. Every Party member should firmly build up this conception in his ideology. This is what we have often spoken of as "Party spirit," "Party conception," or "organizational conception." He should have the Party and the Party's interests uppermost in his mind, and not considerations of a personal character. He should ensure that his personal interests accord with the Party's interests or even merge with them. Thus when his personal interests conflict with the Party's interests, he will be able to submit to the Party's interests and sacrifice his personal interests without the slightest hesitation or reluctance. To sacrifice one's personal interests and even one's life without the slightest hesitation and even with a feeling of happiness for the cause of the Party, for class and national liberation, and for the emancipation of mankind is the highest manifestation of Communist ethics. This is a Party member's highest manifestation of principle. This is the manifestation of the purity of proletarian ideology of a Party member.

In the Party our members should not have personal aims independent of the Party's interests. The personal aims of our Party members can only be part of the Party's aims. For example, our Party members want to study Marxist-Leninist theory, enhance their ability, lead the victorious revolutionary struggle of the broad masses and establish various kinds of revolutionary organizations, etc. If all these are their personal aims they are part of the Party's aims as well, since they are also in the interests of the Party. And the Party certainly needs large numbers of such Party members and cadres. But apart from this our Party members should not have independent aims of their own such as personal position, individual heroism, and so forth. If they have such aims, they may depart from the Party's interests to such an extent as to become opportunists in the Party.

On Inner-Party Struggle

Everyone knows that our Party is a proletarian party, a party that leads the struggles of the broad masses. If the Party is to fulfill the historical tasks it has shouldered, it must fight against the enemies of the revolution at various periods, and must unite with the various revolutionary strata and classes.

From the day of its birth, our Party has never for a single moment lived in any environment but that of serious struggle. The Party and the proletariat have constantly lived inside the encirclement of various nonproletarian classes—the big bourgeoisie, the petty bourgeoisie, the peasantry, and even the remnants of feudal forces. All these classes, when they are struggling against the proletariat or when they are co-operating with it, utilize the unstable elements within the Party and the proletariat to penetrate into the heart of the Party and the proletariat and constantly influence the Party and the proletariat in ideology, in living habits, in theory, and in action. This is the origin of all kinds of erroneous and undesirable tendencies within the Party. It is the social basis of all kinds of opportunism within the Party, and it is also the source of inner-Party struggles.

Inner-Party struggles are a reflection of the class struggles outside the Party.

From the very day of its inception, our Party has struggled not only against the enemies outside the Party, but also against all kinds of hostile and nonproletarian influences inside the Party. These two kinds of struggles are different, but both are necessary and have a common class substance. If our Party did not carry on the latter type of struggle, if it did not struggle constantly within the Party against all undesirable tendencies, if it did not constantly purge the Party of every type of nonproletarian ideology and overcome both left and right opportunism, then such nonproletarian ideology and such left and right opportunism might gain ground in the Party and influence or even dominate our Party. This would make it impossible for the Party to consolidate and develop itself or to preserve its independence. This would endanger the Party and lead to its degeneration. Such nonproletarian ideology and left or right opportunism can corrupt our Party, or certain sections of it, and can even transform the character of our Party or sections of it into that of a nonproletarian organization. For example, it was in this manner that the Social Democratic parties in Europe were corrupted by bourgeois ideology and transformed into political parties of a bourgeois type, thus becoming the main social pillars of the bourgeoisie.

Therefore, such inner-Party struggle is absolutely necessary and cannot be avoided. Any idea of trying to avoid inner-Party struggle, or of refraining from criticizing others' mistakes so that they will not criticize one's own errors, is totally wrong.

Inner-Party struggles consist principally of ideological struggles. The differences and antagonisms among our comrades on matters of ideology and principle can develop into political splits within the Party, and, under certain circumstances, even to inevitable organizational splits; but, in character and content, such differences and antagonisms are basically ideological struggles.

Consequently, any inner-Party struggle not involving differences in matters of ideology and principle and any conflict among Party members not based on differences in matters of principle is a type of unprincipled struggle, a struggle without content. This kind of struggle without principle or content is utterly unnecessary within the Party. It is detrimental and not beneficial to the Party. Every Party member should strictly avoid such struggles.

Inner-Party struggle is absolutely indispensable to protecting the purity and independence of the Party, to guaranteeing that the Party's activities constantly proceed along lines which represent the highest interests of the proletariat, and to preserving the Party's basic proletarian character. With this object in view, inner-Party struggles must be conducted from two sides, or on two fronts. This is because the enemy's ideology influences the Party from two directions, attacking the Party from both the right and the left. This is expressed in the Party by right or left opportunism.

Therefore, our inner-Party struggle must be directed simultaneously against both right opportunism and left opportunism so that our Party can preserve its definite proletarian character. If we fail to do this, if we merely carry on a one-sided struggle, or if we slacken our vigilance and our struggle against either side, then the enemy not only can, but assuredly will, attack our Party from that very side that we have neglected. In that case, it will be impossible to preserve the Party's purity and independence or to consolidate the Party. It is, therefore, in the course of ceaseless inner-Party struggle on two fronts that our Party consolidates and develops itself.

First of all, comrades must understand that inner-Party struggle is a matter of the greatest seriousness and responsibility. We must conduct it with the strictest and most responsible attitude and should never conduct it carelessly. In carrying our inner-Party struggle we must first fully adopt the correct stand of the Party, the unselfish stand of serving the interests of the Party, of doing better work, and of helping other comrades to correct their mistakes and to gain a better understanding of the problems. We ourselves must be clear about the facts and problems by making a systematic investigation and study. At the same time, we must carry on systematic, well-prepared, and well-led inner-Party struggles.

Our self-criticism and inner-Party struggle are not intended to weaken the Party's organization, solidarity, discipline, and prestige, or to obstruct the progress of its work. On the contrary, they are intended to strengthen our Party's organization and solidarity, enhance its discipline and prestige, and accelerate the progress of its work. Thus, inner-Party struggle must not be allowed to follow its own course and lead to ultrademocracy. Inside the Party, neither patriarchy nor ultrademocracy is allowed. These are the two extremes of abnormal life within the Party.

Inner-Party struggle must be conducted with the greatest sense of responsibility to the Party and to the revolution.

Second, comrades must understand that inner-Party struggle is basically a struggle between different ideologies and principles inside the Party. It is imperative to draw a clear line with regard to ideology and principle. But with regard to organization, the form of struggle, and the manner of speaking and criticizing, comrades must be as little antagonistic as possible, must try their best to discuss or to argue over matters in a calm way, and must try their best not to adopt organizational measures and not to draw organizational conclusions.

With regard to different ideologies and principles, comrades' persistence, opposition, and arguments cannot be separated from their obedience to the Party organization, to the majority and to the higher authority; otherwise, there would be no Party unity and no unity in action. Comrades should never, because of their insistence on principle, oppose the Party organizationally, disobey the majority and the higher authority, and begin to take independent action. Such would constitute a violation of the fundamental discipline of the Party.

Third, criticisms directed against Party organizations or against comrades and their work must be appropriate and well-regulated. Bolshevik self-criticism is conducted according to the Bolshevik yardstick. Excessive criticism, exaggeration of others' errors, and indiscriminate name-calling are all incorrect. The case is not that the more bitter the inner-Party struggle, the better; but that inner-Party struggle should be conducted within proper limits. Both overshooting the target and falling short of it are undesirable.

Fourth, the holding of struggle meetings, either inside or outside the Party, should in general be stopped. The various defects and errors should be pointed out in the course of summing up and reviewing work. We should first deal with "the case" and then with "the person." We must first make clear the facts, the points at issue, the nature, the seriousness, and the cause of the errors and defects, and only then point out who are responsible for these defects and errors, and whose is the major responsibility and whose is the minor responsibility.

Fifth, every opportunity to appeal must be given to comrades who have been criticized or punished. As a rule, a comrade should be personally notified of all records or organizational conclusions that may be made about him, and these should be made in his presence. If he does not agree, then after discussion, the case may be referred to a higher authority. (In the case of anyone who expresses dissatisfaction after having been punished, the Party organization concerned must refer the case to a higher authority even if the comrade himself does not want to make an appeal.) No Party organization can prevent any comrade who has been punished from appealing to a higher authority. No Party member can be deprived of his right to appeal. No Party organization can withhold any appeal.

On questions of ideology or principle the Party member concerned may appeal directly to a higher Party committee or even to the Central Committee by going over the head of the Party organization to which he belongs. In making such an appeal the comrade, however, should first fully explain his views, his reasons, and his differences and make all these clear to his Party organization, before making his appeal to a higher authority. He should not keep his mouth shut in his Party organization while indulging in irresponsible talk with a higher Party organization in an attempt to deceive and fool the higher Party organization. Once an appeal has been made, the final decision rests with the higher Party organization, which may cancel, reduce, or increase the disciplinary measures taken against a comrade by a Party committee of a lower level.

Sixth, a clear line should be drawn and a proper link should be established between struggles waged inside the Party and those waged outside the Party. A struggle waged outside the Party must not adopt the same forms as are used in inner-Party struggle, nor vice versa. Particular care should be exercised to avoid taking advantage of outside forces and conditions in waging struggles against the Party or of intimidating the Party. All Party members must take great care to maintain sharp vigilance lest the hidden Trotskyites and counterrevolutionary elements should take advantage of the conflicts and struggles inside the Party to carry on their subversive activities. In conducting inner-Party struggles, Party members must not allow themselves to be utilized by these elements. This can be done by strictly observing Party discipline and by carrying on the inner-Party struggle correctly.

Inside the Party, only open struggles and ideological struggles are allowed. No form of struggle which violates the Party Constitution or Party discipline will be allowed.

Seventh, in order to prevent unprincipled disputes within the Party, it is necessary to lay down the following measures:

a) Party members who disagree with the Party's leading body or any Party organization should submit their views and criticisms to the appropriate Party organization, but should not talk about their disagreement casually among the masses.

b) Party members who disagree with other Party members or certain responsible Party members, may criticize them in their presence or in certain specific Party organizations, but should not talk about their disagreement casually.

c) Party members or Party committees of a lower level who disagree with a Party committee at a higher level, may bring the issue to the Party committee at a higher level, or ask it to call a meeting to study the matter, or should refer the matter to a Party committee at a still higher level, but they should not talk about their disagreement casually or inform Party committees at a lower level about the matter.

d) When Party members discover any other Party member doing something wrong and acting in a manner detrimental to the interests of the Party, they must report such activities to the appropriate Party organization, and should not attempt to cover up the matter or attempt to shield each other.

e) Party members should promote an upright style of work, oppose any kind of deceitful talk and actions, and should severely condemn all those who indulge in idle talk, gossiping, prying into other's secrets, and spreading rumors. The leading bodies of the Party must from time to time issue instructions forbidding Party members to talk about certain specific matters.

f) The leading bodies at all levels must from time to time summon those comrades who indulge in idle talk and unprincipled disputes and talk with them, correct them and warn them, or subject them to discipline in other ways.

g) Party committees at all levels must respect the opinions set forth by Party members. They should frequently convene meetings to discuss questions and review their work, and provide Party members with ample opportunity to express their opinions.

On the Party's Mass Line

The General Program and detailed provisions of the Party Constitution lay particular stress on the Party's mass line. This is another feature of the present revised Constitution, because the mass line is a fundamental political and organizational line of our Party. That is to say that all our Party organizations and all our Party work must be closely linked up with the masses of the people.

Comrade Mao Tse-tung has repeatedly pointed out to us that the mass line should be applied in all our work. In his report to this Congress, he again urged us in most sincere terms to do our work by following the mass line. He said that one striking feature distinguishing us Communists from any other political party was our very close contact with the broadest masses of the people. He asked us "to serve the Chinese people with all out heart and soul, not to become isolated from the masses for a single moment, to proceed in all matters from the interests of the people instead of one's own personal interests or the interests of a small group."

He wanted our comrades to understand that "the highest criterion for all words and deeds of a Communist is whether or not such words and deeds conform to the greatest good of the broadest masses of the people and whether or not they are supported by the broadest masses." He further told us that we are invincible " as long as we rely upon the people, believe firmly in their boundless creative power, have faith in them, and unite as one with them." He pointed out that commandism* is wrong in all phases of work because it goes beyond the level of the consciousness of the masses, violates the voluntary principle of the masses, and is an expression of impetuosity. "In all our work," he added, "tailism* is also wrong, because it lags behind the level of the consciousness of the masses, violates the principle of leading the masses one step forward, and is an expression of sluggishness." All these teachings of Comrade Mao Tse-tung are extremely important and should be carefully studied and grasped and earnestly carried out by every Party member.

This mass line of ours is possible only with a proletarian party. Our mass line is a class line, a mass line of the proletariat. Our views with regard to the people and our relationship to them differ basically from those of the exploiting classes.

Some comrades have committed mistakes of commandism, adventurism, and closed-door-ism.* Some, for instance, have been irresponsible

---

* "Commandism" means issuing commands without taking time to convince the people of the need for them. "Tailism" means blindly following the masses. "Closed-door-ism" means failure to cooperate with other revolutionary forces in a joint effort to overthrow feudalism and imperialism.

toward the masses in their work. They did not believe that it was the masses who were emancipating themselves. Instead, they stood above the masses to fight in their stead, to bestow emancipation on the masses, and to issue orders. Such comrades suffered from impetuosity. Being only superficially active, they did not know how to transform the Party's slogans and tasks into those of the people, or how to enlighten the masses and properly wait for their awakening. Nor did they know how to take steps to bring about a natural revolutionization of the masses. They tried to compel the masses to accept the Party's slogans and tasks simply by issuing arbitrary orders and forcing the masses into action. Thus they violated the voluntary principle regarding the masses. Particularly when slogans too advanced and policies too left had aroused doubts and dissatisfaction among the masses, they sought all the more to carry on their work by means of issuing orders, by coercion, or even by punishment. The worst form of such practices was that wherever they went they would try to find faults, shortcomings, and bad examples, subjecting these to criticism, condemnation, and punishment in order to frighten the people and the cadres, and in order to push forward the work. They refused to see the good points and good examples, to study, develop, and systematize them. They neither commended the heroes and model workers, nor recommended or disseminated the good experiences in order to encourage the progress of the Party members and the people, and in order to overcome errors and defects among the Party members and the people. They struck blows at others everywhere and did things simply by issuing orders. Instead of learning from the masses and benefiting by the people's new ideas and innovations, they forced others to do things in their way. Such a tendency led to serious isolation from the masses, and aroused the resentment of the masses against them or even against the entire Party.

In order to carry out the mass line of our Party and of Comrade Mao Tse-tung thoroughly, the General Program and provisions of the Party Constitution have drawn particular attention to the following points which must be instilled in the mind of every Party member.

First, there is the point that everything is for the masses, and for serving the masses wholeheartedly. From its very beginning, our Party was founded to serve the people. All the sacrifices, efforts, and struggles of Party members have been made for the welfare and emancipation of the masses, and for nothing else. This is our greatest glory as Communists.

Second, there is the point of assuming full responsibility to the masses. As we serve the people, we must hold ourselves responsible to them and enable them to obtain real benefit and emancipation through our service. We must try our best to avoid mistakes or reduce them to a minimum in order not to do harm to the people or cause loss to them. The tasks, policies, and style of work we set forth must all be correct in order to benefit the people; otherwise, harm will be done to the people's interests. In that case, we must earnestly practice self-criticism for prompt rectification. This means that we must know how to serve the people well. Under no circumstances should we adopt an easygoing attitude toward the people. We must be seriously responsible to them.

It is also necessary to understand the unity between responsibility to the people and responsibility to the leading bodies of our Party. This means that our Party members, in carrying out the instructions of a leading body or individual leaders of the Party, must be held responsible to such leading body or individual leaders. But it would be wrong to separate responsibility to the Party leadership from responsibility to the people. Only by holding oneself responsible to the people can one say that one has assumed the highest and final responsibility. It must be understood that the interests of the Party are identical with the interests of the people. Whatever benefits the people also benefits the Party and must be done by every Party member with heart and soul. Likewise, whatever injures the people injures the Party and must be opposed or avoided by every Party member. The interests of people are precisely the interests of the Party. The Party has no particular interests of its own other than the people's interest. The maximum good for the greatest number of people is the highest criterion of truth, and consequently, the highest criterion of all the activities of our Party members. Any Party member who is responsible to the people is also responsible to the Party, and he who is irresponsible to the people is most irresponsible of all to the Party. What must be understood is the unity between responsibility to the Party and responsibility to the people. They should be unified, and must not be separated or set against each other.

The discipline of the Party must be observed and its unity maintained, because maintenance of such discipline and unity is serving the basic interest of the Chinese people. There must be no undermining of the discipline or unity of the Party on the pretext of assuming responsibility to the people. Nevertheless, any shortcoming or error committed by a leading body or individual leaders must be corrected. It is the duty as well as the right of every Party member to help in this respect, for any such shortcomings or errors are disadvantageous to the people, hence also to the Party. Our Party membership's spirit of sincere self-criticism, a critical attitude toward one's own errors and those of the leadership, and a spirit of observing Party discipline, are part of the spirit of being responsible to the people.

Third, there is the point of having faith in the people's self-emancipation. Comrade Mao Tse-tung constantly teaches us that the masses of the people are truly great, that their creative power is inexhaustible, that we are invincible only when we rely on them, that the people alone are the real makers of history, and that real history is the history of the masses. Marx pointed out long ago that the toilers emancipate themselves. Their salvation depends neither upon emperors, gods, nor heroes, but upon themselves, as the *International* says. This means that only through their own struggles and efforts can their emancipation be achieved, maintained, and consolidated. It cannot be bestowed or granted by any outsider. Nor can it be fought for or secured through the efforts of anyone except the people themselves. Hence, the idea of gratuitously bestowing emancipation on the masses or of fighting in their stead is wrong.

The masses of the people make their own history. Their emancipation must be based on their own consciousness and willingness. They select their own vanguard. And, under the leadership of this vanguard, they must organize themselves and fight for their emancipation by their own efforts. Only then can they consciously secure the gains of their struggle and retain and consolidate them. The enemies of the people can be overthrown only by the people themselves. It cannot be done in any other way. Merely through the efforts of the vanguard and without the people's own genuine consciousness and mobilization, emancipation of the people is impossible. History will not move forward, and nothing can be accomplished.

The cause of the Communists is nothing but the cause of the people. However correct our program and policy may be, they cannot be realized without the direct support and consistent struggle of the masses.

With us, therefore, everything is dependent on and determined by the people's consciousness and willingness, without which we can accomplish nothing. But as long as we rely upon the consciousness and willingness of the masses and as long as such consciousness and willingness are genuine, then, with the addition of the Party's correct leadership, every aspect of the great cause of the Party will finally triumph. Therefore, when the masses are not fully conscious, the duty of Communists—the vanguard of the masses of the people—in carrying out any kind of work is to develop their consciousness by every effective and suitable means. This is the first step in our work, which must be well done no matter how difficult it is or how much time it takes.

Fourth, there is the point of learning from the masses of the people. In order to serve the people well, to kindle their consciousness, and to give guidance to their actions, we Communists must first of all possess certain qualities. We must have foresight, or forethought. This means that we must be the harbingers of enlightenment, the only people capable of helping the less enlightened. Aside from our wholehearted devotion to the cause of the people's emancipation, our inexhaustible enthusiasm and our spirit of sacrifice, we must have adequate knowledge and must be sufficiently experienced and vigilant before we can successfully raise the people's consciousness, lead their actions, and serve them well. Learning is indispensable if we are to acquire knowledge, experience, and foresight.

We may enrich our knowledge by studying Marxist-Leninist theories and by studying the history and lessons of the people's struggles in foreign lands. We can also learn from our enemies. But what is most important is to learn from the masses, since their knowledge and experiences are the most abundant and most practical and their creative power is the greatest. This is why Comrade Mao Tse-tung has time and again told us to learn from the masses before we can educate them.

We want to lead the masses forward, but we do not want commandism. We want close relations with the masses, but we do not want tailism. We should start from the level already attained by the masses in developing their consciousness and leading them forward. In our work we must coordinate the highest principles with the closest possible connections with the masses. Such is our mass line. This is, of course, difficult to carry out. But it is the only way to become a good Marxist and Communist.

Our Party is not simply the aggregate of its membership. It is a unified, organic body, established according to a definite principle. It is a combination of leaders and followers. It is an integration of the Party headquarters (the Central Committee), the Party organizations at all levels, and the broad membership, constituted according to a definite principle of inner-Party democratic centralism.

Three Party members in a factory or village do not necessarily constitute a Party organization. They must be organized according to the principle of democratic centralism. Under ordinary conditions, one of the three should be the group leader and the other two the members of the group, so that in all activities there will be a leader and two followers. Only then can this group become a Party organization. This type of organization generates new strength. The strength of the proletariat lies in organization.

As laid down in the Party Constitution, democratic centralism means centralism on the basis of democracy and democracy under centralized leadership. It is both democratic and centralized. It reflects the relationship between the leadership and the followers, between higher and lower Party organizations, between individual Party members and the Party as a whole, and between the Party's Central Committee and Party organizations at all levels on the one hand and the rank and file Party members on the other.

Why do we say that Party centralism is centralism based on democracy? It means that the leading bodies of the Party are elected by the membership on a democratic basis and enjoy their confidence. It means that the directives and resolutions of the Party are centralized from the rank and file upward on a democratic basis as well as decided by them or their representatives, and are then persistently maintained and carried out by the leadership in conjunction with the rank and file. The authority of a leading body of the Party is given by the Party membership. Therefore, it is capable of exercising the power of centralized leadership on behalf of the membership in managing all Party affairs, and of commanding the obedience of its lower organizations and of the Party membership. Order within the Party is built on the principle of the subordination of the individual to the organization, the subordination of the minority to the majority, the subordination of lower organizations to higher organizations, and the subordination of all the constituent Party organizations to the Central Committee. This means that the Party's centralism is based on, instead of separated from, democracy. It is not individual autocracy.

Why do we say that the Party's democracy is democracy under centralized leadership? It means that every Party meeting is to be convened by a leading body and carried through under proper leadership. The adoption of every resolution or ruling is preceded by thorough preparation and careful deliberation. Every election has a carefully prepared list of nominees. The Party as a whole has a unified Party Constitution, unified discipline which all Party members should observe, and a unified leading body which must be obeyed by the entire membership. This means that inner-Party democracy is neither democracy without leadership, ultrademocracy, nor anarchy within the Party.

Democratic centralism within the Party is a system which unites the leadership of the Party with the broad rank and file of the Party membership. In other words, it is a system of crystallization from the rank and file of the membership and of persistently carrying it out among the rank and file. It is the expression of the mass line within the Party.

Some comrades do not understand that centralism of the Party is based on democracy. Consequently, they separate their leadership from inner-Party democracy, and from the rank and file of the Party membership, labelling such a situation "centralism." They think that their authority as leaders needs no mandate from the Party membership but can be arrogated by them. They think their leading positions require neither election nor the confidence of the Party membership and of the lower Party organizations, but can be assumed by themselves. They think that their directives and resolutions need not be centralized and decided from the rank and file upward but can be issued arbitrarily. They stand above the rank and file of the Party membership, instead of joining with the rank and file. They command and control the Party, lording it over the Party organizations, instead of being within the organization of the Party and obeying and submitting to the control of the Party. They want to act independently of the upper Party organizations in the name of inner-Party democracy, but they suppress the democratic rights of the Party membership and lower Party organizations in the name of inner-Party centralism. In fact, they observe neither democracy towards their subordinates nor centralism towards their superiors.

While others must obey and observe majority decisions and Party discipline, they, as leaders, feel entitled to do otherwise. They observe none of the basic organizational principles such as the subordination of the individual to the organization, the subordination of the minority to the majority, and the subordination of lower Party organizations to higher Party organizations. Party rules and resolutions, in their opinion, are written for ordinary Party members but not for those who are leaders. This is an antidemocratic, autocratic tendency in the Party and a reflection of the ideology of the privileged classes in society. It has nothing in common with our Party's centralism. It is a deviation which does, however, exist within our Party and should be completely wiped out.

There are other comrades who do not understand that democracy inside the Party is democracy under centralized leadership. They therefore divorce their actions from the Party's centralized leadership and from the Party as a whole. They pay no attention to the over-all situation or to the long-range interests of the Party as a whole. They act freely within the Party and without restraint, guided solely by their own interests and views. They neither closely observe Party discipline nor carry out the decisions of the Party's leading bodies. They indulge in all kinds of unorganizational, nonpolitical, and unprincipled utterances and actions. They either deliberately resort to exaggeration in order to spread dissension within the Party, or engage in endless gossip or wrangling, never taking the trouble to see whether or not there is a critical situation or an emergency. They even take advantage of the Party membership's temporary lack of understanding due to insufficient consideration, to take votes on their own proposals and to fulfill their own designs in the name of the "majority."

This represents the idea of ultrademocracy which has nothing in common with our Party's democracy. The danger of such an idea, as Comrade Mao Tse-tung has pointed out, is that "it injures or even destroys the Party organization, and weakens or even destroys the Party's fighting power."

The root of this idea of ultrademocracy "lies in petty-bourgeois (small agricultural producers and small urban capitalists) lack of cohesion. It is fundamentally incompatible with the fighting tasks of the proletariat and is indeed, objectively, a kind of counterrevolutionary ideology. Those who embrace it will surely land in the counterrevolutionary groups if they allow it to develop, instead of checking it energetically."*

The tendency to antidemocratic absolutism and the presence of ultrademocracy inside the Party are two extremes of inner-Party life; yet the latter often appears as a kind of retaliation against the former. Thus wherever there is a serious tendency to absolutism, there ultrademocracy may arise. Both are tendencies detrimental to and destructive of genuine Party unity and solidarity. The sharp vigilance of the whole Party is required to guard against their occurrence.

Now we must fully develop the democratic way of life in our Party and bring about a high degree of inner-Party democracy. At the same time a high degree of centralism in Party leadership must also be achieved on the basis of this highly developed democracy.

Inner-Party democracy must be encouraged to proceed along lines beneficial to the cause of the Party, that is, the cause of the people, and it should neither weaken the fighting will and fighting solidarity of the Party nor become a tool for saboteurs, anti-Party elements, splitters, opportunists, and adventurists. Thus the Constitution provides that a thorough review of and debate on the policy and line of the whole Party or of a lower Party organization may be undertaken only under proper leadership, and when conditions permit. In other words, there must not be a state of emergency, and it is so decided by the Party's central or a lower leading body, as the case may be, or it is so proposed by a majority of lower Party organizations or by a higher Party organization.

---

* Mao Tse-tung, *Resolution of the Kutien Conference.*

Inner-Party democracy must be broadened, but Party decisions must be carried out unconditionally. The subordination of the Party membership to the Party organization, of lower Party organizations to higher Party organizations, of the minority to the majority, and of the constituent organizations of the Party to the Central Committee—these principles as laid down in the Constitution must be observed unconditionally.

Document 18

CONSTITUTION OF THE COMMUNIST YOUTH LEAGUE OF CHINA

[Adopted at the Ninth National Congress of the Communist Youth League on June 29, 1964.]

General Principles

The Communist Youth League of China is an organization of the masses of advanced youth, a school for the study of Communism, and an assistant to the Chinese Communist Party. For the realization of Communism in the future, the Chinese Communist Youth League resolutely supports the general program of the Chinese Communist Party, takes Marxism-Leninism and the thought of Mao Tse-tung as its guiding thought, holds aloft the banner of the general line for building socialism, takes an active part in the socialist revolution and socialist construction, and strives to build our country into a socialist power with modern agriculture, modern industry, modern national defense, and modern science and technology.

The basic task of the Chinese Communist Youth League is to educate the young people in Marxism-Leninism and the thought of Mao Tse-tung, guide the young people to temper themselves in the three great revolutionary movements—class struggle, production struggle, and scientific experiment—and bring up the young people of our country as socialist-minded and cultured workers who are patriotic, loyal to the people, educated, disciplined, healthy, industrious, heroic, vigorous, and courageous successors to the cause of Communism.

The Chinese Communist Youth League must put ideological work first and persist in the line of upholding proletarian ideology and eliminating bourgeois ideology. The Chinese Communist Youth

League constantly conducts education on class and class struggle among the young people, and helps them in establishing the proletarian world outlook step by step, in resolutely marching on the road of socialism, and in carrying out revolution to the end. The Communist Youth League educates the young people to inherit and develop the glorious traditions of the Party, to uphold forever the revolutionary spirit of hard struggle, to cultivate the fine quality of Communist morality, and to serve the people wholeheartedly; it educates the young people to love collective labor and physical labor, to learn humbly from the masses of the working people, and to endeavor to bring about prosperity, study hard, and master cultural knowledge and modern science and technology so that they can make contributions to the building and defense of the motherland.

The Chinese Communist Youth League must show concern for the all-around development of young people and help them in achieving the goal of "keeping healthy, studying well, and working well." Centered around the main tasks of the Party, the Communist Youth League constantly unfolds independent activities conducive to the physical and mental development of the young people according to their characteristics in order to enable them to make progress in moral, cultural, and physical education, in a lively manner, and of their own accord.

Democratic centralism is the organizational principle of the Chinese Communist Youth League. In the life of Communist Youth League organizations at all levels, we must fully develop democracy and realistically protect the democratic rights of Communist Youth League members in order to develop their activism and creativity; we must educate the Communist Youth League members and cadres to spontaneously abide by Communist Youth League discipline and executive resolutions adopted by the Communist Youth League, and constantly conduct criticism and self-criticism in order to maintain the political, ideological, and organizational integrity of the Communist Youth League.

The Communist Youth League must persist in the mass line in its work. Communist Youth League cadres must constantly go among the masses, take part in physical labor, conduct investigation and study, sum up the experiences of the masses, and listen to and reflect the opinions of the young people. The Communist Youth League must make full use of persuasive education, representative demonstration, and the method of commending the advanced in order to do its work realistically. The Communist Youth League relies on the young people who come from the workers and poor and lower-middle peasants; and rallies young people who come from middle peasants and other working people, and young people who favor, support, and participate in the socialist cause, and also all patriotic youth of the various nationalities to learn from one another and make common improvements.

The Chinese Communist Youth League resolutely adheres to the general line of the international Communist movement as put forward by the Chinese Communist Party. The Communist Youth League must educate young people of our country to unite with all young people in the socialist camp, to strengthen unity with youth who oppose imperialism and colonialism, new and old, and to step up friendly cooperation with all youth throughout the world. The Communist Youth League resolutely opposes imperialism and reactionaries of various countries headed by the United States, opposes modern revisionism, supports the revolutionary struggle of the oppressed people and nations in all countries, and struggles for the cause of world peace and national liberation and for new victories of People's Democracy and socialism throughout the world.

The Chinese Communist Youth League does its work under the leadership of the Chinese Communist Party. The Central Committee of the Communist Youth League is subject to the leadership of the Chinese Communist Party Central Committee, and the local Communist Youth League organizations are subject to the leadership of the Party organizations at the same or higher levels.

CHAPTER I.   MEMBERSHIP

Article 1. Membership in the Chinese Communist Youth League is open to any Chinese male or female working youth who accepts the Communist Youth League Constitution, joins and works in one of the Communist Youth League organizations, carries out the Communist Youth League's decisions, and pays membership dues as required.

Members who have reached the age of twenty-five and have not been elected to work in the Communist Youth League's leading organizations, or have not been appointed to specialized posts, are not allowed to retain their membership. They may retain their membership until they reach the age of twenty-eight only if they request to remain in the Communist Youth League and continue to participate in the life of the Communist Youth League and fulfill their duties.

Members who have not assumed leading posts or specialized jobs in the Communist Youth League after they have been admitted into the Chinese Communist Party and become regular Party members are not allowed to keep their membership.

Article 2. Members of the Chinese Communist Youth League have the following duties:

1. To strive to study Marxism-Leninism and Mao Tse-tung's thought;

2. To popularize actively and faithfully carry out Party policies and energetically fulfill the tasks assigned them by the Communist Youth League;

3. To play an exemplary role in labor, work, and study; to raise incessantly the level of their cultural, scientific, and technological knowledge; and to strive to improve their physical condition;

4. To protect the interests of the country and the collective, observe communist ethics, and struggle against all illegal practices;

5. To maintain constantly revolutionary vigilance and actively fulfill their duties in safeguarding their motherland; and

6. To learn from the masses and reflect the opinions and demands of the young people, and to help enthusiastically the young people make progress and become their bosom friends.

Article 3. Communist Youth League members enjoy the following rights:

1. To elect and be elected and to participate in voting within the Communist Youth League;

2. To participate in discussion at Communist Youth League meetings or in the Communist Youth League publications on questions regarding Communist Youth League work;

3. To criticize any leading Communist Youth League organization or any functionary at Communist Youth League meetings;

4. To reserve their opinions or submit them to a leading body of the Communist Youth League in case they disagree with any Communist Youth League decision, which, in the meantime, they must carry out unconditionally;

5. To ask to attend in person when a league organization decides to take disciplinary action against them, and to reserve the right to appeal or complain; and

6. To address any proposal, appeal, or statement to any Communist Youth League organization up to and including the Central Committee.

Article 4. Applicants for Communist Youth League membership must undergo the following procedure of admission:

1. An applicant must be recommended by one Communist Youth League member.

2. The Communist Youth League member who recommends an applicant for admission must furnish the Party, with a full sense of responsibility, with truthful information about the applicant's ideology, character, and personal history, and must explain the Communist Youth League Constitution to the applicant.

3. An applicant must submit his membership application to a branch committee of the Communist Youth League. He will be admitted after being accepted by the general membership meeting of the Communist Youth League branch and approved by the next higher Communist Youth League committee; he becomes a full member as soon as the general membership meeting of the Communist Youth League branch approves his membership.

Article 5. When a member is transferred from one organization to another, he must change his organizational relationship according to the regulations of the Central Committee.

Article 6. Communist Youth League members are free to withdraw from the Communist Youth League. When a Communist Youth League member wants to withdraw, he should submit a statement to the branch committee. A Communist Youth League member who, over a period of six months and without proper reasons, fails to take part in the Communist Youth League's organizational life or to pay membership dues is regarded as having withdrawn himself from the Communist Youth League. When a member asks to withdraw or withdraws on his own, the Communist Youth League branch to which he belongs should, by a decision of its general membership meeting, strike his name off the Communist Youth League rolls and report the matter to the next higher Communist Youth League committee for registration.

Article 7. Communist Youth League members who have made significant achievements in building and safeguarding the motherland will be cited and awarded by Communist Youth League organizations.

Article 8. Communist Youth League members who violate Communist Youth League discipline or commit mistakes should be criticized and educated in line with the policy of taking a warning from the past in order to be careful in the future, and treating the illness in order to save the patient. They should be helped to realize and correct their mistakes. Disciplinary measures include warning, serious warning, removal from leading posts in the Communist Youth League, placing on probation within the Communist Youth League, or expulsion from the Communist Youth League.

The period in which a Communist Youth League member is placed on probation is six months or one year. During the probation period, a member has no right to elect or be elected, or to vote on any motion, nor has he the right to recommend youth for Communist Youth League membership. If, after a Communist Youth League member has been placed on probation, facts show that he has corrected his mistakes, his rights as a full Communist Youth League member will be restored as soon as his probation period ends. If he continues to make mistakes or shows unwillingness to correct them, he will be expelled from the Communist Youth League.

Article 9. Any disciplinary action taken against a Communist Youth League member must be decided on by the general membership meeting of the Communist Youth League branch to which he belongs and must be approved by a higher Communist Youth League committee.

Any decision to give a warning or a serious warning to a Communist Youth League member must be approved by the basic Communist Youth League committee. Any decision to remove a Communist Youth League member from his leading post in the Communist Youth League or to place him on probation must be approved by the district committee. In localities where there are no district committees, the approval of the committee of a *hsien,* autonomous *hsien,* or a municipality must be obtained. Any decision to expel a Communist Youth League member must be aproved by the *hsien* committee or a Communist Youth League organization equivalent to a *hsien* committee.

Article 10. All Communist Youth League organizations must exercise the utmost caution in taking disciplinary action against Communist Youth League members. In deciding to take disciplinary action against a Communist Youth League member, the general membership meeting of a Communist Youth League branch must notify the member concerned to attend the meeting, must seriously listen to his opinions, and must forward his appeal immediately; no suppression is permitted. Communist Youth League organizations at all levels must handle and examine such an appeal seriously and promptly.

CHAPTER II. ORGANIZATIONAL STRUCTURE AND
ORGANIZATIONAL SYSTEM OF THE COMMUNIST YOUTH LEAGUE

Article 11. The Chinese Communist Youth League is formed on the principle of democratic centralism. Its fundamental conditions are:

1. The leading bodies of the Communist Youth League at all levels are elected.

2. The Communist Youth League committees at all levels must report on their work to their respective representative meetings or congresses.

3. The leading bodies at all levels must pay constant attention to the views of their lower organizations and the rank-and-file Communist Youth League members.

4. Lower Communist Youth League organizations must present periodic reports on their work to the Communist Youth League organizations above them and ask in good time for instructions on questions which need to be decided by Communist Youth League organizations at a higher level.

5. Communist Youth League organizations and members must carry out Communist Youth League decisions.

Individual league members shall obey the Communist Youth League organizations, the minority shall obey the majority, and the lower Communist Youth League organizations shall obey the higher Communist Youth League organizations.

6. The Communist Youth League organizations at all levels operate on the principle of combining collective leadership with individual responsibility.

Article 12. Communist Youth League organizations are formed in various districts and production units.

The leading bodies of the Communist Youth League are as follows:

1. For the whole country, the leading body is the National Communist Youth League Congress. When the National Communist Youth League Congress is not in session, the leading body is the Central Committee of the Communist Youth League.

2. For a province, autonomous region, or municipality directly under the central authority, it is the provincial, autonomous regional, or municipal Communist Youth League Congress. When the provincial, autonomous regional, or municipal Communist Youth League Congress is not in session, it is the provincial, autonomous regional, or municipal Communist Youth League committee.

3. For an autonomous *chou,* it is the autonomous *chou* Communist Youth League Congress. When the Congress is not in session, it is the autonomous *chou* committee.

4. For a *hsien,* autonomous *hsien,* or municipality, it is the *hsien,* autonomous *hsien,* or municipal Communist Youth League Congress. When the congress is not in session, it is the *hsien,* autonomous *hsien,* or municipal committee.

5. For a primary unit, it is the representative meeting or the general membership meeting. When the representative meeting or the general membership meeting of the primary unit is not in session, it is the primary Communist Youth League committee.

According to the requirements of the work, the committees at all levels can set up relative work departments.

A province, autonomous region, or municipality directly under the central authority can set up their representative bodies—the local committee or the regional committee.

Article 13. When the national, provincial, autonomous regional, or municipal congress is not in session, the central, provincial, autonomous regional, or municipal committee can call its respective representative meeting in accordance with work requirements. The number of representatives and methods for selecting the representatives should be decided by the committees at various levels. The resolutions adopted at the representative meetings cannot be put into effect until they are approved by the committees at their respective levels.

Article 14. Elections in the Communist Youth League are by secret ballot. The list of candidates for election should be fully discussed and accepted by vote of the electors. A Communist Youth League branch may or may not nominate candidates for election. The Communist Youth League organizations must insure that the electors have the right to criticize, reject, or change a candidate.

Article 15. The organizations of the Communist Youth League at all levels must protect the Communist Youth League members' democratic rights, and fully discuss various questions in Communist Youth League work and in Communist Youth League organizations in order to bring their enthusiasm and creativity into full play. They must encourage criticism from the lower level. Special attention should be given to encourage Communist Youth League members to reflect the situation to their upper-level organizations and to put forward criticism and proposals to the Communist Youth League's leading bodies and their functionaries, and to oppose any action which suppresses criticism and retaliates against those who criticize.

Article 16 Communist Youth League members and the Communist Youth League organs at all levels must conscientiously follow all the resolutions adopted by the Communist Youth League and abide by the organizational systems and organizational discipline of the Communist Youth League so as to insure the uniformity of the Communist Youth League's organizational work and activities. Those who disagree with a resolution of the Communist Youth League should convey their opinion to the organization to which they belong or report it to an organization at a higher level. Under no circumstance should they be allowed to take free action.

CHAPTER III.   ORGANIZATIONAL STRUCTURE OF THE CENTRAL COMMITTEE
OF THE COMMUNIST YOUTH LEAGUE

Article 17. The Communist Youth League National Congress is slated to be held once every four years. However, the Central Committee plenum has the right to call a National Congress before or after its scheduled date when a special situation calls for such a change. The Central Committee also decides how many delegates the National Congress should have and how the delegates should be elected.

Article 18. The National Congress has the right to:

1. Examine and ratify the work report of the Central Committee;

2. Discuss and map out guidelines of work and current work tasks for the whole league;

3. Revise the Constitution of the Communist Youth League; and

4. Elect the Central Committee.

Article 19. The Communist Youth League National Congress decides on the question of how many members and alternate members the Communist Youth League Central Committee should have. All the vacancies left by outgoing Central Committee members are to be filled by alternate members according to their eligibility. The removal of any one of the Central Committee's members or alternate members requires the approval of more than two-thirds of the delegates to the National Congress.

Article 20. The Central Committee of the Communist Youth League will call a Plenary Session once or twice a year.

Article 21. At the Central Committee's Plenary Session, the Central Committee will elect its standing committee, which will consist of several members, and it will also elect its secretariat, which will be composed of one first secretary and a number of secretaries. When the Central Committee plenum is not in session, the standing committee and the secretariat act for the Central Committee.

Article 22. The Communist Youth League National Congress has the right to recall some of the members and alternate members of the Communist Youth League Central Committee and to elect new members to replace the recalled. However, the National Congress should not recall more than one-seventh of the total number of the members and alternate members of the Central Committee at one session.

CHAPTER IV.   ORGANIZATIONAL STRUCTURE OF THE LOCAL
COMMUNIST YOUTH LEAGUE ORGANS

Article 23. The Communist Youth League organs in various provinces, autonomous regions, central-government-controlled municipalities, and autonomous *chou* should each call a local congress into session once every two years, while the Communist Youth League organs in various *hsien,* autonomous *hsien,* and municipalities should call local Communist Youth League congresses once a year or once every two years. The number of the delegates to these congresses and how they are to be elected is to be decided by the Communist Youth League committees in the respective areas.

Article 24. Local Communist Youth League congresses held in various localities have the right to:

1. Examine and ratify the work report submitted by the Communist Youth League committees in their respective areas;

2. Discuss and map out current tasks for the local Communist Youth League committees;

3. Elect their own Communist Youth League committees; and

4. Elect delegates for attendance at the Communist Youth League congress at a higher level.

Article 25. The question of how many members and alternate members each local Communist Youth League committee is to have should be decided by the Communist Youth League congress held in the respective area. Vacancies are to be filled by alternate members in accordance with their eligibility. The removal of a member or alternate member of a local Communist Youth League committee, be it in a province, an autonomous region, a central-government-controlled municipality, an autonomous *chou*, a *hsien*, an autonomous *hsien*, or a municipality, requires the vote of more than two-thirds of those present at the local Communist Youth League committee's plenary session. The removal should be submitted to the next higher Communist Youth League committee for approval before action can be taken on it.

Article 26. The Communist Youth League committee of a province, autonomous region, municipality directly under the central authority, or autonomous *chou* shall meet in plenary session once or twice a year. The Communist Youth League committee of a *hsien*, autonomous *hsien*, or municipality shall meet in plenary session at least twice a year.

Article 27. A local committee shall meet in plenary session to elect its standing committee, secretary, and several deputy secretaries. The standing committee exercises the powers and functions of a Communist Youth League committee when the latter is not in plenary session.

Article 28. The formation of a local committee must be approved by a higher committee or by its representative body. The formation of the representative bodies—the local committees and the district committees—of a province, autonomous region, municipality directly under the central authority, *hsien*, autonomous *hsien*, and municipality must be designated by its respective committee.

CHAPTER V. PRIMARY ORGANIZATIONS OF THE COMMUNIST
YOUTH LEAGUE

Article 29. Primary Communist Youth League organizations are the branch, general branch, or Communist Youth League committee in each factory, mine, people's commune, farm, store, People's Liberation Army company, government organ, street, or other primary unit.

1. A unit with more than three Communist Youth League members can set up a branch.

2. A unit with more than fifty Communist Youth League members can set up a general branch. A unit with more than thirty Communist Youth League members can also set up a general branch if its work requires this.

3. A unit with more than 200 Communist Youth League members

can set up a Communist Youth League committee. A unit with more than 100 Communist Youth League members can also set up a Communist Youth League committee if its work requires this.

Branches are formed under a general branch or a Communist Youth League committee. General branches may be formed under the Communist Youth League committee if work requires it. Under a branch, a number of groups may be formed. The establishment of a primary organization must be approved by the next higher committee or its representative body.

Article 30. The primary organization is the foundation of the Communist Youth League and the basic unit for the Communist Youth League's work and activities. A primary organization should fully play its active role of uniting and educating youth and rendering effective help to the Party.

The general tasks of primary organizations are as follows:

1. To carry out ideological-political work among members and young people and to organize them for the study of Marxism-Leninism, Mao Tse-tung's thought, and current affairs as well as policies;

2. To carry out the resolutions and directives issued by the Party or Communist Youth League organizations at a higher level, to induce Communist Youth League members and the young people to actively participate in labor and work hard, and to study culture, science, and technology;

3. To understand and reflect the ideas and demands of youth, show close concern for their life, and see that they have ample rest and are engaged in sports, cultural, and recreational activities;

4. To educate members and youth to sharpen their revolutionary vigilance and resolutely struggle against the disruptive activities of enemies at home and abroad;

5. To educate members on the Communist Youth League Constitution, promote criticism and self-criticism, and to fight against violation of laws and discipline, against corruption and waste, and against bureaucracy; and

6. To recruit new Communist Youth League members, to collect membership dues, and handle procedures for the withdrawal of over-age members from the Communist Youth League.

Article 31. The general membership meeting of a branch shall hold a plenary session at least once every month. The representative meeting or the general membership meeting of a general branch shall hold a plenary session at least once every six months. The representative meeting or the general membership meeting of a Communist Youth League committee shall hold a plenary session at least once a year.

Article 32. A primary committee is elected by a representative meeting or a general membership meeting for a term of six months to one year. A branch with less than seven members only needs to elect a secretary or, in addition, a deputy secretary, but no branch committee needs to be formed.

The Communist Youth League committee can elect a standing committee if necessary.

CHAPTER VI. COMMUNIST YOUTH LEAGUE ORGANIZATIONS IN THE PEOPLE'S LIBERATION ARMY

Article 33. Communist Youth League work in the People's Liberation Army is an important component of the People's Liberation Army political work.

Article 34. Communist Youth League organizations in the People's Liberation Army carry out their work under the leadership of Party committees, political organs, and primary Party organizations and according to the regulations and directives issued by tne Central Committee of the Chinese Communist Youth League and the General Political Department of the People's Liberation Army.

Article 35. Communist Youth League organizations in the People's Liberation Army should maintain close contact with local Communist Youth League organizations, actively participate in their work and activities, and take part in the election of their leading bodies.

CHAPTER VII. RELATIONS BETWEEN THE COMMUNIST YOUTH LEAGUE AND THE YOUNG PIONEERS

Article 36. The Chinese Communist Youth League is entrusted by the Chinese Communist Party with assuming leadership over the work of the Young Pioneers. In leading the Young Pioneers, the Chinese Communist Youth League educates children in the Communist spirit and guides them to "study well" and to "struggle upstream every day" in order to have them become our successors who love the motherland, people, labor, science, and public properties, and who are honest, brave, and united.

Article 37. The Communist Youth League organizations dispatch outstanding Communist Youth League members or invite teachers and other people who are progressive in thinking, show a correct work style, and love children, to be instructors of the Young Pioneers and help them incessantly to raise their political and vocational level. Instructors with significant achievements should be commended and awarded.

Article 38. The Communist Youth League organizations at all levels should strengthen leadership over Young Pioneers, concern themselves with the growth of the children, and fight any practice that impairs the health of the children, mentally or physically.

CHAPTER VIII.   FUNDS OF THE CHINESE COMMUNIST YOUTH LEAGUE

Article 39. Funds of the Chinese Communist Youth League come from membership dues paid by members and other income.

The amount of membership dues shall be fixed by the Communist Youth League Central Committee.

A Communist Youth League member who is also a member of the Chinese Communist Party is exempted from paying membership dues.

Article 40. The Communist Youth League organizations at all levels should make regular reports to their respective representative meetings or their respective general membership meetings on membership dues and other funds of the Communist Youth League, as well as on expenditures.

DOCUMENT 19

CONSTITUTION OF THE CHINESE YOUNG PIONEERS

[Adopted on June 28, 1958.]

1. Name: The Chinese Young Pioneers.

2. Our founder and leader: The Chinese Communist Party.

3. Our aim: To unite youth and children, to study diligently, strengthen the body, love labor, love the motherland, continue the revolutionary traditions of the Chinese Communist Party, and resolve to become builders and protectors of Communism.

4. The flag of our corps: A red flag bearing a five-pointed star and a torch. The five-pointed star represents the leadership of the Chinese Communist Party, the torch denotes brightness, and the red flag symbolizes the victory of the revolution.

5. Our emblem: A red scarf, which represents a section of the red flag. Every member of the corps should wear and cherish the emblem and uphold its honor.

6. Our salute: Raise the right hand above the head, with the five

fingers close together, signifying that the interests of the people are above all.

7. Our slogan: "Be prepared, struggle for the cause of Communism." The reply: "Always be prepared."

8. Our working style: Honesty, courage, vivacity, and unity.

9. Our members: Any one between nine and fifteen years of age who desires to join the Young Pioneers and is willing to abide by the Constitution of the corps may apply to the committee of the corps company. He is admitted as a member after his application has been discussed and approved by the committee.

When admitted to the corps, a member must plant a tree or perform some other public deed. After taking oath in an initiation ceremony, he is given his emblem to wear.

Every member has the right to vote and to be elected, to submit ideas, and make demands in regard to the work and activities of the corps.

Every member must observe discipline, engage energetically in activities, obey the decisions of the corps, do the tasks assigned to him well, and enthusiastically serve other people.

In case of transfer from one regiment to another, a member must present his registration card and become a part of the life of the new regiment.

Upon reaching the age of fifteen, a member officially leaves the corps after an appropriate ceremony at his regiment.

10. Our organization: Our corps is under the direct guidance of the Chinese Communist Youth League. A headquarters office is established in a city, county, district, or village. A regiment or company is established in a school, street, or agricultural cooperative. Platoons are organized below the level of the company. Seven to thirteen members may form a platoon, headed by a commander and two deputy commanders.

Two to five platoons may form a company. The company is governed by a committee, which consists of the company commander, two deputy commanders, and between two and four company committee members.

Two or more companies form a regiment. The regiment committee is composed of the regiment commander, two deputy commanders, and between four and ten regiment committee members.

The commander of the platoon, the company, and the regiment and the committee of the company and regiment are elected by the members annually or semiannually.

The committee of the company or regiment may, according to the needs of its work, designate its members to take charge of flag raising, labor, study, culture, physical training, organizational activities, wall newspapers, etc.

11. Methods of reward and punishment: Corps members or corps units which have shown enthusiasm and initiative or achieved outstanding success in their activities are given citations or awards by the corps or the Communist Youth League.

If a member violates discipline or commits errors in any way, the corps organization should patiently help him to realize and correct them. If after repeated criticism and help he persists in his ways, he should be punished. There are three kinds of punishment: warning, suspension of membership, and expulsion. Warning should be discussed and approved by the company committee. Suspension and expulsion should be discussed and approved by the regiment committee. Expulsion of a member is also subject to the approval of the local branch of the Communist Youth League. A suspended or expelled member may be reinstated after he has rectified his errors, upon approval of the regiment committee.

12. Our advisers: The Communist Youth League appoints some of its most prominent members to serve as advisors and intimate friends of the Young Pioneers. They assist in the work and organizational activities of the company and the regiment. Corps organizations in the junior middle school or the upper division of the elementary school and those in agricultural cooperatives may carry on without the help of advisors.

V

Economic Policy

The purpose of this chapter is not to present up-to-date information about economic growth, or to evaluate the Five-Year Plans for agricultural and industrial development, but to sketch the larger goals and general direction of economic policy and to show the methods used in pursuing the goals.

The Communists call their revolution the "proletarian-socialist revolution." The proletarian aspect is concerned with the class struggle and the hegemony of the working class, while the socialist aspect is concerned with industrialization and the replacement of private ownership with collective ownership and a socialist economy. The documents in this chapter will show how economic plans are made with these two aspects of the revolution clearly in view.

OBJECTIVES

Broadly speaking, Communist economic policy has three specific objectives: agrarian reform, industrialization, and conversion of private enterprises into socialist enterprises. Agrarian reform had its beginning in earlier years and became a well-defined national policy with the promulgation of the Agrarian Reform Law (D20) in 1950. Industrialization was the goal of the Five-Year Plans, and the conversion of private enterprises was carried out according to the "socialist transformation" stipulated in the Preamble of the Constitution of the People's Republic.

The documents chosen for this chapter relate mainly to agrarian reform and the "socialist transformation" of private enterprises. They reflect Communist ideology and show the general direction of economic development under the Communist regime. No documents dealing specifically with the Five-Year Plans are included, partly because they are long and unwieldy, and partly because this volume is more concerned with general patterns and trends than with a detailed presentation of separate sectors of the economy or with statistical data on the amount of production from year to year.

A few characteristic patterns of industrialization may be observed. First, the accent is on socialism. The new industrial enterprises are components of the socialist economy. Although they were inaugurated during the period of the New Democracy, they were products of socialist planning and socialist design. Private ownership and the capitalist pattern of organization were shunned.

183

Second, heavy industry was given first priority. Most of the resources of the First Five-Year Plan (1953-57) were assigned to heavy industry, with minor attention to light industry and agriculture. Consumer goods were produced in small quantities, and so much was exported—partly for the political purpose of impressing China's neighbors with the success of the Five-Year Plan—that the people at home got little benefit. In subsequent years, the decline in agricultural production and the popular discontent over the shortage of consumer goods compelled more attention to agriculture and some forms of light industry directly serving the daily needs of the people. After 1959, economic dislocations created an even more pressing demand for agricultural improvement, and economic planning was revised to adopt the principle that the national economy must develop "agriculture as the foundation and industry as the dominant factor." Industries beneficial to agricultural growth—for example, fertilizers—now received the highest priority. "Agriculture as foundation" continues to be the guiding principle of the Third Five-Year Plan.

Industrialization still remains a major goal. But the Communists now realize that China is basically an agricultural country and no grandiose plans of industrialization can get very far without adequate agricultural growth.

AGRARIAN REFORM

Mao Tse-tung hit upon agrarian reform as a fundamental economic policy as a result of practical reasoning. In China, he said in 1927, no revolution can succeed without the peasants, for the simple reason that they constitute the masses. The most direct way of winning over the peasants is to give them what they want. The peasants want land. The first step in any agrarian reform, therefore, is to give land to the peasants.

The key to the Communist agrarian reform was confiscation of the land and assets of the landlords and an attack upon the landlords as the symbols of feudalism and exploitation. In the rural areas of Hunan in 1926–27, the peasants were given complete license to take what they wanted and to treat the landlords in any way they saw fit. Bloodshed and violence were everyday affairs. In reply to the criticism that "revolutionary action" had gone too far, Mao Tse-tung said:

> A revolution is not the same as inviting people to dinner, or writing an essay, or painting a picture, or doing fancy needlework; it cannot be anything so refined, so calm and gentle. . . . A revolution is an uprising, an act of violence whereby one class overthrows another. . . . In this period . . . it is necessary to bring about a brief reign of terror in every rural area.

The Communists had previously enacted several agrarian laws and shifted between radical and moderate programs according to changing circumstances. The Agrarian Reform Law of 1950 (D20) was not so radical as the laws promulgated before 1930. The principle of confiscating the land of landlords and distributing it to the tillers was unchanged, but some of the detailed provisions of the law reflected the more cautious attitude of a party that now had the responsibility of government. The new regime, in the first place, had to take care not to upset the national economy and, at the same time, avoid arousing greater opposition than it could successfully deal with. To avoid a breakdown in agricultural production, it gave landlords and rich peasants their due share of land, and accorded protection to the interests of rich peasants and middle peasants. At the same time, the law tried to reduce the percentage of the population who would be antagonized by the reform. The landlord class was defined in such a way that it would not exceed 4 per cent of the population. Article 5 makes exceptions for certain classes of people, and Article 6 allows rich peasants to retain land cultivated by hired labor or rented out to other peasants. The provision in Article 3 permitting land owned by mosques to be retained may also be interpreted as a move to avoid antagonizing the strong Moslem minority at this early stage. As Liu Shao-ch'i pointed out,[1] the decision to preserve the rich peasant economy was made for both economic and political reasons: to stimulate agricultural production and to "neutralize the rich peasants politically" so that they would not be on the side of the landlords.

THE CLASS STRUGGLE

Liberals within China and abroad had been attracted by the Communist agrarian reform because they saw in it a positive program to improve the livelihood and welfare of the masses. Peasants supported the reform because they welcomed the opportunity of fulfilling their dream of land ownership. To the Communists, however, the agrarian reform was not primarily a humanitarian program to elevate the living standards of the peasants. Its objectives went far beyond the distribution of land. It may even be said that land distribution was only a means to an end—namely, to achieve the twin goals of the proletarian-socialist revolution.

Liu Shao-ch'i explicitly disputed the view that the agrarian reform was "only designed to relieve the poor people."[2] The first article of the Reform Law states the basic aim as the development of agricultural production as a prelude to industrialization. Teng Tzu-hui, the

[1] D22.
[2] *Ibid.*

head of the rural department of the Central Committee of the Party, went even further. Agrarian reform, he said, was essentially a class struggle.[3]

The reform was not carried out in the whole country at the same time. The country was divided into areas, and a schedule was published for the launching of the reform in each area. One reason for this scheduling is that the Communists did not allow any reform without the direct supervision of their cadres, and there were not enough cadres to cover the entire country at the same time. These cadres were specially trained in the interpretation and implementation of the Reform Law, and they were to carry out faithfully the instructions of the central authorities.

The cadres were virtually superintendents of the class struggle. From the analysis of class status[4] to the mass meetings for the public trial of landlords, they were in complete charge and worked with the full authority of the Party-state behind them. The assignment of class status was a matter of great consequence. Once a person was classified a landlord, he had nothing but grief in store for him. The status of a rich peasant was uncertain. The best that one could hope for was to be called a poor peasant, for then he would not only get land but also be assured of an accepted status in the peasants' association. Once a person had been assigned a class status he could not change it, except by official approval, and his family had to live with it.

It was the duty of the cadres to teach the peasants the meaning of the class struggle and the necessity of liquidating the landlord class. Peasants who did not have sufficient "class consciousness" to "draw a clear line of demarcation between friend and foe"—meaning class allies and class enemies—had to be taught to hate the landlords and led to fight against the landlords, even to abuse them and eliminate them personally. In "struggle meetings," peasants were encouraged to "pour out their grievances" and relate their sorrowful experiences of cruel treatment by oppressive landlords. If some peasants thought their landlords were not so bad, the cadres generally concluded that they had not received sufficient class education and needed further instruction in the class struggle.

The actual distribution of land, which was uppermost in the minds of the peasants, was only secondary to the class struggle. The climax of the struggle was the public trial of the landlords. A vivid description of such a trial is given in D24. Similar reports of actual cases were found in the newspapers. Participation in such experiences was supposed to provide a living lesson in the class struggle. It may be noted

---
[3] D23.
[4] See D21.

in passing that many of China's intellectuals who were in favor of giving land to the peasants were unenthusiastic about the class struggle. As a part of their "thought reform,'" the Communists sent large numbers of college professors and students to the countryside during the agrarian reform to take an active part in the struggle meetings, the classification of class status, and the public trials of landlords. They were asked to join in abusing and attacking the landlords so that they might overcome their "bourgeois sentimentalism" and acquire the emotions of fearless class warriors.

That class struggle is the essence of the Communist agrarian reform is further attested by the fact that while the reform was under way in north China and while rural areas in the south were awaiting their turn, the landlords in some villages voluntarily relinquished their land holdings to the peasants. The peasants were happy enough to get their land, but the central authorities ruled that distribution of land without the proper supervision of cadres could not be considered legal. The peasants were asked to return the land to the landlords, and when the specially trained cadres finally arrived, the villages were put through the whole process of the class struggle. Agrarian reform, it was explained, could not be thorough without the complete liquidation of the feudalistic landlord class, and this liquidation required the physical elimination of the most oppressive landlords of each rural area.

COLLECTIVIZATION

After the violent class struggle and the distribution of land, it remained to attain the other of the twin objectives of the proletarian-socialist revolution: to replace private ownership with collectivism. When land was distributed to the peasants, they were given the right of ownership. The Common Program (Article 27) pledged protection of the new ownership. The socialist revolution, however, demands the eventual liquidation of private land ownership. The initial move to grant private ownership was necessary in order to win the support of the masses. The next step was to devise a number of transitional stages whereby the rural population would step by step be led into advancing forms of collectivization. The Chinese Communists have shown ingenuity in devising the transitional stages.

The first was the mutual aid team.[5] After they were given land, the peasants were told that their small plots placed serious limitations on productivity, and the only way to overcome the limitations was to "get organized" and to cooperate with others. The most elementary form of "cooperation"[6] was the mutual aid team. There were two types of

---

[5] The three-stage plan of agricultural cooperation is outlined in D26.

[6] The term "cooperation" as used here refers to various forms of agricultural cooperation from mutual aid teams to agricultural cooperatives.

mutual aid teams, the seasonal and the year-round. The essential idea behind the transitional forms was to introduce the peasants gradually to successively higher levels of cooperation. In the seasonal mutual aid team, a few farming households were organized to help each other during busy seasons only; they temporarily pooled their labor, even their tools and livestock, but their cooperation ceased as soon as the busy season ended.

After some experience with the seasonal team, the peasants were persuaded to adopt a permanent year-round organization. The year-round mutual aid teams were more stable and provided for more extensive cooperation among the households: some division of labor, elementary group planning, and even common ownership of farm implements which they jointly purchased. According to the Communists, the mutual aid teams gave the peasants the first taste of cooperation and a first lesson in socialism, for in working together the peasants began to acquire "collective thoughts and emotions." At the same time, the teams were unsatisfactory in many ways. Private land ownership was unchanged, and common property was limited to a few tools and implements. Moreover, each household still decided what to plant and took care of the whole farming process—planting, irrigation, etc. A person working on someone else's land was paid for his work. The framework, in other words, was essentially capitalistic.

By 1952, the Communists were already introducing agricultural producers' cooperatives as a more advanced form of cooperation. By the end of 1953, they had decided to shift the emphasis from the mutual aid teams to agricultural producers' cooperatives. Most of the early cooperatives began by merging mutual aid teams. A cooperative was a much larger unit, consisting of forty to fifty households. The participating households pooled their land and offered it as shares in the cooperative. The pooling of land made possible a unified operation and a further division of labor. Land and manpower as well as farm implements and livestock were all placed under unified management. Instead of each household planting its own crops, the cooperative made an over-all plan, which was coordinated with the program of the state.

In joining the cooperatives, the peasants took a big step toward socialism. They surrendered to the cooperative the right to decide what to do with their land. The cooperative set aside a fixed amount of the yield for communal savings. With increased investment in farm implements and livestock for the whole cooperative, there was more collective ownership of property. A definite provision was made for communal savings and welfare funds.

Nevertheless, the Communists considered the cooperatives as only "semisocialist" in character. Some unsocialist features remained. First, although peasants contributed their land as shares in the cooperative, they theoretically retained legal ownership; so private ownership was not entirely abolished. Moreover, the cooperative compensated the owners for the use of their land by distributing income according to the shares. Theoretically, too, a household had the right to withdraw from the cooperative and thus reassert its control and management of the land.[7]

The cooperatives were supposed to have stimulated greater agricultural production. It turned out that many cooperatives, hurriedly organized in response to the drive toward socialism, failed to realize their potentialities because of incompetent management. In late 1953, the authorities issued warnings against undue haste in organizing cooperatives, and also against unfavorable popular reactions resulting from "commandism" and "adventurism."[8] Crop failures in 1954 intensified the controversy regarding the speed of collectivization. Peasants who joined the cooperatives were reported to have shown a "passive attitude." In north China in the spring of 1953, 2,600 cooperatives reverted to mutual aid teams, and many peasants were allowed to withdraw from the cooperatives.

There was a difference of opinion within the Communist Party as to whether the policy of the socialist push was a correct one. Finally, Mao Tse-tung intervened personally to end the controversy. He made known his position in an address (D27) in which he ordered bold action and a steady drive toward socialism. The months following his address saw a feverish drive throughout the country to organize and consolidate cooperatives. By the end of June, 1956, 91 per cent of the mainland's peasant households were reported to have joined agricultural producers' cooperatives. Among them, 62.6 per cent were "higher-level cooperatives" equivalent to collectives.

The so-called "higher-level cooperatives" abolished the "unsocialist" characteristics of the ordinary cooperatives. Private land ownership was now terminated; the peasants, who had only so recently been given land to own with the right to rent or to sell, now gave up all claims to their land; ownership of land was transferred to the collectives. With the guidance and help of the Communist Party and the people's

---

[7] This theoretical right of withdrawal was seriously limited by the fact that the cooperatives enjoyed priorities in the purchase of fertilizers and implements, and in filling other farming needs, while the "lone farmer" would have great difficulty in getting them.

[8] "Commandism" refers to the issuing of orders without regard for the psychological readiness of the people; "adventurism" means hasty action before the time is ripe.

government, the collectives, or "higher-level cooperatives" as the Chinese Communists preferred to call them, became, more clearly than the ordinary cooperatives, an integral part of the state economy. All work was now done on the collectivized land, and remuneration was made on the basis of the maxim "from each according to his ability, to each according to his work." This was socialism,[9] a far cry from the initial policy of "land to the tiller." For the Communists, the collectives marked the final fruition of their agrarian reform; by abolishing the landlord class and private land ownership, they had achieved the rural program of their proletarian-socialist revolution.

THE COMMUNES

A new phenomenon of social-economic organization appeared in 1958—the commune.[10] In a sense, the commune was a further extension of the trend of development from the mutual aid teams to the collectives. The peasants had been inducted into larger and larger units of organization: only a few households in a mutual aid team. 20–50 in an ordinary cooperative, and as many as 200 households in a higher-level cooperative. Now, a commune was to include every person in a geographical area of 20,000 to 50,000 people. It was an oversized collective, but it was more than that.

While the cooperatives and collectives were economic organizations, the commune was hailed as a social-economic-political-cultural organization. It was supposed to take care of collective life in five major areas: agriculture, industry, trading, education, and defense. Each person in a commune was to be concurrently a farmer, a worker, a trader, a student, and a member of the militia. The scope of collective living was broadened to include public mess halls, the public care of infants in nurseries, and common service centers for sewing, mending, laundry, and household services. The functions of the individual family were to be severely curtailed.

The Communists thought that their utopian dream would be fulfilled in the commune. Here collective living would be realized to a full extent. Male and female, young and old, all would work for the commune in any capacity demanded by collective need. Women were to gain their "final emancipation" from the traditional bondage of child care, cooking, and household work; on an equal basis with men, they would work for the commune "with a hoe in one hand and a rifle in the other." Every individual would become the Communist ideal of the "versatile man," ready to work on the farm or the factory or as a member of the militia. There would be "equal obligation of all

---

[9] In the final stage of Communism, the maxim will be "from each according to his ability, to each according to his need."

[10] See D28 and D29.

to work," as stipulated by the Communist manifesto of Marx and Engels, which also advocated "combination of agricultural with manufacturing industries" and "abolition of the distinction between town and country." As a matter of fact, Chinese writers gleefully declared that China was about to advance from the era of socialism to that of Communism.

The ambitious experiment ran into difficulties from the very beginning. Ideologically, the boast of early advance into Communism aroused the criticism of the U.S.S.R. and other Communist countries which maintained that no country had made sufficient progress in socialism to move on to Communism. The Chinese Communists restated their position in reply to this criticism and the Central Committee officially disassociated itself from the views of writers who had earlier hailed the imminent advent of Communism. In a carefully prepared statement in August, 1958 (D29), the Central Committee explained that the transition from socialism to Communism was "a fairly long and complicated process of development and that throughout this entire process society is still socialist in nature" and "any premature attempt" to attain Communism would only fail.

In practice, the communes met with a good deal of resistance from the people. The Chinese family had undergone changes for decades and many old traditions had been modified or discarded. But the abandonment of family life to the extent of the collective life visualized by the Communists was far too radical and too sharp a break from China's past. The people were not disposed to accept it. They had no enthusiasm for the public mess hall, the nurseries, and the common service centers. Economically, the communes were too big to be manageable, and decline in production compelled the adoption of more realistic measures.

The Communists speak of the "three big Red flags" as their major policies: the general line of the state, the Great Leap Forward, and the communes. Theoretically, it is still their major policy to maintain the communes as the "basic units of socialist social structure," but, in practice, the communes that exist today are very different from those proposed in 1958. Administration has been decentralized so that the actual operating unit is the production team,[11] which is no larger than the average agricultural producers' cooperative before the big drive toward collectivism. Small plots are given for peasants to cultivate (but not to own) as private farms, and they are allowed to sell their products in rural fairs which are actually free markets. These private patches of land have become important producers of vegetables, poultry, pigs, as well as "family sidelines" including tung oil, tea, oil, fruit, timber, etc. The Communists consider these as temporary concessions

---

[11] See Section 6, D29.

to necessity and watch them with anxiety and suspicion for fear of the "rebirth of capitalism." Yet, these private lots, constituting no more than 5 per cent of the land, have become essential to the economy of the communes. Almost all the poultry and pigs are raised on them; without them, the communes could not survive. Here lies one of the Communist dilemmas—or "contradictions," as the Marxists prefer to call them—mentioned in the first chapter of this volume.

URBAN CLASS STRUGGLE

As has been repeatedly stated, this volume is concerned more with general plans and major policies than with day-to-day developments. The agrarian reform has been discussed at length in order to show the pattern in which reform was used for the class struggle and agricultural collectivization. It now remains to point out that the same pattern may be observed in the cities.

Just as it promised to protect private land ownership, the Common Program (in Article 3) pledged to safeguard "the economic interests and private property of workers, peasants, the petty bourgeoisie, and the national bourgeoisie." But after the thorough and ruthless class struggle against the landlords, it was only a matter of time before the scene would shift to the urban centers and an attack would be made against the city bourgeoisie. Unlike the landlords, the bourgeoisie had been accorded a place in the favored classes of "people" as represented by the stars on the national flag. On the other hand, Mao had early warned that the "upper bourgeosie" was unreliable and the "national bourgeoisie" would be useful "at a certain period and under certain circumstances" only.[12] Moreover, no clear distinction had been made between the upper bourgeoisie and the national bourgeoisie, and it was easy at any time to condemn any sector of the bourgeoisie class by calling it the undesirable comprador upper bourgeoisie.

The prelude to a fierce class struggle against the urban bourgeoisie was the "three-anti" campaign of 1951, which was at first a sort of house-cleaning campaign to combat the evils of corruption, waste, and bureaucracy in government. In time, however, the Communists discovered that this campaign could be extended into, or merged with, one against the bourgeoisie, who were blamed for having infiltrated the ranks of government and Party personnel and led them astray. Thus was launched the "five-anti" campaign against the city bourgeoisie.[13]

The five evils of the bourgeoisie were declared to be bribery, tax evasion, fraud, theft of state assets, and leakage of state economic

---

[12] See D4.

[13] For a fuller report on these campaigns, see Theodore H. E. Chen and Wen-Hui C. Chen, "The 'Three-Anti' and 'Five-Anti' Movements in Communist China," *Pacific Affairs*, Vol. 26, No. 1, (March, 1953).

secrets. Numerous industrialists, merchants, and business people were found guilty of one or more of these five offenses. Accusations, confessions, denunciations by friends and family, public trials, and sentences marked the campaign. Thousands of investigation teams were organized to expose individual businessmen and to extract confessions from them. The same methods of public trials of the landlords and humiliation by emotionally aroused mass gatherings were now used in the cities. The more fortunate were sentenced to pay heavy fines which depleted their resources but eased the financial problems of the state. The most serious offenders were executed; many were sent to labor camps; some chose to commit suicide.

INDUSTRY AND COMMERCE

Meanwhile, the socialist squeeze on private business followed the same pattern of gradual transition. The 1954 Constitution clearly states that it is the "fundamental task of the state . . . step by step, to bring about the socialist industrialization of the country and, step by step, to accomplish the socialist transformation of agriculture, handicrafts, and capitalist industry and commerce." The story of the socialist transformation of agriculture has been told. The intermediate steps in the socialist transformation of private industry and commerce are the various forms of "state capitalism" (D31). The most advanced form at this moment is the joint public-private enterprise (D32).

In a sense, the liquidation of private property has not been as complete as in the countryside. Visitors to the Chinese mainland are often introduced to China's "millionaires," who live happily under the socialist system. These are the rich industrialists who were permitted to retain 50 per cent of their assets and share with the state "joint ownership" of what used to belong to them exclusively.

Although private capital retains half interest in the assets of the joint enterprises, it does not enjoy the same rights as the state, the owner of the other half. The relation between private capital and the state is not "one of ordinary partnership; it is one between the leader and the led" (D31). The capitalists are actually employed by the state, largely because their know-how is needed, and they are allowed to earn a fixed amount at the rate of 5 per cent per annum on their assets. It was at first announced that interest would be paid for seven years only, but the period was extended in 1962. The state holds the power to terminate the interest payments any time by declaring that the capitalists have been sufficiently compensated. Nevertheless, the urban capitalists do enjoy a respite which the landlords did not have.

They are, however, subject to continuing pressure for ideological reform. The Communists argue that the bourgeoisie has a dual character, with a positive side and a negative side. The positive character is reflected in the willingness to offer assets and technical know-how to the state; the negative stems from a carryover of bourgeois attitudes and ideas. Only by continued effort at reform—by means of physical labor as well as ideological "study"—can the bourgeoisie learn to identify itself with the working class and acquire the proletarian outlook on life. The wives of private industrialists and merchants are in need of reform, too. They must overcome their fondness for a life of ease and their aversion to physical labor. The capitalists themselves do not relish their dual status and some have voiced a preference to give up their income from assets so that they may be fully accepted without reservation. But the ideology-conscious Communists insist on clear-cut class distinctions.

HANDICRAFTS

The handicrafts have also undergone "socialist transformation." The intermediate steps of transition are the small supply and marketing group, the supply and marketing cooperative, and the handicrafts producers' cooperative. By the end of 1956, 90 per cent of the handicrafts in China had been organized in cooperatives. In the following year, a campaign was launched to turn the more advanced cooperatives into state factories. Partly because the handicraftsmen did not have the power of resistance of the rural population or the urban bourgeoisie, the transformation has been swifter and more complete.

THE NATIONAL ECONOMY

The national economy of mainland China looks healthy at some spots and weak at others. Much has been accomplished by virtue of good organization and dogged determination. In view of the severity of the economic crisis in 1960–62, the recovery since then is evidence of a high degree of economic strength and resiliency. Repayment of final installments on the Soviet debt in 1965 must certainly be considered a significant accomplishment. Extension of loans and foreign aid to Asian-African nations further attests to the economic resources the regime has at its command.

Weaknesses in the economic structure result in part from the Communist method of intensive concentration on specific goals at any given time. Concentration on narrow goals and the adoption of "crash programs" do produce impressive results, but often at the expense of other segments of the national economy. The steel drive of 1958 and the neglect of agriculture prior to the economic crisis are examples of the lopsided development that seems to be characteristic of the Communist economy.

In economics, as in education and culture, the dominance of politics is an encumbrance imposed by Communist dogmas. The economic crisis of 1960–62 seemed to have injected more realism into Communist planning, and the initial announcement of the Third Five-Year Plan sounded less pretentious and paid more attention to the needs of agriculture and the consumer. Instead of talking grandly about miraculous achievements, Communist leaders conceded that many years of arduous struggle lie ahead. Said Vice-Premier and Foreign Minister Ch'en Yi in a press conference on September 29, 1965: "It will take decades—thirty to fifty years more of effort—to build up China's industry, agriculture, and national defense and raise them to a higher level."

Nevertheless, politics is still "in command." The "thought of Mao Tse-tung" is held to be the key to the Third Five-Year Plan. Dogmas still pose a threat to the realistic measures that have brought about the economic recovery of recent years. Maoist attacks on "economism" in the course of the cultural revolution could only result in the dominance of blind dogmatism over hard-headed realism.[14]

Production of chemicals, fertilizers, petroleum, and cement continues on a high level. The Third Five-Year Plan, with its emphasis on "agriculture as the foundation and industry as the leading factor," will probably pay much attention to water and soil conservation. But China has been importing wheat and grain from abroad, and the need to import food is likely to continue for some time.

The production of food for the growing population is a serious problem. Statistics of agricultural production do not tell the whole story without reference to population growth. Unless the increase in food production keeps up with population growth, the economic situation will deteriorate. There is no accurate knowledge of the size of the population on the Chinese mainland today, but the best estimate would put it between 700 and 750 million. The government has adopted measures to curb population growth and has been fairly effective. Still, food production has lagged behind population growth.[15]

Another problem is the use of economic resources for defense purposes. Nuclear research, though costly, is given a high priority. The principle of "agriculture as the foundation and industry as the leading factor" does not make explicit the fact that a large portion of industry is oriented to meet defense needs. A writer on Chinese Communist affairs recently noted that "six out of eight of China's Ministries of Machine Building are engaged (though not exclusively) in supervising the production of armaments and military equipment."[16]

---

[14] "Economism" refers especially to the offer of material incentives to stimulate production. The appeal to the profit motive, the Maoists say, is a return to capitalism.

[15] See the next chapter for a brief statement on birth control.

[16] Colina MacDougall, "Peking and the PLA," *Far Eastern Economic Review,* LII (Hong Kong), (June 16, 1966), 563–65.

Document 20

THE AGRARIAN REFORM LAW OF THE PEOPLE'S REPUBLIC OF CHINA

[Promulgated by the Central People's Government on June 30, 1950.]

Section 1. General Principles

Article 1. The land ownership system of feudal exploitation by the landlord class shall be abolished, and the system of peasant land ownership shall be introduced in order to set free the rural productive forces, develop agricultural production, and thus pave the way for New China's industrialization.

Section 2. Confiscation and Requisitioning of Land

Article 2. The land, draft animals, farm implements, and surplus grain and surplus country houses of the landlords shall be confiscated, but their other properties shall not be confiscated.

Article 3. The rural land belonging to ancestral shrines, temples, monasteries, churches, schools, and organizations, and other land owned by public bodies shall be requisitioned. But local people's governments should devise appropriate measures to solve the financial problems facing such schools, orphanages, homes for the aged, hospitals, etc., that depend on the income from the above-mentioned land for their maintenance.

Land owned by mosques may be retained according to circumstances with the consent of the Moslems residing where such mosques are situated.

Article 4. Industry and commerce shall be protected from infringement. Industrial and commercial enterprises operated by landlords, and the land and other properties used by landlords directly for the operation of industrial and commercial enterprises shall not be confiscated. In confiscating feudal land and other properties, no infringement upon industry and commerce shall be permitted.

Land and peasant dwellings in the countryside that are owned by industrialists and merchants shall be requisitioned, but their other rural properties and lawful businesses shall be protected from infringement.

Article 5. Revolutionary soldiers, dependents of martyrs, workers, staff members, professional people, peddlers, and others who rent out small portions of land because they are engaged in other occupations or because they are unable to work shall not be classified as landlords.

196

If the average per capita landholding of such families does not exceed 200 per cent of the average per capita landholding in the locality, it shall remain untouched. (For instance, if the average per capita landholding in the locality is two *mow,* the average per capita landholding of such family members shall not exceed four *mow.)* If it exceeds this proportion, the surplus land may be requisitioned. If the land proves to have been purchased with the earnings of the owners' own labor or if old persons living alone, orphans, invalids, or helpless widows or widowers depend on this land for their livelihood, allowance may be made for such persons according to individual cases even though their average per capita landholding may exceed 200 per cent of the average per capita landholding in the vicinity.

Article 6. Land owned by rich peasants and cultivated by themselves or by hired labor, and their other properties, shall be protected from infringement.

Small portions of land rented out by rich peasants shall remain untouched. But in certain special areas, the land rented out by rich peasants may be requisitioned in part or entirely, with the approval of the people's governments at provincial or higher level.

If the portions of land rented out by rich peasants of a semi-landlord type exceed in size the land tilled by them or by hired labor, the land rented out shall be requisitioned.

When rich peasants rent out land and are also tenants of land, these should be balanced against each other in computing their landholdings.

Article 7. Land and other properties of middle peasants (including well-to-do middle peasants) shall be protected from infringement.

Article 8. Transfer or dispersal of any land that should be confiscated or requisitioned according to this Law by sale, mortgage, gift, or any other means, shall be declared null and void. Such land should be included in the land to be redistributed. But if peasants who took mortgages on the land will thereby suffer any considerable loss, measures should be worked out to compensate them suitably.

Article 9. The legal definition of landlords, rich peasants, middle peasants, poor peasants, farm laborers, and other component classes of rural society will be dealt with separately.

Section 3. Distribution of Land

Article 10. All land and other means of production thus confiscated and requisitioned, with the exception of those to be nationalized as stipulated in this Law, shall be taken over by the *hsiang* peasants' association for unified, equitable, and rational distribution to poor peasants who have little or no land and who have no other means of production. Landlords shall be given an equal share so that they can make their living by their own labor and thus reform themselves through labor.

Article 11. Land should be distributed with a *hsiang* or an administrative village corresponding to a *hsiang* as a single unit, and on the principle of alloting the land to its present tiller. Land should be distributed in a unified manner according to the population, and readjustment in landholdings may be made by taking into consideration the amount, quality, and location of the land. However, *ch'ü* or county peasants' associations may make certain necessary adjustments between various *hsiang* or administrative villages corresponding to a *hsiang*. In areas of extensive territory and sparse population, for convenience in cultivation, the unit for land distribution may be smaller than the level of the *hsiang*. The land lying on the boundary of two *hsiang* shall be allocated for distribution to the *hsiang* where the actual tillers reside.

Article 12. Under the principle of allotting land to the tiller, land owned by the tiller shall not be drawn upon for distribution during land distribution. When rented land is drawn upon for distribution, proper consideration should be given to the tiller. The land he acquires through land distribution plus his own landholding (if he has any) shall be slightly and suitably more than the landholding, after distribution, of the peasants who had little or no land. The principle in this connection should be that the tiller should retain the approximate average per capita landholding in the locality.

If the tiller possesses the surface rights of the land he rents, a portion of land equivalent to the price of the surface rights in that locality shall be reserved for him if the land is drawn upon for distribution.

Article 13. During land distribution, certain special problems of the landless and land-poor population shall be settled as follows:

1. A poor peasant family of one or two members who are able to work may be given more land than the allotment for one or two persons, provided land conditions in the *hsiang* permit.

2. Rural handicraftsmen, peddlers, and professional people and their dependents should be given a certain amount of land and other means of production according to individual cases. But if the earnings from their occupations are sufficient to regularly maintain their dependents, no land shall be allotted to them.

3. If their homes are in the countryside, martyrs' families (the martyr himself can be counted as a family member), officers, men, wounded and demobilized servicemen of the People's Liberation Army, and functionaries of the people's government and people's organizations and their families (including those who travel with the

Army) shall be given land and other means of production equal to those allotted to the peasants. But in the case of the functionaries of the people's government and people's organizations, less land or none may be allotted, in proportion to the amount of their salaries and other income and the degree to which they are able to support their dependents.

4. If local residents take up occupations elsewhere, their dependents still living in the village should be given land and other means of production according to individual cases. But if the income of such persons from their occupations is adequate to regularly maintain their dependents, no land need be allotted to them.

5. Monks, nuns, priests, and other religious personnel should be given shares of land and other means of production equal to those of the peasants if they have no other means of making a living and are able and willing to engage in agricultural work.

6. Unemployed workers and their dependents who return to the countryside with certificates from municipal governments or trade unions should be given shares of land and other means of production equal to those of the peasants if they ask for land and are able to engage in agricultural work, and if local land conditions permit.

7. Landlords who return after running away, persons who once worked for the enemy but who return to the countryside, and families of such persons should be given shares of land and other means of production equal to those of the peasants, provided they are willing to earn a living by agricultural work.

8. No land shall be given to those residing in the countryside whom the people's government has ascertained to be collaborationists, traitors, war criminals, counterrevolutionaries who have committed extremely grave crimes, or criminals who have persistently sabotaged agrarian reform. Members of their families who have not participated in their criminal acts, have no other occupation with which to make a living, and are able and willing to take up agricultural work should be given the same shares of land and other means of production as the peasants.

Article 14. During land distribution, each *hsiang* may reserve a small amount of land, in accordance with the local land conditions, for cultivation by natives of the *hsiang* who have fled and whose whereabouts are unknown but who may return, or for use in adjusting land in the *hsiang*. The land thus reserved shall be placed under the administration of the *hsiang* people's government and rented to peasants for cultivation. However, the total amount of land reserved for this purpose must not exceed 1 per cent of all land in the *hsiang*.

Article 15. During land distribution, the people's governments at or above the county level, in accordance with the local land conditions, may set apart a certain amount of land to be nationalized and used for establishing agricultural experimental stations or model state farms for one or more counties. Prior to the establishment of such farms, the land may be rented to peasants for cultivation.

Section 4.   Treatment of Special Land Problems

Article 16. Confiscated and requisitioned woods, fish ponds, tea groves, tung oil plantations, mulberry fields, bamboo groves, orchards, reed lands, wasteland, and other distributable land should be calculated in terms of ordinary land at an appropriate ratio and distributed in a unified way. In the interests of production, these tracts of land should be allotted as far as possible to the peasants who have hitherto utilized them. Persons receiving this kind of land may be given little or no ordinary arable land. If this kind of distribution is detrimental to production, the land may be operated by the local people's government in a proper manner and under democratic management in conformity with established customs.

Article 17. Confiscated and requisitioned irrigation works, such as dams and ponds, if they are distributable, should be distributed together with the fields. If it is not convenient to distribute them, they should be democratically managed by the local people's governments in conformity with established customs.

Article 18. All great forests, large water conservancy works, large expanses of wasteland, large uncultivated hillsides, big salt fields and mines, as well as lakes, marshes, rivers, and ports, must be nationalized and managed and operated by the people's government. Those in which private capital has been invested and which have so far been privately managed shall continue to be operated by the existing management, according to the decrees promulgated by the people's government.

Article 19. The farms, seedling nurseries, and agricultural experimental stations that are cultivated with machinery or other modern equipment, and the large bamboo groves, large orchards, large tea groves, tung oil plantations, large mulberry fields and large pastures, where technique is essential, shall continue to be operated by their existing managements, and should not be dispersed. But if such land is owned by landlords, it may be nationalized with the approval of the people's governments at the provincial level or above.

Article 20. During the confiscation and requisition of land, all graveyards and woods therein must remain intact.

Article 21. Scenic spots, historical relics, and places of historical interest should be carefully preserved. Ancestral shrines, temples, monasteries, churches, other public buildings, and landlords' houses should not be damaged. Surplus houses of landlords in the countryside that are not suitable for the use of peasants may come under the management of the local people's governments and be used for public purposes.

Article 22. Wasteland reclaimed after the liberation should not be confiscated during land distribution and should continue to be tilled by those who reclaimed it. It should not be included in the amount of land to be distributed.

Article 23. Small plots of land necessary for maintaining bridges and highways in repair, resting places, free ferries, and other public facilities may remain intact according to established customs.

Article 24. Land and houses owned by overseas Chinese should be dealt with in accordance with appropriate measures to be determined by the people's governments (or military and administrative committees) of the various greater administrative areas or by provincial people's governments, with regard for the interests of overseas Chinese and in keeping with the general principles of this Law.

Article 25. Sandy and shoaly land owned by landlords or public bodies should be nationalized and handled in accordance with appropriate measures to be determined by the people's governments at the provincial level or above.

Article 26. Land bordering railways, highways, river banks, and river dykes that is needed for their protection, or land occupied by airfields, harbors, or fortifications should not be distributed. The sites of projected railways, highways, waterways, and airfields whose date of construction has been fixed shall be reserved with the approval of the people's government at the provincial level or above.

Article 27. Private persons managing land owned by the state may not rent it out, sell it, or leave it untended. If the private operators no longer need the land, they must return it to the state.

Section 5. Organizations and Methods for Carrying Out Agrarian Reform

Article 28. In order to strengthen the leadership of the people's governments in the work of agrarian reform, the people's governments at county level or above should organize agrarian reform committees, to be composed of persons elected by people's representative conferences or persons appointed by the people's governments of a higher level. These committees are responsible for directing and handling all matters concerning agrarian reform.

Article 29. Hsiang and village peasant meetings, peasant representative conferences, committees of peasant associations elected at such conferences, the peasant congresses at *ch'ü,* county, and provincial levels, and committees of peasants' associations elected at such congresses are the legal executive organizations for reforming the agrarian system.

Article 30. After agrarian reform is completed, the people's government shall issue title deeds and shall recognize the right of all landowners to manage, buy, sell, or rent out land. All land contracts made before the reform of the agrarian system shall be null and void.

Article 31. The determination of class status shall be carried out according to the decisions on class differentiation in the countryside issued by the Central People's Government. Class status shall be determined by democratic estimation and decision at the village peasant meetings and peasant representative conferences, under the leadership of the village people's governments, by the method of self-assessment and public discussion. If any person concerned is not a member of a peasants' association, he should, nevertheless, be invited to participate in the estimation and decision at the meetings and be allowed to argue his case.

The estimation and decision must be reported to the *ch'ü* people's government for ratification. If any person concerned, or any other person, does not agree with the result, he may, within fifteen days after the announcement of such ratification, lodge an appeal with the county people's tribunal, which shall pass judgment and carry it into effect.

Article 32. A people's tribunal shall be set up in every county to ensure that agrarian reform is carried out. The tribunal shall travel to different places, try hated despotic elements who have committed heinous crimes and whom the masses of the people demand to be brought to justice, and all persons who resist or violate the provisions of the Agrarian Reform Law and decrees, and punish them according to law. Indiscriminate arrest, beating or killing of people, and corporal punishment and the like are strictly forbidden.

The regulations governing the organization of the people's tribunal will be enacted separately.

Article 33. To maintain order during agrarian reform and to protect the people's property, it is strictly prohibited to slaughter draft animals or fell trees, let land lie untended, destroy farm implements, irrigation works, buildings, crops or the like without authorization. Offenders shall be tried and punished by the people's tribunal.

Article 34. To ensure that all agrarian reform measures effectively conform to the interests and wishes of the overwhelming majority of the people, the people's governments at all levels shall be responsible for effectively safeguarding the democratic rights of the people. The peasants and their representatives shall have the right to freely criticize and impeach functionaries of any sphere or level at all meetings. Any one who infringes on these rights shall be punished according to law.

Section 6.   Bylaws

Article 35. This Law shall apply to the rural areas in general, but not to areas in the vicinity of big cities, for which agrarian reform regulations will be formulated separately. The big cities referred to in this article shall be determined by the people's governments (or military and administrative committees) of the greater administrative areas according to the circumstances of the cities.

Article 36. This Law shall not apply to areas inhabited by national minorities. But in areas where the Han nationality is in the majority, scattered inhabitants of national minorities shall be treated in the same way under this Law as the people of Han nationality in carrying out the agrarian reform in those localities.

Article 37. This Law shall not apply to areas where agrarian reform has been nearly completed.

Article 38. All areas that begin agrarian reform after the promulgation of this Law, with the exception of the areas referred to in Articles 35, 36, and 37 of this Law, shall proceed in accordance with this Law. The time for starting agrarian reform in various places shall be regulated by decree and made public by the people's governments (or military and administrative committees) of the greater administrative areas and provincial people's governments.

Article 39. When this Law is made public, each provincial people's government shall formulate regulations for carrying out agrarian reform within its territory, in accordance with the principles as laid down in this Law and the concrete conditions of the territory, and shall submit them to the people's governments (or military and administrative committees) of the greater administrative areas. They shall be put into effect on ratification. They shall also be submitted to the Government Administration Council of the Central People's Government for registration.

Article 40. This Law shall come into force after it is ratified and promulgated by the Central People's Government Council.

HOW TO ANALYZE CLASS STATUS IN THE COUNTRYSIDE

[First promulgated in 1933 and reaffirmed in 1950.]

LANDLORDS

A person shall be classified as a landlord who owns land, but does not engage in labor or only engages in supplementary labor, and who depends on exploitation for his means of livelihood. Exploitation by the landlords is chiefly in the form of land rent, plus money lending, hiring of labor, or the simultaneous carrying on of industrial or commercial enterprises. But the major form of exploitation of the peasants by the landlords is the exacting of land rent from the peasants. The management of landholdings owned by public bodies and the collection of rent from school land also belong to the category of exploitation in the form of land rent.

Some bankrupt landlords who, despite their bankruptcy and their ability to work, do not engage in labor, and whose living conditions are better than those of an ordinary middle peasant, shall continue to be classified as landlords.

Warlords, bureaucrats, local despots, and villainous gentry are the political representatives of the landlord class, and are exceptionally cruel and wicked elements among the landlords. (Among the rich peasants, there are also small local despots and villainous gentry.)

Any person who collects rent, manages property for landlords, and depends on the exploitation of peasants by the landlords as his main means of livelihoood, and whose living conditions are better than those of an ordinary middle peasant, shall be treated in the same manner as a landlord.

RICH PEASANTS

A rich peasant generally owns land. But there are also rich peasants who own only part of the land they cultivate and rent the rest from others. There are others who own no land but rent all their land from others. Generally speaking, they own better means of production and some floating capital and take part in labor themselves, but are dependent on exploitation for a part or the major part of their means of livelihood. Exploitation by rich peasants is chiefly in the form of hiring long-term laborers. They may also let out part of their land for rent, or lend out money, or carry on industrial or commercial enterprises. Most of the rich peasants also manage the landholdings owned by public bodies. Some own a considerable amount of fertile land, engage in labor themselves, and do not hire any laborers. But they exploit the peasants in the form of land rent and loan interest. In such cases, they should be treated in the same manner as other rich peasants. Exploitation by the rich peasants is of a constant character, and in many cases the income from such exploitation constitutes their main means of livelihood.

MIDDLE PEASANTS

Many middle peasants own land. Some possess only a portion of the land they cultivate and rent the remainder. Some of them are landless, and rent all their land from others. The middle peasants own a certain number of farm implements. They depend wholly or mainly upon their own labor for their living. In general they do not exploit others. Many of them are themselves exploited on a small scale by others in the form of land rent and loan interest. But generally they do not sell their labor. Some of the middle peasants (the well-to-do middle peasants) practice a small degree of exploitation, but such exploitation is not of a constant character and the income therefrom does not constitute their main means of livelihood. These people shall be classified as middle peasants.

POOR PEASANTS

Some poor peasants own inadequate farm implements and a part of the land they cultivate. Some have no land at all and own only some inadequate farm implements. In general they must rent land for cultivation, and are exploited by others in the form of land rent, loan interest, or hired labor in a limited degree. These people shall be classified as poor peasants.

In general, the middle peasants need not sell their labor, but the poor peasants have to sell their labor for limited periods. This is the basic criterion for differentiating between middle peasants and poor peasants.

WORKERS

Workers (including farm laborers) generally have neither land nor farm implements. Some of them have a very small amount of land and very few implements. They depend wholly or mainly upon the sale of their labor for their living. These people shall be classified as workers.

DOCUMENT 22

LIU SHAO-CH'I ON THE AGRARIAN REFORM LAW

[Excerpts from a report on June 14, 1950, at the Second Session of the National Committee of the People's Political Consultative Conference.]

We can see from the basic reason for and the aim of agrarian reform that the historical crimes committed by the landlord class in the past are rooted in the old social system. Landlords in general will only be deprived of their feudal landholdings and abolished as a social class, but they will not be physically eliminated. The people's courts should pass sentences of death or imprisonment on only a small number of landlords guilty of heinous crimes—rural despots whose crimes are gross and whose iniquities are extreme, and those criminal elements who persistently resist agrarian reform. As for the others, it is stipulated in the Draft Agrarian Reform Law that after their land and other means of production have been confiscated, the landlords will still be given shares of land and other means of production so that they can also make a living by their own labor, and reform themselves through labor. After undergoing long-term reform through labor, it is possible for landlords to become new men.

The basic reason for and the aim of agrarian reform are different from the view that agrarian reform is only designed to relieve the poor people. The Communist Party has always been fighting for the interests of the laboring poor, but the viewpoint of Communists has always been different from that of the philanthropists. The results of agrarian reform are beneficial to the impoverished laboring peasants, helping the peasants partly solve their problem of poverty. But the basic aim of agrarian reform is not merely one of relieving the poor peasants. It is designed to free the rural productive forces from the shackles of the feudal land ownership system of the landlord class, in order to develop agricultural production and thus pave the way for New China's industrialization. The problem of poverty among the peasants can be finally solved only if agricultural production can be greatly developed, if the industrialization of New China can be realized, if the living standards of the people throughout the country can be raised, and if China finally can embark upon the road to socialism. The mere carrying out of agrarian reform can only solve part, but not all, of the problems of the peasants' poverty.

The basic reason for and the basic aim of agrarian reform are intended for production. Hence, every step in agrarian reform should be a practical one, taking into consideration the development of rural production and closely coordinated with it. Precisely because of this basic reason and aim, the Central Committee of the Communist Party of China has proposed that rich-peasant economy be preserved and protected from infringement in future agrarian reform. This is because the existence of a rich-peasant economy and its development within certain limits is advantageous to the development of the people's economy in our country. It is, therefore, also beneficial to the broad peasant masses.

The various provisions in the Draft Agrarian Reform Law regarding land and other properties of the rich peasants are aimed at preserving the rich-peasant economy, neutralizing the rich peasants politically, and rendering better protection to middle peasants and persons renting out small parcels of land, thus isolating the landlord class and unifying all the people to carry out agrarian reform and eliminate the feudal system in an orderly manner.

If the people's government pursues a policy of preserving the rich-peasant economy, the rich peasants generally can be won over to a neutral attitude. Better protection can then be given to the middle peasants, thus dispelling certain unnecessary misgivings of the peasants during the development of production. Therefore, in the present situation, the adoption of a policy to preserve the rich-peasant economy in the coming agrarian reform is necessary both politically and economically. It will help to overcome our current financial and economic difficulties and thus benefit our country and our people.

The policy adopted by us of preserving a rich-peasant economy is of course not a temporary, but a long-term policy. That is to say, a rich-peasant economy will be preserved throughout the whole stage of New Democracy. Only when the conditions are ripe for the extensive application of mechanized farming, for the organization of collective farms, and for the socialist reform of the rural areas, will the need for a rich-peasant economy cease, and this will take a somewhat long time to achieve.

This is why we advocate the preservation of a rich-peasant economy at present.

Of course, in the areas where agrarian reform has been completed, the rich peasants are not permitted to take advantage of this to regain land from the peasants. If such cases occur, they should be strictly prohibited.

Agrarian reform is a systematic and fierce struggle. Our general line to be followed in future agrarian reform is that reliance should be placed on the poor peasants and farm laborers, while uniting with the middle peasants and neutralizing the rich peasants, in order to eliminate the feudal exploitation system gradually and with discrimination, and to develop agricultural production.

The purity of the leadership of the peasants' associations at all levels should be safeguarded. . . . The term "purity" here means that landlords, rich peasants, and their agents are to be prevented from joining the peasants' associations and, still more important, from holding leading positions in the peasants' associations.

The main leadership of the peasants' associations must be chosen from among the poor peasants and farm laborers. But real alliance with the middle peasants and, above all, real protection of their land and property (including that of the well-to-do middle peasants) is indispensable. At the same time, active middle peasants must be absorbed into the leadership of the peasants' associations.

People's tribunals should be set up to suppress and punish in good time the resistance and subversive activities of despots, secret agents, counterrevolutionary elements, and the landlord class, and to deal with the charges made by the peasants against these elements during the agrarian reform.

The people's tribunals should hand over ordinary criminal and civil cases and especially complicated cases that need a long investigation before settlement can be reached, to the ordinary courts and public security organizations for decision, so that the tribunals themselves can concentrate their efforts on dealing with current breaches of the law during the agrarian reform and preserving revolutionary order in the rural areas.

DOCUMENT 23

THE POLITICAL SIGNIFICANCE OF AGRARIAN REFORM

[The first part of an address by Teng Tzu-hui on December 26, 1950.]

Some comrades look upon agrarian reform as a simple matter of the distribution of land, which in turn they consider purely a technical job, and thus understand the problem of agrarian reform merely as a means for the development of production. This view is incorrect. It must be understood that agrarian reform constitutes the basic content of the New Democratic revolution in China at the present stage. The basic mission of the Chinese revolution is opposition to imperialism and feudalism. The present campaign of resistance against the United States and for aid to Korea is developed in opposition to imperialism. The agrarian reform campaign is, on the other hand, the last and fiercest battle in the series of systematic class struggles to wipe out feudal influences.

We may realize, therefore, that agrarian reform is not carried out merely for the development of production, but is rather a basic task of the Chinese people for the fulfillment of their revolutionary mission and the establishment of China as a member of the modern world. We all know that the landlord class, this feudal force which stands together with our great enemy imperialism, is not a weak and effeminate foe, but one with a history of ruling the country for more than 2,000 years, with deep-rooted ruling powers. *In point of military strength,* this force in the past owned the national army of the Kuomintang and the regional peace preservation corps, as well as local defense units; they also utilized the services of native bandit bands and armed forces of the secret societies, gangsters, and muscle men as stooges. They also owned their own defense units directly. Since the armed forces operating in the open had been eliminated by us, underground armies have been organized in many areas.

In point of political strength, in the past the landlord class had the whole Kuomintang administrative outfit from the highest to the lowest levels, and the *pao chia** system, which extended to each village and each corner in the rural districts. With the abolition of the *pao chia* system by us, these feudal elements immediately caused a change, and exploited their stooges or innocent peasants to serve as chiefs of *ts'un*† and to organize bogus peasants' associations, so that the ruling power in the rural areas remained in their hands and their political superiority was maintained. In the south central region, such a situation still obtained in a large proportion of the rural areas.

In the field of economic strength, this feudal class owns more than 50 per cent of the land and other wealth and controls the materials on which the broad masses of peasants depend for their living. Up to the present moment, the peasants in most areas still depend on the landlords for their living.

In the field of organizational strength, in the past there were the Kuomintang and the San Min Chu I Youth Corps, as well as the various

---

* *Pao chia* was the pre-Communist system of organizing the population in family units.

† *Ts'un* means hamlet.

special service organizations. Even today, various feudal organs such as the secret societies and religious sects are being employed to deceive the peasants, and there are a number of determined counterrevolutionaries who constitute the backbone of these various organizations.

In the matter of ideological influence, these forces are not only adept at arbitrary arguments, fabrication of rumors, deception, threats, instigation, and inducement, but are also in a position to exploit the backwardness, provincialism, superstition, foolishness, and sectarianism that had been created by their long rule over the people. Since the war in Korea, the special agents and despots have been quick to exploit the idea of impending changes that is still in existence among the peasants, and have issued threats about "the third world war," and "the counteroffensive of the Chiang bandits."

Analyzing these various sources of strength, it is clear that it will be no easy task to wipe out the landlord class, this cruel and stubborn foe. The job must be carried out with a fierce class struggle, conducted with measured steps and the systematic coordination of various forces.

DOCUMENT 24

DESCRIPTION OF THE PUBLIC TRIAL OF A LANDLORD DURING AGRARIAN REFORM

[From Hsiao Ch'ien, *How the Tillers Win Back Their Land* (Peking: Foreign Languages Press, 1951), pp. 72-80.]

December 17. The sky was overcast. On the Huilung *hsiang* field paths one could see here and there red flags fluttering against a grey backdrop. Peasants, men and women, beating gongs and drums, once more poured into the open meeting place in front of the ancestral temple. Again a platform was made on the terrace, in front of which were placed two square tables. A horizontal tablet was hung on the spiked railing outside the temple with the characters: "Second Divisional Tribunal of the County People's Tribunal: Meeting for Public Trial" written across it.

At around ten, the judge together with sixteen members of the jury walked to the platform amidst prolonged, enthusiastic applause from the masses. Following them came two cadres to keep a record of the trial. The meeting opened with the singing of the national anthem, with the students of the primary school at the Seven Star Slope in the lead. Then everybody took off their hats and bowed to the national flag and to the portrait of Chairman Mao.

"Today," announced the judge, who rose to his feet, "we are going to pass judgment on three criminal landlords from Huilung *hsiang.*"

At this the three prisoners, handcuffed, clambered up onto the two square tables in front of the platform, under the close surveillance of a squad of militia and six guards from the district government. The guards were armed with rifles or six-shooters with floating silk tassels. Peng Yin-ting* was trembling all over, his head bent low. Lo Pei-jung made a deep bow to the audience when he got up. His face was as pale as the mackerel sky. Peng Erh-hu's mouth was clamped shut, and with cruel bulging eyes he scanned the jostling masses below, expressionless.

"We've caught these rogues," continued the judge. "They couldn't escape if they had wings on them, so you don't need to be afraid of them any more. Now is the time for everyone to pour out the grievance he has kept in his heart for years—murder, swindle, rape, ill-treatment, everything. The final verdict of this tribunal on the prisoners will be based on your evidence and your opinions."

The first to reach the platform was a woman in her early fifties.

"My name is Peng Shu-min," she said, fingering the red insignia pinned on her breast. She was one of the first Huilung *hsiang* women to join the peasants' association.

"I am Peng Kuo-chang's aunt, and I am accusing Peng Erh-hu on behalf of my third brother, Peng Chiang, Peng Kuo-chang's father. In the sixteenth year of the Republic, my third brother was vice-chairman of the local peasants' association. At the return of the reactionaries, he took me and his wife, and their three-year-old son Kuo-chang to the hills, where he became a member of the Red Army. My old father was thus left alone at home.

"Peng Erh-hu had a group of soldiers from the countryside liquidation corps quartered in our house. They ate up everything they could find and burnt and destroyed. What's more, they dragged my father, who was then in his eighties, to the temple where they strung him up, beat him, and trampled on his back, in order to get him to hand over a list of the members of the peasants' association. My father's spine was broken but he died without giving them the list.

"In the twelfth moon of that year, my brother thought he'd come back in disguise and look my father up for the lunar New Year. Before he had a chance to set foot inside the homestead, Peng Erh-hu caught him. He was stabbed several times and left to die. After he died, we still didn't dare collect his body; so finally, we had to ask some coun-

---

* All names follow the romanized spelling of the original text.

try people to stuff it inside a sack and take it to the foot of the hill to be buried. I had a glimpse of him before they lowered him into the grave. His ten fingers were covered with bruises from the bamboo pricks they forced between the flesh and fingernails, and all his upper and lower teeth had been knocked out."

Her face was white with fury. She pointed an accusing finger at Peng Erh-hu. Tears of sympathy trickled down the cheeks of the militia members standing nearby.

With raised fists, the audience below shouted in one voice, "Down with reactionary landlords!" "We demand that Peng Erh-hu be shot!"

Standing there as though rooted to the ground, Peng Shu-min tried to go on, but couldn't, because there seemed to be a lump in her throat. Finally she managed to get these words out:

"Killing one of the chickens we have around the house would practically scare me to death ordinarily. But now I feel I could kill this Peng Erh-hu with my bare hands!"

A young peasant was the next to appear on the platform. Bowing to the audience, he began:

"My name is Tien Yi-che, and I came from Tienchialung in Shih-chiao Village. In 1939, when the KMT [Kuomintang] said they would cooperate with the Communists, the New Fourth Army marched up north to fight the Japanese, leaving behind a People's Livelihood Team, with my father, Tien Chih-cheng, as its captain. The Team was to mobilize the peasants into guerrilla units to fight the Japs.

"Seeing the people organized and armed, Peng Yin-ting began to feel nervous about the security of his own position as village elder, so he sent for a whole regiment of Yang Sen's (a KMT general's) men and made a raid on the Team's headquarters on the night of March 23, taking seven comrades away. Later on they got on the track of my father, the captain, and to this day I've never heard from him.

"The arrival of the Japs made no difference to Peng Yin-ting's position. He still continued as village elder, and not for one instant had he taken his eyes off our family. Without even bothering to give a pretext, he took our ox away from us. It finally got so that we had to take other names and live away from home. We didn't dare come back until after liberation. Nothing short of death is good enough for this traitor, Peng Yin-ting."

Paper flags crackled and the square was a forest of upraised fists. The crowd yelled, "Down with this traitor landlord!" "Wipe out reactionary power!" "A life for a life!"

Mass sentiment continued to run high when Fu-chuan and Grandma Li unburdened themselves of their grievances.

They were followed by a young peasant, Lo Yung-nien. With a deep bow he introduced himself and began: "I'm landlord Lo Pei-jung's nephew. Sometime before the land reform work team came here, Lo Pei-jung once gave me some of his title deeds to be taken to a photographer's shop at the Seven Star Slope to be photographed. 'So that I'll have some evidence on hand once the real deeds are burnt,' he said. Also he hid two of his trunks in the attic of my house. The way I looked at it in the past—well, he's my uncle, isn't he? I hadn't the guts to refuse him. Now I realize that he's a landlord, and I'm a poor peasant. He has fish and meat by the mouthful, and rotten potato is all my family ever tasted. I was a fool. I can't face Chairman Mao if I don't deliver at once to the *hsiang* government the two trunks he asked me to keep for him!"

The masses again shouted in unison. "Down with criminal landlords who hide and disperse their properties!" "Long live the unity of the peasants!"

It had started raining. But the tense atmosphere did not in any way lessen. A woman tearfully told of how Peng Erh-hu had raped her fourteen-year-old daughter. The accusations were practically drowned in the shouts from the masses. Hoarse voices were heard, shaking the half-moist fields:

"Shoot Peng Erh-hu!"

"Shoot Peng Yin-ting!"

"Punish the criminal landlord, Lo Pei-jung!"

"We won't go home until the Peng brothers are shot!"

By four o'clock over twenty peasants had poured out their grievances from the platform. Mass sentiment had surged to boiling point. Over and above there was a curious hush of expectancy. Not one person left or took shelter in spite of the terrific downpour.

After retiring to the inside of the temple to deliberate over the cases, the judge and the jury came back and took their places amidst thunderous applause.

The pale features of the three prisoners standing on the tables suddenly became hard and drawn. Leaning a little to one side, they pricked up their ears to listen to the judge pronounce the final verdict.

"Peasant comrades!" The judge's voice was grave. "We have just heard some of the accusations made by local peasants. From these accusations, it ought to be clear to everyone how the landlord class has always worked hand in glove with the enemy of the peasants— whether it was Japanese imperialism or the KMT—to oppress the peasants themselves. The same motive has prompted them to act as fawning lackeys to American imperialism, since American imperialism is directly opposed to the people's interests too.

"Our verdicts on the three criminal landlords are as follows: Lo

Pei-jung, age forty, native of Hsinlu Village, is charged with rumor-mongering and dispersing of properties, Now these are crimes that the people won't tolerate. Not only has Lo Pei-jung dispersed his belongings, but he had made photostatic copies of his title-deeds, which shows that he is still pinning his hope on the KMT reactionaries. After careful consideration, the jury has unanimously decided on a sentence of seven years. Do you all agree?"

There was a great burst of joyous applause and Lo Pei-jung was led away by militia members to be placed in temporary custody inside the temple.

"Peng Yin-ting, age forty nine, native of Hsinlu Village, has caused the deaths of patriotic youths during the Resistance War. After Liberation, he organized superstitious societies and spread rumors to delude the public. Also, he has hidden firearms with the intent to plan for an uprising. The sentence for him is—death. Do you all agree?"

The sound of applause that came from below the platform was deafening.

"Peng Erh-hu, alias Peng Tien-pao, age forty seven, native of Hsinlu Village, was a captain of an anti-Communist guerrilla team and of the countryside liquidation corps during the First Revolutionary Civil War of 1927, in which capacities he had several times broken up peasant organizations and caused peasant leaders to be arrested or killed. After the defeat of Japan, he succeeded his brother as the bogus village elder and spared no efforts in pressganging men and extorting 'contributions' for the KMT reactionaries, with a view to furthering the war against the people. In addition to these, he has been charged with misappropriating dyke funds, with disastrous results to the welfare of the peasants. For him also the death penalty. Do you all agree?"

The applause which greeted this pronouncement was even more enthusiastic. The militia held their spears way up to express wholehearted support, and voices had almost become strained with the shouting of slogans:

"Abolish the wicked landlord class!"

"Long live the people's government that sides with the peasants in their struggle!"

Peng Yin-ting and Peng Erh-hu were then led off the platform by the militia and the guards. The latter were to see to the actual execution. The masses opened up to let them pass through.

With one arm sheltering his tear-stained face, Peng Yin-ting was hurried along. Intermittent sobs kept issuing from his gaping mouth. Peng Erh-hu's face had taken on an ashen pallor, and his bulging eyes were fixed and full.

When Grandma Li, with her bony fist clenched, edged her way through the crowds and tried to hit him on the shoulder, the guards immediately stopped her. A cordon was quickly formed by them around the prisoners as more blows were about to shower from all directions.

It was now raining harder. Once outside the temple ground, there were not even many trees to take shelter under. But men and women in an uninterrupted stream followed closely behind, almost as though they wanted to make sure that not one prisoner would escape.

The prisoners were escorted to the graveyard south of the temple. From the back of the graveyard came the sound of several shots.

The sound shrilly pierced through the thick, moist atmosphere enveloping Huilung *hsiang*. Sighs of relief were heaved as justice was meted out to the convicted.

"Down with the reactionary landlords!"

"Long live the emancipation of the peasants!"

"Long live the Communist Party!"

"Long live Chairman Mao Tse-tung!"

The masses, for the first time freed from their dread and restraints, let out these slogans with a voice stronger than ever. The poisonous shaft that was thrust in their bosom was at last extracted. With the disappearance of fear came the atmosphere of freedom the peasants had never breathed before.

DOCUMENT 25

PROVISIONAL MEASURES FOR THE CONTROL AND REFORM OF LANDLORDS IN THE SOUTH CENTRAL REGION

[Announced by the South Central Military and Administrative Committee in August, 1952.]

1. In accordance with the provisions of Article 7 of the Common Program of the Chinese People's Political Consultative Conference, all landlords defined as such in accordance with the "Decision on the Differentiation of Class Status in the Countryside" of the Government Administration Council of the Central People's Government shall, after the completion of agrarian reform and in accordance with the law, be deprived of their political rights during a necessary period.

2. Among the landlords, those who are basically members of another class but concurrently landlords (not basically landlords who are con-

currently members of another class) , individuals in a landlord family who had been defined as not being landlords, and young students and members of a landlord family who are under eighteen shall not be treated as landlords, except in cases where they participated in the illegal acts of their families and are thus to be dealt with according to law.

3. Under any one of the conditions mentioned below, a landlord, in addition to being dealt with according to law, shall be placed under control:

a) One who carries out a counterattack or counterstruggle after the conclusion of agrarian reform.

b) One who does not participate in reform through labor service, or engage in some other proper vocation, and is thus an idler given to illegal acts.

c) One who was guilty of despotic or counterrevolutionary activities.

d) One who had judgment passed on him according to law by the people's government and the people's tribunal of a higher level, and handed down to the masses for control.

4. Landlords included in the above article shall be subject to control under the following different measures, according to the individual circumstances of their cases:

a) Within a stipulated period, the landlord shall not receive callers or undertake long journeys without express permission.

b) He shall report at fixed intervals to the peasants' association on conditions relating to labor production, and one who is lazy may have compulsory measures applied against him.

c) With the approval of the people's government of the level above the *hsien,* he may be transferred to another *hsien* or province to be placed under the control of the local government and to carry out compulsory reform through labor service.

5. Landlords in *hsiang* who should be placed under control shall be listed, together with the period of control for each, by the peasants' association and presented within stipulated time to the conference of representatives of the people of the *hsiang* for discussion and examination. Control shall be exercised after approval has been obtained from the *hsien* people's government.

A landlord who seriously abides by the laws and regulations of the government during the period of control, and actively undertakes labor service for reform, may, through the same procedure, have his control period shortened or terminated in accordance with the circumstances of his case. But if such a landlord should be guilty of further illegal acts or should fail to undertake labor production, the seriousness of his case may be considered, and his control period extended or other penalties inflicted on him.

6. A landlord who possesses labor power, is capable of engaging in agricultural labor, and does not have another vocation must be supervised and made to undertake reform through labor service. The land distributed to him shall not be laid waste, sold, mortgaged, or leased.

7. A landlord who really lacks labor power or whose labor power is inadequate, after due discussion of his case by the *hsiang* peasants' association, may be permitted to hire labor for cultivation, or permitted to lease a portion or the whole of the land distributed him, in accordance with the laws relating to the reduction of rent.

8. A landlord who is an intellectual or in possession of other technical skills may be permitted to engage in some other proper vocation (he shall not be compelled to undertake agricultural labor). The locality of his vocation shall be reported to the *hsiang* people's government.

9. After he has thoroughly surrendered all property that can be confiscated according to the Agrarian Reform Law and compensated the peasants for their losses according to law, his surplus assets may be invested in agricultural production or industry and commerce, and no further action shall be taken against him. The income from his labor production and investments shall be his own, and shall be protected.

10. A change in the class status of a landlord shall be effected in accordance with the provisions of Section 11, "Certain New Provisions of the Government Administrative Council," in the "Decisions Concerning the Differentiation of Class Status" of the Government Administrative Council of the Central People's Government. This section provides that: "A member of the landlord class who, after the conclusion of agrarian reform, complies fully with the laws and regulations of the government, exerts efforts at labor production or in other enterprises, and remains free from any reactionary activities for five years continuously, may, in accordance with the nature of his labor service or his enterprise, be changed from his status as a member of the landlord class into a member of the laboring or other class, with the approval of a *hsiang* conference of representatives of the people, and ratification of the *hsien* people's government. One who does not conform with the conditions described above shall not have his status altered.

11. The *hsiang* people's government and the *hsiang* peasants' association shall be jointly responsible for the control and reform of landlords. The security committee and the people's militia may be entrusted with the task of enforcing concrete control measures.

DECISIONS ON MUTUAL AID AND COOPERATION IN AGRICULTURAL PRODUCTION ADOPTED BY THE CENTRAL COMMITTEE OF THE COMMUNIST PARTY OF CHINA

[On December 15, 1951, the Central Committee of the Communist Party of China circulated Draft Decisions on mutual aid and cooperation in agricultural production to Party branches at all levels, to be carried out on an experimental basis. On February 15, 1953, these Decisions were partly amended on the basis of the experience gained in the practical work and officially adopted by the Central Committee.]

1. Following the land reform, peasants show their enthusiasm for production in two ways: in individual economy and in mutual aid and cooperation. This enthusiasm of the peasants for production is one of the basic factors in the speedy recovery and development of the national economy and in the promotion of the country's industrialization. Therefore, the Party's correct leadership in rural production is of tremendous significance.

2. After the liberation, the peasants' enthusiasm for production in the field of individual economy was inevitable. The Party fully understands this characteristic of the peasants as small owners, and points out that we must not ignore or brush aside the peasants' enthusiasm for production in this field. In this respect, the Party persists in the policy of firmly uniting with the middle peasant. The rich-peasant economy is allowed to develop. Under the present economic conditions of our country, the peasants' individual economy will exist to a very large extent and for a considerable length of time. As the Common Program adopted by the Chinese People's Political Consultative Conference points out: "All sectors of the social economy shall, under the leadership of the state-owned economy, carry out division and coordination of labor and play their proper parts in promoting the development of the social economy as a whole." Among these sectors is included the individual economy of peasants and handicraftsmen. In addition to the above, the Common Program has the folowing provision: "In all areas where agrarian reform has been carried out, the ownership of the land acquired by the peasants shall be protected."

3. The Central Committee of the Communist Party of China has always maintained that in order to overcome the various difficulties arising from small-scale farming, to enable the broad masses of impov-

erished peasants to increase production and march rapidly on the road to prosperity, to bring to the state more commodity grain and other raw materials for industry than at present and thereby to increase the purchasing power of the peasants and create a wide market for the industrial products of the nation, the principle of "get organized" must be advocated and the peasants' enthusiasm for cooperation and mutual aid encouraged on the basis of voluntariness and mutual benefit. Cooperation and mutual aid at present means collective labor practiced on the basis of an individual economy (private ownership of property by peasants) ; its future is collective and socialist farming. This policy of the Central Committee of the Communist Party of China has been proved as entirely correct over the years. On the basis of the long experience of the people's liberated areas and in accordance with the policy of the Central Committee of the Communist Party of China, the Common Program of the Chinese People's Political Consultative Conference correctly stipulates:

> In all areas where agrarian reform has been thoroughly carried out, the central task of the people's government shall be the organization of the peasants and of all manpower available for allocation to the development of agricultural production and secondary occupations. The people's government shall also guide the peasants step by step in the organization of various forms of mutual aid in labor and cooperation in production, according to the principle of willingness and of mutual benefit.

It is clear that the policy laid down by the Central Committee of the Communist Party of China and the Common Program has in practice educated the peasant masses, gradually enabled them to understand the vast superiority of mutual aid in labor and cooperation in production over the isolated individual economy, and has inspired them to take the road of gradual transition from individual economy to collective economy.

4. The peasants' mutual aid and cooperative movement has followed different roads and taken different forms, according to local economic developments and the demands of production. However, it may be roughly classified into three main types. The first and simplest type, the mutual aid team, is mainly temporary and seasonal. It has been most widely adopted in the old liberated areas right from the beginning to the present time. This type of mutual aid also tallies with the conventional mutual aid practices of the peasants in newly liberated areas and can be developed on an extensive scale. However, it is generally carried out on a small scale. With rare exceptions, it is desirable for this type of mutal aid team to be organized on a small scale.

The second type is the year-round mutual aid team, a form more advanced than the first. Some teams of this type have begun to combine mutual aid in agriculture with that in subsidiary rural occupations. They have adopted some simple production plans and will gradually combine mutual aid in labor with technical improvements and with a certain degree of division of labor. Some have gradually accumulated a certain amount of common property, such as farm implements and cattle. Mutual aid teams of this type are not yet numerous. However, in areas where the simple mutual aid teams are successful —that is, where the broad masses of the peasants have organized to overcome difficulties and have had some success in increasing their output and improving their living standards—the year-round mutual aid team represents the demand of many peasants, and such teams are therefore increasing year by year. Membership of the above-mentioned two types of mutual aid teams makes up 60 per cent of the peasants in north China and 70 per cent in northeast China.

The agricultural producers' cooperative is the third type. Its special characteristic is that the peasants join the cooperative with their land as shares. Such cooperatives thus earn the name of land cooperatives. This type includes some of the main characteristics of the second type, such as the combination of agriculture with subsidiary occupations, a certain amount of planning in production, division of labor, ownership of more or less improved farm implements for common use and other forms of common property, etc., as described above. But these characteristics are more strongly marked than those of the second type. The joint use of some improved and new types of farm implements, the division of labor and assignment of specialized occupations to some extent, and the building of irrigation projects and reclamation of wasteland have led to the demand for the unified employment of the land for production. This kind of agricultural producers' cooperative is nevertheless built on the basis of the private ownership of land. The peasants may join it voluntarily, with their land as shares, for their mutual benefit. They may likewise withdraw from it if they want to. So far as production is concerned, the agricultural producers' cooperative can either make use of the land according to a unified plan and grow such crops as suit the quality of the soil and promise the best yield, or can make better use of the labor power of its members, who work either full-time or half-time, by carrying out the division of labor so as to promote enthusiasm. These two advantages will gradually bring about the elimination of some of the weak points of a small-peasant economy. The land or the subsidiary occupations managed by this third type of agricultural cooperative can generally yield a much larger crop or income than the ordinary, provided that the society is organized according to the voluntariness of the masses and that the management of the society is reasonable. In general, this kind of agricultural cooperative, which the peasants join with their land as shares, can only be organized on the basis of a relatively successful mutual aid movement and is at present an advanced form of the agricultural mutual aid movement. Today, cooperatives of this kind can only be found in a few districts and in small numbers. However, in north China and northeast China, there are over 300 such cooperatives, and their number is increasing.

The three forms of organization mentioned above do not necessarily have distinct lines of demarcation, nor are they developing evenly from one stage to another. There are some special cases where the peasants pool their land as shares shortly after they have been organized. As the local conditions are varied, the masses organize different cooperatives with some or all of the characteristics of the above-mentioned three types. The development of the cooperative movement within different localities also varies greatly. Generally speaking, the mutual aid movement is advancing on a definite and winding road. It would, of course, be wrong and harmful to the development of the mutual aid and cooperative movement to apply abstract formulas mechanically, regardless of the conditions and actual experience of the masses.

DOCUMENT 27

MAO TSE-TUNG ON AGRICULTURAL COOPERATION

[Excerpts from an address by Mao Tse-tung delivered at a Meeting of Secretaries of Provincial, Municipal, and Area Committees of the Communist Party of China on July 31, 1955.]

Throughout the Chinese countryside a new upsurge in the socialist mass movement is in sight. But some of our comrades are tottering along like a woman with bound feet, always complaining that others are going too fast. They imagine that by picking on trifles, grumbling unnecessarily, worrying continuously, and putting up countless taboos and commandments they are guiding the socialist mass movement in the rural areas on sound lines.

No, this is not the right way at all; it is wrong.

The tide of social reform in the countryside—in the shape of cooperation—has already reached some places. Soon it will sweep the whole country. This is a huge socialist revolutionary movement, which involves a rural population more than 500 million strong, one which has very great world significance. We should guide this movement vigorously, warmly, and systematically, not use all sorts of means that drag it back. In such a movement some deviations are inevitable. That stands to reason, but it is not difficult to straighten them out. Weaknesses or mistakes found among cadres and peasants can be done away with if we actively assist them. Guided by the Party the cadres and peasants are going forward; the movement is fundamentally healthy.

In some places they have made certain mistakes in the work, for example, barring poor peasants from the cooperatives and ignoring their difficulties, and at the same time forcing the well-to-do middle peasants into the cooperatives and interfering with their interests. But these errors have to be corrected by education, not just by reprimands. Mere reprimands solve no problems. We must guide the movement boldly, not act like one fearing the dragon ahead and the tiger behind. Both the cadres and peasants will change themselves as they learn from their own experience in the struggle. Get them into action themselves; they will learn while doing, become more capable, and large numbers of excellent people will come forward. This "fearing the dragon ahead and the tiger behind" attitude will not produce cadres. It is necessary to send large groups of cadres with short-term training into the countryside to guide and assist the agricultural cooperative movement; but the cadres sent down from above will also have to learn how to work from the movement itself. Going in for training courses and hearing dozens of rules explained in lectures does not necessarily mean one knows how to work.

In short, the leadership should never lag behind the mass movement. The present situation is precisely one in which the mass movement is moving ahead of the leadership and the leadership is not catching up with it. This position must be changed.

Now, at a time when the nationwide cooperative movement is taking tremendous strides forward, we still have to argue such questions as: Can the cooperatives grow? Can they be consolidated? As far as some comrades are concerned, the crux of the matter seems to be that they are worried about whether the several hundred thousand existing semi-socialist cooperatives—mostly rather small, averaging twenty-odd peasant households each—can be consolidated. Of course, unless they are, growth is out of the question. Some comrades are still unconvinced by the history of the growth of cooperation in the past few years and are still waiting to see how things go in 1955. They may even wait another year, till 1956, and only if still more cooperatives are firmly established by then will they be truly convinced that agricultural co-operation is a possibility and that the policy of the Central Committee of our Party is correct. That is why the work this year and next is so very important.

DOCUMENT 28

RESOLUTION ON THE ESTABLISHMENT OF PEOPLE'S COMMUNES IN THE RURAL AREAS

[Adopted by the Central Committee of the Chinese Communist Party on August 29, 1958.]

1. The people's communes are the logical result of the march of events. Large, comprehensive people's communes have made their appearance, and in several places they are already widespread. They have developed very rapidly in some areas. It is highly probable that there will soon be an upsurge in setting up people's communes throughout the country and the development is irresistible. The basis for the development of the people's communes is mainly the comprehensive, continuous leap forward in China's agricultural production and the ever-rising political consciousness of the 500 million peasants. An unprecedented advance has been made in agricultural capital construction since the advocates of the capitalist road were fundamentally defeated economically, politically, and ideologically. This has created a new basis for practically eliminating flood and drought, and for ensuring the comparatively stable advance of agricultural production. Agriculture has leaped forward since right conservatism has been overcome and the old technical norms in agriculture have been broken down. The output of agricultural products has doubled or increased severalfold—in some cases more than ten times or scores of times. This has further stimulated emancipation of thought among the people. Large-scale agricultural capital construction and the application of more advanced agricultural technique are making their demands on labor power. The growth of rural industry also demands the transfer of some manpower from agriculture. The demand for mechanization and electrification has become increasingly urgent in China's rural areas. Capital construction in agriculture and the struggle for bumper harvests involve large-scale cooperation, cutting across the boundaries between cooperatives, townships, and counties. The people have taken to organizing themselves along military lines, to work with militancy,

and leading a collective life, and this has raised the political consciousness of the 500 million peasants still further. Community dining rooms,
kindergartens, nurseries, tailoring groups, barber shops, public baths,
"happy homes" for the aged, agricultural middle schools, and "red and
expert" schools, are leading the peasants toward a happier collective
life and further fostering ideas of collectivism among the peasant
masses. What all these developments illustrate is that the agricultural
cooperative with scores of families or several hundred families can no
longer meet the needs of the changing situation. In the present circumstances, the establishment of people's communes with all-around management of agriculture, forestry, animal husbandry, side occupations
and fishery, where industry (the worker), agriculture (the peasant),
exchange (the trader), culture and education (the student), and military affairs (the militiaman) merge into one, is the fundamental policy
to guide the peasants to accelerate socialist construction, complete the
building of socialism ahead of time, and carry out the gradual transition to Communism.

2. Concerning the organization and size of the communes: Generally
speaking, it is at present better to establish one commune to a township,
with the commune comprising about 2,000 peasant households. Where
a township embraces a vast area and is sparsely populated, more than
one commune may be established, each with less than 2,000 households.
In some places, several townships may merge and form a single commune comprising about 6,000 or 7,000 households, according to topo-
graphical conditions and the needs for the development of production.
As to the establishment of communes of more than 10,000 or even
more than 20,000 households, we need not oppose them, but for the
present we should not take the initiative to encourage them.

As the people's communes grow, there may be a tendency to form
federations with the county as a unit. Plans should be drawn up right
now on a county basis to ensure the rational distribution of people's
communes.

The size of the communes and the all-around development of agriculture, forestry, animal husbandry, subsidiary production, and fishing
as well as of industry (the worker), agriculture (the peasant), exchange (the trader), culture and education (the student) and military
affairs (the militiaman), demand an appropriate division of labor
within the administrative organs of the communes; a number of departments, each responsible for a particular kind of work, should be
set up. They should be compactly and efficiently organized and cadres
should take a direct part in production. The township governments
and the communes should become one, with the township committee
of the Party becoming the Party committee of the commune, and the

township people's council becoming the administrative committee of the commune.

3. Concerning the methods and steps to be adopted to merge small cooperatives into bigger ones and transform them into people's communes: The merger of small cooperatives into bigger ones and their transformation into people's communes is now a common mass demand. The poor and the lower-middle peasants firmly support it; most upper-middle peasants also favor it. We must rely on the poor and the lower-middle peasants and fully encourage the masses to air their views and argue it out, unite the majority of the upper-middle peasants who favor it, overcome vacillation among the remainder, and expose and foil rumormongering and sabotage by landlord and rich-peasant elements, so that the mass of the peasants merge the smaller cooperatives into bigger ones and transform them into communes through ideological emancipation and on a voluntary basis, without any compulsion. As to the steps to be taken, it is of course better to complete the merger into bigger cooperatives and their transformation into communes at once; but where this is not feasible, it can be done in two stages, with no compulsory or rash steps. In all counties, experiments should first be made in some selected areas and the experience gained should then be popularized gradually.

The merger of smaller cooperatives into bigger ones and their transformation into communes must be carried out in close coodination with current production to ensure not only that it has no adverse effect on current production, but becomes a tremendous force stimulating an even greater leap forward in production. Therefore, in the early period of the merger, the method of "changing the upper structure while keeping the lower structure unchanged" may be adopted. The original, smaller cooperatives may at first jointly elect an administrative committee for the merged co-op to unify planning and the arrangement of work, and transform themselves into farming zones or production brigades. The original organization of production and system of administration may, for the time being, remain unchanged and continue as before; and later, gradually merge, readjust, and settle whatever needs merging or readjusting and whatever specific questions demand solution during the merger, so as to make sure there is no adverse effect on production.

The size of the communes, the speed of carrying out the merger of small cooperatives into bigger ones and their transformation into communes, and the methods and steps to be taken in this connection will be decided in accordance with the local conditions by the various provinces, autonomous regions, and municipalities directly under the central authorities. But no matter when the merger takes place, whether before or after autumn, in the coming winter or next spring, the small cooperatives that are prepared to merge should be brought together from now on to discuss and jointly work out unified plans for winter capital construction in agriculture and to make unified arrangements of all kinds for preparatory work for an even bigger harvest next year.

4. Concerning some questions of the economic policy involved in the merger of cooperatives: In the course of the merger, education should be strengthened to prevent the growth of departmentalism among a few cooperatives, which might otherwise share out too much or all of their income and leave little or no common funds before the merger. On the other hand, it must be understood that with various agricultural cooperatives established on different foundations, the amount of their public property, their indebtedness inside and outside the cooperatives and so on will not be completely equal when they merge into bigger cooperatives. In the course of the merger, the cadres and the masses should be educated in the spirit of Communism so as to recognize these differences and not resort to minute squaring of accounts, insisting on equal shares and bothering with trifles.

When a people's commune is established, it is not necessary to deal with the questions of reserved private plots of land, scattered fruit trees, share funds and so on in a great hurry; nor is it necessary to adopt clear-cut stipulations on these questions. Generally speaking, reserved private plots of land may perhaps be turned over to collective management in the course of the merger of cooperatives; scattered fruit trees, for the time being, may remain privately owned and be dealt with some time later. Share funds, etc., can be handled after a year or two, since the funds will automatically become publicly owned with the development of production, the increase of income, and the advance in the people's consciousness.

5. Concerning the name, ownership, and system of distribution of the communes: All the big merged cooperatives will be called people's communes. There is no need to change them into state-owned farms. It is not proper for farms to embrace industry, agriculture, exchange, culture and education, and military affairs at the same time.

After the establishment of people's communes, there is no need immediately to transform collective ownership into ownership by the people as a whole. It is better at present to maintain collective owner-ship to avoid unnecessary complications arising in the course of the transformation of ownership. In fact, collective ownership in people's communes already contains some elements of ownership by the people as a whole. These elements will grow constantly in the course of the continuous development of people's communes and will gradually replace collective ownership. The transition from collective ownership to ownership by the people as a whole is a process, the completion of which may take less time—three or four years—in some places, and longer—five or six years or even longer—elsewhere. Even with the completion of this transition, people's communes, like state-owned industry, are still socialist in character, where the principle of "from each according to his ability and to each according to his labor" prevails. After a number of years, as the social product increases greatly, the Communist consciousness and morality of the entire people are raised to a much higher degree, and universal education is instituted and developed, the differences between workers and peasants, town and country, and mental and manual labor—legacies of the old society that have inevitably been carried over into the socialist period—and the remnants of unequal bourgeois rights which are the reflection of these differences —will gradually vanish. Then the function of the state will be limited to protecting the country from external aggression but it will play no role internally. At that time Chinese society will enter the era of Communism, when the principle of "from each according to his ability and to each according to his needs" will be practiced.

After the establishment of the people's communes it is not necessary to hurry the change from the original system of distribution, in order to avoid any unfavorable effect on production. The system of distribution should be determined according to specific conditions. Where conditions permit, the shift to a wage system may be made. But where conditions are not yet ripe, the original system of payment according to work days may be temporarily retained (such as the system of fixed targets for output, work days, and costs, with a part of the extra output as reward; or the system of calculating work days on the basis of output). This can be changed when conditions permit.

Although ownership in the people's communes is still collective ownership and the system of distribution, either the wage system or payment according to work days, is "to each according to his work" and not "to each according to his needs," the people's communes are the best form of organization for the attainment of socialism and gradual transition to Communism. They will develop into the basic social units in Communist society.

6. At the present stage our task is to build socialism. The primary purpose of establishing people's communes is to accelerate the speed of socialist construction and the purpose of building socialism is to prepare actively for the transition to Communism. It seems that the attainment of Communism in China is no longer a remote future event. We should actively use the form of the people's communes to explore the practical road of transition to Communism.

DOCUMENT 29

RESOLUTION ON SOME QUESTIONS CONCERNING THE PEOPLE'S COMMUNES

[Excerpts from a resolution adopted by the Eighth Central Committee of the Communist Party of China at its Sixth Plenary Session on December 10, 1958.]

In 1958 a new social organization appeared, fresh as the morning sun, above the broad horizon of east Asia. This was the large-scale people's commune in the rural areas of our country, which combines industry, agriculture, trade, education, and military affairs, and in which government administration and commune management are integrated. Since their first appearance the people's communes with their immense vitality have attracted widespread attention.

The movement to set up people's communes has grown very rapidly. Within a few months, starting in the summer of 1958, all of the more than 740,000 agricultural producers' cooperatives in the country, in response to the enthusiastic demand of the mass of peasants, reorganized themselves into over 26,000 people's communes. Over 120 million households, or more than 99 per cent of all China's peasant households of various nationalities, have joined the people's communes. This shows that the emergence of the people's communes is not fortuitous; it is the outcome of the economic and political development of our country, of the socialist rectification campaign conducted by the Party, of the Party's general line for socialist construction and the Great Leap Forward of socialist construction in 1958.

Although the rural people's communes were established only a short while ago, the mass of the peasants are already conscious of the obvious benefits communes have brought them. Labor power and the means of production can, on a larger scale than before, be managed and deployed in a unified way to ensure that they are used still more rationally and effectively, and consequently to facilitate the development of production. Under the unified leadership of the commune, industry, agriculture (including farming, forestry, animal husbandry, side occupations, and fisheries), trade, education, and military affairs have been closely coordinated and rapidly developed. In particular, thousands and tens of thousands of small factories have mushroomed in the rural areas. To meet the pressing demands of the masses, the communes have set up large numbers of community dining rooms, nurseries, kindergartens, "homes of respect for the aged," and other institutions for collective welfare, which have, in particular, completely emancipated

228

women from thousands of years of kitchen drudgery and brought broad smiles to their faces. As the result of the bumper crops many communes have instituted a system of distribution that combines the wage system with the free supply system; the mass of peasants, both men and women, have begun to receive their wages, and those families which in the past constantly worried about their daily meals and about their firewood, rice, oil, salt, soya sauce, vinegar, and vegetables are now able to "eat without paying." In other words they have the most important and most reliable kind of social insurance. For the peasants, all this is epoch-making news. The living standards of the peasants have been improved, and they know from practical experience and the prospects of the development of the communes that they will live still better in the future.

The development of the system of rural people's communes has an even more profound and far-reaching significance. It has shown the people of our country the way to the gradual industrialization of the rural areas, the way to the gradual transition from collective ownership to ownership by the whole people in agriculture, the way to the gradual transition from the socialist principle of "to each according to his work" to the Communist principle of "to each according to his needs," the way gradually to lessen and finally to eliminate the differences between town and country, between worker and peasant, and between mental and manual labor, and the way gradually to lessen and finally to eliminate the internal function of the state.

All this has proved the correctness and historic significance of the Resolution on the Establishment of People's Communes in the Rural Areas adopted on the basis of the creativity of the masses by the Political Bureau of the Central Committee of the Chinese Communist Party at its Peitaiho meeting in August, 1958.

People's communes have now become the general rule in all rural areas inhabited by our people of various nationalities (except in Tibet and in certain other areas). Some experiments have also begun in the cities. In the future, urban people's communes, in a form suited to the specific features of cities, will also become instruments for the transformation of old cities and the construction of new socialist cities; they will become the unified organizers of production, exchange, and distribution, and of the livelihood and well-being of the people; they will become social organizations which combine industry, agriculture, trade, education, and military affairs, organizations in which government administration and commune management are integrated. There are, however, certain differences between the city and the countryside.

First, city conditions are more complex than those in the countryside.

Second, socialist ownership by the whole people is already the main form of ownership in the cities, and the factories, public institutions, and schools, under the leadership of the working class, have already become highly organized in accordance with socialist principles (with the exception of some of the family members of the workers and staffs). Therefore, the switchover of cities to people's communes inevitably involves some requirements different from those in the rural areas.

Third, bourgeois ideology is still fairly prevalent among many of the capitalists and intellectuals in the cities; they still have misgivings about the establishment of communes—so we should wait a bit for them.

Consequently, we should continue to make experiments and generally should not be in a hurry to set up people's communes on a large scale in the cities. Particularly in the big cities, this work, except for the necessary preparatory measures, should be postponed. People's communes should be established on a large scale in the cities only after rich experience has been gained and when the sceptics and doubters have been convinced.

The rural people's communes that have already been established have not had time to consolidate their organizations, perfect their working systems, or systematically settle the new questions concerning production, distribution, livelihood and welfare, and management and administration that have arisen with the establishment of the communes. This is because the communes were only recently set up and most of them, immediately after their establishment, threw themselves into the heavy work of the autumn harvest, ploughing and sowing, and the nationwide campaign for iron and steel. There is as yet insufficient experience in successfully running and developing the people's communes. Different approaches to certain questions are unavoidable. The urgent tasks at present are to quickly achieve a unity of views on the communes among all members of the Party and among the people, strengthen the leadership over the communes, check up on and consolidate their organization, define and perfect their working systems, and improve the organization of production and life in the communes. Energetic efforts must be made to strengthen those communes which have already been set up so that they will be in a position to carry out ever more successfully their great mission of promoting the development of the productive forces and the relations of production.

The people's commune is the basic unit of the socialist social structure of our country, combining industry, agriculture, trade, education, and military affairs; at the same time it is the basic organization of the socialist state power. Marxist-Leninist theory and the initial experience of the people's communes in our country enable us to foresee that the people's communes will quicken the tempo of our socialist construction and constitute the best form for realizing, in our country, the transition from collective ownership to ownership by the whole people in the countryside, and the transition from socialist to Communist society. It can also be foreseen that in the future Communist society, the people's commune will remain the basic unit of our social structure.

From now on, the task confronting the people of our country is, through such a form of social organization as the people's commune, and based on the general line for socialist construction laid down by the Party, to develop the social productive forces at high speed; to advance the industrialization of the country, the industrialization of the communes, and the mechanization and electrification of agriculture; and to effect the gradual transition from socialist collective ownership to socialist ownership by the whole people, thus fully realizing ownership by the whole people in the socialist economy of our country and gradually building our country into a great socialist land with a highly developed modern industry, agriculture, science, and culture. During this process, the elements of Communism are bound to increase gradually, and these will lay the foundation of material and spiritual conditions for the transition from socialism to Communism.

This is a gigantic and extremely complex task. In the light of experience already gained, as the concrete conditions now stand in our country, it is possible that socialist ownership by the whole people may be fully realized at a somewhat earlier date than originally expected, but this will not be very soon. Though the pace at which we are advancing is fairly rapid, it will still take a fairly long time to realize, on a large scale, the industrialization of our country, the industrialization of the communes, the mechanization and electrification of agriculture, and the building of a socialist country with a highly developed modern industry, agriculture, science, and culture. This whole process will still take fifteen, twenty or more years to complete.

It should be pointed out that the switch from agricultural producers' cooperatives to people's communes, the transition from socialist collective ownership to socialist ownership by the whole people, and the transition from socialism to Communism are processes which are interrelated but at the same time distinct from each other.

First of all, the switch from the agricultural producers' cooperatives to the people's communes has expanded and strengthened the existing collective ownership and contains certain elements of ownership by the whole people. But this is not to say that collective ownership in the countryside has been transformed into ownership by the whole people. The whole Chinese countryside has now switched over to people's communes, but a certain time will have to pass before ownership by the whole people is realized throughout the countryside.

True, the establishment of the people's communes has added certain elements of ownership by the whole people to the collectively owned economy. This is because the rural people's communes and the basic organizations of state power have been combined into one; because the banks, stores, and some other enterprises owned by the whole people, originally existing in the countryside, have been placed under the management of the communes; because the communes have taken part in establishing certain undertakings in industrial and other construction which are by nature owned by the whole people; because in many counties the county federations of communes, exercising unified leadership over all the people's communes in these counties, have been formed and have the power to deploy a certain portion of the manpower and material and financial resources of the communes to undertake construction on a county or even bigger scale (this has already started in many areas) ; and so on. But at the present time the means of production and the products of the rural people's communes are in the main still collectively owned by the communes and differ from those of the state-owned enterprises which belong to the whole people. Both collective ownership and ownership by the whole people are socialist ownership; but the latter is more advanced than the former because the state, representing the whole people, can directly make a unified and rational distribution of the means of production and the products of enterprises owned by the whole people, according to the requirements of the national economy, while this cannot be done by enterprises run under collective ownership including the existing rural people's communes. To say that ownership by the people's communes as they now exist in the countryside is already ownership by the whole people does not conform to reality.

To gradually promote the transition from collective ownership to ownership by the whole people, every county should set up its federation of communes. In coming years, and on the basis of the energetic development of production and the raising of the people's political understanding, such federations should take suitable steps gradually to increase the proportion of their means of production that is owned by the whole people and the proportion of their products that is subject to unified distribution by the state, and, when conditions are ripe, should change collective ownership into ownership by the whole people. If timely steps are not taken to promote and complete this change and if the existing collective ownership is kept intact indefinitely, restricting the attention of commune members to the relatively narrow scope of the interests of their collective, the continuous development of the social productive forces and the continuous raising of the people's political understanding will be impeded. This is not appropriate. However, it must be pointed out that collective ownership still plays a positive role today in developing production in the people's communes. How soon the transition from collective ownership to ownership by the whole people will be effected will be determined by the objective factors—the level of development of production and the level of the people's political understanding—and not by mere wishful thinking that it can be done at any time we want it. Thus this transition will be realized, by stages and by groups, on a national scale only after a considerable time. Those who, because they fail to understand this, confuse the establishment of people's communes with the realization of ownership by the whole people, making impetuous attempts to abolish collective ownership in the countryside prematurely, and trying hastily to change over to ownership by the whole people, will not be doing the right thing and therefore cannot succeed.

Furthermore, the change from socialist collective ownership to socialist ownership by the whole people is not the same thing as the transition from socialism to Communism. Still less is the change from agricultural producers' cooperatives to people's communes the same thing as the change from socialism to Communism. The change from socialism to Communism will require much more time than the change from socialist collective ownership to socialist ownership by the whole people.

True, the free supply system adopted by the people's communes contains the first shoots of the Communst principle of "to each according to his needs"; the policy carried out by the people's communes of running industry and agriculture simultaneously and combining them has opened up a way to reduce the differences between town and countryside and between worker and peasant, and when the rural people's communes pass over from socialist collective ownership to socialist ownership by the whole people, these Communist factors will grow further. All this must be acknowledged. Moreover, with social products becoming plentiful, thanks to the continuous advance of industry and agriculture throughout the country; with the proportion of what is supplied gratis under the distribution system of the people's communes gradually growing larger and the standards of free supply being gradually raised; with the consistent raising of the level of the people's political understanding; with the constant progress of education for the whole people, the gradual reduction of the differences between mental and manual labor, and the gradual diminution of the internal function of the state power, etc., the conditions for the transition to Communism will also gradually mature. It is of course not proper to ignore or even impede this course of development and relegate Communism to the distant future.

Nevertheless every Marxist must soberly realize that the transition from socialism to Communism is a fairly long and complicated process of development and that throughout this entire process society is still socialist in nature. Socialist society and Communist society are two stages marked by different degrees of economic development. The socialist principle is "from each according to his ability and to each according to his work"; the Communist principle is "from each according to his ability and to each according to his needs." The Communist system of distribution is more rational; but it can be put into effect only when there is a great abundance of social products. In the absence of this condition, any negation of the principle of "to each according to his work" will tend to dampen the working enthusiasm of the people and is therefore disadvantageous to the development of production and the increase of social products, and hence to speeding the realization of Communism. For this reason, in the income of commune members, the portion constituting the wage paid according to work done must occupy an important place over a long period and will, during a certain period, take first place. In order to encourage the working enthusiasm of commune members and also to facilitate the satisfaction of their complex daily needs, the communes must strive gradually to increase the wages of their members and, for a number of years to come, must increase them at a rate faster than that portion of their income which comes under the heading of free supply. Even after the transition from collective ownership to ownership by the whole people, the people's communes will, during a necessary historical period, retain the system of "to each according to his work" owing to the fact that there is not as yet an abundant enough supply of social products to realize Communism. Any premature attempt to negate the principle of "to each according to his work" and replace it with the principle of "to each according to his needs"—that is, any attempt to enter Communism by overreaching ourselves when conditions are not mature—is undoubtedly a Utopian concept that cannot possibly succeed.

On the question of transition from socialism to Communism, we must not mark time at the socialist stage, but neither should we drop into the Utopian dream of skipping the socialist stage and jumping over to the Communist stage. We are advocates of the Marxist-Leninist theory of uninterrupted revolution; we hold that no "Great Wall" exists or can be allowed to exist between the democratic revolution and the socialist revolution and between socialism and Communism. We are at the same time advocates of the Marxist-Leninist theory of the development of revolution by stages; we hold that different stages of development reflect qualitative changes and that these stages, different in quality, should not be confused.

People's communes must go in for industry in a big way. The development of industry by the people's communes will not only accelerate the industrialization of the whole country, but also promote the realization of ownership by the whole people in the rural districts, and reduce the differences between town and country. According to the differing conditions in each people's commune, an appropriate part of the labor force should be transferred, step by step, from agriculture to industry so as to develop, according to plan, the production of fertilizer, insecticides, farm implements and machinery, and building materials; the processing and many-sided utilization of agricultural produce; the manufacturing of sugar, textiles, and paper; and the expansion of mining, metallurgy, electric power, and other light and heavy industries. Industrial production in the people's communes must be closely linked with agricultural production; it should first of all serve the development of agriculture and the mechanization and electrification of farming; at the same time it should serve to meet the demands of commune members for staple consumer goods, and serve the country's big industries and the socialist market. The principles of adaptation to local conditions and obtaining raw materials locally should be fully taken into consideration; in order to avoid increased costs and waste of labor power, industries should not be set up in places where there are no raw materials or where these have to be brought from very far away. With regard to production techniques, the principle should be carried out of linking handicraft with mechanized industry, and indigenous methods with modern methods of production. All handicraft industries which have good foundations and prospects for expansion must continue to be developed, and gradually carry through the necessary technical transformations. The mechanized industries must also make full use of indigenous methods and iron, steel, machine tools, other raw materials and equipment produced by indigenous methods; they will gradually advance from indigenous to modern, from small to large, and from a low to a high level.

Whether in industry or agriculture, people's communes should develop production for their own use which directly meets their own needs, and they should also develop commodity production on as wide a scale as possible. Every people's commune, according to its own characteristics and under the guidance of the state, should carry out necessary division of labor in production and exchange of commodities with other people's communes and state-owned enterprises. Only in this way can the economy of our whole society expand at a faster rate, and every commune get through exchange the machinery and equipment required for the mechanization and electrification of farming, as well as the consumer goods and ready cash required to meet the needs of commune members and pay them wages, thus making it possible to raise wages gradually. To ensure fulfillment of trading plans, an extensive system of contracts should be set up between the state and the communes and among the communes themselves.

It must be stressed that during the course of a necessary historical period, commodity production by the people's communes and the exchange of commodities between the state and communes and among the communes themselves must be greatly developed. Such production and exhange of commodities are different from those under capitalism, because they are conducted in a planned way on the basis of socialist public ownership, and not in an anarchic way on the basis of capitalist private ownership. Continued development of commodity production and continued adherence to the principle of "to each according to his work" are two important principles in expanding the socialist economy. The whole Party should have a uniform understanding of them. Some people, attempting to "enter Communism" prematurely, have tried to abolish the production and exchange of commodies too early, and to negate at too early a stage the positive roles of commodities, value, money, and prices. This line of thinking is harmful to the development of socialist construction and is therefore incorrect.

Communes must ensure the successful running of primary and secondary schools and adult education. Universal primary school education should be instituted in the rural areas throughout the country. Full-time secondary schools and half-time secondary agricultural schools, or other secondary vocational schools, should be well run and universal secondary education should be introduced step by step. Earnest efforts should be made to wipe out illiteracy, organize various kinds of spare-time schools, and conduct political education, cultural classes, and technical education for adults. In reducing the differences between manual and mental labor, the institution of universal education among the working people and the gradual raising of their educational level is an important step which must be carried out conscientiously. The communes, in addition, must also select and send a number of young people to study in senior secondary schools, secondary vocational schools, and institutions of higher learning in the cities, so as to train fairly well-educated working personnel for the state and the communes. The principle of combining education with productive labor must be carried out thoroughly in all schools, without exception. Children above the age of nine may take part in some labor to an appropriate extent so as to cultivate the habit of work in childhood and stimulate their physical and mental development; but full attention must be paid to the health of the children, they must only be given light work for short periods of time, suited to their physical strength and their aptitude.

Ideological and political work among the staffs in community dining rooms, nurseries, kindergartens, "homes of respect for the aged," primary schools, public health centers, clubs, and shops must be strengthened. Efforts must be made to give positive guidance to public opinion so that the whole of society and the whole communes regard the successful running of community dining rooms, nurseries, kindergartens, and other collective welfare undertakings and satisfactory work in the personal services as noble work of service to the people. The attitude of the exploiting classes in looking down on work which concerns the daily life and welfare of the masses and work in the personal services must be criticized and corrected.

The existing old-style houses must be reconstructed step by step; townships and village housing estates with parks and woods must be built by stages and in groups; these will include residential quarters, community dining rooms, nurseries, kindergartens, the "homes of respect for the aged," factories, threshing floors, livestock sheds, shops, post and telecommunications offices, warehouses, schools, hospitals, clubs, cinemas, sports grounds, baths, and public lavatories. The construction plans of townships, and village housing estates should be thoroughly discussed by the masses. We stand for the abolition of the irrational patriarchal system inherited from the past and for the development of family life in which there is democracy and unity. This stand has been warmly received by the masses. Therefore, in building residential quarters, attention must be paid to building the houses so that the married couples, the young and the aged of each family can all live together.

The organizational principle of the people's commune is democratic centralism. This principle must be applied in the management of production, in the distribution of income, in the livelihood and welfare of commune members, and in all other aspects of work.

Unified leadership and management at different levels should be put into effect in the people's commune. The administrative set-up of the commune in general can be divided into three levels, namely: the commune administrative committee, the administrative district (or production brigade), and the production team. The administrative district (or production brigade) is in general the unit which manages industry, agriculture, trade, education, and military affairs in a given area and forms an economic accounting unit, with its gains and losses pooled in the commune as a whole. The production team is the basic unit of labor organization. Under the unified leadership of the commune administrative committee, the necessary powers should be given to the administrative district (or production brigade) and the production team over such matters as the organization of production work, capital construction, and finances and welfare, in order to bring their initiative into full play.

The various levels of organizations of the county federation of communes and of the people's commune must learn to make reasonable distributions and deployments of manpower for the different branches of production (agriculture, industry, transport) and for routine production work, shock production tasks, and service work, so as to avoid situations where there is work without men in one place and there are men without work in another. The organization of labor must be constantly improved, the system of responsibility for a given task at a given level must continue to be applied and reinforced in production and other tasks, and the system of labor inspection and labor awards must be perfected in order to guarantee effectively the steady improvement of labor efficiency and the quality of work.

There must be both discipline and democracy in the organization of labor in the people's commune. What we described as getting organized along military lines means getting organized on the pattern of a factory. It means that the organization of labor in the people's commune should be as organized and disciplined as in a factory or the army; this is necessary in large-scale agricultural production. The forces of large-scale agricultural production, like the forces of large-scale industrial production, constitute an industrial army. The modern industrial army was organized by the bourgeoisie, each factory being like a military camp. The discipline for the worker standing before the machine is as rigid as that in the army. The industrial army in socialist society is an industrial army of a single class, the working class, which has got rid of the capitalists who squeezed surplus value out of the workers and which has put into force in the working class a vigorous and lively democratic centralism based on the voluntary principle. We are now applying this system to the rural areas, thus establishing a socialist industrial army for agriculture based on democratic centralism, which is free from exploitation by the landlords and rich peasants and is elevated above the level of small-scale production.

Militia groups should be set up at corresponding levels of the production organizations in the people's commune. The leading bodies of the militia and production organizations should be separate and, in principle, the commanding officers of the various levels of the militia such as regimental, battalion, and company commanders, should not be concurrently directors of communes and administrative districts (leaders of production brigades) or leaders of production teams. These commanders should take part in the administrative organizations of the same levels in the commune as their members, and they will receive dual leadership: from the administrative organizations of the same level and the superior commanding organizations of the militia. The militia should be equipped with the necessary arms produced by arsenals set up locally. The basic units of the militia should undergo military training according to a set schedule, while the ordinary militiamen should also get appropriate training after work; this is to prepare conditions for turning the whole nation into soldiers. The broad mass of working people in our country greet the militia system warmly, because, in the course of their protracted revolutionary struggle against imperialism and feudalism, and their running dogs, the Kuomintang reactionaries, they came to realize that only by arming themselves would they be able to overcome the armed counterrevolution and become masters of China. After the victory of the revolution, they have come to see further that there are still imperialist pirates abroad who are clamoring every day about wiping out this people's state. Therefore, the whole of our people are determined to continue to arm themselves, and they declare: Be warned, you pirates bent on plundering us; do not dare to make a vain attempt to harm our people engaged in peaceful labor; we are fully prepared! Should the imperialists dare to unleash an aggressive war against our country, then we will turn the whole nation into soldiers; the militia will cooperate with the People's Liberation Army and at any time replenish it to crush the aggressors utterly.

In running a people's commune well the fundamental question is to strengthen the leading role of the Party. It is only by strengthening the Party's leading role that the principle of "politics in command" can be realized, that socialist and Communist ideological education among the cadres and commune members and the struggle against all kinds of erroneous tendencies can be conducted in a thoroughgoing way, and that the Party's line and policy can be implemented correctly. There are some people who think that with the emergence of the commune the Party can be dispensed with, and that they can practice what they call "merging the Party and commune in one." This kind of thinking is wrong.

DOCUMENT 30

TENTATIVE REGULATIONS (DRAFT) OF THE WEIHSING (SPUTNIK) PEOPLE'S COMMUNE

[Published in *Jen Min Jih Pao* (People's Daily), September 4, 1958.]

(*Jen Min Jih Pao* Editor's Note: The Weihsing (Sputnik) People's Commune in Suiping County, Honan Province, was established in April of this year by the merger of twenty-seven agricultural producers' cooperatives of four townships. It has 9,300 households comprising 43,000 people.

These draft regulations stipulate ownership of the means of production in the commune, its economic, cultural, military, and political tasks, its system of distribution, organizational structure, system of management, and service amenities. They are published in full as reference material for all other parts of the country.)

Article 1. The people's commune is a basic unit of society in which the working people unite of their own free will under the leadership of the Communist Party and the people's government. Its task is to manage all industrial and agricultural production, trade, cultural and educational work, and political affairs within its own sphere.

Article 2. The intent and purpose of the people's commune is to consolidate the socialist system and energetically create the conditions for the gradual transition to the Communist system.

To this end, we must exert our utmost effort and press ahead consistently to achieve greater, faster, better, and more economical results in developing industry, agriculture, and cultural and educational work, to carry through the technical and cultural revolutions, and to gradually reduce the differences between town and country and between mental and manual labor.

As the social products become abundant and the people have high political consciousness, so will the transition from the principle of "from each according to his ability, to each according to his work" to the principle of "from each according to his ability, to each according to his needs" be gradually effected.

Article 3. Citizens who are over sixteen years old are admitted as full members. Former landlords, rich peasants, counterrevolutionaries, and other people deprived of political rights may be accepted as unofficial members and, when granted political rights according to law, may be accepted as full members.

All members have the duty to carry out the commune's regulations

240

and resolutions, observe labor discipline, and cherish and protect public property. Excepting mental defectives, full members have the right to elect, to be elected, to vote, and to supervise the commune's affairs. Unofficial members do not have the right to elect, to be elected, or to vote in the commune, but they may enjoy the same economic treatment as full members.

Article 4. When the agricultural producers' cooperatives merge into the people's commune, they must, regardless of excess or deficiency, turn over all their collectively owned property to the commune in the Communist spirit of widespread coordination. Their former debts shall be paid off by the commune, excluding those for use in that year's production expenses, which should be settled by the cooperatives themselves. The share funds contributed by the cooperative members remain registered under their respective names, and bear no interest. Investments made by the cooperative members will be repaid by the commune.

Those who are accepted as commune members, having reached the age of sixteen, or after moving in from other parts of the country, need not make good the contribution of share funds. When a commune member moves away or dies, his share funds shall not be withdrawn.

Article 5. In changing over to the commune, the members of the cooperatives must turn over to the common ownership of the commune all privately owned plots of farmland, house sites, and other means of production, such as livestock, tree holdings, etc., on the basis that common ownership of the means of production is generally in effect. However, the cooperative members may keep a small number of domestic animals and fowls as private property. Privately owned livestock and tree holdings, when turned over to the common ownership of the commune, should be evaluated and counted as the private investment of the cooperative members.

In applying for membership, the peasant households who work on their own should turn over to the common ownership of the commune all their means of production such as land, livestock, tree holdings, large farm tools, etc., with the exception of a small number of domestic animals and fowls. These means of production should be evaluated as share fund payments in accordance with the provisions of the former cooperatives, and the balance will then be regarded as investment by the owners concerned.

Article 6. To ensure a continuously expanding agricultural output the commune must continue to build irrigation works, apply more manure, improve the soil, use good strains of seed over large areas, breed draft animals, prevent and control insect pests and plant diseases, apply rational close planting and practice deep plowing and careful cultivation. It must make vigorous efforts to improve farm implements and carry into effect the mechanization of agriculture and the electrification of the countryside in the shortest possible time.

The commune must develop industry as rapidly as possible. The first things to be done in this field are to set up mines, iron and steel plants, and factories for manufacturing ball bearings, farm tools, fertilizer, and building materials and for processing farm produce, repairing machinery, building hydroelectric power projects, installations for utilizing methane, and other enterprises.

The commune must, in a planned manner, build roads, dredge waterways, improve the means of communications, install telephone service, and gradually build up a network of modern communications. Each production contingent must have one or two postmen to serve the commune members. The postmen shall be paid by the commune.

Article 7. The commune shall establish a supply and marketing department. The supply and marketing department is a basic organ of state trade. It receives funds from the higher state trading organs; its staff shall be paid by the commune. It shall deliver profits to the higher state trading organs, but the commune may retain a certain proportion of the profits. The commune must ensure that the supply and marketing department fulfill the tasks of state purchase and unified purchase and implement the plan and system of the higher state trading organs, while at the same time the commune has the right to give concrete leadership over the business of the supply and marketing department.

The supply and marketing department should set up its branches in all production contingents, and retail departments in the community canteens of the production brigades which, so as to be convenient for the masses, are to render services at the dining hours. The supply and marketing branches shall keep their own accounts, while their gains and losses shall be managed by the supply and marketing department under a unified system. The funds of the supply and marketing branches shall be provided with the share funds contributed to the former supply and marketing cooperative by the members. The deficit shall be made up by the supply and marketing department. No dividends shall be given on the shares.

The supply and marketing department joins the county supply and marketing cooperative as a member organization.

Article 8 The commune shall establish a credit department. The credit department is an agency of the People's Bank. It receives funds from the People's Bank; its staff shall be paid by the commune. It shall deliver profits to the People's Bank, but the commune may retain a certain proportion of the profits. The commune must ensure that the credit department implement the plan and system of the People's Bank, while at the same time the commune has the right to give concrete leadership to the business of the credit department.

For the convenience of the people, the credit department should set up its branches in all production contingents and service centers in all production brigades. The credit branches shall keep their own accounts, while their gains and losses shall be managed by the credit department under a unified system. The funds of the credit branches shall be provided with the share funds contributed to the former credit cooperative by the members. The deficit shall be made up by the credit department.

As a cash treasury of the commune and the different production contingents, the credit department and its branches shall undertake the receipts and disbursement of cash in bulk. The credit department shall undertake book settlement between the commune and other financial departments, and between the various departments in the commune which keep their own accounts. Book settlement is not to be practiced among the commune members.

Article 9. The commune should, step by step, train its members to be cultured working people with professional skill and all-around qualifications.

The commune should institute a system of universal, compulsory education combined closely with labor. Primary schools and spare-time continuation schools should be set up on a wide scale so that by degrees all school-age children may attend school and all young people and the middle-aged may reach the educational level of senior primary school. Measures should be taken to ensure that step by step each production contingent will have a spare-time agricultural middle school to enable all young people and the middle-aged to attain the educational level of senior middle school. Conditions permitting, colleges or universities will be set up to meet the requirements of the commune. The working hours of the members may be duly reduced and their time for study increased when production reaches a higher level.

The commune should encourage and help its members to engage in scientific studies on a wide scale—first of all, studies and experiments in seed cultivation, soil improvement, tree planting, livestock breeding, elimination of insect pests and plant diseases, and the improvement of farming technique and tools.

Article 10. A system of citizen militia shall operate throughout the commune. Young and middle-aged men as well as demobilized servicemen should be organized into militia units that will undertake regular military training and fulfill tasks assigned by the state. The militiamen will be paid the usual wages when they undergo training and carry out tasks.

The commune shall undertake responsibility for compulsory military service and assign work to demobilized servicemen. Families of revolutionary martyrs, of disabled army men and of army men in active service that lack manpower should, to an appropriate extent, be given special consideration by the commune.

Article 11. As the commune has the same confines as a township, that is, one commune to a township, the township should be merged with the commune for the convenience of work. The deputies of the township people's congress will be concurrently representatives of the congress of the commune, members of the township people's council will be concurrently members of the management committee of the commune, the township head will be concurrently the head of the commune, the deputy heads of the township will be concurrently deputy heads of the commune, and the departments under the commune management committee will be concurrently the departments under the township people's council.

Article 12. The highest organization of management in the commune is the congress of the commune, which will discuss and reach decisions on all important matters of the commune. The congress of the commune shall include representatives of all production brigades and all sections of the people, such as the women, youth, old people, cultural and educational workers, medical workers, scientific and technical workers, the personnel of industrial enterprises, traders, and minority people.

The management committee shall be elected by the congress of the commune to take charge of the commune's affairs. It shall be composed of the head and deputy heads of the commune and committee members. Under it there shall be departments and commissions in charge of different jobs such as agriculture, water conservation, forestry, animal husbandry, industry, communications, finance, food supply, trade, cultural and educational work, armed defense, planning and scientific research, etc. The staff of the departments and commissions shall be nominated by the management committee and be subject to the approval of the congress of the commune. The management committee may elect a group of standing members to handle its routine work.

A supervisory committee shall be elected by the commune congress to supervise the commune's affairs. It shall be composed of the chairman and vice-chairmen of the committee and committee members, and operates under the leadership of the state supervisory organs.

The term of office for the members of the commune's congress, its management committee, and its supervisory committee shall be two years. Anyone seriously neglecting his duties may be dismissed by the electorate before the term of office expires.

Article 13. The commune shall institute a system of centralized leadership, with management organs at various levels, in order to operate a responsibility system in production. In accordance with the principle of facilitating production and leadership, the commune shall organize its members into a number of production contingents which will divide up into a number of production brigades. The production contingent is a unit responsible for production and business accounting; its profits and losses are managed by the commune under a unified system. The production brigade is a basic unit for organizing labor. While ensuring the fulfillment of the general plan of the commune, the production contingent has, to a limited degree, the discretion of organizing production, undertaking capital construction, handling production expenses, and distributing awards. The commune and production contingents should give an appropriate award to those production contingents or brigades that have overfulfilled the planned production targets or economized production expenses. When agricultural mechanization is introduced, tractor teams should be organized with the production contingent as a unit. Bigger factories, mines, timber yards, and livestock farms shall be run directly by the commune, while the smaller ones may be left under the care of the contingents. Small machines and equipment such as sewing machines, methane pools, and equipment for making granular fertilizer may be entrusted to the production brigades.

The production contingent shall have a representative conference, composed of the contingent's deputies to the commune congress. The conference shall elect a contingent leader, deputy leaders, and a number of members to form the management committee of the contingent, and a chairman, vice-chairmen, and a number of members to form a supervisory committee. The term of office for the members of these bodies shall be one year.

The general meeting of the members of the production brigade shall elect a brigade leader and deputy leaders to form a committee to lead the brigade's work.

Article 14. The commune shall establish a wage system when it acquires stability of income and adequate funds and when the members are able voluntarily to consolidate labor discipline. Wages of members will be fixed by the masses through discussion, taking into account the intensity and complexity of the work, physical conditions, and technique and attitude towards work. Wages will be paid monthly. Technical allowances may be paid to those who have special skill. One month's wage may differ from another. In months when the commune gets more income and the members need more, the members may get more pay; in other months they may get less. In case of a serious natural calamity the commune may, according to circumstances, pay less to its members.

After the institution of the wage system, there must be periodic reviews and comparisons of work done by the various units and individuals. Those who work energetically and do well should be rewarded, while those who work in a slovenly way and fail to carry out their assignments may be penalized through deductions from their wages. Awards distributed in the commune in a year may amount to a maximum of one-fourth of the total basic wages. The awards are divided into three parts, in charge of the commune, the production contingents, and brigades, respectively. Assignment of work and reviews and comparisons of work done should be on the basis of the average advanced quota.

With the introduction of the wage system, deduction from his wage should be effected when a member absents himself from work. Every member may have two days' paid leave each month and women members three days' paid leave. Women members may have a month's maternity leave during which time they will be paid half wages. Anyone injured in the course of work will be paid full wages during the period of treatment and recovery. Subsidies will be given out of the public welfare funds to anyone whose livelihood is affected by disability due to chronic disease.

Until conditions are mature for the institution of the wage system, the system of piece-work wages may be introduced, with a fixed value calculated per work day. The members may be paid monthly, in part or in full, according to the number of work days done.

The commune should take energetic measures to trim and simplify its administrative departments. The total wages of its administrative personnel should not exceed 1 per cent of the total wages of the members. Meetings should be short and few; they should take a minimum of work hours.

Article 15. A grain supply system should be operated when grain production reaches a higher level and all the members of the commune agree to it. All members as well as each person of their families will then be supplied with grain gratis in accordance with standards laid down by the state, irrespective of how many of the family can work. The institution of the grain supply system should ensure that families with more labor power get more income than before.

To reform those who work in a slovenly way and, despite repeated persuasion, persist in their mistakes, the commune may, with the discussion and approval of its members, exercise supervision over them in work.

Article 16. The principle "from each according to his ability" constitutes the basis for instituting the wage system and the grain supply system. All members shall voluntarily abide by the following disciplinary rules: Take an active part in labor; cherish and protect public property; ensure the quality of work; obey orders and transference; and voluntarily coordinate with one another.

The commune must strengthen political work and education in Communist ideas and, relying on the activists among the poor and lower-middle peasants, initiate Communist labor emulation campaigns, reviews, and comparisons, so that the principle "from each according to his ability" will gradually be executed by members of their own accord.

Article 17. The commune shall set up community canteens, nurseries, and sewing teams to free women from household labor. To facilitate management, these canteens and nurseries shall in general be set up under each production brigade. Members need not use the canteen or nursery services if they do not want to. Those who use the canteen services may have dishes prepared by themselves. The staff of the canteens, nurseries, and sewing teams shall be paid wages and supplied by the commune. The charges for the services they render to the members shall be paid in accordance with the principle of "no losses and no profits." The community canteens should keep kitchen gardens and raise pigs and chickens so as to consistently improve their food supply.

Article 18. The commune will gradually set up and improve the work of medical establishments so that eventually the commune will have a central hospital with in-patient wards for serious cases. Every contingent will have its own clinic for out-patients and every production brigade its own health officer and midwife for the prevention of illness and the care of patients. Sanatoria will be set up when conditions permit.

Medical care shall be given in the commune on a cooperative basis. Members will pay a yearly amount in accordance with the number in the family. No other fees will be charged for any benefits they get from the medical establishments. In exceptionally serious cases beyond the capacity of the central hospital, patients will be sent to the appropriate hospitals for cure, and traveling and medical expenses shall be paid by the central hospital. But this shall not apply, for the time being, to the cases arising from chronic diseases or diseases due to old age. The commune shall provide free medical care when the economic situation allows.

Article 19. The commune shall make necessary arrangements concerning production and living conditions for the aged, the bereft, the disabled members, and people in bad health who have little or no ability to work and nobody to depend on, so that they can be ensured the means of living. It shall set up "happy homes" for the aged who have no children, help them take part in work within the limit of their physical strength, and provide them with necessary supplies so that they can have a happy old age.

Public cemeteries shall be established by the commune. The graves may be removed, with the approval of the family concerned, as required by production and construction.

Article 20. To gradually improve the housing conditions of its members, the commune shall draw up and gradually carry out comprehensive, long-term plans for the laying out of residential quarters and the building of housing estates. In accordance with the principle of facilitating production and leadership, smaller residential quarters may, gradually and in a proper way, be merged into bigger ones.

Material and manpower needed for the building of new houses under the plan shall be supplied by the commune. Existing houses of the members of the commune shall gradually be dismantled and the bricks, tiles, and timber used by the commune as needed. Newly built houses will belong to the commune. Their occupants shall pay rents equivalent to the cost of maintenance and repair.

Article 21. The commune shall encourage cultural, recreational, and sports activities among the masses so as to bring forward Communist people healthy in body and in mind. Steps should be taken to ensure that each commune has its own library, theater, and film projector teams; that each production contingent has its own club room, amateur theatrical troupe, choir, and sports team; and that each production brigade has a small reading room and radio sets.

Article 22. The yearly income of the commune shall be distributed under the following heads: production costs incurred for the current year; depreciation of public property; state taxes; grain supply for members of the commune; basic wages and awards for members of the commune; public welfare funds, in general not exceeding 5 per cent of the total income, to be spent on education, health facilities, culture, and other welfare services; and reserve funds, comprising the remainder of the income, to be used for stockpiling and expanding production (including the construction of transport facilities). The commune should gradually build up grain stocks sufficient for one to two years, and necessary wage funds.

The distribution of income shall be based on the principle of ensuring high speed in expanded production. With the development of production, wages shall be increased every year, but the rate of increase must be slower than the rate of increase in production. When the average wages (including grain supply) of members of the commune rise to a level that guarantees a living standard equivalent to that of the well-to-do middle peasant, the rate of increase in wages should be reduced to ensure the rapid growth of industry, the mechanization of farming, and electrification of the rural areas in the shortest possible time.

Article 23. The commune shall be managed according to plan. It shall work out long-term programs and yearly plans of construction in accordance with the economic plan of the state and the specific conditions of the commune. So as to introduce a strict responsibility system in production and carry through the award and demerit system rationally, the commune should work out concrete plans for output, technical measures, production expenses, and the use of labor power of the contingents, factories, mines, livestock farms, and timber yards. The contingents should also work out similar plans for the different production brigades.

The commune's plans for production, capital construction, sales of products, circulation of commodities, purchase of machinery and equipment, financial affairs, and wages must be submitted to the state pianning organizations and other departments concerned for examination and balancing before being put into practice.

Article 24. Democratic management shall be exercised throughout the commune. A vigorous, regular democratic life must be ensured in the commune, and in all its production contingents, production brigades, factories, mines, timber yards, livestock farms, tractor teams, schools, hospitals, shops, banks, canteens, and militia units. All organizations that keep their own accounts must publish their balance sheets and the accounts of awards distributed regularly and in good time. All administrative staff must take part in productive labor as far as possible. The masses must be encouraged to carry out criticism and self-criticism, commend those who render meritorious service, or put forward suggestions by way of *tatsepao,** so that defects in work can be overcome.

Article 25. The commune must be run in the spirit of industry and thrift, encourage its members to work hard, make full use of its own potential to overcome difficulties, practice economy, lower production costs, oppose waste and extravagance, and, as far as possible, trim and simplify all buildings and equipment not connected with production.

Article 26. The commune must establish a strict system governing financial management. All organizations that keep their own accounts must work out income and expenditure budgets in good time, abide

---

° *Tatsepao* are handwritten posters or "wall newspapers."

by the system and formalities governing the use of cash, and settle their accounts regularly.

Special persons should be appointed to take charge of all public property. Anyone causing loss to public property by negligence must be criticized or dealt with by disciplinary measures by the commune. Cases of corruption, theft, or destruction of public property must be handled in a serious manner; those involved in serious cases should be referred to the higher judicial departments to be punished according to law.

ANNEX TO DOCUMENT 30

ALTERNATIVE ARTICLES CONCERNING THE SUPPLY AND MARKETING DEPARTMENT AND THE CREDIT DEPARTMENT

[Published by *Jen Min Jih Pao* on September 4, 1958.]

Article 7. The commune will establish a supply and marketing department. The supply and marketing department will handle the sales of products and the supply of necessities of the commune under the guidance of state trading organs. The basic form of business of the supply and marketing department is to purchase and sell on behalf of state trading organs. In the purchase or sales of products it should stick to the price fixed by the state trading organs. The service charges for the supply and marketing department in purchasing and selling for state trading organs shall be fixed by the state trading organs in accordance with the principle that "the expenditure incurred plus a small amount of profits" be an allowable deduction. The supply and marketing department may sell in the commune the products left over after the commune has fulfilled the tasks of state purchase and unified purchase. The price and quantity of products sold shall be examined and approved by the state trading organs. The supply and marketing department may, with the approval of the state trading organs, sell to other quarters or buy in certain commodities that the state cannot purchase or supply.

The supply and marketing department shall keep its own accounts, while its profits and losses shall be managed by the commune under a unified system. Its funds shall be provided with the share funds contributed to the former supply and marketing cooperative by the members. The deficit shall be made up by the commune. No dividends shall be given on the shares.

For the convenience of the people, the supply and marketing department should set up its branches in all contingents and retail departments in the fairly distant and out-of-the-way areas. State trading organs should set up wholesale departments in appropriate places and gradually dismiss the retail departments.

The supply and marketing department joins the county supply and marketing cooperative as a member organization.

Article 8. The commune shall set up a credit department. The credit department shall handle the members' deposits, loans, and the utilization of funds of the commune under the guidance of the state banks. The credit department is also an agency of the People's Bank, handling deposits and making loans on its behalf, and charges the latter for the service according to stipulations.

The credit department shall keep its own accounts, while its profits and losses shall be managed by the commune under a unified system. Its funds shall be provided with the share funds contributed to the former credit cooperative by the members. The deficit shall be made up by the commune.

For the convenience of the people, the credit department should set up its branches in all contingents and service centers in the fairly distant and out-of-the-way areas.

As a cash treasury of the commune and the different contingents, the credit department and its branches shall undertake the receipts and disbursement of cash in bulk. Under the leadership of the state banks, the credit department shall undertake book settlement between the commune and other financial departments, and between the various departments in the commune which keep their own accounts. Book settlement is not to be practiced among the members.

DOCUMENT 31

STATE CAPITALISM IN INDUSTRY AND COMMERCE

[Excerpts from Kuan Ta-tung, *The Socialist Transformation of Capitalist Industry and Commerce in China* (Peking: Foreign Languages Press, 1960).

The functions and aims of state capitalism in China were: 1) To gradually transform capitalist private ownership, replacing it with socialist ownership by the whole people; 2) To gradually raise productivity, making use of the beneficial sides of capitalism to serve socialism; 3) To restrict step by step the capitalists' exploitation, blind production, and business management, and place their activities within the orbit of the unified plan of the national economy; and 4) To make arrangements for, educate, and remold the capitalists and gradually change them into working people living by their own labor.

The main elementary forms of state capitalism in industry were as follows:

Processing: The socialist sector (mainly the state trading companies) supplied a capitalist factory with raw materials or semi-finished products to process goods according to the required quantity, quality, and specifications and within a stated time. The state trading company took all the finished products and paid the capitalist factory a sum for the processing that covered its wages, other expenditures of production, the business tax, and a reasonable profit.

Placing orders: The socialist sector placed orders with a capitalist factory which delivered goods according to the required quantity, quality, and specifications and within a stated time and received the price paid for the goods. If necessary, the state trading company might pay in advance part of the price as a deposit or supply part of the raw materials.

Purchasing the entire output of private enterprises: The state, according to the economic needs of society, gave the state trading companies the exclusive right to purchase, on a long-term basis, certain important industrial products at appropriate prices. For the capitalist factories, such purchasing often took the form of processing, but there was a difference. In processing, the capitalist factories, after filling an order, might produce the same goods with their own materials and sell them of their own accord on the market. In the case of the products which were to be purchased exclusively by state enterprises, they were not allowed to sell these products themselves.

Marketing all finished products of private enterprises: The state trading companies undertook to market all or a part of the finished products of capitalist factories, which were sold to the state. In actual practice this often took the form of, or resembled, processing and placing orders. However, the difference was that the additional products or products in excess of the fixed quota as a result of the improvement in production, were to be also sold to the state trading companies.

The elementary forms of state capitalism in commerce were in the main as follows:

Private stores acting as retail distributors for the state: The state trading companies made private retail stores their distributors. These stores paid in cash for the commodities supplied by the state trading companies according to plan and sold them at retail prices set by the companies, making a profit from the difference between the wholesale and retail prices. The retail distributors could purchase the stock of the same commodities for which they acted as state distributors from the free market.

Likewise, private wholesale stores were made wholesale distributors for the state. The wholesale distributors paid in cash for the commodities supplied by the state trading companies and sold them wholesale according to the state plan and other specific conditions, making a profit from the difference in the prices.

Another form somewhat similar to acting as retail distributors, but actually different from it, was that the goods concerned were in general less important and might therefore be sold at prices either set or approved by the state trading companies, and the stock might be purchased, with the permission of the state companies, from the free market.

Private stores acting as commission agents for the state: A commission agent deposited a certain sum with the state trading company as guarantee and sold the commodities on a commission basis, according to the state plan and at the retail prices set by the state trading companies. The commission agent was not allowed to purchase the stock of the same commodities from the free market.

Likewise, private wholesale stores were made wholesale commission agents for the state. A wholesale commission agent deposited a sum with the state trading company as guarantee and sold wholesale the commodities on a commission basis, according to the state plan and other specific conditions.

Another similar form was the private import and export concerns acting as commission agents for the state trading companies. On behalf of the companies, they imported commodities from abroad according to the variety, specifications, quantities, and prices set by the companies and received fixed commissions. They exported commodities on behalf of the companies at the prices set by the latter and received fixed commissions.

The main elementary forms of state capitalism in commerce were the private stores acting as distributors and commission agents for the state.

In 1953, when China began the First Five-Year Plan for national economic construction, a general line for building socialism was popularized among the people. To ensure the successful carrying out of socialist construction and to further the transformation of capitalist industry and commerce, the state adopted two important measures, while vigorously developing the socialist sector of the economy. The first of these was the transformation of private wholesale trade. Wholesale is an important link in commodity exchange. It serves as a bridge between industry, commerce, and agriculture as well as between the socialist, capitalist, and individual sectors of the national economy. The state must control it before it can successfully implement the plan for national economic construction, guarantee a stable market, and strengthen the leadership of the socialist sector over the capitalist and individual sectors of the economy to facilitate their socialist transformation. Hence, the state adopted the policy of gradually replacing private wholesale trade by state trade.

The second was the planned centralized purchasing and marketing by the state of those materials and products which greatly affected the national welfare and the people's livelihood. These commodities could only be handled by the state trading companies or the private stores acting as distributors for the state. Only when they were controlled by the state, could the people's security and the needs of national construction be ensured. In 1953, the state began with the centralized purchase and marketing of grain and edible oil, and in 1954 extended this policy to cotton and cotton cloth. Thus, a radical change took place in the market.

The advanced form of state capitalism in China is called a joint state-private enterprise. This is the principal way through which the transition of capitalist industry and commerce into socialist enterprises is being effected.

A joint state-private enterprise is one in which the state invests and to which it assigns personnel to share management with the capitalists.

In such an enterprise, there are state shares (public shares) and capitalists' shares (private shares); personnel are appointed by the state (representing the state shares) and capitalists or their agents (representing the private shares). But the relationship between these two groups is not the same as that in a capitalist joint-stock company. It cannot be one of ordinary partnership. It is one between the leader and the led. The state representatives combine with the masses of workers in the enterprise to form the socialist force in it. These representatives are in a leading position in the joint enterprise, and this is provided for in the laws of the state. The characteristics of the joint enterprise distinguish it from all elementary forms of state capitalism. In the latter, the cooperation and connections between the socialist and capitalist sectors of the economy generally exist outside the enterprises, while in the former, they exist within them. In the joint enterprise the socialist sector has placed the capitalist sector under its direct supervision and control.

There were two stages in the development of joint enterprises, namely, joint state-private operation of individual enterprises, and joint state-private operation of whole trades.

A fixed rate of interest was paid by the state for the total investment of the capitalists in the joint state-private enterprises. Irrespective of locality and trade, the interest was fixed at a rate of 5 per cent per annum. In the meantime, the state declared that this system would not be changed for seven years beginning in 1956. This was a continuation of the policy of "buying off" the capitalists after the change-over by whole trades, only the form of payment was changed. The fixed rate of interest took the place of the distribution of profit according to definite proportions.

DOCUMENT 32

PROVISIONAL REGULATIONS GOVERNING JOINTLY OPERATED PUBLIC-PRIVATE INDUSTRIAL ENTERPRISES

[Adopted by the Government Administration Council on September 2, 1954.]

CHAPTER I.   GENERAL PROVISIONS

Article 1. These Regulations are enacted for the purpose of encouraging and directing the transformation of capitalist industry beneficial to the national economy and the people's livelihood into state capitalist industry in the form of public-private joint operation, so as to complete their gradual socialist transformation.

Article 2. A public-private, jointly operated industrial enterprise (hereinafter called jointly operated enterprise) is an industrial enterprise with investments made by the state or public-private jointly operated enterprises and jointly operated with the capitalists by cadres assigned by the state.

Public-private joint operation of capitalist industrial enterprises should be based on the needs of the state, practicability of transforming the enterprises, and willingness of capitalists.

Public-private joint operation of enterprises should be subject to approval of the people's government.

Article 3. The socialist sector of jointly operated enterprises shall occupy the leading position but the legitimate rights and interests of private shares shall receive protection.

Article 4. Jointly operated enterprises should obey state plans.

CHAPTER II. SHARES

Article 5. In instituting public-private joint operation of enterprises both the public and the private parties should assess the real assets of the enterprises and clear up the enterprises' credits and debts in order to determine the shares of public and private parties.

Article 6. The real assets of enterprises should be assessed through consultation by public and private parties on a fair and reasonable basis, taking into consideration the number of years in which the assets are actually still serviceable and the effect of the assets on industrial production.

The assets of enterprises should be assessed with participation of office employees and workers; when necessary, the industrial and commercial organ of the people's government shall appoint men to give directions.

Article 7. Jointly operated enterprises may absorb private investments.

Article 8. The shareholders of jointly operated enterprises shall assume limited liability with regard to the debts of jointly operated enterprises.

CHAPTER III. MANAGEMENT AND OPERATIONS

Article 9. Jointly operated enterprises shall be under the leadership of the public party and operated and managed by representatives designated by the competent organ of the people's government in conjunction with the representatives of the private party.

Article 10. Matters bearing on public and private relations in jointly operated enterprises should be dealt with through consultations by representatives of public and private parties; important questions on which no agreement could be reached should be reported to the competent organ of the people's government for decision or referred to the board of directors of jointly operated enterprises for consultations before reporting the questions to the competent organ of the people's government for decision.

Article 11. The administrative duties of the representatives of public and private parties in jointly operated enterprises shall be decided upon through consultations and appointed by the competent organ of the people's government and representatives of the private party. They should have powers according to their functions and should fulfill their responsibility.

Article 12. Jointly operated enterprises should in general continue to employ, according to their talents, the personnel with actual duties who have worked with the enterprises before reorganization, taking into consideration the former conditions, and should give proper care to those personnel who formerly performed meritorious service but who are now deprived of working ability.

Article 13. Jointly operated enterprises should, in appropriate form, introduce systems of management in which workers' representatives will take part.

Article 14. Jointly operated enterprises should gradually improve and gradually bring to the level of state enterprises the wage system and amenity facilities, taking into consideration the systems of wages and amenities of the enterprise before reorganization, the production and operation conditions of jointly operated enterprises, and relevent provisions of state enterprises.

Article 15. Jointly operated enterprises should observe the regulations of the competent organs of the people's government in connection with production, operation, finance, labor, capital construction, and safety and health.

Article 16. Jointly operated enterprises of the same trade or connected in production may, if necessary and possible, be placed under joint management or amalgamated through consultations of public and private parties and with approval of the competent organ of the people's government.

CHAPTER IV. DISTRIBUTION OF PROFITS

Article 17. The balance of yearly profits after payment of income tax should be distributed by the jointly operated enterprises among reserve funds, bonuses, and dividends, according to the following principles:

1. Dividends for shareholders and remunerations to directors, managers, and superintendents may take up about 25 per cent of the yearly profits;

2. An appropriate amount may be taken out as bonuses, taking into consideration the relevant provisions of state enterprises and the amenities formerly provided by the enterprises.

3. The balance left after payment of dividends and bonuses shall be set aside as reserve funds.

Article 18. Dividends accrued to public shares should be remitted to the treasury according to regulations; dividends accrued to private shares shall be placed at the disposal of private shareholders.

Reserve funds should be mainly used for developing production and should be invested by jointly operated enterprises according to state plans either in their own enterprises, in other jointly operated enterprises, or in other private enterprises for public-private joint operation, according to Article 2 of these Regulations.

Bonuses should be mainly used for providing collective amenity facilities for workers and rewarding advanced workers. Budgets should be drawn up by the manager or superintendent together with the trade union and referred to the appropriate agencies as provided in Article 13 of the Regulations and the workers' representative conference for adoption before their use.

[Chapters V, VI, VII of the Provisional Regulations are not included.]

VI
Social Revolution

The Communist revolution is a total revolution that does not stop with economic and political reform, but aims to transform the entire fabric of social and cultural life to conform with Marxist ideas. It is impossible to include in one volume documents bearing upon all phases of the total revolution. Those included in this chapter were chosen to represent various areas of change, to give some idea of the scope of what the Communists have set out to accomplish.

THE FAMILY REVOLUTION

The Marriage Law (D33) is like the visible top of a huge iceberg; its provisions do not begin to convey the depth and scope of the family revolution advocated by the Communists. The Chinese family has been a target of severe Communist attack because it is the cornerstone of the old social order and the depository of old traditions, attitudes, loyalties, and cultural values that the Communists identify with feudal society. The solidarity of the traditional Chinese family is incompatible with the all-embracing collective society which demands the complete surrender of all individuals and the subordination of all loyalties. If the proletarian collective society is to be achieved, the Chinese family must undergo fundamental change.

Most of the provisions of the Marriage Law appear to be reasonable and progressive to the reader. The significance of the law lies in its spirit and in the methods used to enforce its provisions. As a matter of fact, in the family reform as in other phases of their revolution, it is much easier to agree with the Communists on the evils they attack than on the remedies they propose. The beginning articles of the law, for example, list practices that had been condemned by liberal-minded reformers in China for many years before the Communist takeover. For decades, people had talked about family reforms in China. The old clan system was rapidly losing its force, and the large family in which married brothers and their families lived under the same roof with their parents was becoming less and less popular. Concubinage was becoming less common, and money gifts were considered to be distasteful by many educated people in the large cities. More and more young people rejected the arrangement of marriage by parents or matchmakers, and insisted on their right to choose their own mates.

The provisions of the Communist Marriage Law, therefore, are not startingly new in themselves. What is new is the kind of society the Communists aim to establish and the place of the family in that society.

A few examples may help to convey some sense of the revolutionary changes that are being introduced. The articles in Chapter III of the law stipulate that husband and wife have equal status in the home and equal right to free choice of occupations in society. These provisions, however, must be understood within the context of the Communist concept of society, in which every man or women is above all a producer and a revolutionary worker and is judged according to his or her contribution to economic production and political activities. They mean, in actual practice, the transfer of household work—cooking, mending, etc.—from the home to the collective (i.e., the commune) with the result that, while women are indeed relieved of household drudgery, the functions and importance of the home and the family are greatly reduced. They mean that women accept as much responsibility as men for work outside the home and become a part of the national manpower available for production.

Moreover, in the actual enforcement of the Marriage Law, "free choice of partners" has been interpreted to mean freedom to choose provided there is no interference with production and revolutionary work. In line with the argument that the individual must subordinate his personal interests to those of the collective, young people are told that no personal plans, including romance and marriage, should be allowed to detract from full devotion to production and revolutionary work. A campaign has been launched to abolish the wasteful and "feudal" marriage rituals and elaborate wedding celebrations that characterized Chinese life in the past. Instead of making the wedding a big occasion, the newspapers publicize stories of model proletarian youths who choose simple ceremonies after working hours so that not a single hour of production is lost. A marriage is considered desirable if it stimulates both partners to produce more. A person who desires to indulge in the "bourgeois pleasures of family life" instead of giving first priority to production and the revolution is considered an undesirable partner in marriage.

According to Article 3 of the law, "no third party shall be allowed to interfere." But Party and youth organizations take a very positive role in insisting that "politics take command" in love and marriage as much as it does in production, in study, or in any other phase of life. They tell young people in no uncertain terms that they should not marry anyone who is politically incompatible, by which they mean differences in political outlook or "class origin." Cadres and "progressive" youth have been warned not to marry a person of the landlord class or of bourgeois background, for fear of the contamination of feudal and bourgeois ways and ideas. The publications of the youth and women's organizations abound in stories of young people whose production record and revolutionary zeal rise after marriage because the young lovers encourage each other in "ideological improvement" and revolutionary devotion. At the same time, vivid stories are told of good workers and cadres whose revolutionary careers are ruined by marriage because their spouses "seek enjoyment in the intimate circle of the small family"—definitely a bourgeois addiction.

Here we come to a fundamental difference between the pre-Communist family reform and the Communist family revolution. The former was a rebellion against the traditional family, which upheld the rights and the authority of parents and elders. It was an assertion of the twentieth-century demand for individual freedom, expressed in the self-choice of mates and in the preference for the small family of married couples and their own children, living independently of their elders. In attacking the "arbitrary and compulsory feudal marriage system," the Communists and the pre-Communist reformers are in agreement, but the Communists also condemn the "bourgeois individualism" of pre-Communist reform. The new family is to become a part of collective society; it assists the Party-state in the fulfillment of production plans and the execution of revolutionary programs. The Communist family revolution aims to foster collectivism, not individualism.

Many a young married couple in China today are not living together because they have been assigned to work in different places and their "social duty" prevents them from having a home of their own. Until the Party-state reassigns them to jobs in the same city or village or town, they have to remain separated, putting the needs of collectivist society above their personal ambitions. The wedding ceremony is highlighted by talks on socialist construction and is often climaxed by the song "Communism Is Good." "Progressive" bride and groom have been reported to give each other the most precious wedding present of all, the *Works of Mao Tse-tung*. "Let politics take command" is an injunction that applies to the choice of mate, the decision to get married, and life after marriage.

The age provision in Article 4 of the Marriage Law has been modified in practice. As a part of the campaign for population control, men have been urged to postpone marriage until the age of thirty, and women until twenty-five. Family planning is encouraged. Among other measures adopted to slow down population growth are programs to popularize birth-control methods and to make available birth-control devices, the approval of abortion, and the withholding of rations and other benefits from mothers after their third child.

PRODUCING A NEW TYPE OF MAN

The most crucial phase of the Communist revolution is the production of a new type of man, socialist in outlook and collectivistic in behavior, untiring in production and completely loyal to the proletarian revolution under the leadership of the Communist Party. A valiant warrior of the class struggle, he is driven by strong emotions of love and hate, with his love of the Party-state matched only by his intense hatred for all enemies of the revolution. Education, indoctrination, propaganda, and all the media of communication at the disposal of the Party-state are directed toward the same objective: the making of the new socialist man.

The task of making new men with new minds and new loyalties is undertaken on at least three major levels. On the basic level, the thoughts and emotions of the masses must be remolded. The masses must be taught proletarian tastes as well as proletarian thoughts and ideas. From the radio, from the ubiquitous loudspeaker, from the stage and the cinema, from the "propaganda network" of mass persuasion come the daily messages designed to shape the thinking and emotions of the people. They tell the people about world affairs as well as domestic events: the proletarian cause in Cuba, in Vietnam, in Africa; on the home front, the production drive, the collection of fertilizers, the killing of flies and mosquitoes, the ideological struggle against revisionists and counterrevolutionaries, etc.. They tell people how bad conditions were before "liberation" and how life has turned for the better; how, nevertheless, a long arduous struggle still lies ahead and it is necessary for all to work hard, sacrificing the present for the future.

Much is said about a new concept of "happiness." Happiness, it is said, does not consist in personal advancement, material comfort, or a satisfying home life. It consists in making positive contributions to production and the revolutionary cause. Whatever advances the proletarian-socialist revolution should enhance the happiness of all individuals. To lead a happy life under such circumstances requires a remolding of human nature to develop new desires and new tastes. Personal welfare is unimportant. Labor is glorious; the faded overalls of the worker and the patched uniform of the soldier are far more beautiful than the fashions of bourgeois society. "Proletarian aesthetics" see beauty in the rough and calloused hands of the farmer and the wind-beaten face of the laborer.

The masses must be taught to read and write. Adults go to school after working hours so that schooling may not interfere with production. But mass education goes far beyond the three R's. It demands no less than the remolding of human nature to produce the new man needed for the new proletarian society.

A second major level of educational effort is concerned with the youth of the nation. From the young people have come the activists and cadres who are the backbone of the Chinese Communist move- ment. From them must come the successors of the revolution to take over from the rapidly aging present leadership. Educating youth in the proletarian way is therefore a task of paramount importance.

The process of making new men must begin in the cradle and ends only with death. Infants and children must be brought up the Com- munist way. In the nurseries and the schools, children are taught songs and games with clear political import. They are taught to love the Communist Party and to hate the class enemies and the imperialists. It is not yet financially possible to provide enough nurseries and schools for all children. But there is no doubt that the Communists aim to establish day and night nurseries, both to relieve mothers for work and to facilitate the process of molding the thoughts of the children. To insure that this process would take place without the interference of distracting influences, Liu Shao-Ch'i said in 1958[1] that eventually all infants would be placed in state nurseries for "total care" day and night and all elementary schools would become boarding schools.

All education is under the direct and strict supervision of the Com- munist Party. The Party issued a directive in 1958 laying down the basic guidelines: education must serve proletarian politics; it must be combined with productive labor; and it must be directed by the Communist Party. These constitute what the writer calls the three P's of Chinese Communist education: politics, production, Party.[2] In every school, as in every factory or farm, there is a resident representa- tive of the Party known as the "leadership" or the "organization." He and his associates see to it that education serves politics and pro- duction; in fact, his authority is final in all matters, even in curriculum, faculty appointment, and student promotion. Working hand in hand with the Party "leadership" is the branch organization of the Youth League.

It has been noted that the youth organizations work under the direc- tion of the Party. They take an active role in shaping the character of youth, including those who are not members. The recent effort to expand the activities of the youth organizations and to recruit all children between seven and fourteen to join the Pioneers is an indication of greater attention to the education of youth. Rules of Con- duct for Students (D40) may shed some light on the program of character remolding. The Constitution of the Student Federation (D41) is included here to call attention to the fact that there exist

[1] See *Extracts from China Mainland Magazines* (Hong Kong: American Con- sulate General), No. 149 (December 1, 1958), p. 42.
[2] See D42.

other mass organizations to reach the young people who do not belong to the Communist Youth League or the Pioneers.

Third, one of the most difficult problems confronting the Chinese Communists is that of China's intellectuals. In the 1950's, Chinese intellectuals, subjected to vile denunciation and harrassing "thought reform," made humiliating confessions and meek pledges of support to the new regime. They seemed to have succumbed to pressure, but subsequent events showed that beneath the outward conformity there remained deep resentment and a preserve of inner independence of thought unshaken by the attacks and the confessions.

In discussing the baffling question of intellectuals, Chou En-lai said in 1956 that 40 per cent of China's "higher" intellectuals were "progressives who actively supported the Communist Party," 40 per cent would "complete the tasks assigned to them, but were not sufficiently active politically," 10 per cent were "backward intellectuals who lacked political consciousness or ideologically opposed socialism, while less than 10 per cent were counterrevolutionaries or other bad elements." We do not know how accurate this estimate was, or the extent to which the percentages have changed in subsequent years. The 1965–66 attack upon intellectuals who had been actively identified with the new regime, however, suggests that even among the progressive 40 per cent in Chou En-lai's first group there are intellectuals who harbor strong misgivings about the policies and dogmas of the Communists. If this suggestion is valid, the Communists are still a long way from winning over the intellectuals. If, after seventeen years of successive "ideological remolding" campaigns and purges, so many of China's intellectuals can still take a stand against the rulers, they must have within them inner resources which give them strength and enable them to maintain their integrity beneath the outward appearance of meek compliance. Perhaps it was the recognition of this state of affairs that led the Communists to launch in 1966 the "great proletarian cultural revolution" to weed out the cultural heritage from which springs the recalcitrance of the intellectuals.[3]

THE NEW PROLETARIAN HEROES

To popularize the desired virtues of the new socialist man, the Communists have selected many heroes to serve as examples. Model workers, model peasants, model youth, model women, etc., have been invited to national conferences and to tour the country and affirm in public gatherings their readiness to sacrifice for the revolution.

One of the most publicized model new men of recent years is a

---

[3] Unfortunately, space does not permit the inclusion in this volume of documents bearing specifically upon the problem of intellecutals.

soldier named Lei Feng, who was killed in an automobile accident and was glorified after death as the embodiment of the highest virtues. Songs and poems were written about him and a nation-wide campaign was launched to "learn from Lei Feng." According to the officially released story, Lei Feng devoted his entire life to serving the Communist Party and the revolution under its leadership. In *Lei Feng Ti Ku-Shih (Story of Lei Feng)*, published in 1963 by the Literary Department of the People's Liberation Army, we are told that even as a little boy he was filled with deep hatred for the landlords, the capitalists, and the Kuomintang. When he learned to read, he was moved by the picture of Mao Tse-tung on the first page of his book. When he was about to graduate from the elementary school, he declared in an assembly of his teachers and fellow pupils, "Whatever the Communist Party wants me to do, I am ready to do." When the Party called on each person to think of himself as a screw in an intricate machinery, he declared, "I will always be a screw and take care that the screw never rusts."

Another soldier given posthumous honors is Wang Chieh, whose *Diary* is full of pledges of unswerving support to the revolution. Here are some of the statements attributed to him:[4]

> Flowers do not bloom without sunshine, crops do not grow without rain, a revolutionary fighter loses his bearings if he is not armed with Mao Tse-tung's thought.

> The revolutionary army is a big school for tempering men. I will be a piece of coal, to be thrown and burnt in the smelter that is our fighting life.

> The interests of the Party, the revolution, and the masses are identical. I never hesitate to do things in the interest of the revolution. . . . The important thing is to give every ounce of energy wholeheartedly to the revolution.

Chao Meng-t'ao, a girl worker in a textile factory, was glorified after death for having given herself unstintedly to socialist construction. She was described as an indefatigable and absolutely selfless worker, always thinking of the welfare of other people and the advancement of factory work. Despite tuberculosis and failing health, she never relaxed in her effort. Interviewed by reporters on her deathbed, she refused to talk about herself, only of the production campaign and the Communist Party. She said, "My body belongs to the Party. I am not afraid of anything, only of not being able to serve the Party."[5]

---

[4] *Peking Review*, July 15, 1966, pp. 32–35.
[5] *Chung Kuo Fu Nü (Chinese Women)* (Peking), January, 1964.

MASS ORGANIZATIONS

It has been noted in earlier chapters that "mass organizations," or "people's organizations," as the Communists call them, play an important quasi-governmental role in the control of the people. Theoretically, they are "voluntary organizations" representing the interests of their members. Actually, they serve as the eyes and ears of the Party-state in maintaining close contact with the masses, and as the arms of the Party-state in enforcing laws, directives, and official plans.

Reference has been made to the urban inhabitants' committees, the youth organizations, the women's organizations, the peasants' association, etc. The documents on the trade unions (D34, D35) are worthy of note because the workers are supposed to be the favored class of proletarian society. The central purpose of the trade unions, as of other mass organizations, is to "educate and organize" their members so that they may support and obey the government.[6] The expression "labor discipline" appears repeatedly in these documents. To observe labor discipline is to work hard in production, to refrain from demands for purely personal advantages, and willingly to subordinate personal interests to state interests.[7] Furthermore, according to the official line, the interests of the working class are identical with those of the state, which is the workers' state, and the interests of the "working class," of which the Communist Party is the vanguard, transcend those of individual workers. It often becomes necessary, therefore, to "educate" and "discipline" individual workers so that they serve their class instead of themselves.

CONTROL AND REFORM MEASURES

The "democratic" dictatorship frankly uses force and compulsion in dealing with "enemies." D36 and D37 are among the regulations promulgated in the "suppression of counterrevolutionaries" campaign of earlier years. The Common Program states in Article 7 that while counterrevolutionaries must be "severely punished," some reactionary elements may be given a chance to "reform themselves through labor so as to become new men." Such labor service is compulsory and may be of long duration (D38).

FOREIGN POLICY

Communist China's treaties and agreements with other countries have been compiled in various other volumes; several are mentioned in the Preface. There are numerous documents bearing on the ideological background and major guidlines of foreign policy. Only two

---

[6] See Article 8 of D34.
[7] See the preamble of D35.

of immediate interest (D43, D44) are included here. Ch'en Yi's stipu-
lation of conditions for entrance into the United Nations is the clearest
statement that has been made on this touchy question. Even if these
conditions may be subject to negotiation, it is important for the world
to know the specific terms of possible bargaining. Lin Piao's article
on the "People's War" deserves careful reading. Some argue that it is
only public oratory and need not be taken too literally. On the other
hand, the Chinese Communist official news agency hailed it as "the
most historic and revolutionary document of this era." Anyway, in
view of Lin's rising status in the Party heirarchy, his pronouncements
are likely to carry much weight and exert considerable influence on
future events.

DOCUMENT 33

THE MARRIAGE LAW

[Promulgated by the Central People's Government on May 1, 1950.]

CHAPTER I. GENERAL PRINCIPLES

Article 1. The arbitrary and compulsory feudal marriage system, which is based on the superiority of man over woman and which ignores the children's interests, shall be abolished.

The New Democratic marriage system, which is based on free choice of partners, on monogamy, on equal rights for both sexes, and on protection of the lawful interests of women and children, shall be put into effect.

Article 2. Bigamy, concubinage, child betrothal, interference with the remarriage of widows, and the exaction of money or gifts in connection with marriage shall be prohibited.

CHAPTER II. THE MARRIAGE CONTRACT

Article 3. Marriage shall be based upon the complete willingness of the two parties. Neither party shall use compulsion, and no third party shall be allowed to interfere.

Article 4. A marriage can be contracted only after the man has reached twenty years of age and the woman has reached eighteen years of age.

Article 5. No man or woman in any of the following instances shall be allowed to marry:

1. Where the man and woman are lineal relatives by blood, or where the man and woman are brother and sister born of the same parents, or where the man and woman are half-brother and half-sister. The question of prohibiting marriage between collateral relatives by blood within the fifth degree of relationship is to be determined by custom.

2. Where one party, because of certain physical defects, is sexually impotent.

3. Where one party is suffering from venereal disease, mental disorder, leprosy, or any disease that is regarded by medical science as rendering a person unfit for marriage.

Article 6. In order to contract a marriage, both the man and the woman shall register in person with the people's government of the subdistrict or village in which they reside. If the marriage is found to be in conformity with the provisions of this Law, the local people's government shall, without delay, issue marriage certificates.

If the marriage is found not to be in conformity with the provisions of this Law, registration shall not be granted.

CHAPTER III. RIGHTS AND DUTIES OF HUSBAND AND WIFE

Article 7. Husband and wife are companions living together and shall enjoy equal status in the home.

Article 8. Husband and wife are in duty bound to love, respect, assist, and look after each other, to live in harmony, to engage in production, to care for the children, and to strive jointly for the welfare of the family and for the building up of a new society.

Article 9. Both husband and wife shall have the right to free choice of occupation and free participation in work or in social activities.

Article 10. Both husband and wife shall have equal right in the possession and management of family property.

Article 11. Both husband and wife shall have the right to use his or her own family name.

Article 12. Both husband and wife shall have the right to inherit each other's property.

CHAPTER IV. RELATIONS BETWEEN PARENTS AND CHILDREN

Article 13. Parents have the duty to rear and to educate their children; the children have the duty to support and to assist their parents. Neither the parents nor the children shall maltreat or desert one another.

The foregoing provision also applies to stepparents and stepchildren. Infanticide by drowning and similar criminal acts are strictly prohibited.

Article 14. Parents and children shall have the right to inherit one another's property.

Article 15. Children born out of wedlock shall enjoy the same rights as children born in lawful wedlock. No person shall be allowed to harm or discriminate against children born out of wedlock.

Where the paternity of a child born out of wedlock is legally established by the mother of the child or by other witnesses or by other material evidence, the identified father must bear the whole or part of the cost of maintenance and education of the child until it has attained the age of eighteen.

With the consent of the natural mother, the natural father may have custody of the child.

With regard to the maintenance of a child whose natural mother marries, the provisions of Article 22 shall apply.

Article 16. A husband or wife shall not maltreat or discriminate against children born of a previous marriage.

CHAPTER V. DIVORCE

Article 17. Divorce shall be granted when husband and wife both desire it. In the event of either the husband or the wife insisting upon divorce, it may be granted only when mediation by the subdistrict people's government and the subdistrict judicial organ has failed to bring about a reconciliation.

In cases where divorce is desired by both husband and wife, both parties shall register with the subdistrict people's government in order to obtain divorce certificates. The subdistrict government, after establishing that divorce is desired by both parties and that appropriate measures have been taken for the care of children and property, shall issue the divorce certificates without delay.

When only one party insists on divorce, the subdistrict people's government may try to effect a reconciliation. If such mediation fails, it shall, without delay, refer the case to the district or city people's court for decision. The subdistrict people's government shall not attempt to prevent or to obstruct either party from appealing to the district or city people's court. In dealing with a divorce case, the district or city people's court must, in the first instance, try to bring about a reconciliation between the parties. In case such mediation fails, the court shall render a verdict without delay.

In the case where, after divorce, both husband and wife desire the resumption of matrimonial relations, they shall apply to the subdistrict people's government for a registration of remarriage. The subdistrict people's government shall accept such a registration and issue a certificate of remarriage.

Article 18. The husband shall not apply for a divorce when his wife is with child. He may not apply for divorce until one year after the birth of the child. In the case of a woman applying for divorce, this restriction does not apply.

Article 19. The consent of a member of the revolutionary army on active service who maintains correspondence with his or her family must first be obtained before his or her spouse can apply for divorce.

As of the date of the promulgation of this Law, divorce may be granted to the spouse of a member of the revolutionary army who does not correspond with his or her family for a subsequent period of two years. Divorce may also be granted to the spouse of a member of the revolutionary army who had not maintained correspondence with his or her family for over two years prior to the promulgation of this Law and who fails to correspond with his or her family for a further period of one year subsequent to the promulgation of the present Law.

CHAPTER VI.   MAINTENANCE AND EDUCATION OF CHILDREN
AFTER DIVORCE

Article 20. The blood ties between parents and children do not end
with the divorce of the parents. No matter whether the father or the
mother acts as guardian of the children, they still remain the children
of both parents.

After divorce, both parents still have the duty to support and educate
their children.

After divorce, the guiding principle is to allow the mother to have
custory of a baby still being breast-fed. After the weaning of the child,
if a dispute arises between the two parties over the guardianship and
an agreement cannot be reached, the people's court shall render a decision in accordance with the interests of the child.

Article 21. After divorce, if the mother is given custody of a child,
the father shall be responsible for all or part of the necessary cost of
the maintenance and education of the child. Both parties shall reach
an agreement regarding the amount and the duration of such maintenance and education. In the case where two parties fail to reach an
agreement, the people's court shall render a decision.

Payment may be made in cash, in kind, or by tilling land allocated
to the child.

Such agreement reached between parents or a decision rendered by
the people's court in connection with the maintenance and education
of a child shall not prevent the child from requesting either parent
to increase the amount decided upon by agreement or by judicial
decision.

Article 22. In the case where a divorced woman remarries and her
husband is willing to pay the whole or part of the cost of maintenance
and education for the child or children by her former husband, the
father of the child or children is entitled to have such cost of maintenance and education reduced or is entitled to be exempted from
bearing such cost, in accordance with the circumstances.

CHAPTER VII.   PROPERTY AND MAINTENANCE AFTER DIVORCE

Article 23. In case of divorce, the wife shall retain such property as
belonged to her prior to her marriage. The disposal of other household
properties shall be subject to agreement between the two parties. In
cases where agreement cannot be reached, the people's court shall
render a decision after taking into consideration the actual state of
the family property, the interests of the wife and the child or children,
and the principle of benefiting the development of production.

In cases where the property allocated to the wife and her child or children is sufficient for the maintenance and education of the child or children, the husband may be exempted from bearing further maintenance and education costs.

Article 24. After divorce, debts incurred during the period of marriage shall be paid out of the property acquired by husband and wife during this period. In cases where no such property has been acquired or in cases where such property is insufficient to pay off such debts, the husband shall be held responsible for paying these debts. Debts incurred separately by the husband or wife shall be paid off by the party responsible.

Article 25. After divorce, if one party has not remarried and has difficulties in maintenance, the other party shall render assistance. Both parties shall work out an agreement with regard to the method and duration of such assistance; in case an agreement cannot be reached, the people's' court shall render a decision.

CHAPTER VIII. BYLAWS

Article 26. Persons violating this Law shall be punished in accordance with law. In cases where interference with the freedom of marriage has caused death or injury, the person guilty of such interference shall bear criminal responsibility before the law.

Article 27. This Law shall come into force from the date of its promulgation. In regions inhabited by national minorities, the People's Government (or Military and Administrative Committee) of the Administrative Area or the provincial People's Government may enact certain modifications or supplementary articles in conformity with the actual conditions prevailing among national minorities in regard to marriage. But such measures must be submitted to the Government Administration Council for ratification before enforcement.

DOCUMENT 34

THE TRADE UNION LAW

[Promulgated by the Central People's Government on June 29, 1950.]

Section I. General Principles

Article 1. Trade unions are mass organizations of the working class formed on a voluntary basis. All manual and nonmanual wage workers in enterprises, institutions, and schools in Chinese territory whose wages constitute their sole or main means of livelihood, and all wage workers in irregular employment, shall have the right to organize trade unions.

Article 2. Trade unions shall be organized on the principle of democratic centralism, in accordance with the Constitution of the All-China Federation of Labor as adopted by the All-China Labor Congress. Trade union committees at all levels shall be set up by election at general membership meetings or representative conferences.

Members of trade unions shall have the right, in accordance with the constitution of their trade unions, to dismiss and replace at any time any representative or committee member whom they have elected. Trade unions at all levels shall submit reports on their work to the rank and file membership they represent or to their representative conferences, and shall observe the decisions and directives of their respective higher trade union organizations.

Article 3. Trade unions are mass organizations formed in accordance with the resolutions and Constitution adopted by the All-China Labor Congress and various congresses of industrial unions (including the cultural and educational workers' unions and government employees' unions). The trade unions have their own nationwide, independent, and unified system of organization, with the All-China Federation of Labor as the highest body. When trade unions are established, they should submit reports thereon to the All-China Federation of Labor or its affiliated industrial unions or local unions, which, after proper examination and approval, shall undertake to refer the matter to the local people's governments for registration.

Article 4. All other bodies not organized in accordance with Article 3 of this Law shall not be called trade unions, and shall not be entitled to the rights laid down in this Law.

Section II.   The Rights and Duties of Trade Unions

Article 5. Trade unions in enterprises operated by the state or by cooperatives shall have the right to represent the workers and staff members in taking part in administering production and in concluding collective agreements with the managements.

Article 6. Trade unions in private enterprises shall have the right to represent the workers and staff members in conducting negotiations and talks with the employers, in taking part in the labor-capital consultative councils, and in concluding collective agreements with the employers.

Article 7. It is the duty of trade unions to protect the interests of workers and staff members, to ensure that the managements or capitalists effectively carry out the regulations and directives concerning labor protection, labor insurance, wage standards, factory sanitation, safety measures, and other matters as laid down in the laws and decrees of the government, and to take measures for improving the material and cultural life of the workers and staff members.

Article 8. Trade unions at all levels in enterprises operated by the state or by cooperatives shall have the right to ask the managements at the corresponding levels to submit reports on their work to the trade union committees, to the general membership meetings, or to the representative conferences. They also have the right to represent the workers and staff members in taking part in the administrative boards or administrative meetings at the corresponding levels.

Article 9. In order to safeguard the fundamental interests of the working class, trade unions shall carry out the following activities, according to their respective constitutions and decisions:

> 1. To educate and organize the masses of workers and staff members to support the laws and regulations of the people's government, to carry out the policies of the people's government, and to consolidate the people's state power, which is led by the working class;
>
> 2. To educate and organize the masses of workers and staff members to adopt a new attitude toward labor, to observe labor discipline, and to organize labor emulation campaigns and other production movements in order to ensure the fulfillment of the production plans;
>
> 3. To protect public property; to oppose corruption, waste, and bureaucracy; and to fight against saboteurs in enterprises operated by the state or by cooperatives and in institutions and schools;
>
> 4. To promote in privately owned enterprises the policy of developing production and of benefiting both labor and capital, and to oppose violations of government laws and decrees or acts detrimental to production.

Article 10. The people's governments at appropriate levels shall allocate to the All-China Federation of Labor, industrial unions, and local trade unions the necessary buildings and furnishings to enable them to carry out their office work, meetings, educational, recreational, and welfare work. The people's governments at all levels shall also give the trade unions similar preferential treatment in the use of postal, telegraphic, telephone, railway, highway, and navigation facilities, as are enjoyed by government institutions at corresponding levels.

Article 11. When the managements of state-operated enterprises or the owners of private enterprises want to transfer or discharge a trade union committee member elected by the workers, they must obtain in advance the consent of the trade union committee concerned. Such transfer or discharge cannot be carried out until the said trade union committee has reported the matter to a higher trade union committee and has obtained its approval.

Article 12. Committee members or representatives of trade unions at all levels, when provided with credentials issued by their respective trade unions, may inspect the workshops and dormitories of the enterprises, institutions, or schools whose workers and staff members are affiliated to the said trade unions. The managements or the owners may not refuse such inspections except in certain specially stipulated cases.

Section III. The Basic Organization of Trade Unions

Article 13. Factories, mines, business establishments, farms, institutions, schools, and other productive or administrative units with more than twenty-five workers and staff members may set up a basic trade union committee (such as factory, mine, or institution committee). Those employing less than twenty-five persons may elect an organizer, who shall have the same rights as a basic trade union committee. The regulations governing the organization of basic trade union committees shall be formulated by the All-China Federation of Labor or the national committees of the respective industrial unions.

Article 14. Apart from the basic trade union committees approved by the industrial unions or the local unions in accordance with Articles 3 and 13 of this Law, all other organizations in factories, mines, business establishments, farms, institutions, schools, and other productive or administrative units shall not be entitled to the rights enjoyed by the basic trade union committees.

Article 15. The number of full-time trade union functionaries of a basic trade union committee who are to be freed from production in order that they may devote themselves to the work of the trade union shall be determined in accordance with the total number of workers and staff members employed in each factory, mine, business establishment, farm, institution, school, and other productive or administrative unit. The ratio shall be one full-time trade union functionary to each 500 workers or staff members, with a maximum of five full-time functionaries for enterprises employing 2,500 to 4,000 workers.

A further full-time trade union functionary may be added for every additional 2,000 persons in enterprises employing over 4,000 workers and staff members. Basic trade union committees in enterprises employing less than 200 persons may only have a full-time trade union functionary with the authorization of a higher trade union organization.

Article 16. When a basic trade union committee has been elected, the management or the owner must be notified of the names of the committee members. The management or the owner must, in accordance with the decisions of the basic trade union committee, release those members who are required to be freed from production.

Article 17. Full-time trade union functionaries who are freed from production shall be paid by the trade unions, and the amount should not be less than the rate of wages previously paid to them. They shall continue to share in labor insurance and other welfare facilities paid for by the management or the owner. After completing their terms of office, the management or owner shall ensure that they return to their original jobs or be given other jobs at the same wages as formerly.

Article 18. The managements or owners of factories, mines, business establishments, farms, institutions, schools, and other productive or administrative units shall not obstruct the activities of the basic trade union committees or the general membership meetings or representative conferences they convene. But such meetings and conferences called by trade unions should not be held during the prescribed working hours. When such meetings have to be held during working hours as required by special circumstances, the consent of the managements or owners should be obtained. If members of a basic trade union committee who are still engaged in production have to conduct trade union activities during working hours, the trade union must inform the management or owners thereof. But the total working hours thus occupied by any such member shall not exceed two working days per month. In such cases, the wages of such members shall be paid in full.

Article 19. Elections of trade union representatives to a people's representative conference or people's congress, in accordance with the directives of the people's governments at city (county) level or above, or elections of trade union representatives to trade union congresses, in accordance with the directives of the trade union councils at city or provincial levels or above, may be held during working hours if necessary. In private enterprises, representatives of workers and staff members to those and other conferences shall be paid for the period of their attendance by the organizations that call such conferences.

Article 20. The managements or the owners of factories, mines, business establishments, farms, schools, and other productive or administrative units which employ 100 or more workers shall provide the necessary buildings and other facilities (water, electricity, and furniture, etc.) free of charge for office use and other facilities for the basic trade union committees and shall provide, permanently or temporarily, a suitable place for general membership meetings or representative conferences. Those employing less than 100 persons, if unable to provide separate offices for the trade unions, shall provide special trade union desks in rooms in general use. Trade unions may also hold meetings in such rooms.

Article 21. When the managements or the owners of factories, mines, business establishments, farms, institutions, schools, and other productive or administrative units engage workers or staff members, they shall inform the basic trade union committees, which shall have the right to protest, within three days, if they discover that such engagements violate any law or decree of the people's government or run counter to collective agreements. Disputes arising from the managements or owners disagreeing with such protests shall be dealt with in accordance with the Rules of Procedure for Settling Labor Disputes.

Article 22. The managements or the owners of factories, mines, business establishments, farms, institutions, schools, and other productive or administrative units shall inform the basic trade union committees ten days in advance of the name of any worker or staff member they want to discharge, giving reasons for this. The basic trade union committees shall have the right to protest, within seven days, if they discover that such discharge violates any government decree or collective agreement. Disputes arising from the managements or the owners disagreeing with such protests shall be dealt with in accordance with the Rules of Procedure for Settling Labor Disputes.

Articles 21 and 22 shall not apply in the case of personnel appointed by the people's governments at all levels.

Section IV. Trade Union Funds

Article 23. The trade unions must set up their own system of budgeting, drawing up of balance sheets, accounting, and auditing, on the principle of independent administration of their funds.

Article 24. Trade unions funds shall be drawn from the following sources:

1. Membership dues paid by trade union members in accordance with the Constitution of the All-China Federation of Labor;
2. The managements or the owners of factories, mines, business establishments, farms, institutions, schools, and other productive or administrative units shall allocate each month to their respective trade union organizations as trade union funds a sum equal to 2 per cent of the total amount of real wages (including those paid in currency, in kind, and in meals) of all workers and staff members employed (excluding agents of the owners in privately owned enterprises). (Of this sum 1.5 per cent of the total amount of real

wages shall be used for the purpose of promoting cultural and educational activities for the workers and staff members) ;

3. Income from cultural and sports activities sponsored by the trade unions;

4. Subsidies from the people's governments at various levels.

Article 25. Regulations governing the disposal of the funds of the trade union committees at all levels shall be formulated by the All-China Federation of Labor.

Section V.   Bylaws

Article 26. This Law shall come into force after it has been ratified and promulgated by the Central People's Government Council.

DOCUMENT 35

CONSTITUTION OF THE TRADE UNIONS OF THE PEOPLE'S REPUBLIC OF CHINA

[Adopted by the Eighth All-China Congress of Trade Unions
on December 12, 1957.]

General Program

The Chinese working class, led by its vanguard, the Communist Party of China, together with the rest of the Chinese people, after long years of hard struggle and their victory in the people's democratic revolution, has in the main completed the socialist revolution with regard to the ownership of the means of production. In 1957, a new victory was gained in the socialist revolution on the political and ideological fronts. At the same time, tremendous successes have been achieved in socialist construction. The socialist system has been fundamentally established in our country.

The basic task of our working class and the whole Chinese people in the next ten to fifteen years is to carry out the policy of simultaneously developing industry and agriculture on the basis of priority for the development of heavy industry, so as to build our country into a powerful socialist state equipped with a modern industry, agriculture, science, and culture. In order to fulfill this great, historic task, the working class must, under the leadership of the Communist Party of China, raise its class consciousness to a higher level; become better organized and more disciplined; improve its cultural and technical qualifications;

strengthen unity within its own ranks; consolidate the worker-peasant alliance; unite, educate and remold the intellectuals; further develop its fine traditions of diligence, hard work, and thrift; continue to display its noble quality of selflessness; and lead the entire Chinese people by its exemplary action to complete the tasks of socialist construction.

The trade unions of China are the voluntary, broad mass organizations of the working class. Regardless of nationality, sex, or religious belief, all manual or nonmanual workers who depend entirely or mainly upon their wages for the means of life, may join the trade unions.

The modern working-class movement of China has developed under the constant leadership of the Communist Party. The trade unions of China are the mass organizations of the working class, led by the Chinese Communist Party, and are the transmission lines between the Party and the masses. Under the People's Democratic Dictatorship, the trade unions are a school of administration, a school of management, and a school of Communism for the workers.

In building socialism in a country like China, which has an enormous population and backward economy, the fundamental problem is to increase industrial and agricultural production and steadily raise social labor productivity. To achieve that aim, the trade unions must, under the leadership of the Communist Party, better educate the workers in the spirit of Communist principles and carry out the policy of building the country, operating enterprises, and running all undertakings with diligence and thrift. The trade unions should organize socialist emulation and bring the energy and creative ability of all the workers into full play, so that they will voluntarily observe work discipline and ensure fulfillment of the national construction plan and endeavor to overfulfill it. On the basis of developing social production, the trade unions should gradually improve the material and cultural well-being of the workers.

The trade unions are the strongest social support of our People's Democratic Dictatorship. The trade unions should participate actively in the drawing up of state policies, laws, and decrees concerning production, labor, and the material and cultural life of the workers; organize mass supervision over implementation of these policies, laws, and decrees; and fight against all acts which violate state laws and decrees and social and work discipline or damage the interests of the state and the people. At the same time, the trade unions should educate the workers to set a good example in observing the laws and the Constitution of the People's Republic of China and giving firm support to all state policies and decrees.

Under the leadership of the working class, the interests of the state are identical with the common interests of the entire people and also with the fundamental interests of our working class. The trade unions should educate the workers to recognize the unity of interests between the state and the individual and, when these two conflict, realize that individual interests should be subordinated to state interests. At the same time, the trade unions, proceeding from the over-all interests of the state, should support the just demands of the masses, and protect their proper material interests and democratic rights. The trade unions should combat bureaucratic practices which contravene the vital interests of the workers.

Democratic centralism is the fundamental principle of management in our socialist enterprises. All enterprises should, on the one hand, abide by the over-all leadership of the Communist Party and the over-all plans of the state, work under centralized direction, and observe strict discipline; they should, on the other hand, bring into full play the initiative and enthusiasm of the workers in carrying on supervisory activities, and mobilize them to take part in the management of enterprises. The workers' congresses convened by the trade unions in factories, mines, and enterprises are an important means by which the mass line of maintaining close relations between the leadership and the masses is realized. They are also organs through which the workers participate in the management of their enterprises, carry on mass supervision, and improve their self-education. The trade unions must, under the leadership of the corresponding Communist Party committees, do the work of organizing the workers' congresses well and closely link this work with the routine work of the trade unions.

The rectification movement is an important means by which the working class and the rest of the people, under the leadership of the Communist Party, carry on the socialist revolution and socialist construction. The methods used in the rectification movement, including full and frank expression of opinions, the putting up of "posters in big characters," and the unfolding of criticism and self-criticism, make it possible not only to expose and rectify shortcomings and mistakes in work and in the working style of the leadership, but are also good methods for the self-education of the masses. The trade unions should adopt the methods of the present rectification movement as part of their regular working method and integrate them with the system of workers' congresses.

Trade union organizations in joint state-private enterprises should further improve their work in transforming both the enterprises and the capitalists, and gradually enable the capitalists to become people who earn their livelihood by their own labor.

The trade unions of China are formed on the principle of coordinating organization on industrial lines with organization on a local area basis, and on the principle of democratic centralism. They use persuasion and education as their basic method of work. Trade union organizations at all levels should observe the principle of combining collective leadership with division of responsibility.

The maintaining of close ties with the masses is the fundamental condition for the success of all kinds of work by the trade unions. Therefore, all trade union organizations must keep close contact with the masses, and all trade union cadres must be well acquainted with the problems of production and share the joys and sorrows of the masses. All trade union cadres should listen attentively to the views, suggestions, and demands of the masses, make exhaustive investigations into the problems in work, and, in carrying on their work, rely on the masses and the activists. The cadres should fully develop democracy, criticism, and self-criticism, and fight against manifestations of bureaucracy, subjectivism, and sectarianism, which alienate them from the masses. In all trade union organizations, democratic work systems must be set up and improved, especially as regards making regular work reports and financial reports and checking on various aspects of the work. Everything the trade union does should be subject to supervision by the masses.

The building of socialism is the common cause of all nationalities in our country. The trade unions must improve their work in the national minority regions, train trade union cadres from among the various national minority peoples, base their work on Communist principles, and at the same time take cognizance of the special characteristics of the various nationalities. Tendencies to chauvinism and to local nationalism, each of which is detrimental to national unity, must be opposed.

The trade unions must consistently educate the workers in the spirit of patriotism as well as internationalism, help them to study diligently the advanced experience of socialist construction in the Soviet Union and the People's Democracies and the advanced techniques of all other countries, actively support the peaceful foreign policy of the people's government of China, actively participate in the international trade union movement, support the righteous struggles waged by the working class and people the world over, strive for solidarity and cooperation in the international trade union movement, and safeguard world peace and struggle for the cause of human progress.

CHAPTER I. MEMBERSHIP

Article 1. Membership in the trade unions shall be open to all workers whose wages constitute their sole or main means of life, and who accept the Constitution of the Trade Unions, regardless of nationality, sex, or religious belief.

Article 2. Admission to a trade union shall be granted only when a personal application for membership is made and when such application has been discussed and accepted by a trade union group, and approved by the workshop committee or by the primary committee if no workshop committee exists.

Article 3. Trade union members shall have the right:

1. To elect and to be elected;
2. To make proposals and suggestions to trade union organizations for the improvement of their work;
3. To criticize anything that concerns the trade unions and their functionaries at trade union meetings or in the trade union press;
4. To address any question or appeal to any leading body of the trade unions;
5. To demand that the trade union give them all necessary legal protection and support, should an enterprise, institution, or school violate any policy, law, or decree of the state and cause damage to the members' material interests or democratic rights; and
6. To enjoy preferential treatment in all the communal cultural undertakings and welfare services run by the trade unions.

Article 4. It is the duty of trade union members:

1. To observe work discipline and the policies, laws, and decrees of the state; to fulfill enthusiastically their tasks in national construction;
2. To safeguard the socialist system and protect public property; to fight against all antisocialist views and acts, the destruction of public property, violations of law or social and work discipline, and all acts of corruption and waste;
3. To engage assiduously in political, cultural, technical, and professional studies so as to raise their level of class consciousness and ability;
4. To foster class fraternity, unity, and mutual help; and
5. To abide by the Constitution of the Trade Unions, implement trade union decisions, and pay membership dues punctually.

Article 5. The trade union organization shall help by criticism and education any trade union member who violates the Constitution of the Trade Unions. Members whose offence is of a serious nature or who do not correct their mistakes after repeated warnings shall be expelled from the trade union; those members who fail to pay membership dues for more than six consecutive months without good reason may also be expelled.

Article 6. When a trade union wishes to expel a member, the decision for expulsion must be taken by the general membership meeting or the delegate meeting of the primary trade union organization (or, wherever it exists, by the general membership meeting of the workshop) and it must be ratified by the next higher trade union organization.

Article 7. Trade union members may retain their membership while on military service, while working in an industrial or handicraft producers' cooperative or as seasonal workers during the off-season, and when retired, disabled, or invalided, or when they need to retain their membership for some other reason.

CHAPTER II. ORGANIZATIONAL STRUCTURE

Article 8. The trade unions of China are formed on the principle of democratic centralism, that is, centralism on the basis of democracy and democracy under centralized guidance. Its basic conditions are as follows:

1. The leading bodies of the trade unions at all levels shall be elected.

2. The leading bodies of the trade unions at all levels shall observe the principle of combining collective leadership with individual responsibility. All important questions shall be discussed and decided collectively.

3. The trade unions at all levels shall carry on their work in accordance with the Constitution of the Trade Unions and decisions of trade union organizations. At regular intervals they shall submit reports on their work to the membership and pay heed to criticisms and opinions voiced by the general membership and lower organizations.

4. Trade union members shall carry out trade union decisions; the minority shall abide by the decisions of the majority; and the lower trade union organizations shall abide by the decisions of the higher bodies.

Article 9. The trade unions of China are formed on the principle of coordinating organization on industrial lines with organization on a local area basis. To form the trade unions on industrial lines means that all trade union members in the same enterprise, institution, or school shall be organized in one single primary organization.

Trade union members in the same branch of industry or in similar branches of the national economy shall be organized in the same national or local industrial trade union.

The principle of coordinating organization on industrial lines with organization on a local area basis is that trade union councils organized at the level of provinces, autonomous regions, municipalities directly under the central authority, autonomous *chou,* cities under the provincial authorities, counties, and towns shall be the joint leading bodies of their subordinate local trade union organizations and industrial trade union organizations in their locality; the All-China Federation of Trade Unions is the national joint leading body of all local trade union councils and of all national industrial trade union organizations.

Article 10. The highest organs of authority of the trade unions at different levels are: the general membership meetings or the delegate meetings (for primary organizations) ; the congresses (for trade unions at the level of provinces, autonomous regions, municipalities directly under the central authority, autonomous *chou,* cities under the provincial authorities, counties, or towns) ; and the All-China Congress of Trade Unions (for the whole country).

The general membership meetings and congresses at the various levels shall elect the trade union committees at corresponding levels. In the intervals between general membership meetings and congresses, these committees shall be the executive bodies of the trade unions at various levels.

Article 11. Trade union committees at all levels shall elect auditing commissions at their respective levels. These commissions, under the leadership of their respective trade union committees, shall be responsible for auditing income and expenditure and checking on the administration of properties.

Article 12. During the election of trade union officials at various levels, the lists of candidates must be fully discussed at trade union meetings. All those participating in the meeting may nominate candidates and criticize any candidate under discussion. During the voting, electors may reject any candidate, or vote for some other person or persons who are not on the list.

Article 13. Trade union committees above the primary level may convene meetings of representatives in the intervals between congresses, according to the needs of the work, to sum up and exchange experience in different spheres of work, and to remove or fill vacancies among members of the trade union committees; the number of vacancies filled and members removed should not be more than one-fifth of the total number of trade union committee members, and these decisions should be reported to the next higher trade union organization for registration.

Article 14. Primary trade union committees may set up various working committees; trade union committees above the primary level may set up various departments and working committees according to need.

CHAPTER III. THE HIGHEST NATIONAL LEADING BODY OF THE
TRADE UNIONS

Article 15. The highest organ of authority of the trade unions of
China is the All-China Congress of Trade Unions. Its functions and
powers shall be:

1. To hear and approve reports on work and on the income and
expenditure of the Executive Committee of the All-China Federation of Trade Unions;

2. To define the policies and tasks of the trade unions throughout
the country and to hear reports by economic and cultural departments of the Central People's Government, so as to ensure fulfillment of the tasks of national construction;

3. To amend the Constitution of the Trade Unions of the People's Republic of China; and

4. To elect the Executive Committee of the All-China Federation
of Trade Unions.

Article 16. The All-China Congress of Trade Unions shall be convened once every five years by the Executive Committee of the All-
China Federation of Trade Unions. The procedure for election of delegates to the All-China Congress of Trade Unions shall be decided by
the Executive Committee.

Article 17. The Excutive Committee of the All-China Federation of
Trade Unions and its alternate members shall be elected in accordance
with the number of members determined by the All-China Congress of
Trade Unions. Any vacancy which occurs among members of the
Executive Committee shall be filled by alternate members of the Com-
mittee in order of established precedence.

Article 18. In the intervals between sessions of the All-China Congress of Trade Unions, the Executive Committee of the All-China
Federation of Trade Unions shall be responsible for the thorough implementation of the decisions of the Congress and for the direction
of trade union work throughout the country. The Plenary Session of
the Executive Committee shall be convened twice a year by the Presidium. Its basic tasks shall be:

1. To hear work reports made by the Presidium; to define specific
tasks at every stage of work in accordance with the decisions of
the All-China Congress of Trade Unions;

2. To participate in the drawing up of state policies, laws, and
decrees concerning production, labor, and the material and cultural life of the workers; and to educate and organize the working masses to observe and supervise the implementation of these
policies, laws and decrees;

3. To check on trade union work, and to sum up and **exchange**

experience on trade union work throughout the country;

4. To hear reports of the Auditing Commission and to approve trade union budgets and financial reports; and

5. To represent the Chinese trade unions in the international trade union movement.

Article 19. The Executive Committee of the All-China Federation of Trade Unions in Plenary Session shall elect a presidium and a secretariat as well as a chairman and a number of vice-chairmen of the Committee. The Plenary Session of the Presidium shall be convened four times a year by the chairman.

Between sessions of the Executive Committee, the Presidium shall be the leading body of the trade unions throughout the country, responsible for implementing decisions of the All-China Congress of Trade Unions and of the Executive Committee. In addition, it shall direct all the work of the trade unions throughout the country.

Under the guidance of the Presidium, the Secretariat shall attend to the day-to-day work.

Article 20. The highest organ of authority of an industrial union shall be its national congress, which has the following functions and powers:

1. To hear and approve reports on work and on the income and expenditure of its national committee;

2. To define the policies and tasks of the industrial union throughout the country, and to hear reports made by related departments of the Central People's Government so as to ensure fulfillment of the tasks of national construction;

3. To make decisions concerning organizational questions of the industrial union; and

4. To elect its national committee.

The national congress of an industrial union shall be convened once every three to four years by the national committee of the union. The procedure of election of delegates to the national congress shall be decided by the national committee.

Article 21. In the intervals between the national congresses of an industrial union, its national committee shall be responsible for the carrying out of the decisions of the national congress and of the All-China Federation of Trade Unions, and shall elect a chairman, several vice-chairmen, and a number of members to form the presidium to direct the day-to-day work.

The results of election of members of the national committee of the industrial union and the chairman, vice-chairmen, and members of its presidium shall be reported to the Executive Committee of the All-China Federation of Trade Unions for registration.

CHAPTER IV. LOCAL TRADE UNION ORGANIZATIONS

Article 22. Trade union councils of provinces, autonomous regions, municipalities directly under the central authority, autonomous *chou,* cities under the provincial authorities, counties, and towns shall be the joint leading bodies of their subordinate local trade union organizations and industrial union organizations in their locality.

Provincial and municipal trade union councils may, if they deem necessary, set up offices in regions and urban districts in their areas. Acting on behalf of the provincial and municipal trade union councils, these offices shall expedite and check on the activities of trade union organizations affiliated with them.

Article 23. Local industrial union organizations shall be established by trade union councils, in accordance with the existing specific local conditions and in line with the industrial unions' decisions on organization.

Article 24. The highest organs of authority of local trade union councils and local industrial trade union organizations are their respective congresses, whose functions and powers shall be as follows:

1. To hear and approve reports on work and on the income and expenditure of the trade union committees at corresponding levels;

2. To define the tasks of the trade union organizations at their respective levels, and to hear reports on work by the departments of the corresponding people's councils concerned so as to ensure fulfillment of the tasks of national construction; and

3. To elect the trade union committees at corresponding levels.

Congresses of provincial trade union councils, of trade union councils of the autonomous regions, municipalities directly under the central authority, and provincial congresses of industrial unions shall be convened every three years; congresses of autonomous *chou* and cities under the provincial authorities shall be convened every two years; municipal and local congresses of the industrial trade unions shall be convened every year or every two years.

Local trade union congresses at the various levels shall be convened by trade union committees at the corresponding level. The procedure for election of delegates to these congresses shall be decided by the trade union committees at the corresponding level.

Article 25. In the intervals between their respective congresses, the committees of local trade union councils and the regional industrial trade union committees shall be responsible for implementation of the decisions of the congresses and for direction of activities of their subordinate trade union organizations, in accordance with the decisions and directives of the higher trade union organizations.

Article 26. Committees of local trade union councils and regional industrial trade union committees shall each elect a chairman, a number of vice-chairmen, and members to form a standing committee to direct the day-to-day work.

The chairmen, vice-chairmen, and members of standing committees elected by the members of the committees of local trade union councils and regional industrial trade union committees shall be reported to the next higher trade union committee for registration.

Article 27. The regulations governing the formation of trade unions at county and town levels shall be decided by the trade union councils of the provinces or the autonomous regions in accordance with specific local conditions and needs.

CHAPTER V.   PRIMARY TRADE UNION ORGANIZATIONS

Article 28. The primary trade union organizations are the foundation of the trade unions. They are formed by trade union members in the same enterprise, institution, or school, A trade union committee may be set up in an enterprise, institution, or school with ten or more members; when there are less than ten members, they may join the nearest primary trade union organization in a related industry or set up a joint primary organization together with the members of other units.

Article 29. The highest organ or authority of a primary trade union organization shall be the general membership meeting or delegate meeting. Its functions and powers shall be:

1. To hear and approve reports on work and on the income and expenditure of the primary trade union committee;
2. To hear reports by responsible members of the administration of the enterprise, so as to coordinate their efforts in improving work and running their enterprise properly;
3. To define the tasks of the primary trade union; and
4. To elect the primary trade union committee.

General membership meetings or delegate meetings shall be convened regularly by the primary trade union committee. The procedure for electing delegates to the delegate meeting shall be decided by the primary trade union committee.

Article 30. Workers' congresses in factories and mines (meetings of all workers and staff in small enterprises) are the organizations through which the working masses take part in the management of enterprises and supervise their administration, as well as improve their own self-education. The functions and powers of workers' congresses shall be regulated in accordance with the policies of the Communist Party and the laws and decrees of the state.

Article 31. Each primary trade union committee shall elect a chairman and several vice-chairmen, and establish various working committees according to need. It shall draw in as many activists as possible to participate in trade union activities.

The term of office of the primary trade union committee shall be one year, during which the general membership meeting or the delegate meeting may replace any of the committee members if they are found to be seriously violating state policies, laws, or decrees, or the Constitution of the Trade Unions or the interests of the workers.

Article 32. In the intervals between general membership meetings or delegate meetings, the primary trade union committee shall be responsible for implementation of the decisions taken at such meetings, as well as the decisions and directives of higher trade union organizations, and shall guide the day-to-day work of its subordinate organizations. Its basic tasks shall be the following:

1. To organize socialist emulation campaigns among all the workers and the technical and administrative staff; to sum up and exchange advanced working experiences; to encourage rationalization proposals; to strengthen work discipline; to guarantee the fulfillment of the tasks of national construction and try to overfulfill them;

2. To strengthen political and ideological education; to educate all workers in the spirit of Communism through various activities; to promote criticism and self-criticism; to raise consistently the level of social consciousness of the workers and their level of organization and discipline; and to strengthen their solidarity;

3. To assist and supervise the administration in adjusting the wages of the workers, improving labor protection, living and housing conditions, material supplies, and cultural and welfare facilities; to supervise the administration in the full implementation of state policies, laws, and decrees, as well as the decisions of the workers' congress; to fight against all acts that damage the interests of the state and the masses;

4. To show constant concern for the improvement of the material and cultural life and working conditions of the workers; to look after labor insurance and give guidance to mutual aid and savings societies, and to the committees of dependants; to promote mass cultural, recreational, and sports activities, and mutual assistance among the workers; to assist the administration in organizing cultural and technical studies for the workers;

5. To put democratic life on a sound basis; to convene general membership meetings or delegate meetings regularly; to improve the work of the trade union groups; to foster and train activists; to recruit new members; to be always acquainted with the views and

demands of the rank and file and study and deal with these in good time by relying on the wisdom and strength of the masses; and to submit the important questions to the workers' congress for decision and then carry out these decisions by every possible means;

6. To collect membership dues; to check on the fulfillment of the appropriations that the administration in the enterprise, institution, or school should pay to trade union funds and for labor insurance; and to work out budgets and financial reports.

Article 33. The primary trade union committee shall set up workshop (or department) committees to lead trade union activities in the workshops (or departments). Such committees shall be elected at the general membership meetings of the workshops (or departments). Each workshop (or department) committee shall elect a chairman (and several vice-chairmen in the case of a big workshop) and may establish various working committees in accordance with its working needs.

Primary trade union committees in enterprises, institutions, and schools that have women workers may convene, when necessary, a women workers' delegate meeting to discuss and solve their special problems.

Article 34. Under the primary trade union or workshop (department) committee, trade union groups may be formed according to production units or work units. Each trade union group shall elect a group leader and, if necessary, a deputy leader and assistants to help the group leader.

CHAPTER VI. FUNDS

Article 35. The sources of trade union funds are as follows:

1. Membership dues equivalent to 1 per cent of members' monthly wages;

2. Admission fees for new members, equivalent to 1 per cent of their wages for the month previous to their admission;

3. Proceeds from cultural and sports activities sponsored by the trade unions;

4. Appropriations made by the administration of enterprises, institutions, or schools to trade union funds in accordance with the Trade Union Law.

Article 36. The trade union committees at all levels shall work out their budgets and financial reports in accordance with the financial system laid down by the All-China Federation of Trade Unions, and report at regular intervals to the membership and to the next highest trade union committee on their income and expenditure. The report on financial accounts shall be examined and, if approved, signed by the auditing commissions.

Regulations governing the use of trade union funds, budgets, and financial reports, as well as the accounting system of the trade unions, shall be fixed separately by the All-China Federation of Trade Unions.

CHAPTER VII.   APPENDIXES

Article 37. This Constitution shall come into effect after adoption by the Eighth All-China Congress of Trade Unions. The right of interpretation of the Constitution rests with the Executive Committee of the All-China Federation of Trade Unions.

The right to amend this Constitution rests with the All-China Congress of Trade Unions.

Article 38. Primary trade union committees and trade union organizations above the primary level may have their own seals. The design of seals shall be decided by the All-China Federation of Trade Unions.

Article 39. Industrial unions may draw up their own regulations if necessary, but such regulations shall not conflict with the present Constitution.

DOCUMENT 36

REGULATIONS FOR THE SUPPRESSION OF COUNTERREVOLUTIONARIES

[Promulgated by the Central People's Government Council on February 20, 1951.]

In accordance with Article 7 of the Common Program, the following measures are hereby adopted to punish the counterrevolutionary criminals, suppress the counterrevolutionary activities, and to consolidate the People's Democratic Dictatorship. Those who aim at overthrowing the people's democratic power and ruining people's democratic enterprises, and various counterrevolutionary criminals shall be punished according to these measures:

1. Those who rebel against the motherland in collusion with foreign imperialism shall be sentenced to death or life imprisonment.

2. The leading elements who instigate, induce, or bribe public officials, armed troops, or people's militia to revolt or who lead the bands in revolt, shall be sentenced to death or life imprisonment. Others who participate in instigating, inducing, bribing, or revolting, shall be sentenced to a maximum of ten years in prison. Heavier punishment shall be meted out in more serious cases.

3. Chief plotters and directors of armed mass revolt shall be sentenced to death. A minimum penalty of five years in prison shall be meted out to other active participants.

4. Those who engage in one of the following acts shall be sentenced to death:

a) Spying on and stealing state secrets or furnishing intelligence to internal and external enemies;

b) Pointing out bombing targets for enemy planes or vessels; or

c) Supplying arms and ammunition and other war supplies to internal or external enemies.

A minimum of five years' imprisonment shall be meted out in less serious cases.

5. Those who participate in the following counterrevolutionary or espionage activities shall be sentenced to death or life imprisonment:

a) Receiving assignment from internal or external enemies to carry on underground activities;

b) Participating in or organizing counterrevolutionary or espionage activities after liberation;

c) Having organized or led counterrevolutionaries, secret services, or espionage activities and other crimes before liberation, with no intention of redeeming themselves with meritorious services after liberation;

d) Having participated in counterrevolutionary activities, secret services, or espionage activities before liberation and continuing same after liberation;

e) Continued participation in counterrevolutionary activities after surrendering to and registering with the people's government; or

f) Continuing to associate with counterrevolutionaries, secret service agents, and spies after having been educated and released by the people's government.

A minimum of five years' imprisonment shall be meted out to less serious offenders.

6. Those who use feudalistic sects and societies to carry on counterrevolutionary activities shall be sentenced to death or life imprisonment. A minimum of three years' imprisonment shall be meted out to less serious offenders.

7. Death or life imprisonment shall be the penalty for the following kinds of sabotage or killing:

a) Looting or sabotaging military establishments, factories, mines, forests, farms, dams, transportation, banks, warehouses, danger-precaution equipment, and other important public or private properties;

b) Dropping poison, disseminating disease germs, and other

means of causing serious disasters among men, livestock, or agricultural products;

c) Disturbing markets or dislocating currency systems under instructions from internal or external enemies;

d) Attacking, killing, or injuring public officials or the people; or

e) Forging public documents and testimonials by false representation of military organs and democratic parties in order to carry on counterrevolutionary activities.

A minimum of five years' imprisonment shall be meted out in less serious cases.

8. Those who commit, with counterrevolutionary intent, one of the following provocative and delusory acts shall be sentenced to a minimum of three years in prison:

a) Inciting the masses to resist and sabotaging the execution of the decrees of the people's government concerning the collection of grain or taxes, labor service, military service, and other decrees;

b) Undermining the unity of various national minorities, democratic classes, democratic parties, and the unity between people's organizations and the government; or

c) Engaging in counterrevolutionary propaganda or manufacturing and spreading rumors.

Death or life imprisonment shall be the penalty in more serious cases.

9. Those who cross the national boundary secretly with counterrevolutionary intent shall be sentenced to death or life imprisonment. Less serious offenders shall be sentenced to a minimum of five years in prison.

10. Plotters who agitate for jailbreaks or staging a riot shall be sentenced to death or life imprisonment. A minimum of three years' imprisonment shall be meted out to active participants.

11. Those who shelter or protect the counterrevolutionaries shall be sentenced to a minimum of ten years in prison. Life imprisonment or death shall be the penalty for more serious cases.

12. The following shall be mitigating circumstances which may be claimed by those punishable under these measures:

a) Voluntary surrender to the people's government and sincere repentance;

b) Sincere repentance and redeeming of guilt with meritorious deeds before or after the discovery or prosecution;

c) Participation in counterrevolutionary activities not voluntarily, but under pressure and deception; or

d) Having engaged in less serious counterrevolutionary acts before liberation but having since repented and severed all relationships with counterrevolutionary organizations.

13. Those who commit more than one crime shall receive the maximum total penalty as the final puishment.

14. Those who commit counterrevolutionary crimes not listed in these measures shall receive similar penalties.

Those found guilty under these measures may be deprived of their political rights, and all or part of their properties may be confiscated.

These measures shall apply to counterrevolutionary crimes committed before the adoption of same.

Any person shall have the right to inform the government of the counterrevolutionary cases, but they should not report falsely because of personal grudges.

In time of military control counterrevolutionary cases shall be prosecuted by the court martial organized by the local military headquarters, the Military Council, or the Bandit Extermination Command.

These regulations shall become effective on the day of promulgation.

DOCUMENT 37

PROVISIONAL MEASURES FOR THE CONTROL OF COUNTERREVOLUTIONARIES

[Approved by the Government Administration Council, June 27, 1952.]

On July 17, the Ministry of Public Security of the Central People's Government announced "Provisional Measures for the Control of Counterrevolutionaries." The Measures have been approved by the Government Administration Council of the Central People's Government and are enforced as from date of proclamation. Full text of the Measures follows:

Article 1. These Measures are enacted in accordance with the provisions of Article 7 of the CPPCC Common Program and the spirit of the Regulations for the Suppression of Counterrevolutionaires, for the purpose of thorough elimination of counterrevolution, consolidation of the People's Democratic Dictatorship, and strengthening of control of counterrevolutionaries who should be subjected to control measures.

Article 2. The objective of control is to deal out certain punishment and to give certain ideological education to counterrevolutionaries under government control and mass supervision, and to reform them into new men.

Article 3. The following types of counterrevolutionaries who have committed crimes in the past, show no repentance or furnish no proof of repentance but commit no flagrant counterrevolutionary activities after liberation, and whose crime, while deserving certain punishment, is not such as warrant arrest, shall be subject to control by these Measures:

1. Counterrevolutionary special agents;
2. Backbone elements of reactionary parties and groups;
3. Leaders of reactionary secret societies;
4. Landlords persisting in a reactionary viewpoint;
5. Chiang Kai-shek and puppet military and administrative officials persisting in a reactionary view; and
6. Other counterrevolutionaries who should be subject to control.

Article 4. Elements subject to control will be deprived of the following political rights:

1. The right to elect and to be elected;
2. The right to take up administrative posts in state organs;
3. The right to participate in people's armed forces and people's bodies;
4. Freedom of speech, publication, meeting, assembly, correspondence, domicile, removal, and demonstration; and
5. The right to people's honor.

Article 5. Elements subject to control must observe government control provisions, take up proper professions and actively labor to produce, and report instantly on counterrevolutionary activities of others upon discovery.

Article 6. The period of control shall be fixed for less than three years but may be extended if necessary.

Article 7. Elements subject to control who violate control provisions or carry on counterrevolutionary activities may be given an extended period of control or arrested for legal action, according to the circumstances of the case.

Article 8. Under any one of the following circumstances, the period of control may be shortened or control may be lifted in the case of counterrevolutionaries subject to control:

1. Seriously observing government laws and control provisions and showing good behavior;
2. Obeying mass supervision, actively laboring to produce, and achieving genuine reform;
3. Doing meritorious service by actively denouncing counterrevolutionaries to people's government; or

4. Showing other expressions of repentance by meritorious service or making special contributions.

Article 9. Control shall be limited to the person of the counter-revolutionary himself without implicating his dependents, relatives, or friends.

Article 10. Any person shall have the right to supervise and denounce illegal activities of the elements subject to control.

Article 11. With the exception of cases on which the court passes judgment according to law, the right of approval of control of counter-revolutionaries shall belong to public security organs of *hsien* and municipal levels and above. In *hsiang* and *t'sun,* the *ch'ü* and *hsiang* government shall make the recommendations to *hsien* public security bureaus for review and approval. In cities, the public security stations and public security suboffices shall make the recommendations to municipal public security bureaus for review and approval. This also applies to extension and shortening of the period of control and to the cancellation of control. Upon approval of control of a counter-revolutionary, the organ approving the control shall issue official notice to him and make known the decision at some appropriate mass meeting.

Article 12. Counterrevolutionaries sentenced by people's judicial organs to government control shall also be dealt with according to these Measures.

Article 13. These Measures shall be enforced by local public security organs as their responsibility.

Article 14. All provinces and municipalities may, according to the provisions of these Measures and local specific conditions, draw up measures for enforcement and submit them to people's governments of administrative regions for approval and enforcement.

Article 15. These Measures shall be approved by the Government Administration Council and promulgated by the Ministry of Public Security for enforcement.

DOCUMENT 38

REGULATIONS GOVERNING LABOR
SERVICE FOR REFORM

[Passed by the Government Administration Council, August 26, 1954.]

CHAPTER I. GENERAL PRINCIPLES

Article 1. In accordance with the provisions of Article 7 of the Common Program of the Chinese People's' Political Consultative Conference for the punishment of all counterrevolutionary criminals and other criminals and the compulsory reform of these criminals through labor service to become new people, these Regulations have been formulated.

Article 2. The machinery for labor service for reform of the People's Republic of China constitutes a tool of the People's Democratic Dictatorshop, being machinery for the punishment and reform of all counterrevolutionary criminals and other criminals.

Article 3. In the enforcement of labor service for reform, convicted criminals shall be subject to imprisonment and control of different natures, according to the nature of their crimes and the seriousness of the sentences imposed, and be admitted to prisons or Labor Service for Reform Corps.

Criminals not yet sentenced shall be admitted to detention houses for supervision and control.

Juvenile delinquents shall be admitted to juvenile delinquents' institutes for education and reform.

Article 4. Organs enforcing labor services for reform, in dealing with all counterrevolutionary criminals and other criminals, shall thoroughly carry out the policy of coordinating punishment and control with ideological reform, and coordinating labor production and political education.

Article 5. Organs enforcing labor service for reform, in dealing with all counterrevolutionary criminals and other criminals, shall enforce strict control during the period of the imprisonment of the criminals. Lethargic attitudes and relaxation of efforts shall not be permitted. Maltreatment and corporal punishment shall be strictly prohibited.

Article 6. Organs enforcing labor service for reform shall be subject to the leadership of the people's public security organs, the supervision of the offices of the people's procurator at all levels, and in matters connected with judicial activities, the direction of the people's courts at all levels.

Article 7. In dealing with criminals still under investigation or trial, the work of control and education shall be subservient to the work of investigation and trial.

CHAPTER II.   MACHINERY FOR LABOR SERVICE FOR REFORM

Section 1.   Detention Houses

Article 8. A detention house is mainly used for the custody of criminals not yet sentenced.

Criminals sentenced to two years or less, who cannot be conveniently sent to a Labor Service for Reform Corps, may be sent to a detention house for custody.

Article 9. A detention house shall assume responsibility for understanding the conditions of criminals awaiting sentence. Those involved in serious cases shall be placed in individual custody. Those involved in the same crime or in related crimes shall be isolated. These measures are to coordinate with the work of investigation and facilitate the judicial organs in the speedy disposal of cases. Criminals awaiting sentence may be organized for appropriate labor service, provided such service produces no obstacles to the work of investigation and trial.

Convicted criminals placed under the custody of a detention house shall be placed in separate custody from those awaiting sentences, and they shall be forced to engage in labor service and to receive political education.

Article 10. When a criminal awaiting sentence and admitted to a detention house has been sentenced to surveillance or labor service without custody, the affirmed judgment of the people's court shall be upheld, and he shall be returned to his original domicile or to his original work department, and the sentence shall be carried out by the local people's government or the original work department.

Article 11. Detention houses shall be established with the central government, the provinces, the municipalities, and the *hsien* in the country as units, and shall be under the jurisdiction of the public security organs of the corresponding levels.

Detention houses of different units located in the same place may be merged in consideration of actual conditions.

Public security subbureaus in a municipality directly subordinated to the central government, or in a municipality which is a provincial capital, may, if necessary, establish detention houses attached to them.

Article 12. A detention house shall have a chief, one or two deputy chiefs, and a number of secretaries and wardens.

Section 2.   Prisons

Article 13. A prison is mainly intended for the custody of criminals who are not suited to labor service in the open, including counterrevolutionary criminals given the death sentence but having had their execution stayed or given a life term, as well as other important criminals.

Article 14. A prison shall carry out a serious custody of the criminals and exercise rigid precaution, and when necessary may put the criminals in individual confinement. Under rigid control, and in accordance with their different conditions, the criminals shall be made to do compulsory labor service and to receive education.

Article 15. Prisons shall be maintained in all provinces and municipalities in accordance with actual needs, and shall be under the jurisdiction of the relevant provincial and municipal public security organs.

Article 16. A prison shall have a chief warden and one to two deputy chief wardens, and there shall be work departments dealing respectively with control and education, production, and general affairs.

Section 3. Labor Service for Reform Corps

Article 17. Labor Service for Reform Corps shall undertake the custody of convicted counterrevolutionary criminals and other criminals suited for labor service in the open.

Article 18. A Labor Service for Reform Corps shall organize the criminals for planned production in agriculture, industry, and construction projects, and shall coordinate labor production with political education.

Article 19. Labor Service for Reform Corps shall be established in provinces and municipalities in accordance with actual needs, and shall be under the jurisdiction of the relevant provincial and municipal public security organs.

Article 20. On the basis of the number of criminals and the needs of production, Labor Service for Reform Corps may be organized into small companies, medium companies, large companies, branch companies, and General Corps.

A corps shall have a chief and a number of deputy chiefs. Work departments may be established in accordance with the actual needs of control and education and production.

Section 4. Juvenile Delinquents' Institutes

Article 21. A juvenile delinquents' institute shall undertake the custody of juvenile delinquents between the ages of thirteen and eighteen.

Article 22. A juvenile delinquents' institute shall give juvenile delinquents education in politics, in the new moral code, and in basic cultural subjects and production technique. And with due consideration to their biological growth, they shall be made to perform light labor service.

Article 23. Juvenile delinquents' institutes shall be established with the provinces and municipalities as units as necessary, and shall be under the jurisdiction of the relevant provincial and municipal public security organs.

Article 24. A juvenile delinquents' institute shall have a director, one or two deputy directors, and a number of control and teaching personnel as necessary.

CHAPTER III.   LABOR SERVICE REFORM AND EDUCATIONAL REFORM

Article 25. Labor service for reform shall be coordinated with political and ideological education, so that forced labor may gradually be promoted to approach voluntary labor, and the criminals may be reformed into new men.

Article 26. In dealing with the criminals, collective study classes, individual interviews, study of assigned documents, and organized discussions shall be regularly adopted to educate them in the admission of guilt and obedience to law, political and current events, labor production, and culture, so as to expose the nature of the crimes committed, thoroughly wipe out criminal thoughts, and establish a new moral code.

Criminals may be organized for appropriate physical culture, cultural, and entertainment activities, and also organized for the reviewing of their living conditions, labor, and study.

Article 27. Attention shall be paid to the cultivation among the criminals of production technique and labor habits. In the reform through labor of criminals with technical attainments, the fullest use shall be made of their technical capacities.

Article 28. Production competitions may be launched among criminals, to raise production efficiency and to promote the active zeal of the criminals in labor service for reform.

Article 29. For the inspection of conditions relating to the reform of criminals, there shall be established a card index system for the records of criminals, and special personnel shall be placed in charge. There shall be recorded from time to time conditions relating to the maintenance of discipline and their attitude toward labor and study, and periodic inspections shall be carried out.

CHAPTER IV.   PRODUCTION IN LABOR REFORM

Article 30. Production in labor service for reform shall serve the interests of national construction, and be included in the state's general plans for construction and production.

Article 31. Production in labor service for reform shall be subject to the unified leadership of the committees of financial and economic affairs of the people's governments of different levels, and also to the concrete guidance by the relevant agriculture-forestry, industrial, financial, communications, water conservancy, and commercial departments.

Article 32. The central government and the provincial and municipal governments shall establish committees in charge of production in labor service for reform, to lead and supervise the enforcement of the production plans. Such a committee shall be organized with the responsible members of the relevant committee of financial and economic affairs, financial and economic departments, and public security and judicial departments.

Article 33. The direction of development of production in labor service for reform shall be: the concentrated operation of production activities in provinces and municipalities in all-out efforts for agricultural production; the undertaking of industrial, mining, and porcelain production enterprises which have possibilities for development; and the organization of production in water conservation, road building, and other construction projects.

At the administrative district, *hsien* (municipality) levels, major attention shall be paid to the organization of production in the detention houses, and if practical, production in the open may be carried out at the administrative district and *hsien* (municipal) levels.

Article 34. In the organization of the criminals for production, the principle of safety in production shall be upheld, and the necessary safety equipment and systems shall be established. Should a criminal be actually disabled or killed during production or in the suppression of calamities, the circumstances of the case shall be considered and the criminal or his family shall be given appropriate care.

Article 35. The Ministry of Public Security of the Central People's Government may take into consideration the numbers of criminals in different areas, conditions relating to production, and the needs of national construction, and draw up plans for the transfer of criminal manpower, which shall be carried out in a unified manner after approval has been obtained from the Government Administration Council. Temporary transfers of smaller numbers of criminals which affect only a small area may, however, be carried out with the approval of the Ministry of Public Security of the Central People's Government.

CHAPTER V. SYSTEM OF CONTROL OF CRIMINALS

Section 1. Taking into Custody

Article 36. A criminal shall be taken into custody on the basis of a judgment, letter of execution, or certificate of detention, and no prisoner may be accepted without any of the above documents. Where records in the aforementioned documents do not agree with facts, or where they are incomplete, the original organs sending the prisoner shall produce an explanation or make the necessary supplementary records.

Article 37. When a criminal is taken into custody, a physical check-up shall immediately be carried out. With the exception of important counterrevolutionary criminals and other criminals involved in serious crimes, a criminal may not be taken into custody when any one of the following conditions obtain:

1. When the criminal is mentally ill, or suffers from an emergency illness, or suffers from a malignant communicable disease;
2. When the criminal suffers from a serious illness which may endanger his life if placed under custody; or
3) When a criminal has given birth to a child within the previous six months, or is pregnant.

When a criminal cannot be accepted for custody for any of the reasons stated above, the original organ sending the criminal shall consider the circumstances, and send him or her to a hospital, or hand him over to a guardian, or place him in some other appropriate establishment.

Article 38. When criminals are taken into custody, actual conditions shall be considered, and they shall be admitted to mixed cells, individual cells, women's cells, or sick wards for separate custody.

Women criminals shall be supervised by women wardens.

Article 39. A woman criminal shall not be allowed to bring her children into a prison. Where such a criminal has young children with nobody to care for them, the civil affairs department of the local administrative organ of the state shall undertake to have such children taken care of by other residents, or at an orphanage or creche, the expenses incurred to be defrayed out of social relief funds.

Article 40. When a criminal is taken into custody, a strict examination shall be carried out, and contraband found shall be sent to the people's court for confiscation. Non-daily necessities shall be kept on his behalf and a receipt issued him, to be returned on his release, but when there is a legitimate use for such articles, he shall be allowed to use them. Materials that can be used for reference in investigation and trial shall be sent to the organ carrying out the investigation and trial.

A woman criminal shall be examined by a woman warden.

Article 41. In taking a criminal into custody, his name, sex, age, nationality, native place, address, antecedents, vocation, cultural attainment, special capacity, crime committed, length of sentence, health condition, family conditions, and the people's court handing down the judgment on him shall be entered into a book of records of criminals. If necessary, a photograph may also be attached.

Article 42. When a criminal awaiting judgment has been detained for a period in excess of that allowed by law, and the investigations and judgment have not been completed, the detention house shall immediately inform the organ sending the criminal to speed up the case.

Article 43. An organ enforcing labor service for reform, should it discover concrete and reliable data that may affect the case during its supervision and control of a convicted criminal, shall immediately submit such data to the original organ giving the judgment or the local people's court for use as a basis for the reopening of the case.

Section 2. Security Measures

Article 44. Armed security measures against criminals shall be carried out in a unified manner by the people's public security forces, and organs enforcing labor service for reform shall exercise leadership over these armed forces in the carrying out of security measures.

Article 45. Rigid security measures shall be enforced in the outer perimeters of a prison, the outer perimeters of a work site, and during the movement of criminals. With the exception of the security forces and personnal connected with the supervision and control of the criminals, no one shall be allowed to carry arms into a prison, work site, or resting place of criminals.

Article 46. When there is a possibility of the criminals staging an escape, a riot, or other dangerous acts, after a special directive from the investigation organ or with the approval of the responsible personnel of an organ enforcing labor service for reform, a state of emergency may be declared. But when the possibility of dangerous acts has been removed, the emergency shall be called off.

Article 47. Under any of the conditions mentioned below, and when other preventive measures have been exhausted, an organ enforcing labor service for reform and its security forces may resort to the use of arms:

1. When the criminals start a collective riot;
2. When criminals escape, refuse orders to stop, or resist arrest;
3. When criminals armed with weapons or dangerous articles are in the act of commiting a crime or carrying out sabotage, refusing orders to stop, or carrying out resistance;
4. When criminals are being forced or assisted to escape, and orders to stop are unheeded; and
5. When criminals seize the arms of the security guards.

Conditions relating to each occasion when the use of force has been resorted to shall be reported in detail to the competent people's public security organ and the office of the people's procurator for examination.

An organ enforcing labor service for reform and its security forces, if employing arms without correct reason and thereby leading to criminal acts, shall be held responsible for the crime.

Article 48. An organ for the enforcement of labor service for reform and its security forces, on encountering a natural calamity or an accidental development, shall exert efforts to rescue the criminals and at the same time increase security measures.

Article 49. An organ enforcing labor service for reform shall carry out a daily inspection of the criminals and their cells, and a general inspection each week or fortnight.

Section 3.   Living Conditions

Article 50. The standards set for the food and clothing of criminals shall conform with unified specifications, and deductions from the quotas set or the use of the funds for other purposes shall be strictly prohibited.

In supplying food to criminals within the standards set, efforts shall be exerted to achieve variety and quality, and the living habits of national minority criminals shall be taken care of.

Article 51. For the supply of subsidiary foods and daily necessities to the criminals, the practical needs may be considered, and supply centers established within the labor service for reform sites.

Article 52. The actual period of labor for the criminals shall generally be from nine to ten hours, and seasonal production activities shall in no case exceed twelve hours a day. The period for sleep shall generally be eight hours. The period of study shall be provided in accordance with actual conditions, but shall not average less than one hour a day. The periods of sleep and study for juvenile delinquents shall be appropriately extended. Criminals not participating in labor service shall have at least from one to two hours of open air activities.

The criminals shall generally have one rest day each fortnight, and juvenile delinquents shall have one rest day a week.

Article 53. An organ enforcing labor service for reform shall, in accordance with the size of its unit, provide medical facilities such as clinics and hospitals, and shall have the necessary medical equipment. In a *hsien* (municipal) detention house where the number of criminals is not numerous, the *hsien* hospital may be entrusted with medical attention to the criminals.

Criminals shall be given sanitary and health facilities such as baths, haircuts, laundry facilities, disinfection, and plague prevention treatment regularly.

Article 54. When a criminal dies, a medical certificate shall be procured, and an examination made by the local people's court; notification shall also be issued to his family and the organ originally sending the criminal.

Article 55. Expenses incurred in connection with medical and health services, education, physical culture, and cultural and entertainment facilities for the criminals shall be defrayed by the organs enforcing labor service for reform in accordance with stipulated standards and actual needs.

Section 4. Visitors and Communication

Article 56. A criminal may not receive members of his family more than twice a month, and each interview shall not exceed thirty minutes. Under special circumstances and with the approval of the responsible personnel of the organ enforcing labor service for reform, the period may be extended. During an interview, the use of disguised language or foreign languages in conversation shall be banned. Foreign criminals receiving members of their family shall have interpreting personnel present on the occasion.

A criminal awaiting judgment may only receive members of his family with the approval of the original organ sending him or the organ trying his case.

Article 57. Daily necessities or people's currency notes sent a criminal by his family shall be fully inspected by the organ enforcing labor service for reform, and articles not necessary shall not be sent in. Currency notes sent to a criminal shall be registered and placed in the custody of the organ enforcing labor service for reform, and a receipt given the criminal. When the latter has legitimate use for money he may draw from it.

Article 58. A criminal sending or receiving a letter shall have it censored by the organ enforcing labor service for reform. A criminal awaiting judgment shall have a letter he sends out or receives censored by the original organ sending him or the organ trying his case. Letters that contain material leading to complicity in a case or obstructing the education or reform of a criminal shall be detained.

Article 59. In special circumstances, restriction or suspension of a criminal's receiving visitors, accepting gifts, or sending or receiving letters may be ordered.

Section 5. Bail

Article 60. When any one of the conditions mentioned below obtain, a criminal may be permitted to serve his sentence outside a prison on the furnishing of bail, but prior approval shall have to be obtained from the competent people's public security organ, and the people's public security organ in the area of his residence shall be notified to exercise supervision over him. The period spent outside the prison shall be included in the prison term served.

1. When a criminal suffers from a very serious illness which necessitates medical attention outside the prison under bail, with the exception of a criminal guilty of an arch crime; and

2. When a criminal is more than fifty-five or disabled, serving a sentence of more than five years, and incapable of doing further harm to society.

The conditions under paragraph 1 above shall also apply to a criminal awaiting judgment, but the approval of the organ originally sending him must be obtained, and the people's public security organ of the locality of his residence must be notified to exercise supervision over him.

Section 6.   Release

Article 61. A criminal shall be released upon the following conditions:

1. The expiration of his prison term;

2. Notification of release from the organ carrying out the investigation or trial of the case; or

3. On parole.

A criminal who is to be released shall be issued a release certificate by the organ enforcing labor service for reform, and shall be released at the proper time. Before the release, an examination of the case shall be made, and the conclusions recorded in the release certificate.

A released criminal shall be issued traveling expenses to his home by the organ enforcing labor service for reform. If he is seriously ill, his family shall be informed to come and take him home.

Article 62. When a criminal is released on the expiration of his sentence, and voluntarily desires to remain in the Corps for employment, or has no home or vocation to return to, or can be found a place locally in a large and sparsely populated district, the organ enforcing labor service for reform shall undertake the organization of such people for employment. Measures for such organization shall be separately provided.

CHAPTER VI.   SUPERVISORY AND CONTROL COMMITTEES

Article 63. A Committee of Supervision and Control shall be established for a Labor Service for Reform Corps with 3,000 or more members, situated in a desolate area a considerable distance away from a provincial capital.

Article 64. The duties of a Committee of Supervision and Control are to supervise, inspect, and direct the Labor Service for Reform Corps in its work of enforcing labor service, education, control of the criminals, and the implementation of the system of awards and punishments.

Article 65. A Committee of Supervision and Control shall have from five to seven members, with one or two representatives each from the provincial people's public security organ, the people's court, and the responsible members of the Labor Service for Reform Corps.

Article 66. The Committee of Supervision and Control shall periodically make reports to, and obtain instructions from, the relevant provincial people's public security organ, the people's court, and the office of the people's procurator.

CHAPTER VII. AWARDS AND PUNISHMENT

Article 67. There shall be enforced among the criminals a system of awards and punishment that enables them to contribute meritorious service in remission of their sins, and gives awards or inflicts punishment in a just manner.

Article 68. Under any one of the undermentioned conditions, and in accordance with the extent of the manifestations, a criminal shall be awarded by being extolled, given material rewards, credited with a note of merit, having his sentence reduced, or being paroled:

1. When a criminal has consistently abided by discipline, exerted effort at study, and shows real repentance for the crime committed;
2. When a criminal persuades and prevents other criminals from committing illegal acts, or exposes counterrevolutionary organizations and activities within or without the prison, such facts having been verified;
3. When a criminal actively engages in labor service, fulfilling or overfulfilling production tasks;
4. When a criminal exercises economy in the use of raw materials, products, or public property, having registered special achievements;
5. When a criminal excels in technical research, with inventions or creations to his credit, or shows exceptional readiness to impart to others his technical knowledge;
6. When a criminal is responsible for the suppression of calamities or serious accidents leading to the avoidance of losses; and
7. When a criminal has done such other acts as are beneficial to the state and to the people.

Article 69. Under any of the conditions mentioned below and in accordance with the varying degrees of seriousness, a criminal shall be punished through being cautioned, having a note of demerit recorded against him, or being placed in confinement:

1. When a criminal obstructs the reform of other criminals;
2. When a criminal does not treasure and damages production tools;
3. When a criminal is idle during labor service; and
4. When a criminal otherwise violates control regulations.

Article 70. The awards and punishments provided for in Articles 68 and 69, after having been approved by the responsible personnel of the organ enforcing labor service for reform, shall be announced and enforced. Reduction of sentence and parole, however, shall be reported to the competent people's public security organ for review and further sent to the local provincial or municipal people's court for approval before announcement and enforcement.

Article 71. When a criminal under confinement commits any one of the crimes mentioned below, the seriousness of the situation shall be taken into consideration, and the organ enforcing labor service for reform shall report the case to the local people's court for attention according to law:

1. Rioting or acts of violence, or inciting others to acts of violence;
2. Attempting to escape or organizing an attempt to escape;
3. Sabotaging construction projects or important public property;
4. Open resistance to labor service without repentence after repeated education; and
5. Other acts seriously violating the law.

Article 72. When an important counterrevolutionary criminal, a habitual robber, or a habitual thief, during the period of labor service for reform, fails to engage actively in labor service, frequently violates prison regulations, and is factually proved to have failed in being reformed, so that there is the possibility of his continuing to endanger social security after his release, the organ enforcing labor service for reform may, on the approach of the expiration of his sentence, submit views to the competent people's public security organ for examination, and if a judgment is handed down according to law by the local people's court, the criminal may be required to continue his labor service for reform.

Article 73. A criminal who has been punished, on his showing obvious signs of repentance, may, in accordance with the extent of his repentance, have the punishment reduced or revoked.

CHAPTER VIII. FUNDS

Article 74. Funds for the organs enforcing labor service for reform are derived from appropriations from the state budget and income from production of organs enforcing labor service for reform.

Article 75. The expenditures of organs enforcing labor service for reform shall conform with the standards and systems jointly provided by the Ministry of Public Security and Ministry of Finance of the Central People's Government.

Concrete measures for the control of the receipts and expenditures of organs enforcing labor service for reform shall be separately provided.

CHAPTER IX. ADDENDA

Article 76. Detailed rules for the enforcement of these Regulations shall be separately provided.

Article 77. These Regulations shall be promulgated for enforcement after approval by the meeting of the Government Administration Council of the Central People's Government.

DOCUMENT 39

CONSCRIPTION LAW OF THE PEOPLE'S REPUBLIC OF CHINA

[Adopted by the Standing Committee of the National People's Congress on February 7, 1955.]

CHAPTER I. GENERAL PRINCIPLES

Article 1. This Law is enacted in accordance with Article 103 of the Constitution of the People's Republic of China, which states: "It is the sacred duty of every citizen of the People's Republic of China to defend the homeland. It is the honorable duty of citizens of the People's Republic of China to perform military service as required by law."

Article 2. It is the duty of all male citizens of the People's Republic of China who have reached the age of eighteen to perform military service according to provisions of this Law, irrespective of nationality, race, occupation, social status, religious belief, or education.

Article 3. Counterrevolutionary elements, feudal landlords, and bureaucratic capitalists disfranchised by law for a certain period, and other disfranchised persons are not eligible for military service.

Article 4. The armed forces of the People's Republic of China are composed of various arms of the People's Liberation Army.

Article 5. Military service is divided into active service and reserve service.

Those on active service are called servicemen in active service and those on reserve service are called reserve servicemen.

Article 6. Servicemen in active service and reserve servicemen consist of officers, noncommissioned officers, and privates.

Article 7. The terms of active service for noncommissioned officers and privates are as follows: three years for noncommissioned officers and privates of the Army and Public Security Force; four years for noncommissioned officers and privates of the Air Force, Coast Guard Force, and Seaborne Security Force; and five years for noncommissioned officers and ratings of seaborne forces of the Navy.

The term of active service is counted from March 1 of the year subsequent to the year of call-up.

Article 8. Based on the needs of the army, the State Council has the right to extend the term of active service for noncommissioned officers and privates by a period of up to four months; the Ministry of National Defense has the right to transfer the servicemen in active service from one branch of service to another and to change their term of active service accordingly.

Article 9. Noncommissioned officers having served the term of active service may, according to the needs of the army and their desire, perform active service beyond the term; the period beyond the term of active service shall be at least one year.

Article 10. Noncommissioned officers and privates shall end their term of reserve service when they have reached the age of forty, and shall retire at the expiration of their term of reserve service.

Article 11. The Ministry of National Defense has the right to register women with special medical, veterinary, and other technical training for reserve service, and may organize them to receive collective training if necessary.

In wartime women having received such training may be called up to serve in the army. Women with proper qualifications may also be given technical training.

Article 12. The State Council and the administrative organs of the state in provinces, autonomous districts, municipalities directly under the Central People's Government, autonomous *chou, hsien,* autonomous *hsien,* and municipalities shall set up conscription committees to direct conscription work. The organization and duties of the conscription committees shall be determined by the State Council.

Article 13. Conscription bureaus shall be set up in all provinces, autonomous districts, municipalities subordinate to provincial governments, autonomous *chou, hsien,* autonomous *hsien,* and municipalities. Conscription bureaus are military organs in charge of conscription work.

The people's councils of municipal *ch'ü, hsiang,* and *chen* shall undertake conscription work in accordance with the decisions of the conscription bureaus of municipalities directly under the Central People's Government, *hsien,* autonomous *hsien,* and municipalities.

Article 14. Noncommissioned officers and privates who entered their services in the army as volunteers before the promulgation of this Law should, according to orders of the Ministry of National Defense, be demobilized, put on the reserve list, or retired by stages. The state shall issue them different amounts of production subsidies according to the length of their service, and the local administrative organs of the state shall properly resettle them and help them establish themselves in civilian life.

CHAPTER II. CALL-UP

Article 15. The period from March 1 of every year to the end of February of the next year shall be the year of call-up. Male citizens who have reached the age of eighteen before June 30 of the year of call-up should be called up for active service.

Article 16. All male citizens who have reached the age of eighteen before June 30 of the year of call-up should register for military service and take preliminary physical examinations before July 1, upon the notification of the conscription bureaus of municipalities directly under the Central People's Government, *hsien,* autonomous *hsien,* and municipalities. Those registered for military service and having passed preliminary physical examinations are called citizens eligible for conscription. Measures for military service registration shall be drawn up by the State Council.

Article 17. The State Council shall determine the number of persons to be called up for active service each year, measures of call-up, and quotas for provinces, autonomous districts, and municipalities directly under the Central People's Government. The quotas given by provinces and autonomous districts to *hsien,* autonomous *hsien,* and municipalities shall be determined by the people's councils of provinces, autonomous districts, and autonomous *chou.*

Article 18. Regular nationwide call-up should take place from November 1 of each year to the end of February of the following year according to the order of the Ministry of National Defense. Local dates of call-up should be determined by the conscription bureaus of provinces, autonomous districts, and municipalities directly under the Central People's Government.

Article 19. To facilitate call-up, municipalities directly under the Central People's Government, *hsien,* autonomous *hsien,* and municipalities shall be made call-up areas, within which a certain number of call-up stations may be established according to requirements.

Article 20. Following announcement of call-up, every citizen eligible for conscription should report at the date set by the conscription bureau of the call-up area in which he was registered. Citizens eligible for conscription who find it necessary to change their call-up area should complete procedures of transfer prior to August 1 of the call-up year; subsequent to August 1, the call-up area can be changed only if citizens eligible for conscription are transferred to another area on official duties, or if citizens eligible for conscription are removed with their families to another call-up area.

Article 21. At the time of call-up, the conscription committees shall organize state health organs in the localities concerned to give physical examinations on enlistment to citizens eligible for conscription. Examinations shall be conducted according to the standard of physical examination set by the Ministry of National Defense.

Article 22. Conscription may be deferred in the case of citizens eligible for conscription who are found unfit for service on account of illness.

Article 23. Subject to consideration and approval of the conscription committees of municipalities directly under the Central People's Government, *hsien,* and autonomous *hsien,* citizens eligible for conscription who are the sole family support or only sons shall be exempted from active service during peacetime. However, should the above conditions for exemption change, they should be called up for active service for the remaining part of a five-year period counting from the date they are eligible for conscription.

Article 24. Students studying in senior middle schools and schools equivalent to senior middle schools who have reached the age of eighteen shall be called up or deferred in call-up according to order of the State Council.

Students studying in institutes of higher learning shall be deferred in call-up.

Article 25. Citizens liable to conscription who are under arrest, sentenced to prison terms, or placed under surveillance shall not be called up.

CHAPTER III. RESERVE SERVICE OF NONCOMMISSIONED OFFICERS
AND PRIVATES

Article 26. Reserve service of noncommissioned officers and privates shall consist of class I reserve service and class II reserve service.

Article 27. Noncommissioned officers and privates who have fully served the term of active service shall enter into class I reserve service.

Article 28. Citizens liable to conscription who are not called up for active service in peacetime, citizens liable to conscription who are exempted from active service in peacetime, and women aged eighteen to forty who have registered themselves for reserve service in accordance with Article 11 of this Law shall enter into class II reserve service.

Reserve servicemen not called up during the call-up year and entered into class II reserve service may still be called up for active service for the remaining part of a five-year period counting from the date of their being put on the reserve list.

Article 29. Both class I and class II of reserve service shall be divided into grade I and grade II. Grade I shall include those reserve servicemen thirty years of age and under; grade II shall include those reserve servicemen forty years of age and under.

Article 30. Noncommissioned officers and privates on reserve service should participate in collective training according to the order of the Ministry of National Defense.

Article 31. Grade I reserve servicemen of class I selected for noncommissioned officer duties should participate in collective training according to the order of the Ministry of National Defense, and shall enter into reserve service at the expiration of collective training.

Article 32. Grade I reserve servicemen of class I selected to receive the rank of 2d Lieutenant should participate in collective training according to the order of the Ministry of National Defense. Those who have passed examinations at the expiration of their collective training and awarded the rank of 2d Lieutenant shall enter the reserve service of officers; those who have failed in the examinations shall continue to perform the reserve service of noncommissioned officers.

CHAPTER IV. ACTIVE SERVICE AND RESERVE SERVICE OF OFFICERS

Article 33. Officers retired after serving their term of active service, officers retired before fully serving their term of active service, officers given the rank of 2d Lieutenant according to Articles 32 and 54 of this Law, and personnel working in state organs that are not military organizations or in other enterprises who are qualified for officer duties and given the ranks of reserve officers, shall be put on the list of reserve officers.

Reserve service of officers shall be divided into grade I and grade II according to age.

Article 34. The maximum age limits for active service and reserve service of officers are as follows:

1. Officers of the Ground Force, Air Force, and Public Security Force:

    2d Lieutenant: Thirty years of age for active service, forty for grade I reserve service, and forty-five for grade II reserve service.

    1st Lieutenant: Thirty years of age for active service, forty for grade I reserve service, and forty-five for grade II reserve service.

    Senior 1st Lieutenant: Thirty-five years of age for active service, forty-five for grade I reserve service, and fifty for grade II reserve service.

    Captain: Thirty-five years of age for active service, forty-five for grade I reserve service, and fifty for grade II reserve service.

    Major: Forty years of age for active service, fifty for grade I reserve service, and fifty-five for grade II reserve service.

    Lieutenant Colonel: Forty-five years of age for active service, fifty-five for grade I reserve service, and sixty for grade II reserve service.

    Colonel: Fifty years of age for active service, fifty-five for grade I reserve service, and sixty for grade II reserve service.

    Senior Colonel: Fifty years of age for active service, fifty-five for grade I reserve service, and sixty for grade II reserve service.

    Brigadier General: Fifty-five years of age for active service, sixty for grade I reserve service, and sixty-five for grade II reserve service.

    Major General: Sixty years of age for active service, sixty for grade I reserve service, and sixty-five for grade II reserve service.

    Lieutenant General and above: maximum ages to be determined according to specific conditions.

2. Officers of the Navy and Seaborne Security Force:

    Warrant Officer: Thirty-five years of age for active service, forty for grade I reserve service, and forty-five for grade II reserve service.

    Junior Lieutenant: Thirty-five years of age for active service, forty for grade I reserve service, and forty-five for grade II reserve service.

    Lieutenant: Forty years of age for active service, forty-five for grade I reserve service, and fifty for grade II reserve service.

    Senior Lieutenant: Forty years of age for active service, forty-five for grade I reserve service, and fifty for grade II reserve service.

    Captain Lieutenant: Forty-five years of age for active service, fifty for grade I reserve service, and fifty-five for grade II reserve service.

    Captain 3d rank: Fifty years of age for active service, fifty-five for grade I reserve service, and sixty for grade II reserve service.

    Captain 2d rank: Fifty-five years of age for active service, fifty-five for grade I reserve service, and sixty for grade II reserve service. Captain 1st rank: Fifty-five years of age for active service, fifty-five for grade I reserve service, and sixty for grade II reserve service. Rear Admiral: Fifty-five years of age for active service, sixty for grade I reserve service, and sixty-five for grade II reserve service. Vice Admiral: 60 years of age for active service, sixty for grade I reserve service, and sixty-five for grade II reserve service.

Admiral and above: maximum ages to be determined according to specific conditions.

Article 35. Reserve officers shall retire after fully serving their term of reserve service.

Article 36. Reserve officers should participate in collective training during the period of reserve service according to the order of the Ministry of National Defense.

Article 37. Officers' service regulations shall be separately drawn up.

CHAPTER V. RIGHTS AND DUTIES OF SERVICEMEN IN SERVICE AND RESERVE SERVICE

Article 38. Servicemen in active service and reserve service enjoy the civil rights and duties prescribed in the Constitution of the People's Republic of China.

Except for those provided in this Law, the rights and duties of servicemen in active service arising from their military duties shall be prescribed separately by military regulations.

Article 39. Servicemen on active service and reserve service who perform meritorious service should be given state orders and medals and titles of honor.

Article 40. Living expenses and traveling expenses incurred by reserve servicemen during the period of collective training shall be supplied by the state.

Article 41. Workers and office employees should be granted specific leave and paid the usual salaries by the units to which they belong when they attend to business pertaining to registration and conscription.

Article 42. Reserve servicemen among workers and office employees should retain their original posts and should be paid a certain salary by the units to which they belong during the period of collective training of reserve servicemen. The wage standards shall be fixed by the State Council.

Measures for dealing with questions faced by peasants, handicraftsmen, and other laboring people arising from collective training of reserve servicemen shall be determined by the State Council.

Article 43. Reserve officers shall receive subsidies from collective training organs, according to the standard set by the Ministry of National Defense during the period of collective training.

Article 44. Dependents of servicemen in active service who were killed or die of illness on active duty are entitled to pensions and preferential treatment by the state. Servicemen in active service who are disabled on active duty shall receive pensions and preferential treatment by the state. Regulations on pension and preferential treatment shall be separately drawn up.

Article 45. Servicemen in active service and their dependents are entitled to preferential treatment by the state under regulations to be separately drawn up.

Article 46. Servicemen in reserve service are under obligation to observe the discipline of the People's Liberation Army during the period of collective training.

CHAPTER VI. REGISTRATION AND STATISTICS OF SERVICEMEN IN
RESERVE SERVICE

Article 47. Servicemen in reserve service should register for military service at the place designated by the conscription bureaus in the localities where they reside.

Article 48. Servicemen in reserve service who change their place of residence should complete transfer of their conscription records at the same time as completing the transfer of their census records.

Article 49. Registration and statistics of servicemen on reserve service shall be handled by conscription bureaus of municipalities directly under the Central People's Government, *hsien,* autonomous *hsien,* and municipalities.

Article 50. Measures governing registration and statistics of servicemen in reserve service shall be drawn up by the Ministry of National Defense.

CHAPTER VII. WARTIME CALL-UP

Article 51. Wartime call-up shall be ordered by the Ministry of National Defense on the basis of a decision by the State Council, following state proclamation of a mobilization order.

Article 52. Upon proclamation of a mobilization order by the state, all personnel of the People's Liberation Army should carry on their duties until they are freed from active service by order of the Ministry of National Defense; and all servicemen in reserve service should prepare to answer the call-up and should punctually report at the designated place after receipt of orders from the conscription bureaus of municipalities directly under the Central People's Government, *hsien,* autonomous *hsien,* and municipalities.

CHAPTER VIII.   MILITARY TRAINING OF STUDENTS OF SENIOR MIDDLE
SCHOOLS AND ABOVE

Article 53. Students of senior middle schools and schools equivalent
to senior middle schools should receive military training prior to call-up
in schools. The hours and subjects of training shall be decided by the
State Council.

Article 54. Students of institutes of higher learning should receive
military training in school and should prepare to acquire the ranks of
company grade officers and perform the duties of company grade officers. The hours and subjects of training in institutes of higher learning shall be decided by the State Council.

Article 55. Military training of students of senior middle schools and
above shall be conducted by military teachers on the school staff.

CHAPTER IX.   ADDENDA

Article 56. Youths under eighteen years of age who wish to enroll in
military academies of their own account shall not be subject to re-
strictions of the draft liability age for active service stipulated in this
Law.

Article 57. Following enforcement of this Law, people's militiamen
should carry on their tasks of preserving local security and protecting
production and construction.

[Note: In January, 1965, the period of compulsory military service was lengthened
by one year.]

DOCUMENT 40

RULES OF CONDUCT FOR STUDENTS

[Promulgated by the Ministry of Education in February and
May, 1955.]

1. Endeavor to be a good student—good in health, good in studies,
and good in conduct. Prepare to serve the motherland and the people.

2. Respect the national flag. Respect and love the leader of the
people.

3. Obey all the instructions of the principal and teachers. Value and
protect the reputation of the school and of the class.

4. Arrive at the school punctually and attend the classes punctually.
Never be late; never leave school early; never miss a class without
reason.

5. When attending school, bring all the textbooks and stationery required. Before the class begins, prepare all the things required for the lesson.

6. Be orderly and quiet and assume a correct posture during the class. When desiring to leave the classroom, ask the teacher's permission first.

7. During the class, work diligently and listen attentively to the teacher's instruction and to the questions and answers of your classmates. Do not talk unless necessary; do not do anything else except your class work.

8. During the class, when you want to give an answer or to ask a question, raise your hand first. Stand up and speak when the teacher allows you to; sit down when the teacher tells you to.

9. Carefully complete in time the outside work assigned by the teacher.

10. Perform your duties well when it is your day to be the student on duty. Participate actively in extracurricular activities.

11. Respect the principal and the teacher. Salute your teacher when the class begins and again at the end of the class. When you meet the principal or the teacher outside the school, you also salute them.

12. Be friendly with your schoolmates, unite with them, and help each other.

13. When going to school or returning home, do not delay on the way, in order to avoid accidents.

14. Respect and love your parents. Love and protect your brothers and sisters. Do what you can to help your parents.

15. Respect the aged. Give way or offer a seat or any other possible help to the aged, to children, to the sick, or anybody who may have difficulty in movement.

16. Be polite to people. Do not curse. Do not fight. Do not make a lot of noise in public places. Do not disturb people's work, study, or sleep.

17. Do not tell a lie or cheat people. Do not gamble. Do not take away other people's things without their permission. Do not do anything that may be harmful to yourself or to others.

18. Take care of public property. Do not damage or dirty tables, chairs, doors, windows, walls, floors, or anything else.

19. Eat, rest, and sleep at regular hours. Play and take exercise frequently to make your body strong.

20. Keep your body, food, clothes, utensils, bed, and living quarters clean and hygienic. Pay attention to cleanliness and hygiene at public places.

DOCUMENT 41

CONSTITUTION OF THE ALL-CHINA STUDENT FEDERATION

[Passed by the 16th All-China Student Congress on August 6, 1955.]

Article 1. The Federation shall be known as the All-China Student Federation.

Article 2. The objective of the Federation is to unite the students of the higher institutions of learning throughout the country actively to respond to the call of Chairman Mao for "building a good physique, studying well and working well"; to exert efforts to make students into well-rounded, constructive personnel, faithful to the socialist cause of the motherland; to serve the needs of the construction and protection of the motherland; and to unite with democratic students of the whole world in the struggle for peace, democracy, and the beautiful future.

Article 3. All student councils of higher institutions supporting the Constitution of the Federation may apply for membership, and shall become corporate members of the Federation on the approval of the Committee of the Federation.

Members of the Federation have the right to vote and to be elected, the right to make recommendations or criticize the work of the Federation, priority in the enjoyment of the various cultural and welfare enterprises sponsored by the Federation, and the obligation to abide by the Constitution of the Federation, to carry out the resolutions of the Federation, and to pay membership fees.

Article 4. The member student councils of the Federation shall elect representatives to organize the All-China Conference of Representatives of Corporate Members of the Federation, to be held once every three years. Its duties and powers shall be to examine and decide upon the work of the Federation, the formulation and revision of the Constitution, and the election of the Committee of the Federation.

Article 5. In cities with a comparatively larger number of higher institutions of learning, the corporate members of the Federation may organize municipal student federations, that is, joint meetings of the chairmen of the student councils of higher institutions in the same city. The responsibility of such a federation is to promote the work of the student councils and organize the political, cultural, and physical culture activities of the students of the whole city.

A municipal student federation (the joint meeting of the chairmen

, of student councils of higher institutions in the whole city) shall elect a chairman to take charge of its meetings and tasks.

Article 6. The student councils of the various higher institutions of learning shall be the basic organs of the Federation. The normal tasks of a student council are to promote the education of students and organize their social, political, cultural, and physical culture activities, and pay attention to their living conditions and welfare.

The student congress of a school (the general conference of the students of the school) shall examine and decide upon the work of its student council, and elect the committee of the council. A student council shall have a chairman, a number of vice-chairmen, and members of the committee to take charge of routine tasks.

Article 7. The Federation participates as a corporate member in the All-China Federation of Democratic Youth.

Article 8. The income of the Federation shall be derived from membership fees and donations by society.

DOCUMENT 42

EDUCATION MUST BE COMBINED WITH PRODUCTIVE LABOR

by Lu Ting-Yi*

[Excerpts from the English translation of an article published in *Peking Review,* September 9, 1958.]

The educational policy of the Chinese Communist Party has always been that education should serve the politics of the working class and be combined with productive labor; and to apply this policy, education must be directed by the Communist Party. This is the direct opposite of the educational policy of the bourgeoisie. Bourgeois education is directed by bourgeois politicians; it serves the politics of the bourgeoisie—that is, it serves the dictatorship of the bourgeoisie; it is incompatible with proletarian dictatorship. Under the socialist system, the bourgeoisie dare not advocate directly and openly that education should be directed by bourgeois politicians and be a weapon against the proletarian dictatorship; it can only put forward the hypocritical, deceptive propositions that "education should be directed by

---

* In 1958, Lu Ting-yi was director of the Propaganda Department of the Central Committee. He was removed from this position in 1966.

experts" and "education for education's sake," with the aim of preventing education from serving the proletarian dictatorship. In our
socialist country, therefore, the educational policy advocated by the
bourgeoisie is embodied in the propositions "education for education's sake," "mental and manual work are separate" and "education should be directed by experts."

Education is, first and foremost, the transmission and acquisition
of knowledge. But what is knowledge? What is the purpose of trans-
mitting and acquiring knowledge? We Communists interpret these
questions differently from the bourgeoisie. Most bourgeois pedagogues
hold that only book knowledge is knowledge and that practical experience cannot be regarded as knowledge. They therefore take the
view that education means reading books; the more a man reads, the
more knowledge he has, and those possessing book knowledge are of
a higher order. As for productive labor, particularly manual labor and
manual workers, they think all this is demeaning, a "blind alley."
There are other bourgeois pedagogues who maintain that education
is life and vice versa. They do not understand life as the practice of
class struggle and struggle for production, nor do they stress the importance of theory. So in the end, in effect, they write off education.
These two sets of bourgeois views, though they appear to be diametri-
cally opposed to each other, stem from the same root. They imply
that there is no class differentiation among human beings and that
pedagogy is a branch of learning that stands above classes. We Communists view the question differently.

We believe that pedagogy is a branch of the social sciences. All the
social sciences must be guided by politics, and education is no exception. People require education to wage the class struggle and the
struggle for production. We believe there are only two types of knowledge in the world. One is knowledge of the class struggle. The class
struggle is the struggle between groups of men of different economic
status and this has already existed for several thousand years. In the
present period of transition in our country, there is still class struggle.
In the future, when classes no longer exist, even though there will not
be class struggle, there will still be contradictions among the people;
therefore, for tens of thousands of years to come there will still be
poisonous weeds—that is, there will be struggle between truth and
falsehood, between the advanced and the backward, between those who
forward and those who impede the development of the productive
forces.

The other kind of knowledge is the knowledge of the struggle for
production, that is, the knowledge men gain in their struggle against
nature. Philosophy is the summing up and generalization of the two

kinds of knowledge. The importance of philosophy consists in the fact that the philosophy of dialectical materialism provides men with a correct way of thinking. The essential distinction between men lies not in differences of "disposition" or personality, but, first of all, in their different class standpoints and, in addition, their ways of thinking. Class standpoints and ways of thinking are interrelated and at the same time are distinct from each other. Errors always emanate from two sources: class origin and the way of thinking. To avoid making great errors or to commit fewer errors, people must study politics and philosophy.

We are Marxists, and so we maintain that it is necessary to proceed from objective reality. Therefore we must first study our own conditions seriously and have the drive to undertake such research. We also study the experiences of our fraternal countries seriously, and we study history seriously, but our purpose is not to copy or transplant but to understand history and to understand historical materialism in the field of education, so as to have examples to help us in doing our work satisfactorily in accordance with our own conditions. Whatever our sphere of work, we must rely closely on the leadership of the Party because it is indeed the Communist Party, and no one else that understands our conditions best and knows Marxism best. The Communist Party is the highest form of organization of the working class; it must and can give the leadership in everything. From the Central Committee down to the basic organizations, the Communist Party is the organized, disciplined vanguard of the working class. We have relied on this vanguard for victory in the revolutionary war and for success in the socialist revolution on the economic, political, and ideological fronts, and we must rely on it for victory in the technical and cultural revolutions. Our educational workers should accept Party leadership not only in politics, but also in the sphere of educational ideas, policy, and work. Only in this way will it be possible to keep up with the times and avoid mistakes or make fewer mistakes.

In our country's present conditions, we can train people to do many kinds of work, but cannot yet train "people to be capable of undertaking any profession." The essence of all-around development is also that the knowledge imparted to the students must be not one-sided and fragmentary, but comparatively complete knowledge. This requires that education should serve politics and be combined with productive labor. Speaking of his ideal of education in the future, Karl Marx referred to "an education that will, in the case of every child over a given age, combine productive labor with instruction and gymnastics, not only as one of the methods of adding to the efficiency of production, but as the only method of producing fully developed human beings." (*Capital,* Vol. I.) That is, he urged that students acquire comparatively complete knowledge and be able to engage not only in mental labor but manual labor as well. Book knowledge alone, however broad, is still partial and incomplete. People with extensive book knowledge alone and without experience of practical work are what only the bourgeoisie calls "know-it-alls"; they are not what we regard as people of all-around development. Sound physical development is necessary in childhood. In addition, a Communist spirit and style and collective heroism should be inculcated in childhood. This is the moral education of our day. Both are linked with the development of intellectual education. Both are related to manual work and therefore the principle of combining education with labor is unshakable.

In brief, the all-around development we stand for is this: Students should be enabled to acquire comparatively complete, broader knowledge, grow up physically fit, and acquire Communist morals. In his *On the Correct Handling of Contradictions among the People,* Comrade Mao Tse-tung said, "Our educational policy must enable everyone who gets an education to develop morally, intellectually, and physically, and become a cultured, socialist-minded worker." This is our educational principle of all-around development. "A cultured, socialist-minded worker" is a man who is both politically conscious and educated. He is able to undertake both mental and manual work. He is what we regard as developed in an all-around way, both politically and professionally qualified. He is a worker-intellectual and an intellectual-worker.

We insist on the educational principle of all-around development. We consider that the only method to train human beings in all-around development is to educate them to serve working-class politics and combine education with productive labor. We say the only method, because there is no other way to achieve this aim. Bourgeois pedagogues do not agree. They consider the only method to train people to have what they call "all-around development" is to read books and learn by rote. They are absolutely against students learning politics and, in particular, students becoming laborers. According to our educational principle of all-around development, we can and must rely on the masses to run education. According to the bourgeois educational principle of so-called "all-around development," they can rely only on experts to run education; they cannot rely on the masses. According to our educational principle of all-around development, education must be under the leadership of the Communist Party. According to the bourgeois educational principle of so-called "all-around development," education can only be led by the experts; it does not need the leadership of the Communist Party as the Communist Party is "a layman." From this we see that different interpretations of all-around development lead to different and even opposite conclusions. That is why we say that the debate on education in recent years ultimately boils down to the question of "what is all-around development." This is essentially a struggle between proletarian and bourgeois educational ideas.

The chief mistakes and defects in our educational work have been the isolation of education from productive labor. The policy of combining education with productive labor was put forward by our Party early in 1934. Comrade Mao Tse-tung said at that time: "What is the general policy for the Soviet culture and education? It is to educate the broad masses of the toiling people in the spirit of Communism, to make culture and education serve the revolutionary war and the class struggle, to combine education with labor, and to enable the broad masses of the Chinese people to enjoy civilization and happiness." In 1954, when the period of economic rehabilitation was over and the First Five-Year Plan was already in operation, the Central Committee of the Party raised the question of adding productive labor to the curricula of the schools. But the proposal encountered obstruction and was not carried through at that time. The Central Committee of the Party repeatedly stressed its policy that education must be combined with productive labor—at the national conference on propaganda work in March, 1957, in the editorial of *Jen Min Jih Pao* (People's Daily) on April 8 of the same year, and at the Nanning meeting in January, 1958. It is only now that this policy of the Party has been realized on a nationwide scale. Education must serve politics, must be combined with productive labor, and must be led by the Party; these three things are interrelated. Education divorced from productive labor is bound to lead to some degree to the neglect of politics and of Party leadership in educational work, thus divorcing education from the realities of our country and eventually causing right deviationist and doctrinaire mistakes.

The aim of our socialist revolution is to wipe out all exploiting classes and all systems of exploitation, including their remnants. Basic victory has now been won in the socialist revolution on the economic front. On the political and ideological fronts, too, the socialist revolution has achieved decisive victory. As the Second Session of the Eighth National Congress of the Communist Party of China has pointed out in its resolution, our task is "to actively carry out the technical and cultural revolutions while continuing with the socialist revolution on the economic, political, and ideological fronts."

The cultural revolution is to enable all 600 million Chinese people, except for those who are incapable, to do productive work and to study. This means to make the masses of our workers and peasants intellectuals as well, and our intellectuals laborers too. Only as the masses of the workers and peasants and the intellectuals alike develop and make up what they lack is it possible to change thoroughly the irrational legacy of the old society and eradicate the backwardness of each, i.e., eliminate the cultural deficiency of the masses of workers and peasants and eliminate the bourgeois thinking of the intellectuals. This is, therefore, a very far-reaching revolution that demands that education must serve working-class politics, that it be combined with productive labor.

Marx said: "An early combination of productive labor with education is one of the most potent means for the transformation of present-day society." (Karl Marx: *Critique of the Gotha Program*.) It is impossible to carry through the cultural revolution without combining education with productive labor. Cultural revolution is beneficial to the country and to the masses of workers and peasants as well as the intellectuals. Only those who stick to the bourgeois standpoint do not want such a revolution. The bourgeois policy of education for education's sake and of divorcing mental from physical labor is incompatible with the socialist revolution.

The future Communist society will be one of "from each according to his ability and to each according to his needs," a society in which the differences between town and country and between mental and manual labor are eliminated. Our great leap forward in industry and agriculture has made the attainment of Communism no longer a far distant prospect. Marx and Engels formulated ten measures to establish Communist society that "will be pretty generally acceptable . . . in the most advanced countries" 110 years ago in the *Communist Manifesto*. Of these, the first eight have already been carried out in China, through the adoption of methods suitable to the actual conditions of our country; and the last two, namely "the combination of agriculture with manufacturing industries; the gradual abolition of the distinction between town and country" and "the combination of education with industrial production" are beginning to be carried out.

Because the principle of combining education with productive labor is beginning to go into operation, with schools setting up their own factories and farms, and factories and agricultural cooperatives establishing their own schools on a large scale, the phenomenon of students who are at the same time workers and peasants and of workers and peasants who are at the same time students is beginning to appear. This, too, has the embryo of Communist society. It can be imagined that when China enters into Communism, our basic social organizations will be many Communist communes. With few exceptions, each basic unit will have workers, peasants, traders, students, and militia. In the field of education, each basic unit will have its own primary and secondary schools and institutions of higher learning; at the same time everybody will have the time to acquire education as both laborer and intellectual. In *The Housing Question* Engels anticipated this situation when he said:

> And it is precisely this industrial revolution which has raised the productive power of human labor to such a high level that—for the first time in the history of humanity—the possibility exists, given a rational division of labor among all, of producing not only enough for the plentiful consumption of all members of society and for an abundant reserve fund, but also of leaving each individual sufficient leisure so that what is really worth preserving in historically inherited culture—science, art, forms of intercourse—may not only be preserved but converted from a monopoly of the ruling class into the common property of the whole of society, and may be further developed.

To attain this prospect, our educational work must not go in the direction of divorcing mental and manual labor but in the direction of combining mental with manual labor and education with productive labor.

The principle of combining education with productive labor is needed by the working class and all other working people. This principle, which conforms to the people's desires, will certainly prevail. On the other hand, the principle of divorcing mental from manual labor, since it does not conform to the socialist economic base and the people's requirements, will sooner or later be discarded by the people, even though it has a tradition of thousands of years. With politics in command, with leadership by the Communist Party, and the rallying of the entire Party and all educational workers who can be rallied to fight against bourgeois educational policy and for the application of the Party's educational policy, we can carry through our cultural revolution that all of our 600 million people are able to do productive work and all are able to study, becoming new men who are both laborers and intellectuals.

DOCUMENT 43

COMMUNIST CHINA'S FOREIGN POLICY

[Excerpts from an official report of Foreign Minister Ch'en Yi's press conference for nearly 300 Chinese and foreign journalists on September 29, 1965. The English text appeared in *Peking Review, October 8, 1965.*]

ON SHARING NUCLEAR KNOWLEDGE

A London *Times* correspondent asked whether China was prepared to share her nuclear knowledge with any of the developing countries.

In reply, Vice-Premier Ch'en Yi first commented on the western countries' practice of dividing nations into the "developed" and the "underdeveloped." He said, "The western countries have shown a superiority complex by claiming themselves to be 'developed' while degrading some other countries by calling them 'underdeveloped.' I do not agree with these terms. Now they promote the so-called underdeveloped countries by describing them as developing countries. So far as China is concerned, we are not grateful for that. The facts over the past three centuries show that the so-called developed countries have developed by exploiting the colonies, while the so-called underdeveloped countries remain undeveloped as a result of imperialist and colonialist exploitation. No rigid line should be drawn by classifying certain countries as developed and some others as underdeveloped. We hold that, politically, the Asian, African, and Latin American countries which persist in opposing imperialism and colonialism are advanced, while the West European and North American imperialist countries are backward. Economically, we do not believe that the people of Asia, Africa, and Latin America will remain backward forever and that Western Europe and North America forever will be in the vanguard technically. The people of Asia, Africa, and Latin America will overtake the industrially advanced countries within a few decades, once they shake off the control of imperialism and old and new colonialism and start to build their countries by relying on their own efforts. The history of New China over the past sixteen years provides vivid evidence of this. China has achieved great successes in national construction, mainly through the united efforts of the government and the people, self-reliance, hard work, and the exploitation of her own resources. So far there has not been any country in the world which can change its state of backwardness by merely relying on foreign aid."

329

Vice-Premier Ch'en Yi said, "There are two aspects of the question of nuclear cooperation. As for the peaceful use of atomic energy and the building of atomic reactors, China has already been approached by several countries, and China is ready to render them assistance; as for the request for China's help in the manufacture of atom bombs, this question is not realistic.

"In my opinion, the most important task for the Afro-Asian countries today is to shake off imperialist control politically, economically, and culturally, and develop their own independent economy. This task is an acute struggle and its accomplishment will take quite a few years. Any country with a fair basis in industry and agriculture and in science and technology will be able to manufacture atom bombs, with or without China's assistance. China hopes that Afro-Asian countries will be able to make atom bombs themselves, and it would be better for a greater number of countries to come into possession of atom bombs.

"In our view, the role of atom bombs should not be overstressed. The United States has been brandishing the atom bomb for atomic blackmail over the past twenty years, but it has failed. The just struggle of Afro-Asian countries against imperialism and colonialism is the best atom bomb."

ON THE UNITED NATIONS

Concerning the question of restoring to China her legitimate rights in the United Nations, which was raised by the Japanese correspondents, Vice-Premier Ch'en Yi said, "The United Nations has long been controlled by the United States and has today become a place where two big powers, the United States and the Soviet Union, conduct political transactions. This state of affairs has not changed even though dozens of Afro-Asian and peace-loving countries have made no small efforts in the United Nations. China need not take part in such a United Nations.

"During the U.S. war of aggression against Korea, the United Nations adopted a resolution naming China as an aggressor. How can China be expected to take part in an international organization that calls her an aggressor? Calling China an aggressor and then asking the aggressor to join, would not the United Nations be slapping its own face?

"The question now is how to reform the United Nations in accordance with the purposes and principles of its Charter and to free it from the control of the United States and other big powers. If the task of reforming the United Nations cannot be accomplished, conditions will no doubt gradually ripen for the establishment of a revolutionary United Nations.

"Will the present U.N. General Assembly adopt a resolution expelling the elements of the Chiang Kai-shek clique and restoring China's legitimate rights? I think this is impossible as the United Nations is now controlled by the United States. If things really turn out that way, the question will still remain unsolved.

"The United Nations must rectify its mistakes and undergo a thorough reorganization and reform. It must admit and correct all its past mistakes. Among other things, it should cancel its resolution condemning China and the Democratic People's Republic of Korea as aggressors and adopt a resolution condemning the United States as the aggressor; the U.N. Charter must be reviewed and revised jointly by all countries, big and small; all independent states should be included in the United Nations; and all imperialist puppets should be expelled.

"For more than ten years, many countries have in the United Nations firmly demanded the expulsion of the representatives of the Chiang Kai-shek clique and the restoration of China's legitimate rights. China is always grateful for this just and friendly action."

ON KUOMINTANG-COMMUNIST COOPERATION

The Japanese correspondents asked about the possibility of cooperation between the Kuomintang and the Chinese Communist Party. Vice-Premier Ch'en Yi said, "At present there are Revolutionary Committees of the Kuomintang in the provinces and municipalities as well as in Peking, which are cooperating very well with the Communist Party. New China is a country in which eight democratic parties cooperate with the Communist Party and are led by it. We welcome Mr. Li Tsung-jen's participation in this cooperation. Chiang Kai-shek and Chiang Ching-kuo are also welcome to join in this cooperation as Mr. Li Tsung-jen has done. Taiwan Province and any individual or group in Taiwan are welcome to come back to the embrace of the motherland and join in this cooperation. To break away from U.S. imperialist control and be loyal to the motherland—there are no other conditions. In my view, the possibility of Kuomintang-Communist cooperation is great and is, moreover, increasing."

ON CHINA'S THIRD FIVE-YEAR PLAN

The Japanese correspondents asked about China's Third Five-Year Plan. Vice-Premier Ch'en Yi said, "Next year our country will commence its Third Five-Year Plan. During the Second Five-Year Plan, our country met with great difficulties in its national construction because of natural disasters, the blockade imposed by the U.S. imperialists, and the stoppage of aid by Khrushchev. After three years of readjustment, there has been a general turn for the better in the situation, and our industrial and agricultural production has entered a new stage of development, a stage of general upsurge. We shall have a good harvest this year, but there still are natural disasters. It will take decades—thirty to fifty years more of efforts—to build up China's industry, agriculture, and national defense and raise them to a higher level.

"We have laid the foundation for building an independent, integrated, and modern economic system, but many problems remain to be solved. In science and technology, the world's advanced levels have been reached in some branches, but in some others we have reached only the average levels, and there are still a number of gaps. We are optimistic about China's development, but there are still many difficulties to be surmounted.

"In China, too, there are revisionists and people who have illusions about U.S. imperialism. Some people are in the process of remolding themselves, and some have not yet remolded themselves. But these elements play no role in the making of China's policies and exercise no influence among the people. China is stable."

On U.S. Imperialism

"China does not see the question of Taiwan, the question of Hong Kong, and the question of Macao, each on its own; what we see is the global strategy of U.S. imperialism. One must be prepared to wage a worldwide struggle before U.S. imperialism can be defeated. Will the imperialists allow the socialist countries in Eastern Europe and the Soviet Union to live in security? The Khrushchev revisionists place implicit trust in what U.S. imperialism says, and they will sooner or later come to grief for it. . . ."

"The Chinese people are ready to make all necessary sacrifices in the fight against imperialism. It is up to the U.S. President and the Pentagon to decide whether the United States wants a big war with China today. We cherish no illusions about U.S. imperialism. We are fully prepared against U.S. aggression. If the U.S. imperialists are determined to launch a war of aggression against us, they are welcome to come as soon as they want, to come tomorrow. Let the Indian reactionaries, the British imperialists, and the Japanese militarists come along with them! Let the modern revisionists from the north act in coordination with them! We will still win in the end. The great Soviet people and the Communist Party of the Soviet Union will not allow their leaders to take such a criminal decision. Who will meet with destruction— the U.S. imperialists or the people of the world? It can be said with certainty that the U.S. imperialists will perish, while the people of the whole world will win liberation. . . ."

"For sixteen years we have been waiting for the U.S. imperialists to come and attack us. My hair has turned grey in waiting. Perhaps I will not have the luck to see the U.S. imperialist invasion of China, but my children may see it, and they will resolutely carry on the fight. Let no correspondent think that I am bellicose. It is the U.S. imperialists who are brutal and vicious and who bully others too much. They are bullying the Chinese, the Koreans, the Vietnamese, the Khmers, the Laotians, the Indonesians, the Congolese, and the Dominicans. Even their ally France is being bullied by them. Those who are bullied by them have risen against them and become friends of China. This is of the United States' own making.

"Should the U.S. imperialists invade China's mainland, we will take all necessary measures to defeat them. By then, the war will have no boundaries. It is the United States, and not China, that will have broken down the boundaries. We are willing to respect boundaries, but the United States willfully violates boundaries and intervenes wherever it likes. With the defeat of U.S. imperialism, the time will come when imperialism and colonialism will be really liquidated throughout the world. The ideal is bound to come true, with the world truly becoming a community of nations with different social systems coexisting peacefully. China is ready to make all the necessary sacrifices for this noble ideal. She will never take the modern revisionist position of betraying Marxism-Leninism and proletarian internationalism."

DOCUMENT 44

PEOPLE'S WAR

[Excerpts from Defense Minister Lin Piao's article on the twentieth anniversary of the Japanese surrender ending World War II. The English text appeared in *Peking Review*, September 3, 1965.]

Of the innumerable wars against imperialists waged by the Chinese people in the past hundred years, the War of Resistance Against Japan was the first to end in complete victory. It occupies an extremely important place in the annals of both the revolutionary wars of the Chinese people and the wars of the oppressed nations of the world against imperialist aggression.

It was a war in which a weak semicolonial and semifeudal country triumphed over a strong imperialist country.

How was it possible for a weak country finally to defeat a strong country? How was it possible for a seemingly weak army to become the main force in the war?

Comrade Mao Tse-tung's theory of and policies for people's war have creatively enriched and developed Marxism-Leninism. The Chinese people's victory in the anti-Japanese war was a victory for people's war, for Marxism-Leninism, and for the thought of Mao Tse-tung.

Today, the U.S. imperialists are repeating on a worldwide scale the past actions of the Japanese imperialists in China and other parts of Asia. It has become an urgent necessity for the people in many countries to master and use people's war as a weapon against U.S. imperialism and its lackeys. In every conceivable way U.S. imperialism and its lackeys are trying to extinguish the revolutionary flames of people's war. The Khrushchev revisionists, fearing people's war like the plague, are heaping abuse on it. The two are in collusion to prevent and sabotage people's war. In these circumstances, it is of vital practical importance to review the historical experience of the great victory of the people's war in China and to recapitulate Comrade Mao Tse-tung's theory of people's war.

As far back as the period of the First Revolutionary Civil War, Comrade Mao Tse-tung had pointed out that the peasant question occupied an extremely important position in the Chinese revolution, that the bourgeois-democratic revolution against imperialism and feudalism was in essence a peasant revolution, and that the basic task of the Chinese proletariat in the bourgeois-democratic revolution was to give leadership to the peasants' struggle.

In the period of the War of Resistance Against Japan, Comrade Mao Tse-tung again stressed that the peasants were the most reliable and the most numerous ally of the proletariat and constituted the main force in the War of Resistance. The peasants were the main source of manpower for China's armies. The funds and the supplies needed for a protracted war came chiefly from the peasants. In the anti-Japanese war it was imperative to rely mainly on the peasants and to arouse them to participate in the war on the broadest scale.

The War of Resistance Against Japan was in essence a peasant revolutionary war led by our Party. By arousing and organizing the peasant masses and integrating them with the proletariat, our Party created a powerful force capable of defeating the strongest enemy.

To rely on the peasants, build rural bases, and use the countryside to encircle and finally capture the cities—such was the way of victory in the Chinese revolution.

Basing himself on the characteristics of the Chinese revolution, Comrade Mao Tse-tung pointed out the importance of building rural revolutionary bases.

> Since China's key cities have long been occupied by the powerful imperialists and their reactionary Chinese allies, it is imperative for the revolutionary ranks to turn the backward villages into advanced, consolidated bases, into great military, political, economic, and cultural bastions of the revolution from which to fight their vicious enemies who are using the cities for attacks on the rural districts, and to achieve the complete victory of the revolution through protracted fighting; it is imperative for them to do so if they do not wish to compromise with imperialism and its lackeys, but are determined to fight on, and if they intend to build up and temper their forces and avoid decisive battles with a powerful enemy while their own strength is inadequate.*

During the War of Resistance Against Japan, the Japanese imperialist forces occupied many of China's big cities and the main lines of communication. Owing to their shortage of troops, however, they were unable to occupy the vast countryside, which remained the vulnerable sector of the enemy's rule. Consequently, the possibility of building rural bases became even greater. Shortly after the beginning of the War of Resistance, when the Japanese forces surged into China's hinterland and the Kuomintang forces crumbled and fled in one defeat after another, the Eighth Route and New Fourth Armies, led by our Party, followed the wise policy laid down by Comrade Mao Tse-tung. Small contingents boldly drove into the areas behind the enemy lines and established bases throughout the countryside. During the eight years of the war, we established nineteen anti-Japanese bases in northern, central, and southern China. With the exception of the big cities and the main lines of communication, the vast territory in the enemy's rear was in the hands of the people.

In the anti-Japanese base areas, we carried out democratic reforms, improved the livelihood of the people, and mobilized and organized the peasant masses. Organs of anti-Japanese democratic political power were established on an extensive scale, and the masses of the people enjoyed the democratic right to run their own affairs. At the same time

---

* Mao Tse-tung, *The Chinese Revolution and the Communist Party of China,* 1939.

we carried out the policies of "a reasonable burden" and "the reduction of rent and interest," which weakened the feudal system of exploitation and improved the people's livelihood. As a result, the enthusiasm of the peasant masses was deeply aroused, while the various anti-Japanese strata were given due consideration and were thus united. In formulating our policies for the bases, we also took care that these policies should facilitate our work in the enemy-occupied areas.

In the enemy-occupied cities and villages, we combined legal with illegal struggle, united the basic masses and all patriots, and divided and disintegrated the political power of the enemy and his puppets, so as to prepare to attack the enemy from within and without when conditions were ripe.

The essence of Comrade Mao Tse-tung's theory of army building is that in building a people's army, prominence must be given to politics, i.e., the army must first and foremost be built on a political basis. Politics is the commander, politics is the soul of everything. Political work is the lifeline of our army. True, although a people's army must pay attention to the constant improvement of its weapons and equipment and its military technique, it does not rely purely on weapons and technique; it relies mainly on politics, on the proletarian revolutionary consciousness and courage of the commanders and fighters, and on the support and backing of the masses.

During the War of Resistance Against Japan, on the basis of his comprehensive analysis of the enemy and ourselves, Comrade Mao Tse-tung laid down the following strategic principle for the Communist-led Eighth Route and New Fourth Armies: "Guerrilla warfare is basic, but lose no chance for mobile warfare under favorable conditions." He raised guerrilla warfare to the level of strategy, because, if they are to defeat a formidable enemy, revolutionary armed forces should not fight with a reckless disregard for the consequences when there is a great disparity between their own strength and the enemy's. If they do, they will suffer serious losses and bring heavy setbacks to the revolution. Guerrilla warfare is the only way to mobilize and apply the whole strength of the people against the enemy, the only way to expand our forces in the course of the war, deplete and weaken the enemy, gradually change the balance of forces between the enemy and ourselves, switch from guerrilla to mobile warfare, and finally defeat the enemy.

In the initial period of the Second Revolutionary Civil War, Comrade Mao Tse-tung enumerated the basic tactics of guerrilla warfare as follows: "The enemy advances, we retreat; the enemy camps, we harass; the enemy tires, we attack; the enemy retreats, we pursue."

Guerrilla war tactics were further developed during the War of Resistance Against Japan. In the base areas behind the enemy lines, everybody joined in the fighting—the troops and the civilian population, men and women, old and young, every single village fought. Various ingenious methods of fighting were devised, including "sparrow warfare," land-mine warfare, tunnel warfare, sabotage warfare, and guerrilla warfare on lakes and rivers.

In the later period of the War of Resistance Against Japan and during the Third Revolutionary Civil War, in the light of the changes in the balance of forces between the enemy and ourselves, we switched our strategy from that of guerrilla warfare as the primary form of fighting to that of mobile warfare. By the middle, and especially toward the end of the Third Revolutionary Civil War, our operations had developed into large-scale mobile warfare, including the storming of big cities.

War of annihilation is the fundamental guiding principle of our military operations. This guiding principle should be put into effect regardless of whether mobile or guerrilla warfare is the primary form of fighting. It is true that in guerrilla warfare much should be done to disrupt and harass the enemy, but it is still necessary actively to advocate and fight battles of annihilation whenever conditions are favorable. In mobile warfare, superior forces must be concentrated in every battle so that the enemy forces can be wiped out one by one. Comrade Mao Tse-tung has pointed out:

> A battle in which the enemy is routed is not basically decisive in a contest with a foe of great strength. A battle of annihilation, on the other hand, produces a great and immediate impact on any enemy. Injuring all of a man's ten fingers is not as effective as chopping off one, and routing ten enemy divisions is not as effective as annihilating one of them.[*]

In order to annihilate the enemy, we must adopt the policy of luring him in deep and deliberately abandon some cities and districts of our own accord so as to let him in. It is only after letting the enemy in that the people can take part in the war in various ways and that the power of a people's war can be fully exerted. It is only after letting the enemy in that he can be compelled to divide up his forces, take on heavy burdens, and commit mistakes. In other words, we must let the enemy become elated, stretch out all his ten fingers, and become hopelessly bogged down. Thus, we can concentrate superior forces to destroy the enemy forces one by one, to eat them up mouthful by mouthful. Only by wiping out the enemy's effective strength can cities and localities be finally held or seized. We are firmly against dividing up

---

[*] Mao Tse-tung, *Problems of Strategy in China's Revolutionary War*, 1936.

our forces to defend all positions and putting up resistance at every place for fear that our territory might be lost and our pots and pans smashed. Dividing up our forces can neither wipe out the enemy forces nor hold cities or localities.

Comrade Mao Tse-tung has provided a masterly summary of the strategy and tactics of people's war: You fight in your way and we fight in ours; we fight when we can win and move away when we can't.

In other words, you rely on modern weapons and we rely on highly conscious revolutionary people; you give full play to your superiority and we give full play to ours; you have your way of fighting and we have ours. When you want to fight us, we don't let you and you can't even find us. But when we want to fight you, we make sure that you can't get away and we hit you squarely on the chin and wipe you out. When we are able to wipe you out, we do so with a vengeance; when we can't, we see to it that you don't wipe us out. It is opportunism if one won't fight when one can win. It is adventurism if one insists on fighting when one can't win. Fighting is the pivot of all our strategy and tactics. It is because of the necessity of fighting that we admit the necessity of moving away. The sole purpose of moving away is to fight and bring about the final and complete destruction of the enemy. This strategy and these tactics can be applied only when one relies on the broad masses of the people, and such application brings the superiority of people's war into full play. However superior he may be in technical equipment and whatever tricks he may resort to, the enemy will find himself in the passive position of having to receive blows, and the initiative will always be in our hands.

THE INTERNATIONAL SIGNIFICANCE OF COMRADE MAO TSE-TUNG'S THEORY OF PEOPLE'S WAR

The Chinese revolution is a continuation of the Great October Revolution. The road of the October Revolution is the common road for all people's revolutions. The Chinese revolution and the October Revolution have in common the following basic characteristics: Both were led by the working class with a Marxist-Leninist party as its nucleus; both were based on the worker-peasant alliance; state power was seized through violent revolution and the dictatorship of the proletariat was established; the socialist system was built after victory in the revolution; and both were component parts of the proletarian world revolution.

Naturally, the Chinese revolution had its own peculiar characteristics. The October Revolution took place in imperialist Russia, but the Chinese revolution broke out in a semicolonial and semifeudal country. The former was a proletarian socialist revolution, while the latter developed into a socialist revolution after the complete victory of the new democratic revolution. The October Revolution began with armed uprisings in the cities and then spread to the countryside, while the Chinese revolution won nationwide victory through the encirclement and final capture of the cities from the rural areas.

Comrade Mao Tse-tung's great merit lies in the fact that he has succeeded in integrating the universal truth of Marxism-Leninism with the concrete practice of the Chinese revolution and has enriched and developed Marxism-Leninism by his masterly generalization and summation of the experience gained during the Chinese people's protracted revolutionary struggle.

In the last analysis, the Marxist-Leninist theory of proletarian revolution is the theory of the seizure of state power by revolutionary violence, the theory of countering war against the people by people's war. As Marx so aptly put it, "Force is the midwife of every old society pregnant with a new one."

It was on the basis of the lessons derived from the people's wars in China that Comrade Mao Tse-tung, using the simplest and the most vivid language, advanced the famous thesis that "political power grows out of the barrel of a gun."

In view of the fact that some people were afflicted with fear of the imperialists and reactionaries, Comrade Mao Tse-tung put forward his famous thesis that "the imperialists and all reactionaries are paper tigers." He said, "All reactionaries are paper tigers. In appearance, the reactionaries are terrifying, but in reality they are not so powerful. From a long-term point of view, it is not the reactionaries but the people who are really powerful."

The history of people's war in China and other countries provides conclusive evidence that the growth of the people's revolutionary forces from weak and small beginnings into strong and large forces is a universal law of development of class struggle or people's war. A people's war inevitably meets with many difficulties, ups and downs, and setbacks in the course of its development, but no force can alter its general trend towards inevitable triumph.

Comrade Mao Tse-tung points out that we must despise the enemy strategically and take full account of him tactically.

To despise the enemy strategically is an elementary requirement for a revolutionary. Without the courage to despise the enemy and without daring to win, it will be simply impossible to make revolution and wage a people's war, let alone to achieve victory.

It is also very important for revolutionaries to take full account of the enemy tactically. It is likewise impossible to win victory in a people's war without examining the concrete conditions, being prudent and giving great attention to the study of the art of struggle, and adopting appropriate forms of struggle in the revolution of each country and with regard to each concrete problem.

It must be emphasized that Comrade Mao Tse-tung's theory of the establishment of rural revolutionary bases and the encirclement of the cities from the countryside is of outstanding and universal practical importance for the present revolutionary struggles of all the oppressed nations and peoples, particularly those of Asia, Africa, and Latin America, against imperialism and its lackeys.

Many countries and peoples in Asia, Africa, and Latin America are now being subjected to aggression and enslavement on a serious scale by the imperialists, headed by the United States and their lackeys. The basic political and economic conditions in many of these countries are similar to those that prevailed in old China. As in China, the peasant question is extremely important in these regions. The peasants constitute the main force of the national-democratic revolution against the imperialists and their lackeys. In committing aggression against these countries, the imperialists usually begin by seizing the big cities and the main lines of communication, but they are unable to bring the vast countryside completely under their control. The countryside, and the countryside alone, can provide the broad areas in which the revolutionaries can maneuver freely and go forward to final victory. Precisely for this reason, Comrade Mao Tse-tung's theory of establishing revolutionary bases in the rural districts and encircling the cities from the countryside is attracting more and more attention among the people in these regions.

If North America and Western Europe can be called "the cities of the world," then Asia, Africa, and Latin America constitute "the rural areas of the world." Since World War II, the proletarian revolutionary movement has for various reasons been temporarily held back in the North American and West European capitalist countries, while the people's revolutionary movement in Asia, Africa, and Latin America has been growing vigorously. In a sense, the contemporary world revolution presents a picture of the encirclement of cities by the rural areas. In the final analysis, the whole cause of world revolution hinges on the revolutionary struggles of the Asian, African, and Latin American peoples who make up the overwhelming majority of the world's population. The socialist countries should regard it as their internationalist duty to support the people's revolutionary struggles in Asia, Africa, and Latin America.

The struggles waged by the different peoples against U.S. imperialism reinforce each other and merge into a worldwide tide of opposition to U.S. imperialism. The more successful the development of people's war in a given region, the larger the number of U.S. imperialist forces that can be pinned down and depleted there. When the U.S. aggressors are hard pressed in one place, they have no alternative but to loosen their grip on others. Therefore, the conditions become more favorable for the people elsewhere to wage struggles against U.S. imperialism and its lackeys.

Everything is divisible. And so is this colossus of U.S. imperialism. It can be split up and defeated. The peoples of Asia, Africa, Latin America, and other regions can destroy it piece by piece, some striking at its head and others at its feet. That is why the greatest fear of U.S. imperialism is that people's wars will be launched in different parts of the world, particularly in Asia, Africa, and Latin America, and why it regards people's war as a mortal danger.

U.S. imperialism relies solely on its nuclear weapons to intimidate people. But these weapons cannot save U.S. imperialism from its doom. Nuclear weapons cannot be used lightly. U.S. imperialism has been condemned by the people of the whole world for the crime of dropping two atomic bombs on Japan. If it uses nuclear weapons again, it will become isolated in the extreme. Moreover, the U.S. monopoly of nuclear weapsons has long been broken; U.S. imperialism has these weapons, but others have them too. If it threatens other countries with nuclear weapons, U.S. imperialism will expose its own country to the same threat. For this reason, it will meet with strong opposition not only from the people elsewhere but also inevitably from the people in the United States. Even if U.S. imperialism brazenly uses nuclear weapons, it cannot conquer the people, who are indomitable.

However highly developed modern weapons and technical equipment and however complicated the methods of modern warfare may be, in the final analysis the outcome of a war will be decided by the sustained fighting of ground forces, by the political consciousness of the men, and by their courage and spirit of sacrifice. Here the weak points of U.S. imperialism will be laid bare, while the superiority of the revolutionary people will be brought into full play. The reactionary troops of U.S. imperialism cannot possibly be endowed with the courage and the spirit of sacrifice possessed by the revolutionary people. The spiritual atom bomb which the revolutionary people possess is a far more powerful and useful weapon than the physical atom bomb.

History has proved and will go on proving that people's war is the most effective weapon against U.S. imperialism and its lackeys. All revolutionary people will take up arms, learn to fight battles, and become skilled in waging people's war, though they have not done so before. U.S. imperialism, like a mad bull dashing from place to place, will finally be burned to ashes in the blazing fires of the people's wars it has itself provoked.

Suggested Readings

I: THE COMMUNIST REGIME: A BRIEF SURVEY
ADAMS, RUTH (ed.). *Contemporary China*. New York: Pantheon Books, 1966.

BARNETT, DOAK. *China After Mao*. Princeton, N.J.: Princeton University Press, 1967.

II: THE BIRTH OF A NEW REGIME
FITZGERALD, C. P. *The Birth of Communist China*. New York: Frederick A. Praeger, 1966.

JOHNSON, CHALMERS A. *Peasant Nationalism and Communist Power*. Stanford, Calif.: Stanford University Press, 1962.

NORTH, ROBERT. *Chinese Communism*. New York: McGraw-Hill, 1965.

TANG TSOU. *America's Failure in China, 1941–50*. Chicago, Ill.: University of Chicago Press, 1963.

United States Relations with China. Washington, D.C.: U.S. Department of State Publications, Far Eastern Series, 1949.

III: THE ORGANIZATION OF THE GOVERNMENT
JAN, GEORGE P. (ed.). *Government of Communist China*. San Francisco, Calif.: Chandler Publishing Company, 1966.

SCHURMANN, FRANZ. *Ideology and Organization in Communist China*. Berkeley, Calif.: University of California Press, 1966.

TOWNSEND, JAMES R. *Political Participation in Communist China*. Berkeley, Calif.: University of California Press, 1967.

IV: THE CHINESE COMMUNIST PARTY
BRANDT, CONRAD, SCHWARTZ, BENJAMIN, and FAIRBANK, JOHN K. *A Documentary History of Chinese Communism*. Cambridge, Mass.: Harvard University Press, 1952.

HSIAO, TSO-LIANG. *Power Relations Within the Chinese Communist Movement*. Seattle, Wash.: University of Washington Press, 1961.

LEWIS, JOHN WILSON. *Leadership in Communist China*. Ithaca, N.Y.: Cornell University Press, 1963.

RUE, JOHN E. *Mao Tse-tung in Opposition, 1927–1935*. Stanford, Calif.: Stanford University Press, 1966.

TANG, PETER S. H. *Communist China Today*. Rev. ed. Washington, D.C.: Research Institute on the Sino-Soviet Bloc, 1961.

WILBUR, C. MARTIN, and HOW, JULIE LIEN-YING. *Documents on Communism, Nationalism, and Soviet Advisers in China*. New York: Columbia University Press, 1956.

V: ECONOMIC POLICY

CHENG CHU-YUAN. *Communist China's Economy, 1949–1962*. South Orange, N.J.: Seton Hall University Press, 1963.

DUNCAN, JAMES S. *A Businessman Looks at Red China*. Princeton, N.J.: D. Van Nostrand, 1965.

WU, YUAN-LI. *Economic Survey of Communist China*. New York: Twayne, 1966.

VI: SOCIAL REVOLUTION

CHEN, THEODORE H. E. *Thought Reform of the Chinese Intellectuals*. Hong Kong: University of Hong Kong Press; New York: Oxford University Press, 1960.

HEVI, EMMANUEL JOHN. *An African Student in China*. New York: Frederick A. Praeger, 1963.

KLOCHKO, MICHAEL A. *Soviet Scientist in Red China*. New York: Frederick A. Praeger, 1964.

LIU, WILLIAM T. (ed.). *Chinese Society Under Communism*. New York: John Wiley and Sons, 1967.

MU FU-SHENG. *The Wilting of the Hundred Flowers*. New York: Frederick A. Praeger, 1963.

TAYLOR, CHARLES. *Reporter in Red China*. New York: Random House, 1966.

YU, FREDERICK T. C. *Mass Persuasion in Communist China*. New York: Frederick A. Praeger, 1964.

DATE DUE

5-10			
JAN 17			
MAY 3 1 1973			
APR 1 8 1975			
MAY		LP	
GAYLORD			PRINTED IN U.S.A.